TEACHING
IN THE NEW
ELEMENTARY
SCHOOL

WILLIAM B. RAGAN
University of Oklahoma

JOHN H. WILSON
Wichita State University

TILLMAN J. RAGAN
University of Oklahoma

TEACHING IN THE NEW ELEMENTARY SCHOOL

HOLT, RINEHART AND WINSTON, INC.
New York   Chicago   San Francisco   Atlanta
Dallas   Montreal   Toronto   London   Sydney

To Faye and Pauline and Ginny

PREFACE

Dramatic changes are taking place in our society—in knowledge about human development and learning, in forces that have to be considered when groups plan curriculum changes, and in teaching strategies. More imaginative and more effective use of space for learning; team teaching and other organizational schemes designed to make fuller use of the special talents of teachers; exciting new instructional media, both hardware and software; and much more refined procedures for evaluating instruction and learning—these are only a few facets of educational innovation that justify the use of the expression "the new elementary school."

MAJOR FEATURES OF THE BOOK

EMPHASIS ON INNOVATIONS. Teaching strategies, learning resources, and space arrangements that are regarded as innovative today will, no doubt, be commonplace in elementary schools a few years hence. Students who are preparing to teach in elementary schools need to understand innovative programs that already exist in schools throughout the nation and are likely to spread to many other schools in the near future. In brief, the student needs to become familiar with the reform movement that is gaining momentum in elementary education—a movement that is designed to achieve more quality and more equality in childhood education.

The authors identify and discuss innovations in teaching that transcend subject-matter divisions. These include programs for the education of culturally different children; developing useful skills; individualizing and personalizing teaching; working with teacher aides, school volunteers, and other auxiliary personnel; the method of inquiry, simulation, and concept learning; independent study designed to give pupils more responsibility for their own learning; and creative learning.

A REALISTIC APPROACH. The authors describe new types of organization for learning, learning by discovery, the open-space type of instructional area, team teaching, continuous progress, and many other innovations. They realize, however, that for years to come many teachers will be confined to the "egg crate" type of classroom and the rigid type of instructional organization. Instructions are, therefore, provided for improving teaching in situations that are far from ideal. Although the advantages of learning by discovery are recognized, the authors also recognize that there is still a place for exposition on the part of the teacher. They recognize further that *telling* is still an important phase of teaching, although it may be that it is used too exclusively by many teachers.

SITUATIONS. Problems, projects, and discussion questions are provided in the body of each chapter so that students may see the practical application or educational implication of the principles and practices that are discussed in the chapter.

RECOMMENDED READINGS AND FILMS. A text does not provide sufficient material for a college level course. The lists of recommended readings at the end of each chapter will permit the student to explore more deeply the problems and issues treated in the chapter. These readings can be used to encourage students to think critically, evaluate what they read, and engage in independent investigation of problems in which they have a particular interest.

The authors express appreciation to all those who have assisted in this undertaking: to our colleagues and students and to publishers who have granted permission to reproduce their materials. Special recognition is given to Michael Langenbach, who was primarily responsible for three chapters in the book, and to Bonnie Hanson, who assisted with several chapters.

William B. Ragan
John H. Wilson
Tillman J. Ragan

November 1971

CONTENTS

Preface   vii

PART I.   CHANGING TIMES AND CHANGING TASKS   1

1.   LEARNING TO LIVE WITH CHANGE   3
An Era of Constantly Accelerated Change   4
The Impact of Science and Technology   5
Population Trends   7
The Urban Crisis   8
Economic Growth   10
A New Role in International Relations   11
Prejudice and Polarization   13
The Challenge of Leisure   14
Behavioral Technology   15
Summary   16
Recommended Readings   17

2.   CHANGING ESTIMATES OF THE
HUMAN POTENTIAL   19
A Broader Concept of Learning   20
Intellectual Development   20
   *Changing Views about Intelligence 21   Teaching
   Critical Thinking 21   The Critical Years 23   Concept
   Learning 24*
Social Development   27
   Social Characteristics 27
Emotional Development   28
   Emotional Characteristics 28
Studying the Individual Pupil   29
   *Sources of Information about Children 31   Specialized
   School Personnel 32   Regular Classroom Activities 32
   Conferences with Parents 33   Systematic Observation 34
   Work Specimen Folders 35*

Using What We Know about Children   35
Summary   36
Recommended Readings   37

3. **THE CHANGING ELEMENTARY SCHOOL
CURRICULUM   39**
The Nature of the Curriculum   39
    *Planning Learning Experience 40   Developing a
Curriculum Guide 42   The Teacher and the Curriculum 44
The Ability To Participate Effectively in Curriculum
Improvement 45*
Historical Perspective   47
    *Origin of Belief That Schools Should Be a Public
Responsibility 48   The Religious Motive for Education 48
Education as a Foundation for Popular Government 51
The Public School Revival 52   Expanding and
Improving the System 59   John Dewey and the
Progressive Education Association 60   Illustrative
Projects 64   Social Studies Curriculum Projects 65*
Summary   65
Recommended Readings   66

4. **CHANGING TEACHING STRATEGIES   68**
Some Teaching Strategies   69
    *Setting the Stage for Democratic Group Living 70
Evaluating Progress in Group Living 72   A Checklist for
Evaluating Classroom Practices 74*
The Recitation   77
Unit Teaching   78
    The Meaning of a Unit 78   Types of Units 79
The Inquiry or Discovery Strategy   80
    *Advantages of Learning by Inquiry 81   Research
Relating to Discovery 82   Limitations of Inquiry-
Discovery 84*
Situation Games in Learning   84
Summary   85
Recommended Readings   86

PART II.   ORGANIZING AND PLANNING   89

5. **ORGANIZING TO MAXIMIZE LEARNING   91**
Vertical Organization   92

*The Graded School Organization 92   The Multigraded
School Organization 93   The Middle School 93   The
Continuous Progress School Organization 95   The
Appropriate Placement School 96*
Horizontal Organization   98
*The Self-Contained Classroom 98   Departmentalization 99
Team Teaching 100*
Interclass and Intraclass Grouping   101
*Heterogeneous, Interclass Grouping 101   Homogeneous,
Interclass Grouping 102   Modification in Grouping
Organization 103   Combining the Vertical and
Horizontal Organizational Plans 104*
An Additional Consideration: The Open School   105
Some Conclusions   108
Summary   108
Recommended Readings   109

6. **PLANNING FOR EFFECTIVE TEACHING   112**
A Rationale for Planning   113
Long-Range, Unit, and Daily Plans in Perspective   113
*Long-Range Plans 113   Unit Plans 115   Daily
Plans 118   Scheduling Plans   119*
Stating Objectives for Plans   121
Characteristics of Good Objectives 122
A Teaching Unit Plan Problem   124
Summary   130
Recommended Readings   131

7. **UTILIZING EXTRA-TEACHER PERSONNEL   133**
Other Professionals   134
*Teacher Specialists 134   The School Principal 136
The Assistant Principal 137   The School Psychologist-
Guidance Counselor 138   The School Social Worker 139
The Speech and Hearing Clinician 140   The Medical
Personnel 140   The Substitute Teacher 141   The School
Librarian 142*
Other Personnel   142
*Teacher Aides and Parent Volunteers 142   The
School Secretary 144   The School Custodian 145
The School Lunch Personnel 145*
Summary   146
Recommended Readings   147

PART III. CURRENT ISSUES AND PROBLEMS 149

8. **RESEARCH IN THE ELEMENTARY SCHOOL SUBJECTS 151**
   What Is Research? 151
   Limitations of Research 152
   Two Kinds of Theories 153
   Reading 153
      Aims 154   Teacher Role 154   School and Classroom Organization 155   Developmental Reading Practices 155
   Writing 157
      Handwriting 157   Written Expression 159
   Listening 160
   Spelling 161
   Science 163
   Mathematics 164
   Social Studies 167
   Other Research 168
      Books 168   Journals 169
   Summary 169
   Recommended Readings 169

9. **INSTRUCTIONAL TECHNOLOGY 171**
   Education and Technology 173
   Educational Media 175
      Television 175   Commercial Television 175   Motion Pictures 185   Other Instruments of Instruction 187   Tape Recordings and Phonograph Records 191
   Media and Instruction 194
      Programmed Instruction 194   Simulations 196 Implications 198
   Multimedia Instruction 199
      A Procedure for Developing Multimedia Instruction 199
   Summary 204
   Recommended Readings 204

10. **TEACHING CULTURALLY DIFFERENT CHILDREN 207**
    Identification of the Culturally Different 208
       How They Live 208   Characteristics of Slum Schools 210 School Characteristics and Pupil Achievement 211 Disadvantages Suffered by Low-Income Children 212

Quality Education for the Culturally Different   215
    Methods and Materials for the Culturally Different 218
Teachers for the Culturally Different   219
    Successful Teachers of Culturally Different Pupils 219
    Teacher Preparation Programs 222
Summary   222
Recommended Readings   223

11. **CREATIVE WAYS OF TEACHING AND LEARNING   225**
The Meaning of Creativity   226
Characteristics of Highly Creative Children   227
Effects of Creative Teaching on Pupils   229
How Teachers Promote Creativity   233
Creativity in the School Program   234
Summary   236
Recommended Readings   236

PART IV.   NEW APPROACHES TO FAMILIAR
              TASKS   239

12. **EFFECTIVE MASTERY OF SKILLS 241**
A Broader View of Skills   242
Basic Skills of the New Elementary School   244
    Self-Understanding and Creativity 245   Problem-Solving
    Skills 246   Research Skills 247   Communication Skills 250
    Language Arts Skills 252   Mathematics Skills 253   Science
    Skills 255   Social Studies Skills 256   Creative Arts
    Skills 257   Physical Education Skills 258
Summary   259
Recommended Readings   259

13. **INDIVIDUALIZING AND PERSONALIZING
TEACHING   261**
Eight Dimensions of Schooling   262
Preparing for Individualized and Personalized Teaching   267
Another Look at the School Subjects   272
Using Classroom Aides   276
Summary   278
Recommended Readings   278

14. **CLASSROOM MANAGEMENT—DISCIPLINE** 280
What Is Discipline?   281
What about Goals for Discipline? 282
Some Considerations   283
*The System Must Be Developmental 285   The System
Must Be Democratic 287   The System Must Be
Personalized 289   The System Must Be Life Itself 290
The System Must Promote Self-Discipline 291*
Some Common Management Problems   292
*An Unacceptable Learning Climate 292   Organizational
or Personal Management Problems 295   Curriculum
Implementation Problems 297   Stressful Interpersonal
Relations 297   Grouping and Group Membership 298
Continuous Change and Emotional Stress 299   Some
Suggestions 301*
Summary   302
Recommended Readings   `302

15. **EVALUATING AND REPORTING PUPIL
PERFORMANCE**   304
Evaluation Defined   305
*The Complementary Nature of Objectives, Teaching
Strategies, and Evaluative Techniques 305*
The Goals for Evaluation   306
Techniques and Methods for Evaluating Observation   308
*Observation 308   Testing 309   Daily Work 312
Checklists 312   Anecdotal Records 312   Cumulative
Record 313   Sociogram 313*
Some Guiding Principles for Evaluation   314
Reporting the Child's Performance   316
The Report Card 316   Written Report 318
Parent-Teacher Conferences   319
*The Group Conference 320   The Small Group
Conference 320   The Individual Conference 321*
Student Involvement   325
Summary   326
Recommended Readings   327

16. **SCHOOLS FOR TOMORROW**   329
Prospects for the Future   330
   Exciting Prospects and Grave Threats 330
A New Kind of Elementary School   336
   Accelerated Change 336   Enduring Concerns 337
   School Buildings Designed for Learning 339   Greater
   Use of Technological Media 339   The Curriculum of the
   New Elementary School 340   Teachers for the New
   Elementary School 342   The Syracuse University Model 342
   The University of Florida Program 343   What Educators
   Believe May Happen in the Schools 344
Summary   345
Recommended Readings   346

Appendix   349
Indexes   357

CHANGING TIMES AND CHANGING TASKS

Changing Times and Changing Tasks

Learning To Live with Change	The Changing Elementary School Curriculum
Changing Estimates of the Human Potential	Changing Teaching Strategies

Part I explains how rapid change in our society poses new tasks for the elementary school. Chapter 1 summarizes some changes that have been taking place in several facets of American life and how these changes influence the task of teaching in the new elementary school. Chapter 2 introduces a broader concept of learning that has emerged in recent years; summarizes significant insights that have been gained into intellectual, social, and emotional development; and stresses the importance of using what we know about children. Chapter 3 explains what is meant by "curriculum"; reviews the historical development of the American elementary school; emphasizes the importance of national curriculum-improvement projects; and presents a brief statement concerning the impact of instructional technology. Chapter 4 presents the principal features of four teaching strategies: the recitation, the unit of work, the inquiry or discovery strategy, and simulation and games.

Chapter 1

Learning To Live with Change

The two great themes of "the new education" are intellectual excellence and individualization.

Glen Heathers, "The Role of Innovation in Education,"
The National Elementary Principal, September 1963,
pp. 8–14.

Reform movements in American elementary education began soon after the first legislation in America requiring that towns establish schools was passed by the General Court of the Massachusetts Bay Colony in 1647. Indeed, the Old Deluder Satan Act itself was based on a revolutionary idea—that the education of children should be a public rather than a private enterprise. The history of education in the United States is replete with illustrations of the fact that a changing society requires continuous changes in school programs.

The current reform movement in elementary education is concerned primarily with helping children develop intellectual and social skills for a lifetime of learning and living and with individualizing and personalizing teaching. It has been accelerated by significant changes in our society, by new knowledge about child development, and by expenditures for research

3

and development by federal, state, and private agencies. Substantial changes have already taken place in school organization, curriculum, teaching strategies, learning materials, and school buildings. This chapter examines the impact of societal changes on teaching. Other phases of the reform movement will be treated in the chapters that follow.

AN ERA OF CONSTANTLY ACCELERATED CHANGE

An analysis of tasks—old and new—that confront the elementary school teacher cannot overlook the restless sea of social forces that surround and condition the elementary school. Every generation of teachers has had to plan learning experiences in terms of the social medium in which the school existed—to take into consideration the changes that were taking place in the society. The rate of change has now become so rapid that it is difficult for teachers to understand the play of social forces upon the school and to plan instructional programs accordingly.

> **SITUATION 1.1**
> *The Rate of Change*
>
> Consider the lives of two men. The father was born in 1860 and died in 1912. His entire life was spent on a farm. His son was born in 1900 and is still living. He has spent his entire life in urban communities. Compare the changes that these two men witnessed in family life, recreation, communication, transportation, and education.

A study of the various stages in the history of civilization reveals that each age has been shorter than the preceding one. The stone age covered hundreds of thousands of years; the bronze age lasted for several thousand years; the iron age lasted about one-half as long; and the steel age is a little more than a hundred years old. Only three decades ago, educators were asking the question: "Can we, the last generation of the earthbound, provide an adequate education for the first generation with wings?" Peter F. Drucker wrote in 1957—the same year that Soviet Russia launched the first artificial earth satellite—that:

> Indeed anyone over forty lives in a different world from that in which he came to manhood, lives as if he had emigrated, fully grown, to a new and strange country.[1]

[1] Peter F. Drucker, *Landmarks of Tomorrow* (New York: Harper & Row, Publishers, 1957), p. ix.

He said that we had moved out of the "modern age" into the "post-modern" world and that the old view of the world made no sense anymore. When members of the crew of Apollo 11 set foot on the moon on July 20, 1969, we entered another, as yet unnamed, era in the history of civilization. There can be little doubt that this giant leap forward by mankind will pose new challenges and hazards for those who teach America's children.

THE IMPACT OF SCIENCE AND TECHNOLOGY

Science is primarily concerned with understanding our physical environment and living creatures, including man himself. Technology is the application of scientific knowledge to practical concerns. Science and technology have increasingly revolutionized our lives; they have profoundly influenced cities, transportation, communication, leisure, government, family life, and education.

THE CONQUEST OF DISTANCE. One of the most spectacular achievements of science and technology has been in the field of travel. It took our forefathers sixty-six days to cross the Atlantic Ocean in the *Mayflower*; it took Lindbergh and the *Spirit of St. Louis* thirty-three hours and thirty-two minutes to fly across it in 1927; a supersonic jet plane can now cross it in less than three hours. According to our grade-school history books, it took Magellan's crew three years to circumnavigate the globe; astronauts now make the trip in ninety minutes. We had historically emphasized the obligation of the schools to participate in the development of intelligent citizens of the United States; we had made some progress in developing programs that emphasized global interdependence; we must now become concerned about our relation to other planets.

THE COMPUTER AND THE LASER BEAM. Another amazing technological development of the 1960s has been the increasing use of computers. The computer has already become an indispensable item in industry, business, medical practice, government, and education. The speed and capacity of computers are expected to increase rapidly during the 1970s. Their services will be extended to homes—it will be possible for anyone to plug into a central installation and obtain complete data on any topic that concerns him. The concentrated beam of light that is called the *laser* promises to achieve within the next ten years wonders comparable to those of the computer. It is expected to revolutionize television and other communication media; provide more safety in air travel and underwater navigation; and become standard equipment in medical and surgical wards.

COMFORTS AND CONVENIENCES. Advancements in science and technology have added new dimensions to life in the home. Central heating and air conditioning, the all-electric kitchen, color television, stereophonic sound equipment, long-distance telephone dialing, an abundance of reading material for adults and children, talking books (records) for the blind, educational toys and picture books for children, and special purpose rooms arranged to fit the habits and needs of members of the family have provided more leisure time and more opportunities for enjoyment in the home.

SITUATION 1.2
Differences in Homes

Children who enter school for the first time from homes like the one described above may already have learned most of what the school ordinarily teaches to first-year pupils. What is the school's responsibility in this case? What about the child whose home does not provide these advantages?

THE BIOLOGICAL REVOLUTION. This revolution is older and in some respects more crucial than the aerospace revolution or the computer revolution. It has enabled man to increase his numbers, to gain a better understanding of himself, and to manipulate his environment. It has made great strides toward the elimination of communicable disease, the transplanting of human organs, and finding new cures for mental illness. It has uncovered more efficient methods of converting solar energy into human food, laid the foundations for using the oceans as sources of food and entertainment, and found new methods of killing harmful pests.

Man's ability to manipulate the environment has, however, outstripped his ability to understand the consequences. Changes in weather patterns, disastrous floods caused by deforestation, the destruction of natural predators of harmful pests by indiscriminate spraying with insecticides, the harmful side effects of some new drugs, the growing hazards of air and water pollution, types of irrigation that ruin the soil, and the depletion of our coal and oil resources illustrate the price that mankind pays for progress.

Ehrlich has described an "understanding gap" that could lead us to self-destruction. While a rather small portion of the population has the information and the means to achieve scientific and technological breakthroughs that benefit mankind, the average individual has only a small fraction of the information needed to make constructive use of these breakthroughs. The urgent need to select curriculum content that is relevant to crucial problems of our times could hardly be stated more concisely than Ehrlich has stated it:

Most people are simply the victims of a general 'understanding gap.' If they comprehended the situation and had the equipment I think most people would act in a socially responsible way.[2]

SITUATION 1.3
Current Social Problems

It has been argued that elementary school children are too immature to profit from a study of crucial problems confronting our people. On the other hand, the idea is widely accepted that any subject can be taught in some intellectually honest fashion to any child at any stage of development. As a member of a committee to prepare a curriculum guide for the social studies in a certain school system, what stand would you take on including such topics as conservation, air and water pollution, and the use of insecticides in the program?

POPULATION TRENDS

An understanding of population phenomena is essential to intelligent educational planning. The population of the United States was 151,718,000 in 1950; 180,007,000 in 1960; and 203,185,000 in 1970. Enrollments in public and nonpublic day schools, grades K–8, increased from 22 million in 1949–1950 to 33 million in 1959–1960 and to 38 million in 1969–1970. The mobility of our population also poses problems for schools. It has been estimated that only 26 percent of our people have lived in the same house for ten years or more and three of every ten people have moved from their native states in recent years. Between March 1966 and March 1967, 18 percent of the population moved. The number of people sixty-five years of age and over increased from 16 million in 1960 to 20 million in 1970. The population boom of the 1960s resulted in a temporary shortage of qualified elementary school teachers. Seventy-six of the nation's largest school systems reported in August 1969 that they had a total of 2665 unfilled positions in their elementary schools. Within a few years, however, the shortage of teachers was followed by a surplus of teachers. If school systems could reduce enrollments from twenty-eight to twenty pupils per teacher—and if the 9 percent of the nation's elementary school teachers who hold no degrees could be replaced by fully qualified teachers —the teacher surplus would be greatly reduced if not eliminated.

It is not likely that schools will be able to employ as many well-qualified teachers as would be needed to meet the needs of every boy and

[2] Paul R. Ehrlich, "The Biological Revolution," *Stanford Review*, September–October 1965, p. 46.

girl in the elementary schools. Several plans for making better use of the talents of well-qualified teachers have been developed. The team-teaching arrangement enables each teacher to specialize in those areas in which she is most competent; teacher aides and school volunteers relieve teachers of many nonteaching chores; instructional television makes it possible for more pupils to receive help from master teachers; and programmed materials enable pupils to learn with less help from the teacher. These innovations will be explained in the chapters that follow.

THE URBAN CRISIS

The best known population phenomenon of recent decades has been the rural-urban migration followed by migration from the central cities to the suburbs. In 1920, about 50 million people, or one-half the population of the United States, lived in metropolitan areas; by 1965, 130 million people, or two-thirds of the population, lived there. Between 1966 and 1968 the central cities decreased in population by 381,000 while the suburbs increased by 1,566,000.

METROPOLITANISM. The large city and, particularly, the metropolitan area are comparatively recent developments in America. No city in the United States had a population of 100,000 people until 1820; by 1968 we had one city with a population of 8 million whose metropolitan area had a population of more than 16 million; and two-thirds of the American people lived in 219 metropolitan areas. The Bureau of the Census has defined a Standard Metropolitan Statistical Area (SMSA) as a city of 50,000 or more with the surrounding area that is economically and socially integrated with it.

As technological developments have made it difficult for an individual family to earn a living either as farm owners or as farm workers the rural poor have moved to the cities in unprecedented numbers in search of employment. The cities were not prepared to provide decent jobs, housing, and schools for this influx, not only from rural America but from other countries. A type of polarization developed that is known as the "urban crisis," and this is recognized as one of the major problems confronting the nation.

As poor people moved into the central cities, urbanites who could afford to do so moved to the suburbs. The central cities developed slums, dilapidated housing, substandard schools, and juvenile delinquency. Old buildings, poorly prepared teachers, and high dropout rates generally characterize the schools in the central cities. The Bureau of the Census estimates that 4,716,000 or 13.6 percent of young adults 14–24 years of age had not graduated from high school and were not enrolled in 1967.

Local school administrative units in metropolitan areas have simply evolved over the years, without any rational design or master plan. One can find in almost any SMSA in the United States a pattern of school districts that defies any logical explanation. Several school districts may exist within the city limits, the city school district may extend beyond the city limits, and the schools in the SMSA may lie in several counties, each of which has a county superintendent of schools. Cunningham reported in 1968 that within the SMSA of Chicago there were 339 autonomous elementary and secondary school districts, plus six county school governments.[3]

Studies of school district reorganization within metropolitan areas generally recognize the following principles:

1. Some educational functions can best be performed by a large school district; other functions can best be performed by small administrative units.
2. The school administrative unit should be large enough to permit a wide range of educational programs.
3. The administrative unit should be large enough to provide for equalization of educational opportunities and tax burdens.
4. School district organization should facilitate change and innovation in existing programs in an era of rapid change.
5. The organization should provide opportunities for citizen participation in decision making.

A new pattern of educational government for metropolitan areas designed to accomplish these objectives has been suggested. It calls for the creation of a metropolitan school district with a board of education, and the creation of a number of local districts, each with its own board of education with limited power.[4]

SITUATION 1.4
Large versus Small School Districts

You would like, after graduation, to teach in an elementary school in a metropolitan area. Compare the services provided by one of the smaller districts in the area with those offered by the larger school district. Consider such services as those provided by school psychologists, social workers, supervisors, nurses, and remedial-reading specialists. List advantages and disadvantages of teaching in the larger school district.

[3] Luverne L. Cunningham, in National Society for the Study of Education, *Metropolitanism: Its Challenge to Education* (Chicago: University of Chicago Press, 1968), p. 96.
[4] Cunningham, p. 109.

ECONOMIC GROWTH

A vigorous, growing economy has moved to the center of the stage among the concerns of Americans. We depend upon economic growth for maintaining high standards of living, reducing unemployment, caring for the poor and aged, supporting educational programs, and for discharging our obligations abroad. The Gross National Product (GNP) refers to the market value of all the goods and services produced in any one year by our nation's economy. It stood at $197 billion in 1947, $343 billion in 1957, and $860 billion in 1968. The estimate for 1975 is $1.3 trillion.

We live in a rich and powerful nation. It has been estimated that if all the people in the world were condensed into a community with a population of 1,000, sixty of these would be Americans. These sixty Americans would have one-half the income and the other 940 people would share the other half. Our economic growth has been influenced by an abundance of natural resources, competent business managers, the development of power-driven machines, and a liberal government that has encouraged private initiative. But investments in human resources in the form of education have been having an increasing influence on economic growth. Between 1909 and 1929 education accounted for only one-eighth of our economic growth; between 1929 and 1957 it accounted for one-fifth of our economic growth.

Millions of Americans, however, do not share in our general prosperity. According to the definition of poverty used by the Office of Economic Opportunity, we had 30 million people living in poverty in 1969. The fact that this figure is a few million less than it was in 1960 provides little ground for complacency. The presence of substandard schools in city slums and depressed rural areas is a reflection on our cherished ideal of equality of opportunity and a waste of our human resources. Seventy-five percent of the upper-middle and upper-class youth who rank in the upper quarter in intellectual ability finish four years of college; only 25 percent of the lower-class youth with comparable mental ability do so. A situation in which millions of our young people are unemployed because they lack the educational qualifications for the only jobs that are available represents social dynamite.

Underinvestment in human resources extends far beyond the city slums and depressed rural areas. Quality and equality are lacking in many schools outside these areas. Bright children are bored by a single-track curriculum geared to the mythical average child and soon grow restless; slow learners become discouraged by a program that is not geared to their rates of learning; research relating to the importance of the early years of a child's life is wasted when schools do not provide programs for children under six years of age. In fact, the National Education Association recommended several years ago that school entrance age be lowered to four years of age. Innovations designed to remedy these weaknesses are treated in the chapters that follow.

SITUATION 1.5
Teacher Education Programs

You are enrolled in a program leading to a certificate to teach in elementary schools. Examine the program to find out what opportunities you will have to learn about programs for the gifted child and for slow learners. What preparation will you have for adapting materials to individual differences in children? What experiences are provided for helping you understand the effects of poverty on a child's concept of himself, his community, and his school?

A NEW ROLE IN INTERNATIONAL RELATIONS

The policy of isolationism, enunciated by our first president, dominated the foreign policy of the United States until the end of World War II. This policy served us well when we were a young nation, separated from the rest of the world by two great oceans, and relatively free to develop a unique civilization here on the North American continent. Woodrow Wilson saw clearly the need for international cooperation at the end of "the war to end wars" when he persuaded the major nations of the world to join the League of Nations. His dream of a cooperative world order was shattered, however, when the Senate of the United States refused to go along.

By the end of World War II, however, leaders of both the major political parties were convinced that we did not inhabit the earth alone. Science and technology had made the world so much smaller, nations had become so interdependent, and the weapons of warfare had become so destructive that most people realized that joining other nations in an organization designed to maintain peace constituted our only hope for survival.

Two developments since the end of World War II have intensified the need for international cooperation: Communism has extended its control over one-third of the world's population, and forty-eight new nations have come into existence. The people of these developing countries have an intense desire for political independence and economic develop-

Children must learn to live in a changing world. (Photo courtesy Norman Public Schools.)

In a rapidly changing world, "knowing the right answer" is becoming less important than "being able to find the right answer." (Photo courtesy Oklahoma City Public Schools.)

ment. The development of a modern industrialized economy depends in the beginning stages upon savings and the accumulation of capital. This is difficult for a people who are living at the bare subsistence level. Without schools and universities, the leaders needed to maintain a stable government are not available and, without technical training, skillful industrial managers are lacking.

Brameld has suggested that the overarching purpose of schools and colleges should be ". . . to channel and release the full resources of education in behalf of the creation of a world civilization. . . ."[5] Hanna has suggested that the problems that the citizens of the United States will face in our lifetime will revolve around three new communities of men: (1) the Inter-American community, (2) the Atlantic community, and (3) the Pacific community. He says that these regions-of-nations communities lie between the national communities and the world community.[6]

Instructional programs in the area of international understanding are generally designed to promote (1) respect for the worth of people of all races and nationalities, (2) understanding of the likenesses and differences of peoples in different lands, (3) understanding of the services performed by the different departments of the United Nations, and (4) understanding of world economic and social interdependence.

PREJUDICE AND POLARIZATION

Prejudice has generally been explained in terms of attitudes; it can also be regarded as a form of behavior. Prejudiced behavior excludes certain racial, religious, and ethnic groups from the chance to attain equality of opportunity and status. Prejudiced individuals and groups do not recognize individual differences; they treat all individuals as indistinguishable parts of a stereotyped group. Prejudice extends beyond the groups listed above. It leads to polarizations such as the rich versus the poor, the educated versus the uneducated, and the young versus the old.

The most serious type of polarization arising from prejudiced behavior exists between white people and black people in our society. Prejudiced behavior is seen in housing restrictions, discrimination in employment practices, and disparity in educational opportunities. The consequences of prejudiced behavior have been stated by Raab and Lipset as follows:

[5] Theodore Brameld, in Stanley Elem, *New Dimensions for Educational Progress* (Bloomington, Ind.: *Phi Delta Kappan*, 1962), pp. 3–4.

[6] Paul R. Hanna, in National Society for the Study of Education, *The United States and International Education* (Chicago: University of Chicago Press, 1969), p. 258.

The opportunity for every man to develop his capacities is no longer just an abstract ethical precept that attaches to democracy. It is a practical condition of a modern industrial society. Such a society can function efficiently only if opportunity for full development and participation is not removed from large groups of its population.[7]

The same authors also point out in their chapter on "The Prejudiced Community" that patterns of community action are more influential in maintaining polarization as opposed to integration in our society than prejudiced attitudes on the part of individuals; that prejudiced behavior has generally been reduced in communities where segregation has broken down. The social situation in which an individual lives largely determines his attitudes and behavior. Substantial progress has been made in desegregating the armed forces, public housing, and industries receiving contracts from the government. Human Relations Institutes located at universities have helped many communities study their race relations situation and work out a program for a more harmonious settlement of disputes, particularly in the field of school desegregation. Many voluntary community organizations have also performed useful services in the field of racial relations. Chapter 10 examines steps that have been taken and steps that need to be taken in order to provide adequate educational opportunities for culturally disadvantaged children as well as to provide programs in intercultural education for all American children.

THE CHALLENGE OF LEISURE

New technological developments have increased the amount of time men have available to use as they please and have provided more choices in the way free time may be used. They have made it possible to increase standards of living, to provide a higher quality of education, and to relieve men of much drudgery. They have, however, created a situation in which new concepts and new systems of management are necessary in industry, government, and education.

The hours in the work week for industrial laborers have decreased from eighty in 1800 to sixty in 1900 to less than forty in 1970, and the estimate for 1979 is a twenty- to thirty-hour work week. Forty-eight men, with modern equipment, can now make an engine block that used to take 400 men twice as long. It has been predicted that, within twenty-five years, 2 percent of our people will be able to produce all the food and other goods that the other 98 percent will need.

[7] Earl Raab and S. M. Lipset, *Prejudice and Society* (New York: Anti-Defamation League of B'Nai B'Rith, 1963), p. 9.

The situation with regard to leisure time today is a reversal of conditions that previously existed, when laborers worked long hours and leisure was enjoyed by only a few aristocrats; we have now created more leisure for the masses and more work for the classes. It is not unusual for managers, proprietors, and members of the professions to work fifty-three hours a week, while workers have more and more leisure time.

Emphasis on education for the worthy use of leisure is not new in American education. It was one of the Seven Cardinal Principles of Education developed by the National Education Act in 1918; it appeared again in the statement of the purposes of education issued by the Educational Policies Commission of the National Education Association in 1938—"The educated person has mental resources for the use of leisure." More recent publications have examined the impact of automation on the amount of leisure time available, the way people spend their leisure time, and the implications for education.[8] As automation continues to produce more leisure for the masses, it becomes more essential for school programs to help children develop resources for the enjoyment of leisure. Several aspects of the new elementary school that are discussed in the chapters that follow are related to this problem: teaching children to think independently, emphasis on the critical years of the child's life, individualizing and personalizing instruction, and teaching the culturally disadvantaged child are a few examples.

BEHAVIORAL TECHNOLOGY

Hope for the solution of such problems as war, poverty, overpopulation, prejudice, and pollution must spring from a faith in the improvability of human beings. There is no basis for the belief that conditions that have always existed must continue to exist. The application of human intelligence to the problem of unlocking the secrets of the physical environment has brought many benefits to mankind. The new frontier lies in the field of human relations. Behavioral technology—based on discoveries in neurology, physiology, genetics, psychology, anthropology, sociology, and political science—has already increased our power to control the social forces that surround us. Much greater progress in behavioral technology is expected in the next few decades.[9]

[8] See Walter Buckingham, *Automation: Its Impact on Business and People* (New York: Harper & Row, Publishers, 1961), p. 27; also Ernest Havemann, "Leisure, the Great New Challenge," *Reader's Digest*, August 1964, p. 125.

[9] Ithiel de Sola Pool, in Foreign Policy Association, *Toward the Year 2018* (New York: Cowles Education Corporation, 1968), p. 88.

Innovations in education that are discussed in the chapters that follow promise to lay the foundations for a truly educated society—a society in which statesmen will govern with greater insight and in which citizens will be better prepared to make decisions based on an understanding of issues rather than on impulse or emotion. When Horace Mann left the legal profession to enter the field of education, he said, "I have faith in the improvability of race—in their accelerating improvability." The public school system that he was instrumental in establishing is today charged with tremendous social responsibility.

SUMMARY

1. The current reform movement in elementary education has been accelerated by significant changes in our society.

2. The rate of change in our society has been so great that it has been difficult for teachers to understand the play of social forces upon the school and to plan instructional programs accordingly.

3. The technological revolution has influenced the growth of cities, methods of transportation and communication, the amount of leisure time available, international relations, economic growth, and education.

4. The biological revolution is older and in some respects more crucial than the aerospace revolution and the computer revolution.

5. The understanding gap between the few who have developed the new technology and the masses who do not have the information needed to understand its consequences could lead us to self-destruction.

6. The population boom of the 1960s has resulted in a shortage of qualified elementary school teachers; the schools have had to devise ways of dealing with the problems posed by this shortage.

7. Two-thirds of the American people live in metropolitan areas; the urban crisis is one of the major problems confronting our people.

8. The presence of substandard schools in city slums and depressed rural areas is a reflection on our cherished ideal of equality of opportunity and a tragic waste of our human resources.

9. Releasing the full resources of education in behalf of creating a world civilization is now recognized as essential for national survival in an interdependent world.

10. Prejudiced behavior based on race, religion, and national origin divides and weakens our society; the schools have a responsibility for providing programs of intercultural education for all American children.

11. As automation provides more leisure time for workers, the schools have a responsibility for helping children develop resources for the wholesome use of leisure.

12. Behavioral technology has already increased our power to control the social forces that surround us; much greater progress in behavioral technology is expected in the next few decades.

RECOMMENDED READINGS

Buckingham, Walter, *Automation: Its Impact on Business and People*. New York: New American Library of World Literature, Inc., 1961. Chapter 9 deals with the social and economic revolution, including the impact of automation on leisure.

Collier, C. C., W. R. Houston, R. R. Schmatz, and W. J. Walsh, *Teaching in the Modern Elementary School*. New York: Crowell-Collier and Macmillan, Inc., 1967. Chapter 1 deals with "Society in Transition"; "The Changing Elementary School."

Hartford, Ellis Ford, *Education in These United States*. New York: Crowell-Collier and Macmillan, Inc., 1964. Chapter 4 explains the relation of education to individual well-being and to economic progress.

Havighurst, Robert J., Bernice L. Neugarten, and J. M. Falk, *Society and Education: A Book of Readings*. Boston: Allyn and Bacon, Inc., 1967. Explains the changing shape of American social structure, socializing agencies, the school in the community and in the wider society, conflicts in role expectations relating to the teacher.

Hillson, Maurie, *Current Issues and Research in Education: Elementary Education*. New York: The Free Press, 1967. The prologue explains some forces that have accelerated change in elementary education and some new lines of development. Chapter 19 summarizes innovations that are taking place in elementary schools.

Hunter, David R., *The Slums: Challenge and Response*. New York: The Free Press, 1964. Chapter 2 explains some conditions existing in the slums; Part Two explains what is being done in response to these conditions.

National Society for the Study of Education, *Metropolitanism: Its Challenge to Education*. Chicago: University of Chicago Press, 1968. Chapter 1 explains the meaning of metropolitanism; other chapters deal with problems involved in living in metropolitan areas and efforts to solve these problems.

———, *The United States and International Education*. Chicago: University of Chicago Press, 1969. Section III, "Interacting Powers and Forces on the International Scene," is particularly valuable.

Project on the Instructional Program in Public Schools, *Education in a Changing Society*. Washington, D.C.: National Education Association, 1963. Explains the impact on education of trends in international relations, economic growth, population growth, science and technology, and the mass media.

Raab, Earl, and S. M. Lipset, *Prejudice and Society*. New York: Anti-Defamation League of B'Nai B'Rith, 1963. Explains the consequences of prejudiced behavior; cites examples of promising efforts to deal with it.

Schultz, Theodore W., *The Economic Value of Education*. New York: Columbia University Press, 1963. Documents the idea that education is an important factor in the economic strength of the nation.

Toffler, Alvin, *Future Shock*. New York: Random House, 1970. Explains the need for learning to live with chance.

Chapter 2

Changing Estimates
of the Human Potential

*Science has at last turned its attention to the central question of
human capability, has begun the search for a technology as well
as a science of the human potential. Men in varied fields,
sometimes unknown to each other, sometimes disagreeing on
method, philosophy, and even language, are coming to
startlingly similar conclusions that make pessimism about the
human prospect far more difficult than before.*

> George B. Leonard, *Education and Ecstasy* (New York:
> Delacorte Press, 1968), p. 25.

Teachers have become increasingly concerned in the last few decades
about the problem of releasing the potential of children. This concern
extends beyond the problem of making special provisions for the gifted
child and for the disadvantaged child. In fact, it has created a new concept of teaching as a process of releasing human potential. Teachers have
a much greater understanding than ever before of the ways that environmental forces mingle with the individual's biological inheritance to release
his potential for learning.

Most teachers understand that learning is the central concern of the
school; that the environment in the school can be structured so that
certain kinds of learning will be fostered while other kinds will be inhibited;
and that pupils vary in rates of learning to such an extent that differenti-

ated materials and methods are required if all pupils are to have equal opportunity to learn.

A BROADER CONCEPT OF LEARNING

Learning was for many years regarded as identical with knowing. This concept influenced teaching in many ways. If the child could recite the names of the bones of the human body and trace the circulation of blood, the teacher considered that he had learned in the area of health, regardless of whether he was learning to live more healthfully from day to day. Learning was divorced from living; the proof of learning was the ability to reproduce the words of the teacher or the textbook; and learning was motivated primarily by rewards and punishments. Annual promotions, minimum grade standards, examinations designed to test recall of information—the whole mechanized procedure of the traditional elementary school harmonized with this narrow, static concept of learning.

A broader concept of learning has been gaining increasing acceptance in recent decades. Learning is now regarded as the modification of behavior that takes place as the child interacts with the environment. The acquisition of knowledge and skills is important, but this represents only one phase of the learning process. In the broader sense learning takes place only when an individual has an experience that influences his behavior and makes him a different person.

The teacher in the new elementary school is concerned with the contribution of psychology to effective teaching; he is also concerned with the contributions of other behavioral sciences. He is concerned with new insights into the problem of learning school subjects; he is also concerned with finding out how children become adequate, fully functioning persons. He is concerned with new insights into intellectual development; he is also concerned with learning more about the social and emotional factors that influence growth and learning. This chapter presents only a brief treatment of these problems. Other chapters, particularly those dealing with individual differences and with the multimedia approach to teaching, contain additional information about learning.

INTELLECTUAL DEVELOPMENT

We are living in an era when many challenging questions are being raised about the intellectual development of children. Information relating to these questions is needed by the teacher in making wise decisions about teaching strategies. Can intelligence be altered by changing the learning environment? Can many children actually begin the learning of difficult subjects much earlier than we had thought? Is there a critical period in the life of an individual when his pattern of achievement in school subjects and his personality traits are largely determined? What is known about concept development?

Changing Views about Intelligence

Since 1945 psychologists have been investigating the potential of the human brain. Their research has provided a basis for much optimism regarding the possibility of raising the average level of intelligence of our people during one generation. More importantly, these psychologists have provided a new concept relating to the nature of intelligence. The traditional view of intelligence was that it was inherited and that it could not be changed by altering the learning environment. Most psychologists now take the position that intelligence grows as the individual interacts with his environment. Joseph McVicker Hunt has been quoted by Langemann as follows: "So, intelligence can be defined as the techniques that a child acquires for processing information furnished by his senses."[1] Hunt also believes ". . . that we might raise the average level of intelligence during the next generation or two by about 30 points of IQ—provided we reach the children early enough."[2] It would be difficult to estimate how much more effective teaching could become in terms of releasing human potential if all teachers gained a better understanding of the nature of intelligence.

THE SELF-FULFILLING PROPHECY. This is a term that is used to explain the effects of teacher expectations on pupil performance. There is considerable evidence to support the idea that when the teacher believes that pupils are slow learners the pupils will perform in harmony with the teacher's expectation.[3] Minority-group children in particular may frequently be deprived of the opportunity to develop their full potential because of the low expectations of teachers.[4]

Teaching Critical Thinking

A significant phase of the reform movement in elementary education during the 1950s and 1960s was the effort to do more about helping

[1] Quoted in John K. Langemann, "Can We Make Human Beings More Intelligent?" *Reader's Digest*, May 1966, p. 78.

[2] Langemann, p. 77.

[3] Robert Rosenthal and Lenore Jacobson, *Pygmalion in the Classroom* (New York: Holt, Rinehart and Winston, 1968).

[4] William B. Ragan and George Henderson, *Foundations of American Education* (New York: Harper & Row, Publishers, 1970), Chap. 6.

children to think critically. It was realized that citizens of a free society need to think clearly about the great problems and issues that influence their lives; that the rapid growth of automation increased the demand for individuals who could think, analyze, and make decisions; and that the schools had a responsibility for doing something to counteract the trend toward anti-intellectualism in our society.

Some very significant books dealing with this important aspect of human development have been published since 1960.[5] These books deal with a wide range of topics: what critical thinking is, the abilities that are involved in critical thinking, the extent to which critical thinking can be taught, and to what extent the ability to think in one area can be transferred to another. In addition to these books on critical thinking, the materials produced by the national curriculum projects in the various elementary school subjects have supplied a great many suggestions for teaching students to think, to solve problems, and to discover concepts and principles.

Research in the area of children's thinking has provided much valuable information for teachers. Studies have revealed that (1) curiosity is an outstanding trait of young children, (2) children acquire a vast amount of information by asking questions, (3) the idea that fantasy holds a predominant place in the mental life of children has no foundation, and (4) critical thinking manifests itself early in the life of many children and grows gradually throughout their grade school, high school, and college experience. Children need a great deal of information on a wide variety of topics in order to think clearly; critical thinking begins with problems that are closely related with the child's previous experience; children need opportunities to discover for themselves how to solve problems instead of having adult models imposed upon them; and evaluation procedures exert a powerful influence upon the child's thinking processes.

The Ohio Association for Supervision and Curriculum Development produced a useful bulletin on the teaching of critical thinking in 1964. The bulletin explains the steps in problem solving or critical thinking, and suggests procedures for teaching critical thinking in the language arts, social studies, science, mathematics, the arts, and physical education.[6]

---

[5] See particularly William H. Burton, Ronald B. Kimball, and Richard L. Wing, *Education for Effective Thinking* (New York: Appleton-Century-Crofts, Inc., 1960), and Irving E. Sigel and Frank H. Hooper (Eds.), *Logical Thinking in Children* (New York: Holt, Rinehart and Winston, Inc., 1968).

[6] Ohio Association for Supervision and Curriculum Development, *Teaching Critical Thinking in the Elementary School* (Columbus, Ohio: Ohio Education Association, 1964).

SITUATION 2.1
Encouraging Critical Thinking

A sixth-grade social studies class in a low-income area in a large city was planning a city. They had a central committee and separate committees for every service the city would need to provide. They were planning the number and location of schools, churches, industrial areas, and residential areas. One student called the teacher's attention to the fact that they had located the industrial area on the west side and the residential area on the east side. He said, "Last night after I went to bed I got to thinking. The prevailing winds here are from the west. I imagined I could smell packing town." What light does this situation throw on the problem of encouraging critical thinking? Can you think of other situations that the teacher could create to encourage critical thinking?

The Critical Years

Every year that the child spends in the elementary school is a critical year as far as the responsibility of the school is concerned. Research, however, has highlighted the importance of the first four years—kindergarten through the third grade. One of the most useful studies of child growth and achievement has been reported by Bloom.[7] Bloom examined and interpreted data from hundreds of longitudinal studies on the shaping of human beings from infancy to adulthood. Some of his findings point out clearly some new directions for the elementary school programs.

1. By age nine (grade 3), at least 50 percent of the achievement pattern (general achievement, reading comprehension, and vocabulary development) to be attained by age eighteen (grade 12) has already been attained.

2. When the student starts to school at age six, he has attained about one-third of his general learning pattern.

3. The first three years that the child spends in school (grades 1–3) constitute the most crucial period available to the public schools for the development of general learning patterns.

4. Most stable human characteristics have negatively accelerated growth rates—growth begins very rapidly and then slows down. In terms of intelligence measured at age seventeen, 50 percent of the development takes place between conception and age four, about 30 percent between

[7] Benjamin S. Bloom, *Stability and Change in Human Characteristics* (New York: John Wiley & Sons, 1964). See particularly pp.104, 105, 176, and 177.

ages four and eight, and about 20 percent between ages eight and seventeen. School achievement and deep-seated personality traits follow the same pattern.

5. Several studies have indicated that development at one period influences the nature of later development. Moss and Kagan found, for example, that achievement strivings during the early years were a good index of future achievement behavior. For boys particularly, the period between ages six and ten was the crucial time for developing the desire for task mastery and intellectual competence.[8]

Worth has reviewed these and other studies relating to the critical years and has suggested the following implications for elementary school procedures:

1. Extending school services to children under six years of age;
2. Broadening the scope of pupil personnel services;
3. Facilitating more individualized instruction; and
4. Providing a well-qualified teacher for every elementary classroom.[9]

SITUATION 2.2
Equalizing Educational Opportunity

Suggest ways that extending school services to children under six years of age would help to equalize educational opportunities for culturally disadvantaged children. How would other procedures listed above contribute to this objective?

Concept Learning

A concept consists of the meaning that a person attaches to the symbol for a class of things, events, or ideas. A concept is necessarily abstract because it consists of meaning associated with all members of a class rather than with any particular member. A student's concept of *automobile* is an abstract notion of what attributes all automobiles have in common; it is a mental process that gives unity to diverse members of a class; and it is subjective—each student builds his own concept of anything from his own experience.

---

[8] H. Moss and J. Kagan, "Stability of Achievement and Recognition Seeking Behaviors From Early Childhood Through Adulthood," *Journal of Abnormal and Social Psychology* (December 1961), No. 62, pp. 504–513.

[9] W. H. Worth, "The Critical Years," *The Canadian Administrator* (Edmonton, Canada: University of Alberta, January 1965), pp. 13–16.

Curriculum-planning groups at the national, state, and local school system levels now generally list content in the social studies in the form of a conceptual framework. The National Council for the Social Studies took a step in this direction in 1958 in *A Guide to Content in the Social Studies*. The publication listed fourteen themes around which the social studies program for grades K–12 could be organized. The historical, geographical, economic, political, and sociocultural aspects of each theme could then be presented in spiral fashion as pupils progressed from kindergarten through grade 12.[10] A *Conceptual Framework for the Social Studies* presented major social studies concepts to be developed in the K–12 sequence.[11] The trend toward listing curriculum content in the form of concepts to be learned has not been limited to the social studies—it is evident also in mathematics, science, and other areas. It is not difficult to discover the rationale for the emphasis on concepts. One obvious reason lies in the explosion of knowledge in practically every curriculum area. In the field of science, for example, the amount of knowledge has been doubling every ten years and it is expected to increase even more rapidly in the future. It is, therefore, not feasible to undertake to teach children in the elementary school all the facts available. The school has become increasingly a place for equipping every student with the resources, skills, and understandings that will enable him to process information and to investigate a field of knowledge on his own.

Since the new curricula emphasize concept development, it becomes the responsibility of the teacher to learn as much as possible about concept learning and about teaching procedures that foster effective concept learning. It is one thing for specialists in the various disciplines to list important concepts to be learned; it is quite another matter for teachers to assist students in making adult concepts their own—to help students form their *own* concepts.

STAGES IN CONCEPT DEVELOPMENT. Jean Piaget, the Swiss psychologist, and his colleagues have provided a great deal of information about the way concepts develop. Other psychologists have used the findings of Piaget's experimentation to explain the sequential development of concepts. For example, Bruner has identified three stages in concept development.[12] During the first stage, which ends about ages five or six, the child is con-

---

[10] National Council for the Social Studies, *A Guide to Content in the Social Studies* (Washington, D.C.: The National Education Association, 1958).

[11] *A Conceptual Framework for the Social Studies* (Madison, Wis.: Wisconsin Department of Public Instruction, 1967).

[12] Jerome S. Bruner, *The Process of Education* (Cambridge: Harvard University Press, 1962), pp. 34–42.

cerned with manipulating objects on an intuitive level, by trial and error. This is called the *preoperational* stage. The second stage, which occurs after the child has entered school, is called the *concrete operations* stage. The operation is a means of getting data about the real world into the mind so that they can be organized and used selectively in the solution of problems. The third stage, which generally occurs between ages ten and fourteen, is called the *formal operations* stage. The child acquires the ability to operate on hypothetical propositions rather than being limited to what he has experienced or to what is apparently before him. This is the type of mental process that is the stock-in-trade of the scientist and the abstract thinker. It should be noted that although all children follow this sequence in concept development, the chronological ages vary greatly from one child to another. Bruner recognized this when he stated:

> Precisely what kinds of materials should be used at what age with what effect is a subject for research—research of several kinds. . . . Nor do we need to wait for all the research findings to be in before proceeding, for a skillful teacher can also experiment by attempting to teach what seems to be intuitively right for children of different ages, correcting as he goes.[13]

TEACHING CONCEPTS. Detailed suggestions relating to instructional procedures designed to help pupils understand concepts may be found in teachers' manuals that accompany series of textbooks, curriculum guides prepared by state and local school systems, and recent publications that deal with effective teaching.[14] Principles emphasized generally include the following:

1. Not all concepts require direct teaching; the student acquires many concepts on his own independently of the teacher.
2. Teachers generally try to help students progress gradually from learning that involves the use of concrete objects to abstract thinking.
3. Each concept is introduced in a way that causes it to be significant and interesting to students.
4. Pupils can be motivated to learn abstract concepts by being shown how they are related to activities in daily life.
5. Students can generally be motivated to study concepts by providing opportunities for them to explore, discover, and verify hypotheses.

---

[13] Bruner, p. 53.
[14] See particularly Marlin L. Tanck, "Teaching Concepts, Generalizations, and Constructs," in Dorothy McClure Fraser (Ed.), *Social Studies Curriculum Development: Prospects and Problems* (Washington, D.C.: National Council for the Social Studies, 1969), Chap. 4.

SITUATION 2.3

Concepts of Preschool Children

The reference by Johnston and Burns (see Recommended Readings) provides the following information: 80 percent of the five-year-olds studied responded accurately to situations requiring an understanding of largest, smallest, tallest while only 50 percent recognized situations describing the terms shortest, few, and some. Eighty-nine percent were able to name the clock while only 51 percent could name the calendar. Suggest ways that research relating to children's concepts can be used by teachers. (Johnston and Burns, p. 279.)

SOCIAL DEVELOPMENT

Although no national norms exist for the social development of children, the teacher can find a great deal of information concerning types of social behavior normally displayed by children at various age levels. The student will certainly want to explore in depth this fascinating subject of how immature individuals struggle to meet their developmental needs, and at the same time try to learn the rules of the game in the ever-expanding number of groups in which they hold membership.

Social Characteristics

1. During early childhood, children are more interested in the approval of their parents and teachers than they are in the approval of other children; after they have been in school a few years, their interest in playmates of their own age increases and their interest in adults decreases; the child who had once considered it a treat to accompany his parents on picnics and family gatherings now considers it a bore. In late childhood, the influence of the group on the social behavior of the child continues to increase; the group sets the style in clothing, the kind of play engaged in, and the patterns of right and wrong behavior.

2. In early childhood, the choice of a companion is likely to be another child of his own age or a year or two older, someone who can do the things he likes to do. Such factors as sex, intelligence, and status in the group do not influence his choice much at this time.

3. In later childhood, interest in team games increases; loyalty to the group, a feeling of superiority over those who are not members, and unwillingness to play with members of the opposite sex become dominant traits.

4. Negativism and resistance to adult authority become noticeable between the ages of two and four years; after age four they generally begin to decline.

5. By the time pupils reach the sixth grade, their ethical and moral standards are fairly well established. They exhibit a keen interest in social, political, and economic problems, but they frequently have vague and incorrect notions about the terms they use rather glibly in their routine school work.

6. During late childhood, girls are generally more mature than boys and tend to frown upon the youthful antics of boys of their own age.

7. The elementary school child grows gradually in his ability to work in groups. His social development is influenced by home, school, peer groups, the mass media, and other forces. "The Changing American Child" is a title that is used for an explanation of how a changing society has brought about changes in the intellectual and social development of children.[15] Suggestions for guiding the social development of children are presented in Chapter 4.

EMOTIONAL DEVELOPMENT

How a child feels about himself, other people, his home, and his school determines to some extent how well he will do in school. Emotional maturity is the result of many factors, but the child's experiences during the first few years of his life are perhaps the most important. The teacher who understands the factors that influence emotional development may be influential in helping children gain confidence, security, and satisfaction.

Emotional Characteristics

1. Changes in emotional behavior take place most rapidly during the early years of a child's life; emotions and feelings have become fairly well stabilized by the time the child enters school.

2. Although emotional behavior has an innate basis, people learn to emote in a specific manner as a result of life experiences.

3. Primary emotional behavior patterns are those that are based on innate factors; universal emotional behavior patterns are those that emerge from the universal experiences of the race.

4. Primary emotional behavior patterns have become fairly well established by the age of three; most of the changes thereafter are the

---

[15] Urie Bronfenbrenner, "The Changing American Child—A Speculative Analysis," in Robert J. Havighurst, Bernice L. Neugarten, and Jacqueline M. Falk (Eds.), *Society and Education* (Boston: Allyn and Bacon, Inc., 1967), pp. 67–74.

result of environmental influences. They are, therefore, said to be the result of learning.

5. To the extent that vastly different people all over the world treat their children alike in some circumstances, universal emotional behavior patterns emerge.

6. Emotional learning is influenced to a great extent by the emotional climate in the home and at school.

7. There is evidence that children from culturally disadvantaged homes frequently have to overcome a negative image of self.

8. One of the most important emotional needs of children is a feeling of confidence—confidence in oneself and confidence in others. Confidence in oneself increases as one has successful experiences. Confidence in others comes with the feeling that they will accept us as worthy persons with all our mistakes and shortcomings.

9. The school has an important responsibility for teaching children to express emotions in ways that are acceptable to others.

SITUATION 2.4
Emotional Maturity

What does emotional maturity mean? How does the behavior of an emotionally mature nine-year-old differ from that of an emotionally immature one? Can teachers influence emotional maturity?

10. Children need help in learning to get along with people whose "emotional dialects" differ from their own.[16]

11. Although children cannot be expected to achieve complete emotional maturity while they are in elementary school, adequate emotional support and guidance can help them attain sufficient maturity to use emotions effectively to establish satisfying relations with other people.

STUDYING THE INDIVIDUAL PUPIL

In many elementary schools today, there are children whose intellectual, social, and emotional needs are not being met by the school program. Some are failing to achieve as much in school subjects as their abilities should permit; some have negative feelings about themselves, their class-

[16] Horace B. English, *Dynamics of Child Development* (New York: Holt, Rinehart and Winston, Inc., 1961). See the discussion of emotional shadings of the language of everyday life, pp. 152–155.

Our study of human learning and development is making direct contributions to individualized instruction. (Photo courtesy Norman Public Schools.)

mates, and their school; and others never seem to be able to enter fully into the group life of the school. These children are described as trying to say something to adults who do not understand.

Many school systems now employ school psychologists, guidance specialists, social workers, and other specialized personnel. These specialists perform valuable services by helping teachers learn how to identify children who need special attention, suggesting ways of meeting the needs of children in the regular classroom, and providing clinical services for severely maladjusted children. It is the teacher, however, who has daily contacts with the pupils, and who is in a unique position to put sound psychological principles into practice. Indeed, a study of the individual child is an integral part of the work of the elementary school teacher, not merely an additional chore.

It cannot be assumed that dividing the pupils in any grade or year in school into groups based on test scores solves the problem of meeting individual needs. It should be recognized that children who have been placed in one of these groups on a narrow academic basis still differ widely in many attributes that influence success and satisfaction, and that each child must be understood and treated as an individual. Studies reported by Otto and Sanders indicate that dividing the pupils in a classroom into two groups on the basis of general ability reduced variability by 7 percent;

dividing them into three groups on the basis of general ability reduced variability by 17 percent.[17]

Sources of Information about Children

Successful teaching in the new elementary school involves getting enough information about each child to understand why he behaves as he does in certain situations and how his achievement in school subjects is influenced by various factors in his environment. The teacher cannot be expected to be as proficient in the use of child-study instruments and procedures as the school psychologist; he cannot be expected to administer all the tests and gather all the information needed about all the children he teaches. But he can be expected to examine and interpret the information already available; refine and extend his techniques for studying individual pupils; and utilize opportunities arising in connection with regular classwork to gain a better understanding of each pupil.

CUMULATIVE RECORDS. Most school systems today maintain a system of cumulative records. These records, when systematically maintained, provide much information about children that the teacher can use in guidance, instruction, grouping, and reporting to parents. Some school systems provide written instructions to principals and teachers designating when certain information is to be recorded on cumulative record forms and explaining how the information is to be summarized and used. The information contained in cumulative-record folders varies from one school system to another. Certain types of information however are generally included:

Family background. Address, marital status of parents, age, nationality, educational level, and occupation of each parent; number, sex, and age of siblings; and data on others living in the home.

School history. Date of entrance into school; schools attended; times retained in a grade or given double promotion; marks in school subjects; ratings on conduct, citizenship, effort, and work habits; reports of interviews with parents or parental visits to school; referrals to specialized personnel; records of special abilities, interests, or accomplishments; and data concerning social adjustment and emotional maturity.

School health record. Periodic recordings of height, weight, and general nutritional status; reports on vision, hearing, and speech; record of inoculations, diseases, and illnesses; and recommendations of physicians and nurses.

---

[17] Henry J. Otto and David C. Sanders, *Elementary School Organization and Administration,* 4th ed. (New York: Appleton-Century-Crofts, 1964), p. 104.

Test results. Scores on intelligence and achievement tests and rating on personality, interests, and special aptitude scales.

THE PRINCIPAL AND OTHER TEACHERS. By talking with the principal and two or three former teachers of a pupil the current teacher can determine whether the child's present behavior represents a continuation of his previous behavior or whether it represents a new development. If the school is departmentalized, the principal and all the teachers who work with the child may hold a conference for the purpose of pooling information. These contacts not only serve as data-collecting devices but also help the teacher to understand the experiences the child is having in other phases of the school program. Frequently one teacher will recognize in a child potentials that other teachers have overlooked and thus open the way for the other teachers to provide more positive guidance for him.

It is important, however, for the teacher to distinguish between descriptions of a child's behavior and conclusions that another teacher may have reached about the child—between a single episode and behavior that has been exhibited over and over for a considerable length of time. Unless each teacher is diligent in getting specific information about his behavior, a child may carry over from year to year and from classroom to classroom a reputation concerning a trait that has long since disappeared.

Specialized School Personnel

Many school systems employ specialized personnel who can help the classroom teacher gain information that is needed in order to adapt instruction and guidance to individual abilities and needs. The guidance worker, the school nurse, the school physician, the school psychologist, the attendance officer, the social worker, the speech and hearing therapist, and others can provide useful information if the teacher establishes an effective working arrangement with them. If the school system does not employ specialized personnel, these services can sometimes be secured from community agencies.

Regular Classroom Activities

Regular classroom activities provide the teacher with many opportunities to learn about individual pupils. When these opportunities are used, teachers are less likely to regard child study as an extra chore, and the chances are increased that the information will be put to use. The language arts class provides a natural setting for the pupil to express his feelings about himself and his school and to reveal his interests, goals, and problems. The social studies class provides data for a sociogram when children are allowed to express their preferences regarding pupils with whom they would like to work on committees. Health classes provide opportunities for pupils to discuss their own health problems, concepts, and practices. Classes in physical education provide opportunities for the teacher to gain information about the pupil's ability to play with others and to observe symptoms of abnormality. Classes in art, music, and homemaking frequently reveal special abilities or aspects of personality that are not brought out by other classes. It seems reasonable that the vast amount of information about pupils that can be obtained from regular classroom activities should be used before extra time is devoted to special techniques of child study.

Conferences with Parents

The idea that the whole child comes to school is generally accepted by teachers of young children. Most of them realize that they cannot understand a child unless they know something about the home in which he is growing up. Teachers have developed many effective ways of working with parents in groups and as individuals. The success of any method depends to a large degree upon the attitude of the teacher. If he is suspicious of parents, if he is afraid they will criticize his methods of teaching, no method he uses is likely to succeed. On the other hand, if he believes that parents and teachers have a common interest, if he welcomes suggestions from parents, almost any method is likely to bring about wholesome results.

A profitable type of group meeting is the one in which the parents of the children in a certain room meet regularly with the teacher. The children help arrange the chairs and decorate the room before they leave in the afternoon. The parents decide what problems they want to discuss; they exchange experiences and express their opinions. The teacher suggests books, pamphlets, and magazine articles dealing with the problems in which parents are interested. He guides the discussion in an unobtrusive manner, attempts to clarify issues, and provides whatever facts he may have regarding the problem. He avoids making any member of the group feel deflated or ignorant and frequently states that he does not know any one best method of handling a certain problem. When these meetings continue for the entire period that the child remains in the elementary school, each child has several adults in the community, in addition to his teachers, who know him well and who are interested in his progress.

The individual conference is regarded by many as the most effective single method of working with parents. Many teachers arrange to hold a conference with the parents of every child in the room during the first month of school, and as frequently as possible thereafter. The value of the individual conference depends largely upon the preparation the teacher has made for it and the skill with which he conducts the conference. The teacher is fortunate, of course, if his preservice preparation has included both theory and practice in the art of interviewing individuals. If the interview is to be successful in establishing better working relationships between the home and the school, certain fundamental principles must be observed:

1. The teacher must be relaxed and comfortable and must make the parent feel comfortable also.

2. Instead of presuming to know all the answers, the teacher should approach the interview with the attitude that the parent can give him much information he can use in working with the child.

3. The teacher should give the parent a chance to ask questions about how the child is getting along in school, why certain procedures are used in the school, and what the parent can do to help the child make better use of his opportunities.

4. Before the interview begins, the teacher should review the child's school record, so that he can supply information for the parent and raise specific questions for discussion.

5. The teacher should not look upon the interview as a means of completing a neat plan for working with the child. At best, it can provide only a few new insights and give the parent a chance to talk. By talking, the parent may supply useful information, clarify his thinking about the child and the school, and go away with a better understanding of what the school is trying to do.

Systematic Observation

It is easy to underestimate the value of systematic observation as a source of information about the individual pupil. There are many phases of growth for which we do not have standardized measuring instruments. Moreover, the measuring instruments we have are used primarily for making cross-sectional studies of groups, rather than for tracing the course of development of an individual child over a period of time. These cross-sectional data are obtained quickly, are easy to summarize, and show readily the differences that exist among children with respect to a given trait at a given time. Although requiring more time, longitudinal studies provide insight into developmental patterns that cannot be gained by any other procedure.

The teacher must, therefore, become a skillful observer. This requires knowledge of what types of behavior to look for, skill in record-keeping, and ability to interpret and use the evidence collected. Forms for recording observations vary from the extremely simple to the most complex. The anecdotal record, for example, usually contains spaces for jotting down weekly comments concerning evidence of physical, mental, social, and emotional development. Other forms consist merely of a list of items to be checked, such as: Does he show evidence of impaired vision? Is he taller or heavier than the rest of his group? Does he like most of his school subjects? Does he get along well with other children in the group? Does he seem well balanced emotionally?

Work Specimen Folders

Some teachers maintain for each pupil a folder in which are filed specimens of his work in spelling, handwriting, drawing, arithmetic, and other subjects. These folders should be maintained over a three-year period, in order to indicate pupil growth over an extended period. Pupils participate in filing, arranging, and evaluating specimens of their own work. They should be encouraged to date each piece of material filed in the folder.

USING WHAT WE KNOW ABOUT CHILDREN

A substantial amount of information about the characteristics and needs of children is available to the elementary school teacher. The *Encyclopedia of Educational Research,* the yearbooks of professional societies, the journals dealing with child development, and the textbooks used in professional education courses reveal how vast this store of information has become. However, in elementary education, as in other fields of human endeavor, we are not putting to use all that we know.

The traditional attitude toward educational research was that individuals who were exceptionally well trained in research techniques should investigate educational problems scientifically; that they should not be concerned about the changes in practice that might result from their findings; and that the application of research findings to practice in schools should be left to administrators, supervisors, and teachers. There is no doubt that published information resulting from traditional educational research has through the years slowly influenced educational practice. Publishers incorporate the findings into books written for children; courses of study and curriculum guides recommend learning activities and teaching procedures based on research data; and teachers, administrators, and supervisors sometimes read research reports and modify practices accordingly.

In recent years there has been increasing concern about the lag between what is being done in schools and what research indicates should be done. Some believe that the difficulty lies in inadequate communication. They suggest that research reports contain more illustrations and state more clearly the implications for practice. Some professional associations have attempted to surmount the communications hurdle by publishing pamphlets, written in untechnical language, that point out the implications of research for teaching various school subjects. Others believe that the difficulty is deeper than communication. They suggest that action research, in which teachers and other practitioners attempt to study their problems scientifically, will lead to better decisions and more effective practices.

By putting to use what they have learned about children, both from research done by others and by themselves, many teachers and administrators have found ways to serve the individual child instead of trying to fit every child into a rigid school program. They have found that many traditional school practices had to be modified or eliminated before each child could receive the kinds of educational experiences he needed as an individual.

SUMMARY

1. Teachers are becoming increasingly aware that teaching is a process of releasing human potential.

2. Because children vary in rates of learning, differentiated methods and materials are required if all pupils are to have an opportunity to learn as much as they are capable of learning.

3. Learning is now regarded by many as the modification of behavior that takes place as the individual interacts with the environment.

4. The teacher in the new elementary school is concerned about learning as it applies to school subjects; he is also concerned with helping children learn to become adequate, fully functioning persons.

5. There is evidence that the average level of intelligence can be raised by about 30 points of IQ in a generation or two provided children are reached early enough.

6. When a teacher believes that pupils are slow learners, the pupils tend to perform in harmony with the teacher's expectation. This is called the "self-fulfilling prophecy."

7. National curriculum-improvement projects have supplied a great deal of material and a great many procedures for teaching children to think, solve problems, and develop concepts.

8. The first three years that the child spends in school constitute the most crucial period available to schools for the development of general learning patterns.

9. Child development at one period influences the kind and amount of development that can be attained at a later period.

10. Research findings relating to the critical years support the policy of providing school services for children under six years of age, broadening the scope of pupil personnel services, providing more individualized instruction, and providing well-qualified teachers for elementary schools.

11. Curriculum-improvement projects at the national and state levels

have been listing content in the various elementary school areas in terms of concepts.

12. Psychologists have identified stages in concept development as pre-operational, concrete operations, and formal operations. All children seem to follow this sequence in concept development, but the ages at which they enter a new stage vary significantly.

13. The teacher can obtain a great deal of information about the types of social behavior children normally display at different age levels.

14. The child's experiences during the first few days of his life are the most influential factors in determining his emotional development.

15. How a child feels about himself, other people, his home, and his school determines to some extent how well he will do in school.

16. The teacher must study the individual pupil objectively if the needs of the pupil are to be met.

RECOMMENDED READINGS

Bloom, Benjamin S., *Stability and Change in Human Characteristics*. New York: John Wiley & Sons, Inc., 1964. Traces the course of development of a large number of human characteristics including intelligence, achievement, and personality. Concludes that change in many characteristics becomes more and more difficult with age.

English, Horace B., *Dynamics of Child Development*. New York: Holt, Rinehart and Winston, Inc., 1961. Chapters 4 and 5 deal with the development of emotional maturity.

Frazier, Alexander (Ed.), *The New Elementary School*. Washington, D.C.: Association for Supervision and Curriculum Development and Department of Elementary School Principals, N.E.A., 1968. Part I deals with new knowledge about children, understanding, conceptual development, and the acquisition of language.

Gagné, Robert M., *The Conditions of Learning*, 2d ed. New York: Holt, Rinehart and Winston, Inc., 1970. Chapter 1 presents the implications of a view of learning for education. Chapter 2 relates types of learning to instruction.

Havighurst, Robert J., Bernice L. Neugarten, and Jacqueline M. Falk, *Society and Education: A Book of Readings*. Boston: Allyn and Bacon, Inc., 1967. Part 1 presents a discussion of "The Changing American Child," and explains the influence of the family, peer group, and school on the socialization of the child.

Johnston, A. Montgomery, and Paul C. Burns (Eds.), *Research in Elementary Curriculum*. Boston: Allyn and Bacon, Inc., 1970. Chapter 5 reports some research relating to children's arithmetic concepts.

Leonard, George B., *Education and Ecstasy*. New York: Delacorte Press, 1968. Chapter 2 reports experimentation designed to alter the functioning of the brain; states that education can be as effective in increasing mental powers as other devices. Points out promising developments designed to expand human potentials.

Passow, A. Harry, and Robert R. Leeper (Eds.), *Intellectual Development: Another Look.* Washington, D.C.: Association for Supervision and Curriculum Development, 1964. Contains articles by leading authorities on intellectual development in early childhood, cognitive structures, the inquiry process, and the development of mathematical concepts.

Ragan, William B., and George Henderson, *Foundations of American Education.* New York: Harper & Row, Publishers, 1970. Chapter 6 contains a summary of the social characteristics of elementary school children; explains changing views of intelligence.

Rosenthal, Robert, and Lenore Jacobson, *Pygmalion in the Classroom.* New York: Holt, Rinehart and Winston, Inc., 1968. Reports evidence that teacher expectations influence student performance.

Sigel, Irving E., and Frank H. Hooper (Eds.), *Logical Thinking in Children.* New York: Holt, Rinehart and Winston, Inc., 1968. Reports research relating to cognitive development during the period between six and twelve years based on the theories of Piaget.

Tanck, Marlin L., "Teaching Concepts, Generalizations, and Constructs," in Dorothy McClure Fraser (Ed.), *Social Studies Curriculum Development: Prospects and Problems.* Washington, D.C.: National Council for the Social Studies, 1969. Explains the meaning of a concept; outlines a procedure for teaching concepts in the social studies.

Chapter 3

The Changing Elementary School Curriculum

Curriculum reform of the late 1950s and of the 1960s has resulted in many innovations both in content and process. That this reform has given us excellent new resources to use if we can but learn to use them with insight seems no longer to be a debatable matter.

> Paul R. Klohr in Alexander Frazier (Ed.), A *Curriculum for Children* (Washington, D.C.: Association for Supervision and Curriculum Development, 1969), p. 91.

The curriculum reform movement that has been accelerated since 1957 has been a reflection both of a better understanding of the changing society in which we live and of new insights into child development and learning. The curriculum of the elementary school has been changing significantly during the decade of the 1960s; it is expected to change even more rapidly and more significantly during the 1970s and 1980s.

THE NATURE OF THE CURRICULUM

The word "curriculum," in the usual sense, refers to the whole body of courses offered by an educational institution or by a department thereof. The elementary school curriculum is regarded by some writers as a collection of subjects to be taught; by others, as all the experiences that children have under the influence of the school. The second concept is used in this text. Although the selection of appropriate content to be taught is an important phase of curriculum planning, the curriculum includes much more than content; it includes teacher-pupil relationships, methods of teaching, evaluation procedures, the so-called extracurricular activities—in short, the whole life and program of the school.

The curriculum is concerned with providing an environment that will help each child achieve self-fulfillment and at the same time prepare for social service by acquiring useful information, skills, and attitudes. The school curriculum is a specialized rather than a chance environment. Instead of being as broad as life itself, it is an environment that has been simplified, systematized, and edited.

Planning Learning Experiences

Curriculum planning for American elementary schools takes place at several different levels: national, state, county, local school system, the

The teacher's contribution to the curriculum can often be neither predicted nor specified. (Photo courtesy Norman Public Schools.)

individual elementary school, and the individual classroom. There is no legally constituted national body for curriculum planning. Voluntary groups at the national level have, however, made studies and published reports that have influenced curriculum planning. State, county, and city school systems have also published courses of study or curriculum guides that establish a broad curriculum framework within which the teacher plans specific learning experiences.

It is in the individual classroom, however, that the most crucial phase of curriculum planning takes place. It is here that the teacher's knowledge of content in the various fields, his information relating to the realities and ideals of the culture, his insight into the nature of human growth and learning, and his understanding of the purposes of education in American democracy are incorporated into actual learning experiences for boys and girls. Others have participated in setting up broad educational goals, but the teacher and the pupils with whom he works must make a multitude of decisions within the limits of these broad goals.

SITUATION 3.1

Changing the Curriculum

Some authorities regard the curriculum as a document that is prepared by a committee and handed to the teacher before he has ever met the class. Thus, curriculum planning takes place before teaching begins. This text regards the teacher-pupil planning that goes on in the classroom as the most important phase of curriculum planning. Explain what would be involved in changing the curriculum in line with the first concept; the second concept.

PRINCIPLES OF CURRICULUM ORGANIZATION. The practical problem confronting the staff of an elementary school is not that of deciding which of the many well-known types of curriculum design to adopt; it is rather a problem of developing a design through which the objectives accepted by that school can best be attained. Experience indicates that certain principles serve as useful guides to elementary school groups that are engaged in the cooperative enterprise of developing and improving the design of the curriculum.

Developing the design of the curriculum should be a cooperative enterprise. The principal of a school may decide without consulation what type of curriculum organization is best for the school; he may even label the plan "our life-centered curriculum" and have it distributed to teachers and parents. This procedure, however, does not work out well in practice. The principle of the consent of the governed is deeply embedded in our culture. People contribute more to an enterprise when they have a part in planning it. The design of the curriculum is the concern not only of the principal, but also of teachers, pupils, parents, and other citizens of the community. It is the function of educational leadership to help all who are concerned with the enterprise to develop an organization through which each can make his own unique contribution.

The school program should be conceived and operated as a whole. The basic subjects, the special subjects, health services, recreation, the school lunch program, school clubs, and guidance services should be planned so that each supplements the others rather than being allowed to develop piecemeal. The term "horizontal articulation" is frequently used to designate the plan for seeing that studies at any particular grade level are interrelated.

Curriculum organization should foster continuity in learning experiences. The learning activities in which a child engages during any school year should be related to those of previous years and to those that are to follow. The plan for providing year-to-year continuity in the learning experiences is frequently called "vertical articulation."

Learning experiences should be organized on the basis of the needs of children who are growing up in contemporary American society. The needs of children cannot be understood apart from an understanding of problems of living in the culture. Successful living in modern America demands not only acquisition of an increasing number of facts, but skill in human relations, respect for the opinions of others, ability to use leisure time constructively, and skill in problem solving. Curriculum design should, therefore, center the life of the school around basic problems of cooperative living.

Opportunities should be provided for teachers and pupils to select and plan specific learning activities within the general curriculum framework. Selecting and planning learning activities is an important phase of the educative process. Children, together with their teacher, should have an important part in curriculum planning, but this planning should be done within the general framework of the curriculum that has been agreed upon by the school staff.

Developing a Curriculum Guide

The results of preplanning of the curriculum are made available to teachers in the form of a curriculum guide or framework. For example, a system-wide committee may work for a year or more to produce a tentative curriculum guide for the social studies. After the tentative guide is used on a trial basis in selected schools, it is revised, reproduced, and distributed to teachers. The curriculum guide, or framework, may be a useful tool for the teacher provided it is presented as a resource rather than as a set of rigid requirements to be met or specific content to be covered by all students in the same length of time.

Although these documents vary greatly in length, format, and contents, the following features are found in most of them:

1. Curriculum guides generally contain a statement of the objectives of the subject. The trend in recent years has been toward the statement of more explicit objectives and toward the statement of objectives in terms of changes in behavior. Those who develop curriculum guides today generally expect more of students than the acquisition of isolated bits of information. Social studies guides, for example, emphasize (a) learning about the world as it is and as it is becoming and (b) the development of inquiry skills that can be used to gain social understanding throughout a lifetime.

2. Curriculum guides generally suggest the scope of topics to be studied and other learning experiences for the course. The older documents (generally called courses of study) listed in great detail the content to be covered. The course of study for elementary school science, for example, listed areas such as the earth, the universe, living things, physical and chemical changes, conditions necessary to life, and man's attempts to control his environment. Listed under each of these areas were many specific topics to be studied. The typical course of study was content-centered rather than process-centered. The new curricula in elementary science, on the other hand, are process-centered; observation, measurement, experimentation, interpretation of data, and prediction are some of the processes that are explained and illustrated in the curriculum guide.

3. Curriculum guides generally provide suggestions concerning the sequence in which various learning experiences are to be undertaken. Curriculum-planning groups are interested in the sequence of learning experiences because it is considered desirable to provide for continuity in the learning experiences of children; what students are expected to study today will depend upon what they have already learned, and what they learn today will determine to some extent what they can learn tomorrow.

4. Curriculum guides generally suggest appropriate types of instructional resources for the convenience of the teacher. Although the teacher is the final judge of the materials to be used, the media specialist can provide valuable service by examining, testing, and recommending instructional media to be listed in the curriculum guide. He can also demonstrate how these media can be used most effectively.

5. Curriculum guides generally suggest appropriate evaluation instruments and procedures and explain how to make the most effective use

of information gained from evaluation. Recent developments in the area of educational evaluation are examined in Chapter 15.

SITUATION 3.2
Trends in Curriculum Guides

Examine some curriculum guides produced by state and local curriculum committees several years ago; others that have been produced in the last five years. Note differences in these guides. Cite evidence of a trend toward process-oriented curricula; of emphasis on developing inquiry skills.

The Teacher and the Curriculum

Increased curriculum-improvement activity at the national level has not diminished the time and attention given to this activity at the local school-system level. This has happened because programs developed at the national level have had to be adapted to local circumstances and resources, because leaders have found that participation in curriculum-improvement projects is an effective means of promoting the professional growth of teachers, because serving on curriculum-improvement committees has frequently promoted innovations in individual schools, and because the influence of experienced teachers is needed to keep instructional planning close to reality.

If teachers are to be effective in the decision-making process relating to curriculum improvement, they must be willing to state clearly what they regard as good about the current program and what is in greatest need of improvement, and be prepared to support their position with research findings, practices in other schools, and the judgment of specialists.

There are several important elements in the teacher's relationship to the curriculum. The teacher should be free to adapt and revise the curriculum guide within reasonable limits, to cross departmental lines, and to adapt the program to the varying capabilities and needs of students. The teacher should also be free to take advantage of special "teachable moments." These moments occur when there is a presidential election; when a famous musician, writer, or statesman comes to town; and when there has been an unusual happening in the community. These unplanned experiences add joy, zest, and enthusiasm to learning. Another important element is what Gould has called "the wisdom factor." Speaking of the teacher, he says,

> Regardless of the subject matter involved, the whole should be surrounded by the aura of his personal values, his personal experiences, his

own wisdom. There is no way to put these into the curriculum outline, nor can the teacher purposefully plan when and where he can exert such influences transcending the course content.[1]

THE "SELF-AS-INSTRUMENT" CONCEPT. The "wisdom factor" is closely akin to the "self-as-instrument" concept. According to Combs:

> The effective professional worker is no longer regarded as a technician applying methods in a more or less mechanical fashion the way he has been taught. We now see him as an intelligent human being using himself, his knowledge, and the resources at hand to solve the problems for which he is responsible.[2]

Those who hold this view of the relationship of the teacher to the curriculum are concerned about the dangers of regimentation that lead to stultification and stagnation—about such expressions as "teacher-proof" materials. They would like to see a curriculum influenced by what the teacher puts of herself into the enterprise—a curriculum that is characterized by flexibility and vitality.

SITUATION 3.3
*Preparation for Participation
in Curriculum Planning*

If we accept the "self-as-instrument" concept in relation to teaching, what consequences will this have for teacher education? What will it mean in terms of individualization of instruction? In terms of creativity? In terms of the concept of the "good teacher." (See Combs [1965], pp. 8–9.)

The Ability To Participate Effectively in Curriculum Improvement

The curriculum of an elementary school reveals, to some extent at least, the desires that the adults of a community have for their children; it is the instrument for bringing to bear on the lives of children the most wholesome influences in the culture. The overall design of the curriculum is influenced, in a democracy, by many individuals and groups. In previous

---

[1] Samuel B. Gould, "The Teacher's Impact on the Curriculum," in Edmund C. Short and George D. Marconnit (Eds.), *Contemporary Thought on Public School Curriculum* (Dubuque, Iowa: Wm. C. Brown Company, Publishers, 1968), p. 350.

[2] Arthur W. Combs, *The Professional Education of Teachers* (Boston: Allyn and Bacon, 1965), p. 8.

generations, when teachers were poorly prepared, the major decisions concerning the curriculum were made by experts in the various subject-matter fields. Courses of study were prepared by experts, and teachers were expected to follow them regardless of their own ideas or the abilities and needs of the particular group of children they were teaching.

Increased information about the learning process and the characteristics and needs of children, rapid changes in the culture, and improvements in teacher education have resulted in many changes in the elementary school curriculum and have increased the responsibility of classroom teachers for helping to make decisions. Curriculum planning is now regarded as a continuous, cooperative enterprise in which the teacher plays a major role. Teachers are expected to serve on committees and participate in the deliberations of the entire staff in determining the over-all design of the curriculum. Furthermore, the overall design of the

Children at Westwood School, Oklahoma City, are developing appreciation for our American heritage. (Photo courtesy Oklahoma City Public Schools.)

curriculum developed by the entire staff usually leaves a great deal of freedom for the individual teacher to make adaptations to his own classroom situation. Much of the significant curriculum planning, therefore, goes on in the individual classroom.

Programs of teacher education, both preservice and in-service, are placing a great deal of emphasis on preparation for participating in curriculum planning. Techniques of formulating educational objectives, organizing learning experiences, developing units of work, studying the individual child, surveying the community, selecting and using learning materials, and evaluating pupil progress are integral phases of the professional preparation of teachers.

HISTORICAL PERSPECTIVE

The student can gain a better understanding of recent innovations in the elementary school curriculum if he takes a brief look at the historical development of the American elementary school. Indeed, one writer has stated that no one is competent to teach in America's schools unless he has a reasonably broad understanding of "the growth and changing functions of the school as a social institution."[3] Another writer has stated that curriculum theorists and practitioners should "engage in dialogue not only among themselves, but with their professional forebears."[4]

Although the common schools established in the American colonies were descendants of the vernacular schools of Europe, they were soon tranformed into truly American institutions. The American elementary school that developed during the nineteenth century was a unique social experiment; no previous society had deliberately established a single school system for the education of everyone's children. In no other country has the school their children attended been so responsive to the desires of the people in the local community. The people in the various states, through their representatives, created the public elementary school; it was theirs and theirs it remains.

The elementary school has come to be associated in the minds of the people with the ideal of human freedom. The dream of a social order in which every child could grow up and achieve success, freedom, respect, and a measure of economic security has come closer to realization here than anywhere else because it has been supported by a system of free public education. Although some critics maintain that we have sacrificed

[3] William E. Drake, *The American School in Transition* (Englewood Cliffs, N.J.: Prentice-Hall, 1955), p. v.

[4] Arno Bellack, "History of Curriculum Thought and Practice," *Review of Educational Research*, June 1969, Chap. 1.

quality in our effort to educate all American children, few would deny that the experiment has helped to underwrite the democratic way of life.

Origin of Belief That Schools Should Be a Public Responsibility

The student interested in the origin of the idea that the education of children should be a public rather than a private responsibility should study certain developments that took place in Europe long before our Puritan forefathers passed the Old Deluder Satan Act. A school of medicine was established at Salerno in southern Italy in the eleventh century, and a little later a school of law was established at Bologna in northern Italy. Before 1200, a great university, which eventually became the principal center for the study of theology, began to develop at Paris. Universities were soon established in other European cities, to prepare the sons of members of the ruling classes for the professions. Because instruction in the universities was in Latin, secondary schools teaching Latin were soon established to prepare students for the universities. The children of the common people, however, had no share in the education provided in the universities and secondary schools.

The art of printing from metal type was put into practice about 1450, making it possible to produce a hundred books for what had been the cost of three. When books written in the vernacular became more readily available, schools for children of the common people increased. The invention and spread of printing was possibly the most important single factor in the rise of the common school.

One of the earliest pleas for education as a public responsibility was made by Martin Luther. His letter of 1524, to the mayors and aldermen of German cities, has been called "the charter of the common schools."[5] He made it clear that schools were needed for the sake of Christianity, the maintenance of civil order, and the proper regulation of the household. Furthermore, he called upon the city officials to take this matter into their own hands or "be obliged to feel in vain the pangs of remorse forever." The work of Martin Luther, John Calvin, and other leaders of religious reform in Europe had a profound influence on the colonial and early national development of education in this country.

The Religious Motive for Education

Virginia and most of the Southern colonies were settled by English royalists. These people believed that the business of the poor was to

---

[5] See J. D. Russell and C. H. Judd, *The American Educational System* (Boston: Houghton Mifflin Company, 1940), pp. 19–21.

work rather than to think. "To make society happy," they said, "it is requisite that great numbers should be ignorant as well as poor." Governor Berkeley wrote in 1671, "I thank God there are no free schools or printing presses, and I hope we shall not have them these hundred years." His hope was more than realized, for Virginia did not develop a system of free schools until the middle of the nineteenth century.

The Puritans in New England, however, regarded schools in a different light. Although it cannot be said that they visualized a great system of state schools to support a democratic society, they did recognize the necessity for schools to support their religious beliefs. They believed that the Bible was the guide to salvation, that each person should be able to read the Bible, and that this required that schools be established. Drake has stated, "It will be observed that there was much of missionary zeal in this period, but that such was more a zeal for the church than for humanity." [6]

In 1647 the General Court of the Massachusetts Bay Colony passed a law now generally known as the "Old Deluder Satan Act." The law required that every township that had fifty householders should appoint someone to teach "all such children as shall resort to him to read and write." The wages of the schoolmaster were to be paid in part by the parents or masters of the children and in part by the inhabitants in general. The law also provided that every township that had a hundred families or householders should set up a grammar school, "the master thereof being able to instruct youths so far as they shall be fitted for the university." The university in this case was Harvard, which had been established in 1636.

The law provided a fine of five pounds for failure to establish schools. The fine was raised to ten pounds in 1671 and to twenty pounds in 1683. The law did not compel parents to send their children to school, and since it was difficult to arrest and fine a town, it was reported near the close of the century that the law was "shamefully neglected by divers towns." The details of erecting school buildings, levying school taxes, and hiring teachers were left to the people of the various towns. Another law, passed in 1693, gave the selectmen authority to levy taxes for schools when a majority of the people of the town so voted, and another series of laws was passed providing that the grammar schoolmaster should be examined and certified by a majority of the ministers of his and adjoining towns and that elementary school teachers should be examined and certified by the selectmen. As the people moved from the compact communities into more remote areas, it became necessary to organize schools on a district rather than a town basis. Thus, Massachusetts and other New England colonies provided a precedent for taxation for school pur-

[6] Drake, p. 64.

poses, for the certification of teachers, for the district school, and for the local board of education.

The religious motive for education in colonial times is revealed by the reasons stated for establishing schools, in the content of instructional material, in the control of the school by the church, and by the type of discipline practiced in the schools. The reason for establishing schools is revealed by the language used in the preamble of the Massachusetts law of 1647: "It being one chief purpose of that old deluder Satan, to keep men from a knowledge of Scripture. . . ."

Additional evidence of the religious motive for education is found in the famous *New England Primer*, which was the most-used schoolbook in the American colonies, and which continued to be widely used for more than a hundred years. The contents of this book, the total sales of which have been estimated at 3 million copies, have been described in practically every history of American education that has been written. It contained an illustrated alphabetical rhyme beginning with, "In Adam's fall we sinned all," and ending with, "Zacheus he did climb a tree his Lord to see." The Lord's Prayer, the Apostles' Creed, the Ten Commandments, a list of the books of the Old and the New Testaments, and the Shorter Catechism were included to make sure that children would be well equipped to defeat the schemes of the old deluder Satan. Reisner has suggested that it was not only a religious book, but that it was religious in "the strict and narrow sense of Calvinistic orthodoxy."[7]

The discipline in colonial schools was influenced by the theological beliefs of the times. The Puritans believed that children were conceived in iniquity and born in sin, and that they could be regenerated only by the "rod of correction." It was the duty of the colonial schoolmaster, therefore, to beat the devil out of them with rod or switch. The expression, "beat the devil out of them," which is frequently heard today, was taken literally in colonial times. The whipping post and the dunce cap were familiar objects in colonial classrooms, and fear was the chief means of maintaining control of pupils. These practices reflected the harshness and brutality of the times. New England laws permitted young people to be put to death for disobedience of parents, and a young Harvard student was publicly beaten in the library in the presence of all the students for using blasphemous words. The event was preceded and followed by prayer offered by the president of the university. The close relationship of school discipline to the theology of the time is aptly illustrated by the statement, "It is possible to imagine a child cringing in fear before one dressed in ministerial black holding a rod in his hand."[8]

    [7] Edward H. Reisner, *The Evolution of the Common School* (New York: Crowell-Collier and Macmillan, Inc., 1930), p. 49.
    [8] Drake, p. 92.

This brief account of the small beginnings of elementary education during colonial times gives the reader some idea of the changes that had to take place before the common school of that period could become the American elementary school as we know it today.

A PERIOD OF DECLINE IN EDUCATION. The Massachusetts type of school was adopted in all the New England colonies except Rhode Island, where the devotion of the colonists to religious freedom was too strong to permit the establishment of schools dominated by one religious sect. Outside New England, colonial legislatures showed little interest in education, and schools developed more or less at random. The law of 1647 was followed by a period of educational decline in Massachusetts and in other New England colonies.

Several developments contributed to the decline of the New England town school. When the Commonwealth government was established in England, the migration of Puritans to the New World practically ceased. The unity of religious belief, which made the Massachusetts law of 1647 possible, gradually gave way to a divergence of beliefs and to the toleration of other sects. When people moved into remote sections of a township, they demanded that the school be brought nearer to them; this gave rise to the "moving" school and finally to the district school. The last step in the decline of the town school was reached when each district within the town established its own school. School districts were not able to maintain as good schools as the towns had provided, and when the Revolution began, New England had poorer schools than those that had existed a century earlier.

Education as a Foundation
for Popular Government

During the Revolutionary and early National periods, the idea that free public education was the foundation of popular government began to emerge. The emphasis on liberty, equality, and the rights of the individual expressed in such documents as the Declaration of Independence, the Preamble to the Constitution, and the Bill of Rights provided a new motive for education. The Ordinance of 1785 provided that the sixteenth section of each township in the Northwest Territory be set aside for school purposes. Madison wrote, "A popular government without popular information, or the means of acquiring it, is but a prologue to a farce or a tragedy or perhaps both." Jefferson wrote from France to his former teacher, "Preach, my dear sir, a crusade against ignorance; establish and improve the law for educating the common people."

As early as 1779, Jefferson drafted a plan for a system of public education and tried to get it adopted in Virginia. The only part of his plan that he lived to see established was the University of Virginia, and it was not until the Public School Revival got under way during the era of Jacksonian Democracy that state legislatures began to enact laws in keeping with the ideas of Jefferson and Madison.

The Public School Revival

In 1826, just two years before Andrew Jackson was elected President, there was only one institution in the United States for the preparation of teachers, and no pedagogical book had yet been printed in this country. Although Jefferson and others had urged that universal public education was the foundation of a free society, the idea had little support in the state legislatures. The inadequate facilities that did exist for the education of children were provided by private schools and by church schools. The practice of granting public funds to private schools was common, and some states passed laws to permit certain localities to establish "pauper" schools for children of poor parents. The opposition, from private schools, from religious sects, and from those who believed that it was unjust to compel people who had no children to pay taxes to support schools, had to be overcome before public schools could be established in the various states.

By 1876, the principle of universal free public schools had been accepted in all the states, state systems for administering the schools had been established everywhere except in the Southern states, public normal schools had been generally established, and the system had been extended to include four years of high school. Why so pronounced a change in American education came about in fifty years can only be understood by examining the movement known as the "Public School Revival" and the forces that contributed to its success.

What was the Public School Revival? Some say that it was merely the lengthened shadow of Horace Mann. Although he was the most outstanding leader in American education during this period, other men prepared the way for him, and significant developments in American life contributed to the success of the movement to which he gave intelligent, effective, and courageous leadership. The Public School Revival is a collective term used to describe a great many events and movements occurring during the period and ultimately resulting in the improvement of education. It involved changing long-established attitudes of those who influenced school legislation, persuading voters to cast their ballots for increased school expenditures, getting schools established where none had existed, establishing state departments of education, making provision for the preparation of teachers, and enriching the curriculum.

THE INFLUENCE OF THE FRONTIER. Before the Public School Revival could succeed, changes that broke through the traditions and precedents of the past had to occur. The Constitution of the United States made no mention of education. Few of the liberal leaders of the period were present at the Constitutional Convention in 1787. Jefferson was in Paris, Patrick Henry refused to attend, and Samuel Adams was not chosen. The men who framed the Constitution were motivated by the desire to establish a strong central government, capable of protecting property, and to provide bulwarks against simple majority rule. Washington revealed his antidemocratic convictions when he wrote, "My opinion is that you could as soon scrub the blackamoor white as to change the principles of a professed Democrat, and that he will leave nothing unattempted to overturn the government of the country." John Adams described democracy as "the most ignoble, unjust, and detestable form of government"; and added that, "There never was a democracy that did not commit suicide."

However, the aristocratic ideas of Washington and Adams could not prevail long after the democratic spirit of the frontier began to be felt. The first settlements in the territory west of the Appalachians were established before the American Revolution. By 1790 the territory had a population of two hundred thousand; by 1803 four new states had been admitted from this territory; and by 1810 the population had reached a million. It was here that the traits commonly considered the most characteristically American developed; that the restrictions and conventions of the older settlements were abandoned; and that new ideas, customs, and institutions were developed. "For the frontier states," says Agar, "democracy was not an ideal; it was an inescapable condition, like the weather."[9]

All the states west of the Appalachians, except Mississippi, framed constitutions that omitted property qualifications for voting and holding office. Eventually the older states followed suit, although some delayed until the middle of the nineteenth century. Other reforms that indicated increasing confidence in the people followed. There was an increase in the number of offices to be filled by popular vote, representation in state legislatures was changed from the basis of wealth to the basis of population, and eventually United States senators were to be elected by popular vote rather than appointed by state legislatures.

As the right to vote was extended to all white male citizens, agitation for free public schools increased; citizens who were to have a part in determining the policies of the government had to be qualified to vote intelligently. The growth of democracy and the extension of suffrage

[9] Herbert Agar, *The People's Choice* (Boston: Houghton Mifflin Company, 1933), p. 109.

called for a system of public schools strong enough to meet the needs of a democracy and consistent with its ideals.

SECURING TAX SUPPORT FOR SCHOOLS. Gaining financial support for needed extensions of educational effort has never been easy in America. The quarrel with King George over taxation was one of the principal causes of the American Revolution. The principle that the state has a right to raise funds for the support of schools by taxation is so widely accepted today that it is easy to forget the long and bitter struggle required to get this principle accepted. State governments used many devices, such as tuition fees, rate bills, fines, lotteries, and taxes on liquor, before they finally realized that the safest and most certain plan was a direct tax on property.

The leaders of the Public School Revival faced bitter opposition to the idea of direct taxation on property for school purposes. A member of the legislature in Rhode Island told Henry Barnard that the state tax for schools could not be enforced even at the point of the bayonet, and a farmer of the same state threatened him with violence if he were ever caught preaching such "heresy as the partial confiscation of one man's property to educate another man's child." In 1829 a Raleigh newspaper published an open letter to members of the legislature of North Carolina in which the writer stated that more advantage would redound to young persons "if they should pass their days in the cotton patch, or at the plow, or in the cornfield, instead of being mewed up in a schoolhouse, where they are earning nothing." In answer to the argument that North Carolina was behind other states in the matter of education, he said, "We shall always have reason enough to crow over them . . . that our taxes are lighter than theirs." [10]

The experience of the schools in New York City illustrates the gradual acceptance of the idea of tax-supported schools. The Free School Society of New York City was organized in 1805, by a small group of philanthropists, to provide schools for children who did not attend private or church schools. The society received funds from both the city and the state. It received a new charter in 1826, changed its name to the Public School Society, and was granted permission to charge a fee for children whose parents could afford it. Various religious sects soon began demanding that their schools be granted a share of the public funds. Finally, in 1842, the legislature established a Board of Education for New York City to be elected by the people and to administer the school funds, no part of which was to be shared by a sectarian school. The principle of tax-supported, state-controlled, nonsectarian schools was gradually gaining acceptance.

---

[10] See Edgar W. Knight, *Education in the United States*, 3d rev. ed. (Boston: Ginn & Co., 1951), pp. 243–244.

FOREIGN INFLUENCES. The foreign influence most directly felt during the time of the Public School Revival came from Germany. During the twenty-five years following the Treaty of Tilsit in 1807, the state of Prussia established a thoroughly efficient national system of educational adminis- tration, headed by a Minister of Religion, Education, and Health in the king's cabinet. Each of the ten provinces had a division of education, a system of training teachers, and a Schulrath who supervised the folk (common) schools. Financial support came from fees levied on parents and property owners.

A great many intelligent Germans emigrated to the United States after the Revolution of 1848 and became strong advocates of the idea of school systems supported and controlled by the states. Furthermore, many of the leaders of the Public School Revival, including Horace Mann, visited Prussia and other German states and published reports on the school systems they had observed in operation.

Johann Heinrich Pestalozzi, born in Zurich, Switzerland, in 1746, has been called the father of the modern elementary school. His concept of child growth and development was an organismic rather than a me- chanical one. He recognized that the narrow, mechanical exercises in reading that were in use in the common schools of his time were inade- quate to prepare children for intelligent citizenship. In the schools he conducted in Switzerland, he introduced the practice of grouping children according to their abilities and achievements; expanded the curriculum; and developed methods of instruction that emphasized the use of concrete materials, cooperative procedures, thinking, and doing. His work influenced to a great extent methods of teaching children and of preparing teachers in Prussia, and later in the United States.

The Prussians, after their defeat by Napoleon in 1806, were deter- mined to establish a national system of education as a means of building a stronger nation. The young men who were sent to observe the work of Pestalozzi returned to establish teachers' seminaries and to work out instructional procedures in harmony with those they had seen him using. When Calvin E. Stowe, Horace Mann, and other leaders of the Public School Revival visited Prussia, they found the Prussian-Pestalozzian sys- tem in operation; they returned to this country to publish elaborate reports, which were distributed in all states. In 1861, in Oswego, New York, Edward A. Sheldon organized a teacher training class, which be- came the Oswego Normal School in 1863. The introduction of the ideas of Pestalozzi into this normal school was an important step in the develop- ment of better methods in elementary education in this country.

The Infant School Movement. Three educational movements that originated in England influenced the development of the elementary school in the United States. The infant school first appeared in Scotland, where Robert Owen established a school at Lanark in 1815 for children who were working in the factories. The children were taught cleanliness, plays and games, and the art of working and playing together, rather than reading and writing. An English reformer, Samuel Witherspin, organized the Infant School Society in 1824, and reading, writing, arithmetic, geography, and natural history were added to this program. Infant schools were established in Boston in 1818, in New York and Philadelphia in 1827, and in Providence, Rhode Island, in 1828. The infant school, which at first was distinct from the elementary school, became the primary department of the elementary school when both were taken over by public authorities.

The Sunday School Movement. The Sunday school, as it was first organized, was not a church institution; it was an agency for educating the poor in secular as well as religious subjects. It made a contribution by getting people accustomed to the idea of secular education for all children. The Sunday school was imported from England, where Robert Raikes organized the first one in 1780 for the purpose of providing factory children with instruction in reading and the catechism. Sunday schools of the secular type existed in this country for nearly a half century after they were introduced about 1790. After the churches took them over, secular instruction was dropped.

The Monitorial System. A third movement, originating in England, played an important role in getting public elementary schools established in the United States. Andrew Bell, a clergyman in the Established Church, developed, in an orphan asylum in India, a system of teaching based on the use of pupils as monitors; and Joseph Lancaster, a Quaker schoolmaster, used a similar plan with industrial classes in England. A Lancasterian monitorial school was opened in New York City in 1806, and soon Philadelphia, Pittsburgh, Baltimore, Washington, and Louisville had schools operating on the Lancasterian plan. Lancaster himself came to the United States in 1818 to help promote the movement.

By using pupils as monitors and by reducing classroom routine to military precision, it was possible for one teacher to direct the instruction of several hundred children. Lancaster published manuals giving minute directions for the conduct of recitations and for classroom management. Monitors assigned pupils to classes, checked attendance, taught lessons, inspected written exercises at the signal "Show slates," and performed other duties assigned by the teacher. One of Lancaster's mottoes was, "A place for everything and everything in its place." The problem, for example, of caring for children's hats was solved by tying the hats around the children's necks and having them come on and off at a prescribed signal.

The monitorial system was received with enthusiasm by proponents of public education in the United States. Governor De Witt Clinton said in 1809, ". . . when I perceive one great assembly of a thousand children under the eye of a single teacher, marching with unexampled rapidity and with perfect discipline to a goal of knowledge, I confess that I recognize in Lancaster the benefactor of the human race." In order to get any system of public education at the time, it was essential that the expense be very small. As late as 1834, Philadelphia had an average of 218 pupils per teacher, and the annual per pupil cost was only five dollars.

The weaknesses of the monitorial system were soon recognized; it was too mechanical, it gave too little attention to individual differences in pupils, and it consisted primarily of using those who knew little to teach those who knew less. By the middle of the nineteenth century the people were looking for something better, and enthusiasm for the monitorial system began to wane. It had, however, served a useful purpose by getting people accustomed to having tax-supported schools for their children to attend.

EDUCATIONAL LEADERSHIP. The success of the Public School Revival depended to no small degree upon the work of intelligent, persistent educational leaders. Samuel R. Hall established the first private normal school at Concord, Vermont, in 1823 and in 1829 wrote the first pedagogical book to be published in the United States—*Lectures on School Keeping.* James G. Carter was instrumental in achieving legislation creating the first State Board of Education in Massachusetts in 1837 and the first state normal school at Lexington, Massachusetts, in 1838. The legislature appropriated $10,000 to match a gift from Edmund Dwight for the establishment of the normal school, and Horace Mann sold his law library to add to the fund.

No man better epitomized the leadership of the Public School Revival than did Horace Mann, who accepted the position of Secretary of the Massachusetts State Board of Education in 1837. He had been a member of the state legislature, had worked for social reforms, and as president of the senate had signed the act creating the position for which he was selected. When he accepted the position, he said, "I have abandoned jurisprudence and betaken myself to the larger sphere of mind and morals." His decision was a fortunate one for the cause of public education. During the twelve years he spent in the office, the attitude of the people of Massachusetts toward public schools changed from one of apathy to one of active enthusiasm. He collected and published information about the condition of the schools, visited Prussia and other places in Europe to study school systems, and traveled up and down the state addressing public meetings and conventions. His annual reports were models of readability, directness, and simplicity. His achievements included the establishment of three public normal schools, the addition of a full month to the average school term, the gradual substitution of public high schools for private academies, the doubling of appropriations for schools, the development of school libraries, and the adoption of new methods of instruction based on the ideas of Pestalozzi.

Other leaders who contributed to the success of the Public School Revival included Henry Barnard, who in 1867 became the first Commissioner of Education for the United States; Calvin E. Stowe; Victor E. Cousins; Calvin H. Wiley; Caleb Mills; John D. Pierce; William F. Perry; and John Swett. Educational journals contributed to the success of the Public School Revival by promoting the establishment of public schools, the improvement of methods of teaching, and the development of more adequate facilities for the preparation of teachers. By 1861, the number of educational journals in the United States reached 121, the most widely used being Horace Mann's *Common School Journal*, Henry Barnard's *Connecticut Common School Journal*, and Calvin Wiley's *North Carolina Journal of Education*.

The rise of the factory system, the increased use of machinery, and the growth of cities altered conditions of living during the nineteenth century and provided a new motive for public education. Industrialists supported the establishment and improvement of public schools for a number of reasons: the development of the resources of the state and region, teaching sound economic principles to safeguard property rights, and making sales campaigns more effective by educating the masses.

The labor unions of the time were active supporters of the Public School Revival. Two-fifths of all laborers in factories in 1832 were children, few of whom could read and write. Laborers desired public schools as a means of securing economic and social justice, to provide better opportunities for their children, and to avoid the class stigma attached to children who attended charity schools. They gave active support to the cause of public education in their newspapers, in their conventions, and by their votes.

A WINNING COMBINATION. Factors discussed in the preceding paragraphs, together with other favorable developments, combined to make the Public School Revival a success. The first major breakthrough came in the state of Pennsylvania, when Thaddeus Stevens won the historic battle for free public elementary schools in the legislature in 1835. The legislature had enacted a law in 1834 making tax support of schools optional with the school districts. In the 1835 session of the legislature a bill was introduced that would repeal the essential features of the act of 1834 and substitute a measure entitled "An act making provision for the education of the poor gratis." Stevens moved to substitute for this bill another, which greatly strengthened the law of 1834. The Stevens bill was passed, and the public school system was saved from defeat. Stevens' speech to the members of the legislature in favor of public tax-supported schools for every child was perhaps the strongest and most effective defense of the principle of free public education that had been given up to that time. By 1876 the principle of public elementary education had been accepted in all the states, and schools had been established everywhere except in the Southern states, where economic conditions following the Civil War left the states too poor to support schools.

Expanding and Improving the System

The period between 1876 and 1929 was one of expansion and reform in business and industry, in government, and in education. The growth of factories, of cities, and of corporations produced a complex, industrialized society in place of the agriculture-based society of former years. The influence of wealthy individuals and corporations on government, the exploitation of natural and human resources, and the growth of slums and sweatshops brought the issue of reform into American politics. Reform movements were not merely the creations of political leaders; they represented to a great extent a revolt of the American people against the trends of the times, and a determination to use the machinery of government in the interest of human welfare.

This was also an era of expansion and reform for the elementary school. The enrollment more than doubled during this period; many new subjects were added to the curriculum; the length of the school term increased by more than 30 percent; supervisors and directors of research were added to the school staff; and per-pupil expenditures increased manyfold. The two-year normal schools for teachers, which existed in practically all the states in 1861, became four-year teachers' colleges by 1929, and schools or colleges of education were established in virtually all universities. Requirements for certificates to teach in elementary schools, which as late as 1900 had consisted of passing an examination on the subjects taught in elementary schools, by 1929 had expanded to include work in child psychology, educational measurement, history of education, philosophy of education, curriculum development, special methods, and student teaching.

Between 1929 and 1945 two periods of national emergency—the Great Depression and World War II—stimulated new developments in science and technology, increased the tempo of American life, and placed new responsibilities on the doorstep of the school. The stock market crash of 1929 was followed by unemployment, business failures, and social unrest. It was an era when many unorthodox schemes were suggested for ending the economic depression: the "technocrats," who advocated production for use rather than for profit; the Townsend Movement, which advocated that everyone over 65 years of age be paid $2,000 a year by the government; and other schemes for altering the economic system through government action. These movements represented efforts of a free people to provide a maximum of economic security without destroying the entire system. Frederick Lewis Allen has suggested: ". . . when the ship of state was not behaving as it should, one did not need to scrap it and build another, but by a series of adjustments and improvements, repair it while keeping it running—provided the ship's crew were forever alert, forever inspecting and tinkering with it."[11] The stresses and strains of the culture were reflected in education. It was suggested that the schools should build a new social order, that school subjects be eliminated, and that radically different curriculum organizations be adopted. Many of these ideas were impractical, but they did center attention on the need for curriculum reform.

John Dewey and the Progressive Education Association

John Dewey (1859–1952) exerted a wide influence on liberal movements and practices in American elementary schools through his writings, his teaching, and the laboratory school that he established at the University of Chicago in 1896. This school was important not only because it was the first experimental laboratory school in America, but because it demonstrated a new teaching strategy. Joy Elmer Morgan, who was for many years editor of the journal of the National Education Association, said that Dewey's *My Pedagogical Creed*, published in 1897, was as important for the revolution that was taking place in education as Thomas Paine's *Common Sense* was for the political revolution of 1776. Dewey's pedagogical beliefs included the following: (1) the only true education was that which stimulated the child's powers by the demands of the social situation in which the child found himself, (2) education must begin with insight into the child's capacities, interests, and habits, (3) subject matter was anything that helped a student solve a problem, (4) education should help a child learn to use his intellectual powers for social ends, and (5) subjects taught in school were frequently too far removed from the day-to-day experiences of children.

---

[11] Frederick Lewis Allen, *The Big Change* (New York: Harper & Row, Publishers, 1952), p. 105.

SITUATION 3.4
Dewey's Ideas in the "New" Curricula

Examine Dewey's ideas in greater detail in a history-of-education text. Examine the pedagogical principles upon which the "new" science is based. Discuss the extent to which Dewey's ideas are implemented in the "new" science program.

The Progressive Education Association (1919–1955) deserves a great deal of credit for helping to make the American elementary school a more democratic, enjoyable, and effective environment for living and learning. It was never a large organization—the membership was never more than 10,000—and it certainly never did gain control of American schools, as is sometimes supposed. During its existence it had the support of many of the most capable and courageous leaders in American education, published an excellent journal, held conventions, sponsored experimental programs in public schools, and initiated the workshop as a new and effective device for the in-service education of teachers. No group has ever been adversely criticized and judged by so many who have never consulted a single source that sets forth the principles for which it stand or the research findings concerning the results achieved in the experiments that it has conducted. *Progressive Education* for May 1941 carried an article entitled, "Progressive Education: Its Philosophy and Challenge," which set forth in detail the beliefs of the Association. These included: (1) the dominant ideals of our democratic culture, continuously reinterpreted and refined, should provide the basic direction for American education, (2) every child should have the fullest opportunity possible for achieving his potential, (3) education should make people aware of social changes that make it necessary for schools to break with tradition and open up new possibilities for the future, (4) it is only in the process of living and working together that the optimal development of the personality can be achieved, (5) physical and mental health should be a major concern of the school, (6) children should have many opportunities for self-expression at all stages of their development and in many diverse areas of the curriculum, and (7) the child should have increasing freedom to direct his own behavior as his knowledge and experience increase.

The same issue of *Progressive Education* contained an abstract of the report of a committee appointed by the Association to evaluate the achievement of children who were attending schools in which newer practices were used. This abstract carried the title, "New Methods vs. Old in American Education." Studies were made in Lincoln School, Teachers College, Columbia University; Winnetka, Illinois; Roslyn, New York; and

Santa Monica, Pasadena, and Los Angeles, California. The studies showed that in general pupils achieved higher scores in academic subjects in schools where the newer procedures were used. There was increased interest in learning, initiative, self-direction and social understanding and responsibility on the part of pupils in the schools where the newer procedures were used.

> SITUATION 3.5
> *The Workshop Way of Learning*
>
> Read Earl C. Kelley, *The Workshop Way of Learning* (New York: Harper & Row, Publishers, 1951). Summarize briefly the purposes, procedures, and outcomes of the workshop procedure.

The twelve-year period between 1945 and 1957 has been called an age of miracles. More spectacular changes were packed into this period than had been witnessed in any previous period of this length. These changes increased the role of the United States in world affairs, reduced the size of the world in terms of travel time, and increased the interdependence of the people of the whole world. The scope of the curriculum had to be broadened to include a second language, the use of polar projection, and education for international understanding. The single textbook gave way to a wide variety of learning resources and equipment; by 1954 central libraries were maintained in 57 percent of the elementary schools in cities with a population of 100,000 or more; and there was an 83 percent increase in schools offering special education services between 1948 and 1953. Some national curriculum-improvement projects were initiated during this period, and there was an increase in the amount of research devoted to factors influencing teacher effectiveness.

The period from 1957 through 1969 will be remembered for many exciting developments, but best of all perhaps for being the period during which the United States placed men on the moon. It will also be remembered as the period during which a massive curriculum-reform movement was launched. This movement involved many new developments in education. The most unique feature was the emergence of curriculum improvement from the top down. Previous changes in the curriculum had been initiated by state and local school system groups. It has been possible for groups operating at the national level to obtain financial support and top-level personnel that were not available to local curriculum-planning groups. The salient features of the new curricula have been summarized as follows:

1. National curriculum-improvement projects, located on university

campuses throughout the country, have been generously supported with funds from the federal government and from private foundations.

2. Attention has been sharply focused on single subjects, so that local school systems have been left with the problem of maintaining balance in the curriculum. Many school systems have therefore found it necessary to adapt, rather than adopt, the materials produced by these projects.

3. The groups that have been responsible for directing these projects have generally included staff members from the colleges of liberal arts and sciences, colleges of education, and the public schools.

4. Although the movement began with mathematics, science, and foreign languages, new courses have also been developed in English, social studies, anthropology, geography, and economics.

5. The sponsors of the new curricula generally advocate a "spiral" arrangement for the grade placement of content in the various curriculum areas. For example, instead of teaching geometry only in the tenth grade, elements of this subject are introduced in the elementary school and the subject is "revisited" at successive grade levels. The same arrangement is used for economics, geography, anthropology.

6. Most of the new curricula expect more of students than the mere acquisition of information; students are expected to learn the structure of each discipline and thus to think like a scientist, a mathematician, or an economist. Something more lasting than the learning of bits of information has been sought; the new procedures emphasize concept formation, learning by discovery, and the development of the ability to think. The goal is a kind of education that will enable students to become increasingly self-propelling during a lifetime of learning.

7. There is little question that these national projects have developed vastly improved content and procedures in many curriculum areas; the questions that are raised generally deal with how these new programs can be implemented in elementary and secondary schools. Since most of the teachers now employed in the schools have not been taught the new science and the new mathematics, the new curricula place a heavy burden on the in-service education budgets of public school systems. Summer institutes, operating under federal grants, have helped.

8. Teaching procedures necessary to implement the new curricula involve an understanding of newer insights into the nature of the learning process; if the new programs are to achieve their maximum potentials, classroom teachers must become much more proficient as practicing psychologists.[12]

[12] William B. Ragan and George Henderson, *Foundations of American Education* (New York: Harper & Row, Publishers, 1970), pp. 117–118.

Illustrative Projects

Curriculum-improvement projects are moving at such a pace that what may be described today as current may be outdated tomorrow. What follows is a description of some illustrative projects in mathematics, science, and the social studies. There are many other curriculum projects in each of these fields and in other areas of the elementary school curriculum. The references listed at the end of this chapter describe many of these projects.

SMSG. The School Mathematics Study Group was located at Stanford University. The Director was E. G. Begel and the National Science Foundation provided approximately $8 million to finance the project. SMSG prepared sample textbooks for grades K–12 which were regarded as suitable for today's children and youth. The writing team consisted of elementary school teachers, college teachers of mathematics, mathematics supervisors, mathematics educators, and psychologists. The program for elementary school pupils contains the usual arithmetic topics plus some work in nonmetric geometry and informal algebra. SMSG has been the most widely used of all the new mathematics programs. The most innovative aspect of the program is the emphasis on sets of numbers as structured systems, but emphasis is also placed on the use of precise mathematical language. Even though commercially prepared textbooks and teachers' manuals are now available using the SMSG approach, intensive in-service education programs are needed if teachers are to use the materials effectively.

SCIS. The Science Curriculum Improvement Study at the University of California at Berkeley has been funded since 1959 by grants from the National Science Foundation. Robert Karplus (University of California at Berkeley) is the director of the program. The program emphasizes science concepts, pupil observation and experimentation, and skill in manipulating equipment and recording data. Instructional units for grades K–6 have been tried out in selected schools in the San Francisco Bay area; in the area of Teachers College, Columbia University; the University of California at Los Angeles, the University of Oklahoma, and the University of Hawaii. The course outline makes provision for learning at each level to prepare the student for learning at succeeding levels. The abstractions at the first level relate to variations in one property among similar objects and growth in living matter; abstractions at the second level relate to interaction, relativity, and ecosystem; those at the third level relate to energy, equilibrium, behavior, reproduction and evolution of living organisms, to mention only a few. A college text, *Teaching Science in the Elementary School*, provides detailed suggestions for using the

SCIS approach.[13] The impact of this and other projects on the teaching of elementary science has been significant.

Social Studies Curriculum Projects

The United States Office of Education, through its cooperative Research Program, initiated a program in 1962 to improve instruction, research, and teacher education in the social sciences. According to Goodlad, Von Stoephasius, and Klein, fourteen more projects were initiated. All of them shared the objectives of (1) redefining the scope and goals of the social studies program, (2) developing techniques and materials designed to achieve these goals, (3) submitting materials to a sequence of experimentations, evaluations, and revisions, and (4) disseminating the materials and relevant information. The centers have these characteristics in common:

a. They are located at universities and headed by professors.

b. They seek to identify the structure of social science disciplines and to develop new curricula around social science concepts.

c. They involve the collaboration of university scholars with public school teachers.

d. They usually employ the inquiry approach and emphasize the importance of critical thinking and sequential and cumulative learning experiences.

e. They are using the multimedia approach, trying out new materials in classrooms, and developing evaluative procedures.[14]

SUMMARY

1. The elementary school curriculum has been changing significantly during the last decade; it is expected to change more rapidly during the next two decades.

2. The elementary school curriculum is composed of all the experiences that children have under the influence of the school.

3. Curriculum planning occupies the attention of groups at the national, state, local school system, and individual classroom levels. It is in the individual classroom that the most crucial phase of curriculum planning takes place.

4. Those who participate in the development of curriculum guides gener-

[13] John W. Renner and William B. Ragan, *Teaching Science in the Elementary School* (New York: Harper & Row, Publishers, 1968).

[14] Adapted from John I. Goodlad, Renata Von Stoephasius, and M. Frances Klein, *The Changing School Curriculum* (New York: The Fund for the Advancement of Education, 1966), pp. 57–58.

ally expect more of students than the memorizing of isolated bits of information; they expect them to develop inquiry skills which can be used to gain understanding during a lifetime of learning.

5. The "Self as Instrument" concept views the teacher as an intelligent human being who uses himself—his knowledge and resources—to solve problems for which he is responsible.

6. The overall design of the curriculum developed by the school staff generally leaves a great deal of freedom for the individual teacher to make adaptations in terms of his particular group of students and his own set of capabilities.

7. Teachers in American schools need to understand the changing functions of the school as a social institution.

8. The religious motive for education was dominant during the colonial period; the idea of education as the foundation of popular government emerged during the national period 1776–1876.

9. After 1957 changes in the curriculum began to originate at the national level to a greater extent than ever before.

10. National curriculum projects located at universities have been generously supported by the federal government and by private foundations. They have been sharply focused on single subjects, and have involved active participation from faculty members of liberal arts colleges.

RECOMMENDED READINGS

Goodlad, John I., Renata Von Stoephasius, and M. Frances Klein, *The Changing School Curriculum*. New York: The Fund for the Advancement of Education, 1966. Section II explains the curriculum-improvement projects that have been developed at the national level.

Inlow, Gail M., *The Emergent in Curriculum*. New York: John Wiley & Sons, Inc., 1966. Part II presents an analysis of "Newer Curriculum Directions."

Kelley, Earl C., *The Workshop Way of Learning*. New York: Harper & Row, Publishers, 1951. Explains the purposes, procedures, and outcomes of the workshop procedure.

Michaelis, John U., Ruth H. Grossman, and Lloyd F. Scott, *New Designs for the Elementary School Curriculum*. New York: McGraw-Hill Book Company, 1967. Chapter 2 examines "Key Components of New Curriculum Designs."

Pulliam, John D., *History of Education in America*. Columbus, Ohio: Charles E. Merrill Publishing Company, 1968. Pages 97–111 present a discussion of experiments and innovations in the twentieth century.

Ragan, William B., and Gene D. Shepherd, *Modern Elementary Curriculum*, 4th ed. New York: Holt, Rinehart and Winston, Inc., 1970. Chapter 1 presents an account of more than 300 years of curriculum development in this country.

Renner, John W., and William B. Ragan, *Teaching Science in the Elementary*

School. New York: Harper & Row, Publishers, 1968. Provides vivid comparisons of the "new" science with the "old."

Short, Edmund C., and George D. Marconnit, *Contemporary Thought on Public School Curriculum.* Dubuque, Iowa: Wm. C. Brown Company, Publishers, 1968. Part IV contains two excellent articles on the construction and use of curriculum guides.

Chapter 4

Changing Teaching Strategies

More teachers must learn to envision themselves as more than idea-givers. They must learn to feel as much satisfaction in leading the student to reason out ideas independently as in demonstrating their own command of information and ideas.

Norris M. Sanders, in Dorothy McClure Fraser (Ed.),
Social Studies Curriculum Development: Prospects and Problems (Washington, D.C.: National Council for the Social Studies, 1968), p. 172.

The decade of the 1960s witnessed increasing attention given to the improvement of teaching. Several circumstances combined to produce a post-Sputnik revolution in instruction. The contributions that schools can make to national survival became more generally recognized; evidence accumulated concerning the relation of education to economic growth; and the quest for excellence in all segments of American life influenced thinking about teaching strategies.

Although progress has not been as rapid or as widespread as most people would like, elementary schools have changed in many respects since 1960. Indeed, it has been suggested that parents who have children attending one of the innovative elementary schools need a glossary in order to understand some of the terms used by the teachers. The following are only a few of these terms: team leader, carrel, resource center, open-space construction, egg-crate construction, auto-instruction device, programmed learning, multimedia, teacher aide, and cluster plan.

SITUATION 4.1

A New Vocabulary in Teaching

List 15 or 20 new terms that have been added to the vocabulary of teachers during the last decade or so. Give definitions for each term. (See *Ladies Home Journal*, September 1968, p. 74.)

SOME TEACHING STRATEGIES

Teachers generally find it desirable to understand several teaching strategies. Many strategies (or methods) of teaching can be identified. The fact that a few have been selected for treatment in this chapter does not mean that no others deserve attention. When a teacher adopts a new teaching strategy, this does not mean that she abandons the one that she has been using before. The new strategy may have unique elements, but it will generally involve many of the practices that have been familiar for years. The difference is, in part at least, a difference in emphasis. One strategy may emphasize questions which require only memory; another may use questions which require higher mental processes.[1]

Shifts in emphasis that are closely related to successful teaching in the new elementary school are:

More emphasis on developing enthusiasm for learning and less emphasis on information giving.

More emphasis on critical thinking and less emphasis on memorization.

More emphasis on self-instructional and self-testing media and less dependence upon a single textbook.

More emphasis on learning how to function effectively as a member of a teaching team and less emphasis on learning how to operate independently of other teachers.

More emphasis on the use of specialized professional personnel—media specialists, counselors, social workers, school psychologists, curriculum consultants, and others.

More emphasis on using noncertified personnel—teachers aides, school volunteers, and others.

More emphasis on the processes of learning and less emphasis on the products.

[1]See Norris M. Sanders, *Classroom Questions: What Kind?* (New York: Harper & Row, Publishers, 1966), p. 10.

More emphasis on learning by discovery and less emphasis on memorizing the answers provided by others.

More emphasis on involving students in decision making and less teacher domination.

More emphasis on developing skill in human relations and appreciation of democratic values by guiding group work effectively.

More emphasis on individualizing and personalizing teaching.

Greater emphasis on questions that require thinking rather than mere recall.

More emphasis on evaluation for guidance purposes and less emphasis on using it to judge students.

Setting the Stage for Democratic Group Living

The teacher in the modern elementary school sets the stage for democratic living by helping pupils become acquainted quickly, learn to trust one another, and learn to work effectively together. Adequate classroom space, movable furniture, abundant materials, an attractive classroom, and a teacher who understands the children are important factors in democratic living, but they are no substitutes for mutual understanding and mutual respect. By studying individual records so that names can be called without hesitation, by remembering the names of older brothers or sisters whom she may have taught, by discovering through school records the special interests or accomplishments of individuals, by letting the children tell about their hobbies or activities, and by making them feel at ease, the teacher helps to create a social climate that is conducive to democratic living.

SITUATION 4.2

Helping Pupils Get Acquainted

Mary Brown knew that each of her pupils had done something during the summer vacation that was of particular interest to him and that would help others to become acquainted with him. She asked them one after another to tell about something they had done. Billy told about his fishing trip to the Ozark Mountains, Susan told about her visit to a Rhode Island beach, Tim told about looking out over San Francisco from the Top of the Mark. After each child had told about some experience during summer vacation, Miss Brown knew that they were well on their way to mutual understanding. Explain how various learning experiences (speaking, writing, and so on) could grow out of an activity such as the one reported above.

Any group enterprise needs organization. But an organization that is forced upon a group by the teacher may hinder the work of the group because the pupils do not understand its purpose. The task of the teacher, therefore, is not to organize the class, but to help the pupils form their own organization in terms of their own goals and the interests and abilities of members of the class. Group rapport depends in part on the formation of committees consisting of pupils who like to work together. Because friendships among children of elementary school age change rapidly, it is necessary to change the composition of committees frequently. If children have no opportunity to select class members with whom they work, the development of rapport necessary for effective group work is difficult.

Any teacher who has had experience in working democratically with a group of pupils knows that many interesting and worthwhile plans are initiated by members of the class. When learning activities are selected entirely by the teacher, the pupils are not only denied the educative experience of planning activities, but the activities themselves are likely to be somewhat narrow and lacking in childlike qualities.

The teacher works with the group in planning the activities necessary to attain the goals that have been formulated. Each step is planned with the pupils, but not for them. Pupils engage in many activities in connection with group projects. They read books, take field trips, hold interviews, carry on experiments, conduct surveys, view films, listen to the radio, and compare ideas in discussion groups. Pupils who have been working in different ways share the results of their efforts with classmates by telling stories, painting pictures, building models, and preparing graphs and charts.

There are many advantages to cooperative planning of activities. Experience has shown that a group of people working together can make better plans than can be made by one person, that an idea presented by one member of a group sets off a chain of ideas from other members, and that cooperative planning contributes to group morale and unity. Teachers have found that children in a group frequently know a great deal about special abilities of other children that the teacher does not know, that they can suggest sources of information or resources for learning that would never occur to the teacher, and that human relations in the classroom improve through group interaction. For example, one class was studying the growth of plants. One boy had a bulletin on the growing of beans that his parents had obtained from the County Agricultural Agent. The class decided to experiment with the growing of beans, following the directions about soil, water, and sunshine that were given in the bulletin. Another pupil suggested that the County Agricultural Agent might have bulletins about growing other plants, and the class decided to follow the suggestion and find out. One child working alone would not have thought of all the ways to use the services of the agent that the combined thinking of the group produced.

Evaluating Progress in Group Living

Citizens of a democracy participate in many common undertakings involving group discussion, group planning, group decision, group action, and group evaluation. Although not always labeled as such, group evaluation is a common activity in adult life. It is an integral part of cooperative action by a school faculty, it is used in staff meetings of business concerns, and it is a regular phase of the work of those who are responsible for the administration of various units of government. In these and in many other adult activities, the questions arise: How are our plans working out? Are we making the best use of our resources? Are we learning to work together effectively?

It has been suggested earlier in this chapter that unit work is not an educational panacea, that it does not constitute a pattern into which all the activities of the class must be forced, and that many other methods of teaching are used to achieve the objectives of the modern elementary school. Learning the ways of democracy, however, is one of the *fundamentals* for which the schools of a democratic society are responsible, and learning to participate in the evaluation of progress is an integral phase of this learning.

It is recognized, of course, that group evaluation is only one of the many forms of evaluation that are used in the modern elementary school. The broader problem of evaluating and reporting pupil progress is presented in another chapter. This section is concerned with evaluation as an integral phase of cooperative learning in the classroom. It is concerned with techniques for helping children verbalize what they have learned from a given experience, for helping them identify the strengths and weaknesses in their planning, for helping them weigh the evidence of individual growth, and for helping them evaluate the progress made in learning to work together.

EVALUATION HELPS CHILDREN VERBALIZE WHAT THEY HAVE LEARNED. One important outcome of working together democratically, although by no means the only one, is that children acquire a quantity and variety of useful information. Cooperative planning includes having the children list the things they wish to learn from the undertaking. It frequently happens, however, that they learn a great many things that they did not have in mind when they started.

The technique for evaluating this aspect of cooperative learning will vary with the age level of the group and with the nature of the project.

One simple technique that can be used even with pupils in the primary grades is to ask the pupils what they have learned. The teacher presses for as many answers as the pupils can give, and writes the list on the board. He points out that they have learned many things that they did not start out to learn, asks them to tell how they learned these things, and points out how this information may be useful to them.

Evaluation can also help pupils verbalize other forms of growth that have taken place. For example, John may say, "I learned that the group leader must let everyone participate in deciding what to do, rather than insisting on having the group do what he wants them to do." Mary may say, "I learned that working with other members of the class makes me more interested in doing the best that I can." Henry may say, "I learned that James can do many things that I didn't know he could do." Helen may say, "I learned that reading to find out things for the group is more interesting than just reading an assignment."

EVALUATION HELPS THE GROUP IMPROVE ITS PLANNING. Group evaluation relates to the goals set up by the group and the efficiency of the processes used to achieve these goals. Evaluation that emerges from the experience of working together helps children improve the process of planning so that subsequent activities will produce better results.

A third-grade class decided to prepare an exhibit of their work in various subjects and to invite their parents and members of another class to see what they had done. Although the teacher, the parents, and members of the visiting class thought the exhibit was an outstanding success, the evaluation session that was held the following day revealed that the pupils themselves were not satisfied with the results. Ralph pointed out that the exhibits had to be too close together in the regular classroom and suggested that they should use the assembly room next time. Henry suggested that the program should begin earlier in the day to avoid so much rushing to see all the exhibits. Mary said that more time should be used in getting the exhibits ready.

EVALUATION PROVIDES EVIDENCE OF INDIVIDUAL GROWTH. Because respect for the individual is the essence of democracy, the growth of each child is a basic criterion for evaluating democratic living. As each child makes his own contributions to group enterprises and sees his ideas incorporated in the planning of the group, he gains self-confidence and strives harder to improve his own skills and make progressively better contributions. Working alone to improve his own skills would not give him the same satisfaction that he gains from making a contribution to group living and gaining recognition from the group.

The references listed at the end of this chapter contain many suggestions for evaluating individual growth. Two of the most commonly used techniques are group discussion and checklists. When group discussion is used for this purpose, attention is focused on the contributions each has made to the success of the group project and on the changes in the behavior of individuals that indicate growth in the skills of group living. When negative comments are made, the teacher tactfully redirects the discussion toward constructive suggestions for improvement. Checklists may either be devised by the teacher or developed cooperatively by the teacher and the class. Some checklists are developed for use by the teacher; others are to be used by the pupil.

EVALUATION MAKES CHILDREN AWARE OF THE VALUES OF DEMOCRATIC LIVING. The students in a graduate-level course in school supervision had been working in groups on various phases of the problem and reporting to the class. After several reports had been given, a student said to the instructor, "Some of us have been talking about what has happened to us as a result of this way of working together. We know each other better, we have learned to respect the contributions of each member, we take pride in the accomplishments of the group, we have accumulated a great deal of material as a result of our combined efforts, and all of us have read more than we ever have in other classes. We would like to have a class session set aside for talking about what has happened to us as a group. We would like to try to identify the factors in our process of working together that have made these things possible."

This is an example of the desire for evaluating group processes originating from members of the group. Children who are working in groups need help in finding signs of improvement that have occurred in their group living, in identifying the ways of working that have been successful, and in deciding how this process may be useful in other school and out-of-school situations. Cooperative group work must be linked with cooperative evaluation if children are to be made aware of the importance of democratic living both in the classroom and in later life when they are adult citizens.

The following checklist is presented as an illustration of the kind of instrument that can be developed cooperatively by teachers, principals, and supervisors and then used to help teachers evaluate their practices in terms of democratic values.

A Checklist for Evaluating Classroom Practices

Instructions for scoring: Use the blanks after each statement to rate the conditions and practices in your classroom as follows: check under M if the condition or practice is missing, under 1 if it exists to a limited degree, under 2 if it exists to a considerable degree, and under 3 if it exists to a great degree.

I. *Self-Fulfillment for Every Pupil.* The teacher is concerned with what is happening to each pupil, evaluates practices in terms of their effect on the pupils involved, and tries to release the potentials of each pupil.

M 1 2 3

1. The teacher works patiently with a pupil who is having difficulty in adjusting to group life.
2. The teacher is so well acquainted with each pupil that he can help him to understand himself, plan intelligently, and make full use of the school's resources.
3. The teacher tries to find some tasks at which the slower pupils can experience some measure of success.
4. The teacher challenges abler pupils to accomplish as much as their ability permits.
5. The teacher gives encouragement to all pupils— not merely to the talented few.
6. A wide variety of learning materials is available.
7. Pupils are helped to establish worthwhile purposes.
8. There is evidence of real concern for identifying and meeting individual needs.

II. *Working Together for the Common Good.* The democratic classroom is a place in which pupils develop the skills involved in group living, share their efforts and ideas with classmates, and take pride in group accomplishments.

9. The teacher helps pupils develop skills in group leadership and group membership.
10. The teacher helps pupils become well acquainted.
11. Pupils exhibit an attitude of mutual respect and mutual confidence.
12. There is evidence that group living in the classroom fosters the achievement of individuality.
13. There is evidence that pupils are developing the skills involved in group evaluation.
14. There is evidence that pupils are selected to serve on committees on the basis of their special abilities to make contributions to group goals.

15. There is evidence that the class organization is dynamic rather than static—that it is frequently changed in response to felt needs.

III. *Participation by All Members of the Class.* Effective teaching in a democratic society involves organizing learning activities so that every pupil takes a responsible part in the life and work of the class.

16. Pupils participate in formulating plans, in working them out, and in evaluating results.

17. Pupil participation takes place in activities relating to school subjects as well as in routine chores.

18. The teacher makes a careful appraisal of the readiness of each pupil for assuming responsibilities.

19. The teacher helps pupils evaluate their own progress toward effective participation in group enterprises.

20. The teacher uses effective procedures for encouraging timid pupils to participate in classroom activities.

21. Members of the class participate in establishing rules for the orderly transaction of class business.

22. There is a free exchange of ideas before the class makes decisions on matters of procedure.

23. Members of the class take turns at serving as leaders for various group enterprises.

IV. *Freedom To Experiment.* In the democratic classroom, pupils are encouraged to think for themselves, to find proof, and to work out unique solutions to problems.

24. Pupils have many opportunities to try out new ways of doing things.

25. The teacher provides enough direction to give pupils a feeling of security, but not enough to discourage initiative.

26. Materials and resources are well organized, so that pupils do not experience frustration in trying to find answers for themselves.

27. Both the material and human resources of the community are utilized in the learning process.

28. The teacher encourages pupils to collect evidence and to base decisions on facts rather than on prejudice.

M 1   2   3
___ ___ ___ ___

29. Pupils are encouraged to ask questions and to work out solutions to problems that are important to them.

    ___ ___ ___ ___

30. The teacher avoids providing ready-made solutions to children's problems.

    ___ ___ ___ ___

THE RECITATION

The teaching strategy that has represented majority practice in elementary and secondary schools in this country for almost two centuries is known as the recitation. Before 1800, the prevailing method of instruction was individual. The master would summon pupils to his desk one at a time to recite. One pupil reported that in 1800 he had forty minutes of teaching daily and 320 minutes of playing, whispering, and wasting time. It should be pointed out that no definite dates can be set for the end of individual instruction and the beginning of the form of group instruction called the recitation. For example, as late as 1855 a writer in *Barnard's Journal* deplored the time wasted by teaching individuals instead of classes.[2] It is interesting to find that group instruction, initiated early in the 1800s, has not eliminated wasted time in all classrooms. Jackson reported in 1968 that his visits to several classrooms convinced him that *delay* was an outstanding feature of life in classrooms. He reported that it was not unusual for one or more students to have their hands raised, waiting patiently for the teacher to get around to them.[3]

Common features of the recitation include a question by the teacher, a response by a pupil, and frequently a comment by the teacher on the response. At the close of the recitation, the teacher assigns a lesson for the next day; the student takes the textbook home to study the lesson; and the teacher gives the student an opportunity the following day to display how much or how little he has learned. James Hoetker and William P. Ahlbrand, Jr., have summarized more than a dozen observational studies of the recitation procedure and classroom questioning. One of the earliest major studies was made by Romiett Stevens in 1912 and one of the most recent was made by Arno Bellack et al. in 1966.[4] What these

---

[2] V. T. Thayer, *The Passing of the Recitation* (New York: D. C. Heath and Company, 1928), pp. 1–2.

[3] Philip W. Jackson, *Life in Classrooms* (New York: Holt, Rinehart and Winston, Inc., 1968), pp. 14–17.

[4] James Hoetker and William P. Ahlbrand, Jr., "The Persistence of the Recitation," *American Educational Research Journal*, March 1969, pp. 145–167.

two studies revealed has generally been confirmed by other studies; when the recitation procedure is used, teachers generally talk about 64 percent of the class time; about 80 percent of the classroom talk is used for asking, answering, and reacting to questions; the average number of questions asked is about two per minute; the type of questions generally require only rote memory to answer; and the answers to the questions can generally be found in the textbook. Regardless of the subject taught or the grade level, the teacher does most of the work, leaving little opportunity for pupils to become self-reliant, independent workers. Thayer characterized the recitation as follows:

> Traditional procedures, as embodied in what is generally termed the recitation method, are found to be out of harmony with the objectives of modern education. These procedures seem to have been developed under the dominance of a psychology of learning no longer accepted and are the expressions of social ideals which no longer accord with the fundamental aspirations of democratic citizenship.[5]

UNIT TEACHING

For more than a half-century, educators have sought teaching strategies that would represent basically different and more functional situations than the stereotyped assign-study-recite-test procedure known as the *recitation*. They have sought to produce more unity, more reality, more democracy, and more self-direction in the learning experiences of children. One of the most widely used of these strategies is the *unit*.

The Meaning of a Unit

The term *unit* has been used erroneously to mean a block of subject matter, a topic to be studied, or a chapter out of a textbook. It is broader than any of these concepts. Hanna, Potter, and Hagaman have stated: "A unit, or a unit of work, can be defined as a purposeful learning experience focused upon some socially significant understanding that will modify the behavior of the learner and enable him to adjust to a life situation more effectively."[6] Essential features of a unit include the following: (1) learning activities are many and varied, (2) activities are unified around a purpose or theme, (3) opportunities are provided for the socialization

[5] Thayer, p. iii.

[6] Lavone A. Hanna, Gladys L. Potter, and Neva Hagaman, *Unit Teaching in the Elementary School*, rev. ed. (New York: Holt, Rinehart and Winston, Inc., 1963), p. 117.

of students through participation in group enterprises, and (4) the teacher serves as a leader rather than as a taskmaster.

Types of Units

Units have been classified on the basis of the principal outcomes expected and on the basis when they are developed. When the primary emphasis is placed on content to be learned, when the content to be learned lies primarily within the boundaries of a single discipline, the learning experience is called a *subject matter unit*. When learning activities are organized around the problems, purposes, and needs of pupils; when socially useful content is selected from a variety of sources and used in the solution of problems that are understood by students; and when the outcomes expected include information, attitudes, modes of inquiry, and intellectual and social skills, the learning experience is called an *experience unit*.

SITUATION 4.3
Subject Matter versus Experience Units

It can be argued that the distinction between subject matter and experience units is meaningless since any unit involves subject matter and any unit involves experience, however narrow and meaningless the experience is. Describe a subject matter unit and an experience unit in detail to illustrate the difference.

A unit that has been developed before it is used by a class is generally called a *resource unit*. Plans for teaching certain units are developed by committees and then reproduced and distributed to teachers in the form of curriculum guides. Teachers are generally advised to regard these resource units as material that may be useful in developing their own units with and for a particular group of students. *Curriculum records* consist of descriptions of what went on in certain classrooms in which teachers and students worked together in selecting units, formulating objectives, planning and carrying out objectives, and evaluating progress.

The resource unit is written before it is used in the classroom; the curriculum record is written after it has been experienced by the students. A term which has been widely used for the type of emerging unit that comes from cooperative planning in the class is the *teaching unit*. This type of learning experience could be called a *dynamic unit*, which would suggest that everything had not been preplanned before the teacher and the students met in the classroom; rather the most important phase of

The "Discovery Approach" helps children learn how to ask productive questions in a problem-solving framework. (Photo courtesy Norman Public Schools.)

unit planning emerges from cooperative planning on the part of the teacher and the students as the unit progresses. No curriculum committee can possibly anticipate all the activities that a group of students may invent as the activity gets under way, all the materials that may be found to be useful, and all the outcomes that may be worthwhile. Unit teaching is discussed in greater detail in Chapter 6.

THE INQUIRY OR DISCOVERY STRATEGY

Until recently the most commonly used strategy for introducing students to new subject matter has been *exposition*. This procedure consists primarily of telling or information-giving. The teacher presented the students with information that they were expected to remember and be able to give back to the teacher upon demand. As far as the student was concerned, his role was a passive rather than an active one. Although few would deny that there will always be a need for teachers to spend some time on exposition, several developments have made it feasible to reduce the amount of time given to this phase of teaching and increase the amount of time given to other phases. Instructional technology has made it possible for students to acquire information with much less help from teachers; librarians and directors of learning resource centers teach students how to find information that they need; and newer teaching strategies place more responsibility on the student for acquiring the information that he needs to solve problems. Although it is perhaps an exaggeration to say that teaching is what is left after a teacher stops transmitting information, this is the direction in which we are moving.

The inquiry approach is concerned with helping the student develop the intellectual tools which he can use as he seeks solutions to problems, with the development of his reasoning powers, and with learning how to learn. It has been used most extensively in elementary school science, but its influence is also seen in other elementary school subjects. The inquiry process generally has been described as consisting of (1) identification and exploration of a problem, (2) statement of hypotheses, (3) experimenting and gathering data to support or disprove the hypotheses, (4) selecting a tentative solution to the problem, and (5) subjecting the tentative solution to the rigors of disproof.[7] An excellent example of using the inquiry approach in planning a social studies program is the California Social Sciences Framework. The inquiry process is described in terms of three "modes of thinking"—analytic, integrative, and policy. By the end of the 12th grade the student is expected to become proficient in all three modes of inquiry.[8]

Advantages of Learning by Inquiry

1. When students discover generalizations rather than having adult generalizations imposed upon them, they are developing their reasoning powers and learning how to learn.

2. Students who use the inquiry approach discover for themselves the structure of the discipline.

3. When the inquiry approach is used, motivation comes from within rather than from rewards and punishments.

[7] John W. Renner and William B. Ragan, *Teaching Science in the Elementary School* (New York: Harper & Row, Publishers, 1968), p. 35.

[8] Statewide Social Sciences Study Committee, *Preliminary K–12 Social Sciences Framework* (Sacramento, Calif.: State Department of Education, April 1968), pp. 3–21.

4. The inquiry approach allows students to collect, classify, and interpret data to arrive at their own solutions to problems.

5. The inquiry approach provides students with experiences in using the processes by which new facts, principles, and techniques are developed.

6. The inquiry approach is process oriented—instead of requiring students to memorize great amounts of factual information, the emphasis is on acquiring the intellectual skills needed for a lifetime of learning.

Research Relating to Discovery

Friedlander reported in 1965 that research findings related to discovery and self-directed study were highly inconclusive. In regard to memory of what has been learned he stated:

> First, I do not know of any extensive "hard" evidence that the insights which the student develops on his own have a higher likelihood of being remembered than insights he learns about from others, although we base much of our faith in the discovery method of teaching on the assumption that this is true.[9]

Some rather encouraging evidence relating to the influence of the discovery strategy of teaching has emerged since Friedlander made the above appraisal.

Wilson studied (1) the frequency of pupil involvement in five "essential science experiences" in classes taught by SCIS-educated teachers (Science Curriculum Study which emphasizes discovery) as compared with classes taught by teachers who were not educated in the SCIS Project's methods and (2) the extent to which inquiry-educated teachers asked more questions that required analytical thinking than did other teachers. Essential science experiences were regarded as observation, measurement, experimentation, data interpretation, and prediction. Wilson found that:

1. Students taught by the inquiry-educated teachers were provided significantly more of the essential science experiences than were the students taught by other teachers.

2. A significantly larger number of questions requiring only recognition and recall were asked by the traditional group of teachers than by the inquiry-educated teachers.

3. The inquiry-educated teachers asked a significantly larger number of questions calling for analysis and synthesis than did the traditional teachers.

---

[9] Bernard Z. Friedlander, "A Psychologist's Second Thoughts on Concepts, Curiosity, and Discovery in Teaching and Learning," *Harvard Educational Review*, Winter 1965, pp. 18–38.

4. The inquiry-educated teachers tended to ask more demonstration of skill-type questions while traditional teachers tended to ask more comprehension-type questions.[10]

Schmidt conducted a study using as his subjects sixteen teachers who taught both elementary school science and social studies. He reported modifications in the behavior of these teachers after they had attended a "new science" workshop. The modifications were:

1. Teachers asked fewer recall and convergent questions.

2. The questions asked by the teachers who attended the workshop required pupils to use higher-level mental processes.

3. A greater number of essential science experiences were provided by the teachers who attended the workshop.

4. The modifications in teacher behavior listed above appeared in the social studies classes taught by the same teachers as well as in the science classes.[11]

Commenting on the Schmidt investigation, Renner and Stafford stated:

> The teachers Schmidt observed were using inquiry-centered materials in science following their workshop experience, but they were using traditional materials in their social studies classes. These results seem to suggest that the deviation from the traditional mode of teacher education and not the materials is the significant factor in changing the teachers' instructional patterns.[12]

Porterfield investigated whether teachers who had been prepared to use the inquiry-centered approach in teaching elementary science asked a significantly greater proportion of questions that called for higher levels of thought than did teachers who had not been so prepared.[13]

While the studies mentioned above encourage the belief that an inquiry-centered experience in science education predisposes a teacher to use this approach when teaching other subjects, the belief should be subjected to additional testing.

[10] John H. Wilson, *Differences Between the Inquiry-Discovery and the Traditional Approaches to Teaching Science in Elementary Schools* (Unpublished doctoral dissertation, University of Oklahoma, 1967).

[11] Frederick B. Schmidt, *The Influence of A Summer Institute in Inquiry-Centered Science Education Upon the Teaching Strategies of Elementary Teachers in Two Disciplines* (Unpublished doctoral dissertation, University of Oklahoma, 1969).

[12] John W. Renner and Donald G. Stafford, "Inquiry, Children, and Teachers," *The Science Teacher*, April 1970.

[13] Denzil Porterfield, *The Influence of Preparation in the Science Curriculum Improvement Study on the Questioning Behavior of Selected Second and Fourth Grade Reading Teachers* (Unpublished doctoral dissertation, University of Oklahoma, 1969).

Limitations of Inquiry-Discovery

The inquiry-discovery strategy is not an educational panacea. Sanders has stated the case well:

> Even without the testimony of research, many teachers using discovery have learned the following in their own classrooms:
>   1. Students can learn by discovery. They can also learn by exposition.
>   2. Some ideas to be taught lend themselves better to learning by discovery than other ideas.
>   3. Some students thrive on a considerable amount of discovery and others wilt under the responsibility.
>   4. Students vary in the kind of discovery strategy which they perform successfully.
>   5. Some teachers enjoy a style of instruction featuring more discovery and usually do it well while others neither enjoy it nor consistently succeed in it.
>   6. There is an interaction between affective climate within a class and the success of various discovery strategies.[14]

SIMULATION GAMES IN LEARNING

Conventional methods of teaching do not give students much preparation for making decisions in life outside of school. Simulation games place students in situations which require them to make decisions based on the data available. They can then evaluate these decisions without fear of having to suffer the consequences that would be involved in real life.

Simulation games are available from commercial sources, and some teachers design their own games. Teachers who are interested in designing their own games may find useful suggestions in an article by Gearson.[15] Games that are available from commercial concerns vary greatly in the number of students who can play, the amount of time required to complete the game, the aspect of life depicted by the game, and the level of maturity required of the players.

Opinions vary greatly on the educational value of simulation games. Among the advantages claimed are (1) students become highly motivated, (2) they develop a more realistic understanding of how things are done in life outside the school, (3) they learn the need for cooperation, (4)

[14] Norris Sanders, "Changing Strategies of Instruction: Three Case Examples," in Dorothy McClure Fraser (Ed.), *Social Studies Curriculum: Prospects and Problems* (Washington, D.C.: National Council for the Social Studies, N.E.A., 1969), pp. 150–151.

[15] John D. Gearson, "Labor vs. Management: A Simulation Game," *Social Education*, October 1966, pp. 421–422.

they gain an appreciation of the complexity of real life situations, and (5) they become more excited about learning.[16]

A source of information about new games that are being developed is Project Simile, "Occasional Newsletter about Uses of Simulations and Games for Education and Training," Western Behavioral Sciences Institute, 1121 Torrey Pines Road, La Jolla, California 92037.

Another desirable feature of simulation games that are available for the social studies is that they deal with important topics: international relations, economic problems, the legislative process, people of other cultures, and home and family living. For example, the two games described below can be obtained from The Simulation Corporation, 16 E. 41st Street, New York, New York 10017.

Community Response Game. Simulates some important problems with which individuals are faced when a community is hit by a disaster. Each player is given a role in the simulated community. This role includes the player's location at the beginning of the game, the relatives and friends he has in the community, his job, and eventually such special obligations or interests as appointments to keep and property owned. Number of players per game—eight to ten; time—two to four hours. Can be divided into two sessions.

Consumers. A model of the consumer buying process involving players in the problems and economics of installment buying. Consumers compete to maximize their utility points for specific purchases while minimizing their credit charges. Number of players per game—twelve to fifteen; time—forty-five minutes to one and one and one-half hours.

SUMMARY

1. Changed circumstances in our society have caused many of our citizens to expect changes in teaching strategies.

2. Differences in teaching strategies are frequently differences in emphasis rather than the emergence of something entirely new.

3. Teachers in the new elementary school generally emphasize critical thinking, the process of learning as well as the product, skill in human relations, and learning by discovery.

4. When the recitation procedure is used, teachers generally talk about 64 percent of the class time; about 80 percent of the class time is used for questions, answering questions, and commenting on answers; the average number

[16] For a more detailed discussion of the value of games and simulations, see S. Boocock and James S. Coleman, "Games with Simulated Environments in Learning," *Sociology of Education*, Summer 1966, pp. 215–237.

of questions asked per minute is two; and the types of questions asked generally require only rote memory to answer.

5. When unit teaching is practiced, (a) learning activities are many and varied, (b) activities are unified around a purpose or theme, (c) opportunities are provided for the socialization of students, and (d) the teacher serves as a leader rather than as a taskmaster.

6. Units have been identified as subject matter units, experience units, resource units, curriculum records, teaching units, and dynamic units.

7. Time that is spent in orienting students to the study of a unit is worthwhile when it leads to enthusiastic participation in unit activities.

8. Children gain experience in democratic group living through participating in planning for a unit of work.

9. Evaluation goes on all the time that the unit is in progress. Pupils have opportunities to evaluate their own progress and that of the group.

10. A unit of work provides opportunities for learning skills that are needed for democratic group living, provides unity in the school experiences of children, provides opportunities for the use of skills in functional situations, and helps the teacher make better provision for individual differences.

11. The inquiry or discovery approach to teaching is concerned with helping the student develop the intellectual tools which he can use in solving problems, with the development of reasoning powers, and with learning how to learn.

12. The use of simulation games helps students to become highly motivated, learn the need for cooperation, get a more realistic understanding of life outside the school, gain an appreciation of the complexity of life situations, and become more excited about learning.

RECOMMENDED READINGS

Beyer, Barry K. (Ed.), *Concepts in the Social Studies*. Washington, D.C.: National Council for the Social Studies, 1971. The meaning of concepts, why we teach concepts, and how concepts can be taught.

Boocock, Sarane S., and E. O. Schild (Eds.), *Simulation Games in Learning*. Beverly Hills, Calif.: Sage Publications, Inc., 1968. A comprehensive treatment of the rationale and status of simulation games in learning.

Fraser, Dorothy McClure (Ed.), *Social Studies Curriculum Development: Prospects and Problems*. Washington, D.C.: National Council for the Social Studies, N.E.A., 1969. Chapter 5 explores changing strategies in instruction.

Hanna, Lavone A., Gladys L. Potter, and Neva Hagaman, *Unit Teaching in the Elementary School*, rev. ed. New York: Holt, Rinehart and Winston, Inc., 1963. Chapter 4 explains how learning experiences are organized in a unit; Chapter 9 suggests procedures for developing skills of inquiry and research.

Hoetker, James, and William P. Ahlbrand, Jr., "The Persistence of the Recitation," *American Educational Research Journal*, March 1969, pp. 145–167. Provides a brief account of the origin and development of the recitation; cites research relating to the use of questions in recitations.

Mager, Robert F., *Preparing Instructional Objectives*. Palo Alto, Calif.: Fearon Publishers, 1962. Emphasizes the importance of being explicit, communicating well, and explaining what pupils will be doing (behavioral).

Renner, John W., and William B. Ragan, *Teaching Science in the Elementary School*. New York: Harper & Row, Publishers, 1968. Chapter 8 describes the inquiry-centered classroom.

Sanders, Norris M., *Classroom Questions: What Kinds?* New York: Harper & Row, Publishers, 1966. Explains how to prepare questions for various processes involved in thinking.

Thayer, Vivian T., *The Passing of the Recitation*. New York: D. C. Heath and Company, 1928. Chapters 1 and 2 explain the origin of the recitation and some educational principles which are taken for granted when the recitation is used.

ORGANIZING
AND PLANNING

Organizing and Planning

**Organizing
To Maximize
Learning**

**Planning
for Effective Teaching**

**Utilizing
Extra-Teacher
Personnel**

*Part II is concerned with the relationship between school
organization and effective learning, types of planning that
facilitate effective teaching, and the importance of cooperation
with nonteaching personnel. Chapter 5 describes several types of
organization and draws certain conclusions regarding grouping
for instruction. Chapter 6 explains the need for long-range plans,
unit plans, and daily plans; tells why objectives, activities, and
evaluation should be related; and emphasizes the nature of
teaching strategies and evaluation techniques. Chapter 7
characterizes the roles played by nonteaching personnel.*

Chapter 5

Organizing To Maximize Learning

The difference between the school we now have and the one that will emerge from this era of change is difficult to visualize. But, surely we can tell from the present trends that it will be a school that uses team teaching and team learning in combination with nongraded patterns of education established on differing learning bases that will ensure the greatest growth for the individual child.

> Maurie Hillson, *Elementary Education: Current Issues and Research* (New York: The Free Press, 1967), p. 5.

The organization of the elementary school is not an end in itself; it is a means of maximizing the development of each child and releasing the special talents of each teacher. Innovations in elementary school organization began soon after the first graded elementary school was established in the Quincy School in Boston in 1848. Several famous plans designed to eliminate the evils and shortcomings involved in the lock-step (graded) system appeared during the first two decades of the twentieth century: the Gary Plan, the Dalton Plan, the Winnetka Plan, and others. Of more recent duration, the decades of the 1950s and 1960s have witnessed the emergence of many innovations in elementary school organization that are intended to foster quality, equality, individualization, and personalization in learning experiences. This chapter examines these plans, using as major headings (1) vertical organization, (2) horizontal organization, and (3) interclass and intraclass grouping.

VERTICAL ORGANIZATION

There are two distinct ways in which elementary schools are organized—vertically and horizontally. The vertical organization of the school determines how the learner will move upward through the hierarchy of school experiences from the time he is admitted until the time he is to leave the elementary school. Five such plans for moving the elementary learner through the elementary school will be discussed in this chapter: graded; multigraded; middle school; continuous progress (nongraded); and appropriate placement.

The Graded School Organization

The graded school is based upon a classification system, usually chronological age. Children who are six years old by the first day of November are expected to begin the first grade, and by experiencing normal annual promotions to the next grade level, one would have progressed through the graded elementary school by age twelve years. While November 1 is not the cutoff date subscribed to by all school systems, some such date must be used. As you would expect, members of the same grade level will vary in age from a very few days to a full year.

Virtually all materials that are produced for use in the elementary school are prepared for grade levels. That is, these materials are written and designed for use by "the average third grader, fourth grader," and so forth. At the beginning of the typical school year, in most third-grade classrooms, every learner picks up the same set of materials and turns to the first page as each text is introduced and begins his work from that point. What each teacher does about the individual differences that must exist in every class is his choice. Just the intimation that a set of learners, classified by chronological age, might be taught effectively by a single set of materials suggests questions that should be raised by such an organizational plan. It can be noted, though, that this is the most popular vertical plan of organization in the United States.

One question that is asked concerns the efficacy of the graded plan in relation to the influence rendered upon the children's personality development. Some children who are legally old enough for a particular grade level are not physically or psychologically ready for the experiences that are designed for this grade. The *readiness* level these youngsters bring to the school may be inadequate for many reasons, for example, environmental deprivation, physical impairments, emotional difficulties, and so on.

Age alone cannot dictate readiness, and the frustrating experiences such young learners will experience with graded materials can bring about a lack of self-confidence that may permanently impair learning for the future.

Other children housed in the graded structure who find the materials and experiences of the "package" relatively easy to satisfy may also be experiencing frustrations. Unless they are encouraged to move on in their studies, both in depth and in breadth, they may fall victim to a boring, challengeless, elementary curriculum and never be revived to their full potential at some later time. In this sense, the graded elementary school has been likened to the fabled Procrustean bed, with similar consequences.

The Multigraded School Organization

A plan that is designed to reduce the obvious regimentation of the graded school, the multigraded organization typically included classes of learners with age differences of three or more years. For example, a primary multi-grade class would contain an equal number of children from each of the first three grade levels. An emphasis is placed on the differences one would expect to find in existence among members of a group with such an age span. Learners are expected to gain from those who are so different, and in a three-year period one can enjoy being the youngest, the middle, and the oldest member of his class, with accompanying privileges.

This plan presents an interesting opportunity for personal, social, and attitudinal development. By planning for individual differences, teachers expect to employ a wide variety of learning aids and materials, and thus individualized instruction is personified. One possibility under this plan is for a single pupil to be working at one level in math, another level in language, and yet another level in social studies, and never once with the same group of classmates. Less of a stigma would be attached to the assignment of different texts since several levels of texts are commonly used in this classroom. Grouping is flexible, tentative, and designed to take advantage of, not reduce, the individual differences that exist.

The multigraded plan is not a commonly accepted organization for the elementary school, but there is some evidence that academic achievement for learners in these classes is somewhat higher than for lock-step graded classes.

The Middle School

Another modification of the pure graded structure in the elementary school is the middle school, still incorporating gradedness, but reducing the number of grade levels. The most common middle school plan includes kindergarten and the first four grades in the elementary school. Upon completion of this experience, the students would move to the middle school for the next four years before graduating to the high school for their final four years.

While there are no hard data to support evidence of a definite movement to middle school organization, many school systems are experimenting with ways to improve the articulation of students from the elementary schools to the present junior high or intermediate schools. Alexander reports a review of such studies, noting, "We may conclude, I believe, that there is a movement toward a 4-4-4 and 5-3-4 ladder development in various large school systems and that scattered throughout the country there are many individual school districts and schools whose personnel are trying very seriously to find a better educational organization than the now traditional 6-3-3 one."[1]

Historically, the elementary school was planned to provide educational experiences for the child while the high school was designed for the adolescent. The junior high school was given the formidable task of educating the youngsters making this transition from childhood to adolescence. Unfortunately, the typical junior high school is organized and programmed almost exactly like the high school; thus, the move from the elementary school to the junior high school has seldom been smooth and well planned.

Today's concern for individual progress and continuity of learning experiences is not enhanced by such a disjointed articulation. Supporters of the middle school suggest that a more likely time for changing schools comes at the time a child is ten or eleven years old, immediately before or very early in pubescence. These four or five years between ages ten or eleven and fourteen or fifteen find youngsters experiencing perhaps the greatest range of differences in physical, emotional, social, and psychological growth. The middle school would house a vast majority of young people who are caught up in these exciting changes and could be designed to provide relevant educational experiences for these students.

At least two other arguments are commonly presented in favor of the change to a middle school organizational plan. First, some school districts have found it easier to implement innovations to instructional practices, curriculum organization, and staff utilization when they have introduced this new vertical organizational plan. Second, school districts that have been placed under pressure to deal with school desegregation cite the change to middle school organization as an effort toward solution of this problem. The middle school may be seen as a compromise between arguments for the neighborhood school as opposed to a move to total

---

[1] William M. Alexander, "New Organizational Patterns for the Middle School Years," *The New Elementary School* (Washington, D.C.: A.S.C.D.-N.E.A.), p. 55.

school integration that would involve abandonment of the neighborhood school.

The Continuous Progress School Organization

This plan is usually referred to as nongraded vertical organization and should be viewed synonymously, except that continuous progress implies a more absolute abstention from gradedness in every sense. A continuous progress system suggests that both teachers and children interact in the learning situation most effectively when all artificial and formal barriers are removed. Characterized by flexibility, this plan allows each child to progress in every academic area at his own speed.

Strong students are encouraged to work up to their capacity, and slower students enjoy the privilege of progressing at their maximum comfortable rate. Every learner can experience daily success and yet know the thrill of a challenge. Unmarked materials for every need are commonplace, and the stigma attached to working "below your grade level" is reduced. Boredom, loss of interest, and misbehavior are less likely to occur when students are guided in activities that provide self-competition and assure intrinsic rewards of success feelings.

Chronological age grouping, beginning school at a set date on the calendar, and an average time of six years spent in what had been the first six grades of the elementary school are common characteristics of this plan. But annual promotions and retentions, neat packages of curricula, and all members of a single class starting at the same place each new school year are eliminated. With the continuous progress plan each child begins at the first of a new year where he left off the previous spring, without repeating work in some subjects and playing catch-up in others.

A common organizational grouping for the continuous progress plan is by primary and intermediate units. The new pupil would enter the primary unit at the age of six and expect to spend three years with either the same or three different teachers. Upon completion of each of the first three years, the youngster would take up from where he had left off the following year. After completing the primary unit, which usually takes three years, he would move into the intermediate unit. The teachers in the intermediate unit would plan their work with each pupil according to his achievement level in each subject. Satisfactory completion of this second three-year unit would earn the pupil the privilege of continuing his education at the junior high school.

It is worthy of note that John Dewey, in 1902, suggested that schools

> abandon the notion of subject matter as something fixed and ready made in itself, outside the child's experience; cease thinking of the child's experience as also something hard and fast; see it as something fluent,

embryonic, vital; and we realize that the child and the curriculum are simply two limits which define a single process.[2]

There may be a hierarchical order in difficulty of subject matter as well as a hierarchical order of readiness for learners, but these cannot be packaged and matched in grade-level units without placing indefensible pressures on elementary youngsters. The nongraded, continuous progress organization takes this into account, allowing for the existing differences in pupil readiness for each academic area.

The Appropriate Placement School

Organizational plans that reduce the lock-step nature of gradedness in the elementary school have been more extensively employed in the earlier grades than in the later school years. An exception to this is the plan currently being used by the Melbourne High School in Florida, a school that is well known for its successful implementation of a nongraded plan for grouping students in high school. The Melbourne plan, which also takes advantage of a multiphased curriculum, is called *The Appropriate Placement School* and is hailed as an innovative nongraded curricular organization. This plan should be examined carefully for the potential it holds in terms of improving the vertical organization of the modern elementary school.

The appropriate placement organization adds new dimensions to the grouping procedures that are used in the nongraded plan. It is particularly manipulative of the various phases of the curriculum and the expenditure of time given for instruction. The Multiphased Curriculum, as it is organized for the high school, is described as follows:

> Phase 1—Subjects are provided for students who perform from 0-20th percentile on standardized achievement tests, indicating that they need special assistance in small classes.
>
> Phase 2—Subjects are organized for students who range between the 20th and 40th percentile in achievement and who need more emphasis on fundamentals.
>
> Phase 3—Courses are arranged for students who score between the 40th and 60th percentile on standardized achievement tests, indicating that they have an average background of accomplishment.
>
> Phase 4—Subject matter is planned for extremely well-prepared students who achieve between the 60th and 80th percentile and desire education in depth.

[2] John Dewey, *Experience and Education* (New York: Crowell-Collier and Macmillan, Inc., 1938), p. 75.

Phase 5—Courses are available for students who attain above the 80th percentile and are willing to assume responsibility for their own learning, pursuing college level courses while still in high school.

Phase 6—Students whose creative talents are well developed should give consideration to the Quest phase of the curriculum. This is an important dimension of the phased organization which gives thrust in the direction of individual fulfillment. In this phase, a student may research any area in which he is deeply and sincerely interested.[3]

A reasonable facsimile of this type of organization could be designed for the elementary school; in fact, the plan may be even more appropriate for younger learners whose readiness level must be accounted for to more nearly assure successful school experiences in the early school years.

To further complement the total program of the appropriate placement school, the following distribution of class time is suggested:

1. Presentation of materials comprises approximately 20 percent of the time in the course. (This includes time spent in viewing films as well as lecturing.)

2. Discussion in analysis groups constitutes approximately 40 percent of the class time.

3. Individual work and reading encompass roughly 40 percent of the class time.[4]

Obviously, this use of time is submitted for implementation in the high school. Emphasis is placed upon changing the role of the teacher from expositor to one of coordinating group and independent learning activities. The learner becomes much more involved in the learning process, spending far less time as a listener and much more time as an active participant in discussions and as an independent learner. These kinds of changes are just as important in the elementary school and must be given prime consideration when vertical organizational plans are selected.

SITUATION 5.1
Meeting Educational Needs

Jerry is a ten-year-old fourth grader who just completed the annual achievement test. His grade-equivalent scores were: math 4.3; language 2.9; work-study 3.8; and reading 5.1. What strengths and/or limitations do you believe are inherent in each of the five vertical plans of organization, in relation to Jerry's educational needs?

[3] B. Frank Brown, *The Appropriate Placement School: A Sophisticated Nongraded Curriculum* (West Nyack, N.Y.: Parker Publishing Co., Inc., 1965).

[4] Brown.

HORIZONTAL ORGANIZATION

The horizontal organization of the elementary school controls the distribution of the students to the classroom teachers and determines the make-up of the class groups. Three major plans will be explained in this section—self-contained, departmentalized, and team-taught classes. Several modifications of these plans are discussed briefly.

The Self-Contained Classroom

The teacher in the self-contained classroom is responsible for directing the instruction in all, or virtually all, subjects. He is a specialist in a grade level, but a generalist in the curriculum for that particular level. He remains with the same group of learners every day for an entire school year and can be expected to become very well acquainted with each individual. Perhaps the greatest strength of this plan rests in this opportunity to know the individual characteristics and differences of the pupils. The self-contained classroom is the most common horizontal plan currently in use in today's elementary schools.

An advantage of the self-contained classroom is that the teacher can design his instruction to show the interrelatedness of the subject-matter fields. Also, there tends to be a greater flexibility in the schedule which allows the teacher to pursue a topic while the interest is high instead of bringing the lesson to a halt so that classes can move. Field trips or other experiences that take more than one instructional period are more easily arranged in the self-contained classroom. Finally, it is more likely that self-contained classroom teachers will become isolated from the other teachers in the building, with fewer occasions for working as a building or unit team.

One severe limitation of this plan is the tendency to keep the teacher in charge of his class from opening exercises to dismissal, without even a planning session during the regular school hours. In fact, the schools using the self-contained plan often expect these teachers to supervise playground, lunchroom, and tend halls before and after school. Many schools, mostly through the efforts of the local school associations, are demanding and gaining release time from such noneducation duties to be allowed planning and evaluation time.

Another difficulty presented by the self-contained plan is the presumption that any teacher can teach every subject, with competence, enthusiasm, and interest. By stretching an educator's imagination and energy in so many directions, can any one teacher have time to be really competent in any one subject area? And, let us not forget the pupil. All of his eggs are in one basket for a full school year. If he draws a strong teacher, good fortune has smiled upon him, but if he should be assigned to a weak teacher, nine months of trauma, dissatisfaction, and frustrations can be his fare. Once assigned, most classes remain intact for the year. Those who criticize this organizational plan cite the learner's need to have experiences with many teachers as a prime argument.

Departmentalization

In this plan both the teachers and the pupils are arranged in groups according to subjects. A teacher may become a specialist in one or more subjects and have classes with pupils working at one or more grade levels. He may teach science and math to all of the sixth-grade youngsters in a large elementary school or only math to fourth, fifth, and sixth graders in a smaller school. Pupils may have only two teachers who have separated the subjects evenly, or they may have a different teacher for each major subject. The combinations are limitless and are usually dictated by the size of the school's enrollment as well as the interests and talents of the teachers.

Departmentalization, or some modification, is especially popular for intermediate grade organization. One report in 1965 points out that almost one-half of all elementary schools were using some form of departmentalization and that one in twenty-five were completely departmentalized (N.E.A., *The Principals Look At Schools*).

This plan tends to exaggerate the importance of subject matter in contrast to a more general concern for the total development of the child. Opponents of departmentalization advise that this approach to learning is not in keeping with accepted findings in learning theory, that is, it is fragmentary and lacks integrative qualities. An example of this is the lack of occasion to teach units that cut across subject-matter divisions. Full departmentalization would make it virtually impossible for a teacher to get well acquainted with all of his students, and its relatively inflexible time schedule places the teacher at a disadvantage when additional time is needed or when motivation is running high.

A departmental plan will be encouraging to those wishing to specialize in a favorite subject field, and it could be responsible for attracting more men to elementary teaching. The demands placed upon the classroom teacher by fast-changing curricula, methods, and media create a favorable disposition toward the concentration of one's efforts to one subject. Also, the special materials and equipment that are used for one subject can be housed in a central location for easy access by that teacher. With this plan the pupil benefits from the instruction of more than one teacher and will probably be able to identify well with at least one, who can make the school situation a very positive experience.

Team Teaching

It is not entirely defensible to place team teaching in the category of horizontal organization because it can be employed vertically as well. Since its unique characteristics are more accurately aligned with horizontal concerns, team teaching will be viewed here in this light.

As a strategy for deploying teachers, usually in groups of three to five, teaming distributes the responsibility for instructing a large number of pupils among members of the team. The number of learners per teacher is essentially the same as the ratio for the self-contained or departmental teacher. Typically, a team includes a team leader or coordinator who accepts additional responsibility beyond the usual subject specialization. Other teaching members of the team lead instruction in one or two subjects and work with the other team members in planning and supporting. Quite often, paraprofessionals are employed to aid the team with lesser duties.

Several benefits can accrue from a team-teaching plan. Exemplary teachers can be used to direct the education of a large group of children and serve as a model for newer, inexperienced teachers. These teachers can demand higher salaries, enjoy the prestige of leadership, and provide an important professional service. Beginning teachers can profit from the opportunity of working with an experienced teacher and not have the burden of complete responsibility for a group of pupils. The new teacher will have more time to develop a strong proficiency in one subject area, under the supervision of the team leader. Nor will it be necessary for any group of students to receive all of their instruction from an inexperienced teacher.

Time is available for cooperative and individual planning. The pupils work in large and small instructional settings as well as directed independent study and gain important experience. Even though the basic unit of pupils consists of a large number, each teacher can concentrate on becoming especially familiar with a smaller group and be sharing information with other members of the team; all of the team members can eventually know the children even better. The pupils have the advantage of working with more than just one teacher during the year.

Team teaching must be complemented with a great number of meetings to ensure coordination of plans, projects, activities, and ideas. Often the efforts of the team are successful in direct relation to how well the members can work together, both personally and professionally. Countless teams have failed simply because of petty personal grievances. The ability of the team leader to arrange and administer the talents and interests of team members is a crucial factor. There is no guarantee that a highly successful classroom teacher will make a good team leader. Occasionally the team leader, appointed because of his strength as a teacher, will have little contact with the pupils because of the increased administrative load he bears. These are but a few of the problems that can limit the effectiveness of teaming.

> **SITUATION 5.2**
> *Modifying Horizontal Options*
>
> It should not be expected that one must go "all the way" in selecting a horizontal organizational plan of one type or another. Show how you might incorporate the unique strengths of either two or three of the above plans and adapt your own horizontal organization. How would you support your choice to a group of educators?

INTERCLASS AND INTRACLASS GROUPING

Plans for grouping elementary children, both within and between classes, are exercised after the more general horizontal and vertical organization is determined. In this section an examination of heterogeneous and homogeneous grouping practices, and modifications of each of these, is undertaken.

Heterogeneous, Interclass Grouping

This is an organizational plan whereby students are intentionally grouped as a cross-section of the population that makes up a whole grade level. Teachers would expect to have slow, average, and fast learners; youngsters exhibiting a full range of emotional and psychological characteristics; and students representing virtually all physical and social determinants. Students in these classes will experience just as many personal and academic differences as there will be likenesses.

Heterogeneous grouping provides a more natural social situation for elementary school youngsters. Children of varied and diverse talents have the opportunity to learn to work together, much as they will in real-life situations out of school. Learners do not have to live with the stigma of categorical labels that represent their intellectual prowess nor are parents forced to submit explanations to their youngsters about the reasons for such arrangements.

Heterogeneous grouping strongly suggests that criteria other than simply academic achievement are important. Social, emotional, and interpersonal development are considered equally as important as academic excellence. The pupil's right to be different is not only enhanced, but honored—a mark of the democratic setting.

Homogeneous, Interclass Grouping

In an effort to reduce the individual differences that exist among members of a single-grade level, some schools group the learners according to ability to learn and/or their achievement level in basic skills. Mental maturity (IQ), composite achievement score, and reading achievement are commonly used to determine such groups. Usually only one criterion is selected to make this judgment; thus, variability is reduced only slightly. Questions are raised concerning how homogeneous any group can be, when one considers the number of variabilities that create individual differences.

Teachers tend to prefer this method of grouping elementary children, at least teachers who do not receive the assignment for teaching the slower pupils. There seems to be a popular misconception that grouping by ability has reduced the individual differences significantly, and teachers who accept this notion often fail to provide for the vast differences that persist. Working with a limited set of materials, teachers may believe that they can control the instruction for a more carefully selected group of learners. Too little attention may then be given to the development of important traits and skills other than those used to determine the groups. For example, groups that have been determined on the basis of reading-achievement scores provide little assurance of homogeneity in math, science, or social studies achievement levels. A teacher who would assume a high correlation between reading achievement and any other academic area labors under a very questionable assumption. Instruction planned with the notion that a common homogeneity exists among all subjects could indeed prove frustrating to the teacher and learners alike.

When the objective of instruction is limited to a specific skill development or academic excellence in one subject area, homogeneous grouping could provide optimal conditions for learning by reducing the differences among learners. For example, in a departmentalized program this type of grouping might prove advantageous.

Research is inconclusive about the effect ability grouping has on the child's self-concept, except that such practices do not enhance the development of self-concept of young learners and members of the slower groups often report negative feelings about their placement. Homogeneous grouping was generally abandoned in the 1930s as a result of a lack of evidence to support its use.

Once again, a careful examination of the goals of elementary education must be made before any organizational plan can be sustained. It is questionable whether one can defend ability grouping within one of the major institutions of a democratic society, the public schools.

Modification in Grouping Organization

Many plans are in existence that allow for adaptation of the major organizational plans. In fact, it is rare to find any school employing a *pure* organizational plan such as those discussed above in a single elementary school. A school might choose to use heterogeneous grouping for all grades in all subjects except reading and mathematics. In these two subjects the pupils might be grouped according to their achievement level, with considerable overlapping of chronological age and/or grade levels. Another variation is the school that uses homogeneous grouping in the intermediate grades and heterogeneous grouping in the primary grades. An elementary school could use departmentalization in only the intermediate grades with homogeneous grouping in one or more subjects. The possible combinations are innumerable.

Whatever *interclass* grouping plan is adopted, there still remains the inevitability of grouping within the class; that is, *intraclass* grouping. At least one whole textbook is devoted to the subject of grouping procedures within a given class, and much needs to be said about the advisability of grouping the members of a single class of learners. While there is probably no one plan that is best for intraclass grouping, according to the objectives of the instruction in a given subject, improved instruction can be more nearly assured with grouping that reduces the differences of the pupils in this particular area. Children can be grouped solely to improve social and interpersonal relations; to take advantage of unique interests and talents of individuals; for preserving the unity of the class; to accommodate the facilities and materials of the classroom; for discipline and classroom management; to effect instruction in different subject areas; and for a host of other educationally sound reasons.

A guiding principle is that any grouping practice must remain open to continuous revision, entirely flexible and dynamic. Actually, the goal of grouping is not to reduce individual differences, but to create a learning environment that will encourage the exposure of every child's unique talents and contributions as well as present the most comfortable setting.

SITUATION 5.3

Satisfying Goals by Grouping

You are a fourth-grade teacher, working with two other teachers assigned to this same level. There are eighty-six fourth graders. The principal has suggested that you help design a plan for grouping these youngsters, both between and within the three classes to which you three teachers will be assigned. What will your suggestions be? Toward what educational goals would your plan move? What important criteria would you cite to guide your decisions?

Combining the Vertical and Horizontal Organizational Plans

No elementary school is organized in only one way. The number of options and combinations that can be derived by using horizontal and vertical choices, as well as grouping within these patterns, is almost limitless. Every elementary school evidences the use of a combination horizontal and vertical organizational plan. The most common combination plan is the graded school with self-contained classrooms. The recurring findings from every dependable resource suggest that neither of these alternatives should head their respective category. And, certainly, a combination of the two refutes much of what education has learned from psychology, curriculum and instruction theory, the field of school administration, and public relations experience.

What are other choices that one can select? Only a few will be reviewed here, but the reader is encouraged to let his imagination run free as he envisions the great number of possible modifications and alternatives that are available to the creative administrator and improvement-conscious faculty.

Using the graded, vertical organization, several combinations can be constructed: graded with departmentalization; graded with team teaching; graded with team-taught primary grades and departmentalized intermediate grades. Using the graded structure and modifications within the horizontal plan can produce several more combinations: a graded school can use self-contained classrooms with homogeneous grouping; graded with departmentalized teaching using heterogeneous groups; and graded with variations of inter- and intraclass grouping, using modifications of departmentalized, self-contained, and team-taught horizontal organization. It is easy to see the great number of possibilities when working within only the graded, vertical structure.

Equally as many combination choices exist when the continuous progress or multigraded vertical organizations are used. A few examples include: continuous progress and self-contained; continuous progress with departmentalization, plus modifications; continuous progress supported with team teaching; multigraded and semidepartmentalization.

The question remains, what horizontal and vertical organizational combination can provide the best educational opportunities for elementary school age youngsters? At the present, there is no clear-cut evidence to support a superior organizational plan for the modern elementary school. There are too many contingencies for this problem to be dealt with universally. Several questions inevitably arise. What limitations do your physical facilities impose? What teaching talent is available? How knowledgeable and capable is the school leadership? What is the capacity of the school for provision of the necessary materials? How receptive are the patrons to innovative ideas? How much extra time are those who will be involved willing to sacrifice while getting the new organizational plan started? These are but a few of the questions that must be considered.

It should not be overlooked that the teachers' and administrators' dispositions toward any organizational plan will largely control its effectiveness. Care must be taken to prevent placing any teacher or administrator in a situation that he cannot accept, philosophically. For this reason, the people who will be responsible for effecting instruction in any organizational plan should be actively involved in the selection of the plan. A one- to two-year period of in-service education is recommended to precede any major organization change. Moving too quickly without careful planning and in-service work is almost sure to create difficulties.

SITUATION 5.4
Creating a Vertical—Horizontal Combination

Your advice has been solicited by a member of the committee responsible for recommending a new organizational plan for the elementary schools. What vertical and horizontal organizational combination would you support? Give several reasons for your choice. Suppose two other plans have been submitted (choose your own two plans for this assignment) for your consideration. Give arguments against their advisability compared to your choice.

AN ADDITIONAL CONSIDERATION: THE OPEN SCHOOL

The idea of discussing, even briefly, the poorly defined concept of the open or informal school in a chapter designed to explain the organization of the elementary school is suspect. Perhaps more accurately defined as a learning environment creation, the open school can be identified with some basic organizational characteristics.

This reform in the organization of the elementary school answers to many names, most common of which include the informal approach, open school, open classroom, and informal education. By whatever name, the approach attempts to satisfy the following criteria:

1. A child's education must be centered upon his own experiences, his needs and interests, and involve him as an active participant in the direction of his learning activities. The conviction that learning will be more effective when it interests the child and not the teacher or some curriculum guide is accepted. Organizational flexibility must complement this basic criterion.

2. Individualized and personalized learning opportunities are assured,

especially by providing a variety of learning environments that are appropriate to the age of the children. Skills, understandings, and appreciations are developed in these interest centers that make use of a multiplicity and variety of curriculum materials, learning tools, and other stimuli which the children can make and operate. The centers promote student interaction in small to large groups, but also reward independent behavior. The child's performance is evaluated by considering the rate that is appropriate to his capacity, interest, and stage of development rather than by comparing his performance to a national norm, the teacher's expectations, a curriculum guide, or graded groupings.

3. There is a deemphasis placed upon formal instruction by the teacher. With direct teaching being limited, the teacher assumes the roles of observer, stimulator, assistant, and resource person. The demands placed upon the teacher more nearly resemble those expected of a diagnostician, one who determines a child's learning problems and draws upon a repertoire of alternatives that may support him.

4. The physical arrangement of the classroom is limited only by

Team teaching is facilitated when a large instructional area without partitions is provided. (Photo courtesy Norman Public Schools.)

the imagination of the teacher and the children as they seek to structure a setting that is most conducive to pursuit of their current "educational" interests and needs. It is not uncommon to find rooms that contain fewer chairs than students; all (or no) large tables as desks; large open spaces for freedom of movement and activities; individual learning carrels; carpeted "comfort" stations with upholstered chairs or divans; and considerable use of the hallways and corridors adjoining the room.

5. Extensive cooperation among the teachers is considered an important strength. At least two, usually more, teachers cooperatively provide for the learning environments that a child may experience. The children in a new school may cross traditional grade-level or age divisions for learning interactions with children of various grades or ages; thus, the teachers must coordinate their plans to take advantage of this option. Groups of teachers often work together to develop long-range plans for

Tutorial services supplement the work of regular teachers in the new elementary school. (Photo courtesy Oklahoma City Public Schools.)

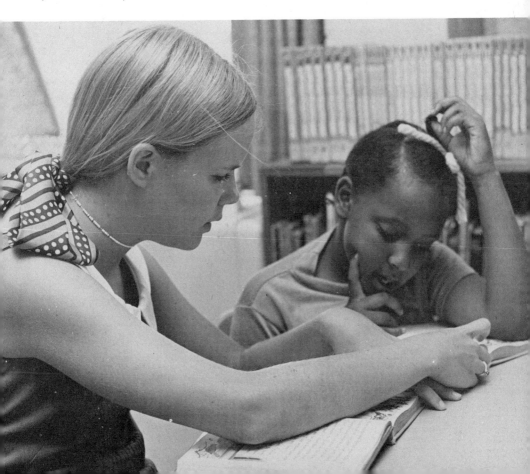

single-subject areas; coordinate their use of study trips or resource people; integrate complementary learning experiences that may be available through different subjects; procure and utilize materials; share information that may provide keener insights for evaluation; develop teaching units; and engage in professional growth activities. This cooperative behavior tends to become a professional attitude which enhances the total program by more nearly assuring an *esprit de corps* among members of the teaching team.

This brief sketch and cursory presentation of basic criteria that define the "informal school" approach is not satisfactory in detail. The reader is invited to search out additional information about the movement, reminded that much of what is being practiced in the United States emanated from the British Infant School idea.

SOME CONCLUSIONS

The organization of the elementary school is best seen as only an administrative device; it is in no sense a panacea that, by definition, guarantees quality education. Sound programs, exemplary teachers, effective leadership, good materials and conditions must accompany the best-designed organizational plan. But, the plan that effectively complements other curricular components is indispensable for facilitating the total school program. The organizational plan is the framework within which important educational objectives can be experienced and must always reflect the ultimate concern the schools hold for every learner. With this in mind, every elementary school faculty must determine which way it can best organize its school to assure optimal teaching and learning conditions. Continuous and comprehensive appraisal of the current organizational plan is demanded and deserves an annual "state of the school organization" report, complete with recommendations for active consideration in terms of future plans.

As our knowledge about learning, the teaching process, mental hygiene, and child growth and development increases, so must the organization of our educational institutions be prepared to change. Organization is never a finished product; it should evidence flexible, dynamic characteristics that are designed to meet the needs of the times.

SUMMARY

1. The basic criteria for selecting the organizational plan of the elementary school are quality, equality, and individualization.

2. Every elementary school is organized both vertically and horizontally. Common vertical plans are graded, multigraded, middle school, continuous progress, and appropriate placement. Horizontal plans include self-contained, departmentalized, and team-taught.

3. There are numerous combinations of horizontal and vertical plans.

4. Further grouping of learners takes place within the general organization of the elementary school.

5. Homogeneous, or ability, grouping is a technique for selecting groups according to likeness in ability or achievement. This practice is commonly used to determine members of classes within a grade level.

6. Heterogeneous grouping is a deliberate effort to pick members of classes according to their differences.

7. Intraclass grouping is used to place pupils in like groups within a single class for various reasons, both academic and personal.

8. The best horizontal and vertical organizational plan, with the necessary modifications within and between classes, must be determined by each unique elementary school according to its needs, goals, and potential.

9. There is no single best organizational plan for all elementary schools.

10. The organization of the elementary school must always remain open, flexible, and receptive to change.

RECOMMENDED READINGS

Association for Supervision and Curriculum Development, *The Self-Contained Classroom.* Washington, D.C.: A.S.C.D., 1960. This rather short booklet is assigned to a comprehensive coverage of the self-contained classroom, accentuating the characteristics of a good educational program in the self-contained classroom setting.

Beggs, D. W., *Team Teaching: Bold New Venture.* Bloomington, Indiana: Indiana University Press, 1964. An early but comprehensive treatment of team teaching that is appropriate for elementary schools.

Blair, Medill, and Richard G. Woodward, *Team Teaching in Action.* Boston: Houghton Mifflin Company, 1964. A very practical explanation of the many facets of team teaching.

Brown, G. Frank, *The Appropriate Placement School: A Sophisticated Nongraded Curriculum.* West Nyack, N.Y.: Parker Publishing Company, Inc., 1965. This book presents the multiphased appropriate placement curriculum as a modification of the nongraded school plan.

Faber, Charles F., and Gilbert F. Shearron, *Elementary School Administration: Theory and Practice.* New York: Holt, Rinehart and Winston, Inc., 1970. Chapter 2 examines the development of elementary school organization from a historic perspective, noting both the vertical and horizontal plans. Chapter 3 extends this study by discussing a variety of currently popular organizational plans, most of which are introduced in this chapter.

Franklin, Marian P., *School Organization: Theory and Practice.* Chicago: Rand McNally, 1967. Includes selected readings on grading, nongrading, multigrading, self-contained classrooms, departmentalization, team teaching, homogeneous and heterogeneous grouping.

Goodlad, John I., *Planning and Organizing for Teaching* (Project on the Instructional Program of the Public Schools). Washington, D.C.: N.E.A., 1963. Ways of organizing the curriculum, the classrooms, the schools, and instructional resources are discussed in this source book.

————, and Robert H. Anderson, *The Non-Graded Elementary School,* rev. ed. New York: Harcourt Brace Jovanovich, Inc., 1963. A thorough examination of nongradedness in the elementary school, this book is probably the best-known source about this vertical organization alternative.

Gross, Beatrice and Ronald, *Radical School Reform.* New York: Simon and Schuster, 1969. This book includes writings by many contemporary critics of America's schools. Alternative, innovative school programs are described and evaluated in relation to the present schools.

Hillson, Maurie, *Change and Innovation in Elementary School Organization, Selected Readings.* New York: Holt, Rinehart and Winston, Inc., 1965. This reader contains a complete treatment of important organizational alternatives, citing advantages and limitations of each plan. This may be the most thorough presentation of the topics introduced in this chapter.

Jarvis, Oscar T., and Haskin R. Pounds, *Organizing, Supervising, and Administering the Elementary School.* West Nyack, N.Y.: Parker Publishing Company, Inc., 1969. Chapter four presents some principles of organizing for instruction in the elementary school as they relate to various vertical and horizontal organizational plans.

Kohl, Herbert R., *The Open Classroom.* New York: Vintage Books, 1969. The author reports a candid account of his experiences while organizing and effecting an open classroom learning environment. The book is defined as a practical guide to a new way of teaching.

National Education Association, *Ability Grouping—Research Summary 1968 S3.* Washington, D.C.: N.E.A., 1968. Discusses grouping practices, the place considered for ability grouping in overall school organization, the schools' capacity for ability grouping, and the strengths and limitations of ability grouping.

Otto, Henry J., and David C. Sanders, *Elementary School Organization and Administration,* 4th ed. New York: Appleton-Century-Crofts, 1964. Chapters three and four present information about organization alternatives and grouping plans.

Ragan, William B., and Gene Shepherd, *Modern Elementary Curriculum,* 4th ed. New York: Holt, Rinehart and Winston, Inc., 1971. A chapter is given to reporting about current organizational plans that have found favor in the elementary schools. Strengths and disadvantages of each are presented.

Stoddard, George W., *The Dual Progress Plan: A New Philosophy and Program in Elementary Education*. New York: Harper & Row, Publishers, 1961. Introduces and carefully explains the dual progress plan as a new approach to dealing with subject matter in the elementary classroom. Two New York schools' use of this plan is reported.

Chapter 6

Planning for Effective Teaching

Whether the unit of work uses all or a part of the day, it is the core of the curriculum and provides the integrative experiences that give meaning to many of the skills, helps the child understand the world in which he lives, and gives him socializing experiences so that he learns to work and live with others democratically.

Lavone A. Hanna, Gladys Potter, and Neva Hagaman, *Unit Teaching in the Elementary School*, rev. ed. (New York: Holt, Rinehart and Winston, Inc., 1963), p. 115.

There are so many reasonable and logical arguments in support of planning to assure effective teaching that it seems almost unnecessary to introduce this chapter in such a defensive fashion. One does not need experience in teaching to recognize the importance of carefully formulated plans for any course of action. Planning forces the teacher-actor to define his direction, determine his goals, select his strategies, but first of all it provides him with a basis for making decisions. Most of the objectives teachers seek can be reached in more than one way, and most of a teacher's energy is given to satisfying more than one objective at a time. Planning often becomes an effort to meet more than one goal at a time in the most expedient and productive manner. Expertise in planning is learned, never accidentally, but because the path toward this important facility is carefully planned.

A RATIONALE FOR PLANNING

The teacher plans because he wants to provide his students with the best educational experiences as he faces severe limitations in time, materials, facilities, energy, and professional support. He plans because he realizes that all three elements in the teaching-learning triangle depend upon his ability to organize and integrate each element with the other two. The *objectives* must be reached through thoughtfully selected teaching *procedures*, which, in turn, must take into account the availability of appropriate *evaluative techniques*. If he teaches in a self-contained classroom, the elementary teacher plans because he knows that only by thorough planning can he maximize the correlative combinations available in such an organizational plan. If he teaches with a team of teachers he plans cooperatively to take advantage of the varied skills, interests, backgrounds, and motives of the different team members as they execute each day's experiences with the students. He learns that his planning assures a more adequate resolution of individual differences, just as planning makes the learning experiences continuous and interrelated. A reward of well-organized plans is the feeling of confidence a teacher experiences. Finally, the conscientious teacher plans because he knows he does not have the right to waste the time of a class of young learners who have placed the responsibility for their learning upon his shoulders.

LONG-RANGE, UNIT, AND DAILY PLANS IN PERSPECTIVE

The well-prepared elementary teacher is using three types of plans in concert, each serving a little different purpose, but each closely related to the others. The complementary nature of these plans, as sources of guidance to the teacher and students, will be stressed in this section of the chapter.

Long-Range Plans

Long-range plans represent a kind of structure upon which the remainder of the teacher's plans rest. They are more tentative and remain flexible to adjustment, but they do provide a sense of stability for the yearly program. The continuity, scope and sequence, balance, and perspective of the year-long program are more nearly assured when long-range plans are formalized. Unit and daily plans evolve from the teacher's long-range plans; thus, the total program is synchronized and logically integrated.

There are a number of sources available to the teacher from which his long-range plans can be determined. State and local curriculum guides are essential for the identification of broad objectives and the major areas of study that should be covered during the entire year. Often, individual school personnel will elect to meet in grade- or multigrade-level groups to discuss their plans to complement the suggestions set forth in curriculum guides. These meetings are usually scheduled during the summer break so that time is available for each teacher to formulate his own long-range plans from his cooperative planning.

Teacher's editions of the texts that are used provide an excellent source for long-range planning. The overall objectives of the course of study that is contained in a text are presented in the teacher's edition. Broad, general objectives are explained, later to be broken down into unit and daily type objectives. Supplementary books that have proven appropriate to supporting a subject often provide similar aid to the teacher. Standardized achievement tests contain insights about the goals held for the various grade levels in the major areas of study. Fears that the teacher may "teach for the test" if he is familiar with its content are usually unfounded.

Long-range plans are necessary to the teacher so that decisions about timing the presentation of certain units to coincide with similar activities in other subjects will effect the best use of time. Problems that occur as a result of day-by-day planning can be prevented by advanced scheduling of materials, facilities, and people. For example, arrangements can be made for study trips well in advance so that disappointment caused by a full calendar can be prevented. The audio-visual media that would be most advantageous to a unit planned for later in the year can be scheduled before school begins. Special resource people who can add much to the school program can be invited weeks in advance, giving them time for preparation and allowing the teacher time to adjust his plans to fit the guests' if the suggested date cannot be met. Other resources can be anticipated and sought out when the teacher is thinking in terms of year-long plans for his class.

Perhaps the strongest argument for long-range planning is that the school year will not conclude with certain parts of the curriculum untouched and other parts covered in a redundant fashion. There is too much for a teacher to remember without expecting him to recall which, and to what extent, specific objectives were dealt with in the fall as May rolls around. An experience typical to most teachers during their second year of teaching in the alarming realization that something he felt sure had been done this year was really done last year and vice versa. This problem becomes decidedly more complicated with additional teaching experience. Thus, the suggestion that more experienced teachers have less need for formal, long-range plans is quite unsupportable.

SITUATION 6.1

Long-Range Plans: Strengths and Limitations

Secure a state or local school system "Curriculum Guide" and a teacher's edition of the same subject, for the same grade level. Examine the guide and text and identify the year-long or long-range objectives that are cited. Do these objectives present an overview of what is expected of a learner as he studies this subject? Are these objectives highly structured? Do you find evidence that the long-range objectives and plans might limit the teacher's flexibility in adapting this curriculum to his class and its unique needs? How do you feel that the long-term plans cited in these materials might be helpful to a teacher? How might they prove limiting?

Unit Plans

The unit plan is a teaching guide that contains an outline of objectives, the content, organized ideas, learning experiences, and the necessary instructional materials. Keying from this guide, the teacher and students select the most useful and interesting experiences they wish to have. There are certain characteristics of the unit plan that make it the important unifying learning experience that it is. These characteristics will be discussed here to show how unit plans are extensions of the long-range plans and are, in turn, extended to serve as a teacher's daily plans.

UNIT DESCRIPTION. The unit is usually entitled in such a way that the area of study is implied, but most unit introductions are more descriptive in an effort to inform the teacher about the nature of the study that is planned. Titles, alone, may express a theme, topic, or problem. The unit description may be a few short paragraphs about the more specific concerns that will be taken up by the unit study. Usually, enough information is given here to aid the teacher in deciding whether a particular unit would contribute significantly to the long-range plans that have been selected. A list of key ideas, a summary of major generalizations, an outline of content, or a set of suggested activities are examples of information that may be contained here.

OBJECTIVES. The objectives for a unit are usually categorized in some manner. If the unit is a single-subject unit, the major divisions of objectives for that subject would serve as category headings. For example, the objectives for a social studies unit might be listed under the areas of: concepts and generalizations, attitudes and appreciation, and basic skills. If the unit is multidisciplinary the objectives would probably be cited according to each subject contained in the unit. There might be objectives for language arts, social studies, and science within the same unit.

Unit objectives are an important part of the structure of long-range planning. The unit is a major division of the total year's instruction, yet to be broken down further to the daily objectives that are carefully planned to contribute to the long-range or yearly plans. Technique in stating objectives will be discussed later in this chapter.

ORIENTATION OR INTRODUCTION. Upon deciding which unit of study will most nearly satisfy the long-range plans, it becomes the teacher's responsibility to arrange or create an orientation to the unit that assures student motivation. Interest in the unit will be maximized when the students recognize the importance of the study, can relate their past experiences to the unit's goals, and can identify something about the unit study that will have some personal value to them. In fact, the introduction to a unit is largely a matter of personalizing the potential the unit holds for every member of the class.

The teacher who enjoys success in staging the orientation of a unit of study practices one important characteristic of every effective teacher, that is, he knows his students extremely well. He also is aware of a number of helpful sources that aid in the introduction of a unit. Some reliable sources include: discussions between the students and the teacher during other units of study; audio-visual media (films, recordings, flat pictures, and so on) that might generate interest in the topic; a local resource person who would make an introductory-type presentation; a display or exhibit made up of materials and artifacts collected from children's homes, local businesses, service organizations, or other people in the community; a current event, either on the national or local scene; or a popular book or periodical accessible to the students.

Often, the teacher must rely upon his skill in raising meaningful and challenging questions about the unit topic as the primary technique to introduce the unit. The right questions, asked in the proper manner, can set the stage for the entire study of the unit, especially when care is taken to complement the objectives with the questions.

TEACHER-STUDENT PLANNING. With the guiding support of the teacher, students should be encouraged to become involved to a significant extent in the planning of the unit. Cooperatively, the objectives of the unit can be modified to fit the needs and interests that are unique to the class. The students can help select committee assignments, determine meaningful activities, volunteer for various responsibilities, help clarify the teacher's role, and add their ideas about other procedures that may be useful to satisfying the objectives cited for the unit. Together, teacher and students should agree upon the evaluative techniques that will most adequately determine whether and to what extent the unit's goals have been met.

Planning together to organize the unit of study is an excellent opportunity for the students to experience democracy in action. The teacher is not just mouthing the characteristics of a democratic situation, he is involving the students in the process of resolving a learning situation by democratic means. As ideas presented by members of the class or the teacher conflict, the demand to settle the conflict is met, for real. The students can see how rational thinking is employed in a reasonable manner to mediate differences, compromise positions, and make decisions for the common good.

These processive experiences, such as the orientation activities and the student-teacher planning, are important to the long-range objectives and plans. During these times, continuous and comprehensive evaluation of the students' behavior will reveal performance criteria that bear upon important educational goals.

THE ACTIVITY PERIOD. The time has come for the plans to be effected. The plans that have evolved from the orientation to the unit are set in motion, usually with a variety of activities. Whole group, small group, and independent study is practiced as the students read, gather materials, view films, write reports, take study trips, entertain resource people, prepare skits, make puppets, practice panel presentations, make collages, paint murals, and otherwise work toward evidencing their acquisition of new knowledge, skills, and attitudes.

The activity time is a period in which the teacher will probably be hard pressed to remain cool and collected. There can hardly be meaningful activity without noise. The more enthusiastic and excited the learners are about the activities selected for the unit, the higher the level of noise is likely to be. An important consideration for the teacher to remember is to discuss this very concern with the students during the student-teacher planning periods. Cooperatively, the class can decide upon a healthy, acceptable set of guidelines for the activity period that should prevent embarrassing or uncomfortable confrontations during this otherwise enjoyable period.

THE CULMINATING PERIOD. The unit must eventually be terminated. During the planning period the students and teacher can decide upon a meaningful and interesting way to bring the unit to a close with a culminating activity. This activity can be something as informal as small group reports to the rest of the class or as formal as a convocation program for parents and other students in the school. The culminating period can be made up of a variety of activities, each determined by the small groups that work up expressive experiences for the rest of the class. Informative and/or entertaining skits, art-related projects, music-supported dramatizations, a carefully explained exhibit, a mock radio or TV program are examples of such activities. The culminating period is usually a fairly comprehensive activity that attempts to summarize and allow the students an opportunity to give evidence of having met the objectives of the unit.

THE EVALUATION. The evaluative techniques assigned to the unit are not reserved for a time following all of the other activities. Evaluation began as the unit was introduced and continued throughout the teacher-student planning, the activity period, and the culminating period. Appropriate evaluative procedures were selected and used as each occasion was presented. The controlling determinant of the methods for evaluation is the set of objectives that was accepted early in the unit study. This aspect of the unit was at least partially cared for during the student-teacher planning, at which time the evaluative techniques that seemed appropriate to the unit were reviewed and decided upon.

The activities selected for the activity period, the experiences planned for the culminating period, and the evaluative techniques are all coordinated and organized to contribute to the long-range plans that the teacher has accepted in a more general context for the school year. Unit plans are an intermediary device for assuring this coordination.

Daily Plans

Obviously, a teacher's daily plans are a natural extension of the long-range and unit plans, designed to assure coverage and a degree of continuity to the more comprehensive list. Daily plans are not entirely circumscribed by longer ranged plans. Unit and year-long plans provide a structure within which the teacher may operate with quite a lot of flexibility as he executes the daily routine. In fact, it is the daily planning that provides a teacher the greatest opportunity for finally personalizing the curriculum.

A teacher may be well advised to have developed a daily lesson-plan form that provides further structure for a day's activities. This planning form should allow space for a description of the objectives, the instructional procedures the teacher will employ, the materials that are necessary to the lesson, and an explanation of the evaluative techniques that will be used. An estimation of the time that each teacher and/or student activity will demand should be included on the planning form. Space for notes about the lesson, especially as they may pertain to the unit or long-range plans, may be helpful. The daily lesson-plan form included here is an example that may be useful to the elementary teacher.

DAILY LESSON PLAN FORM

Subject _____ Date _____

Objective(s):
  (See the section in this chapter concerning objectives.)

Procedures:

Teacher Activities	Time	Student Activities
(What is the teacher doing as he interacts with the students? What does he do as the students act?)	(approximation in minutes)	(What behavior is expected of the students? What are they doing when the teacher is in charge?)

Evaluation:
  (What evaluative techniques, methods, strategies are used to assure the objectives have been met? What performance criteria are demanded and how are these assessed and reported?

Materials:
  (Include the materials that will be necessary to complete the lesson; where they may be secured.)

Notes:
  (Could include additional considerations about individuals; relationship of this lesson to the unit or long-range plans; information relative to tomorrow's lesson; a brief evaluation of the daily lesson; or notes about the relationship of this subject to another academic area or another part of the curriculum.)

Scheduling Plans

Many school systems issue a suggested allotment of time to be spent teaching each part of the elementary curriculum. There are typically 1800 minutes of instructional time per week in the elementary school and, often, a conditional breakdown of this time is proffered for teachers' consideration as long-range, unit, and daily plans are organized. The distribution of time is usually different according to the grade level taught. An example of a plan for time allotment is shown on page 120.

Teachers are invited to manipulate the time that is available, on a daily, unit, or long-range basis, but a general adherence to the suggested time distribution is expected. For example, the teacher may choose to virtually exclude formal writing instruction for a period of two weeks so

A Suggested Weekly Program of Studies

SUBJECT	MINUTES PER WEEK		
	Grades 1–2	Grade 3	Grades 4–5–6
Reading	600	600	300
English	150	175	250
Spelling	100	100	75
Writing	50	75	50
Math	100	150	225
Social Studies	100	150	300
Science	75	75	125
Fine Arts:			
Music	100	100	100
Art	100	100	100
Phys. Ed. and Health	150	100	100
Recess	75	75	75
*Planning Time for Day's Activities	75	75	50
*Evaluation Time for Day's Activities	50	25	0
*Time for Special Activities	75	0	50
	1800	1800	1800

* Primary grades dismiss a little earlier. Take time from areas starred.

that this time could be used for other purposes, but this time missed should be made up some time within that evaluation period. When a multidiscipline unit is being taught the teacher may have complete freedom to integrate the different subjects and not worry about accounting for the expenditure of time for each separate subject as long as he is fairly sure that the time distribution is reasonably close. Of course, this carries over to daily plans, and there is little excuse for a teacher chopping off a lesson at a precise time just because his time allotment has run out. When the interest is high and an activity should be continued the teacher has the option of using time from another area and reciprocating this later.

Scheduling also includes such considerations as a balance of physically active versus relatively quiet learning situations. While there is little evidence to support the notion that any one subject should be taught at a particular time of the day, there may be circumstances persistent in a classroom that make certain types of study more appropriate. For example, if the school band is practicing next door for a half-hour on Tuesday, this may be an ideal time to schedule small group buzz sessions in science.

Occasionally changing the scheduled routine may generate some interest from the class, simply because of a felt need for change.

SITUATION 6.2

A Weekly Schedule Problem

Choose a grade level, use the suggested weekly program of studies, consider the following conditions, and set up a week's schedule. The conditions: (1) three of your students spend two half-hour sessions per week in speech therapy; (2) the nurse would like a forty-five minute block of time for hearing tests on Tuesday; (3) eight of your students are in the beginning band which practices on Friday, 2:30 to 3:15 P.M.; (4) two students have regular appointments with the counselor, your choice of times; (5) five of your students serve on the school Safety Patrol and must leave class ten minutes before dismissal at noon and at the end of the school day; (6) there is a special assembly on Thursday, 10:15 a.m.; (7) you exchange-teach with another teacher, taking her art while she takes your music; (8) physical education and health can be scheduled only three days a week, your choice of days. Explain your rationale for designing our schedule in whatever way you have to allow for: the speech-therapy students; the loss of forty-five minutes to the nurse; the two students going to the counselor; the loss of time experienced by the Safety Patrol members and members of the band; the time you took for the special assembly. The reader should be reminded that this does not represent an unusual week on the elementary calendar.

STATING OBJECTIVES FOR PLANS

The objectives that are accepted for each of the three different types of plans discussed here should be stated in relation to the learning that is expected to occur. Since learning is generally considered a "change in behavior" the statements of objectives should reflect this type of expectation, that is, a *behavioral* statement. During the past few years a great deal of interest has been shown in stating objectives in terms of more precise, observable behavior. The advantages of more specific behavioral statements include clearer direction in planning, more definitive selection of procedures, and improved criteria for the selection of proper evaluative techniques.

Since the objective is a suggested change in a learner's behavior as a result of an educational experience, the statement of the objective should identify the attributes that can be observed in the learner's behavior at the conclusion of the experience. A clear statement of this sort will help the teacher know which teaching strategies are most appropriate and what type of evaluation methods will most likely assess the learning, as well as aiding him in the selection of meaningful materials and content. More exactly defined observable behavior is an essential dimension of well-stated objectives.

Characteristics of Good Objectives[1]

THE OBJECTIVE COMMUNICATES ACCURATELY. The first test of a well-stated behavioral objective is that it conveys the same message to the receiver and to the sender. Challenged by the rather limiting nature of words and symbols, the teacher must be guaranteed that his statement relates his intent to others exactly as he perceives it. Any distortion of the teacher's intention for the learner's ultimate behavior detracts from the meaningfulness of the objective. A technique for checking the communicative nature of an objective statement is to challenge each alternative to the desired goal and try to eliminate these alternatives in the statement.

THE OBJECTIVE IDENTIFIES PERFORMANCE. The objective statement must explain what the child can actually do as a result of what he has learned. The demand is for performance by the learner that reflects behavior of an acceptable nature. The child may be able to intellectualize or verbalize the expected behavior, but a well-stated behavioral objective refuses to accept anything less than *performance* from the one being evaluated. For example, an elementary learner may be able to define and explain how one develops open-mindedness, but this is no assurance that he himself has learned to develop open-mindedness. Stated behaviorally, the learner may be expected to *identify* points on all sides of an issue, *distinguish* facts from opinions, *consider* and *use* ideas of others, and *gather* information to settle arguments. These criteria establish more precise expectations of his behavior, in performance terms. They strengthen an objective statement.

THE OBJECTIVE DESCRIBES ITS CONDITIONS. The behavior expected of the learner can be more precisely identified when the situational conditions are exposed in the statement. It may be necessary to exclude the kinds of behavior that could not be accepted as evidence that the objective has been satisfied. For example, a student may be expected to "estimate distances on a map by using the scale of miles found in a map legend." This statement does not include some important conditions that would make it more explicit. An expectation more appropriate to determining whether the learner can use a scale of miles to estimate distances would be, "Given

[1] See Robert F. Mager, *Preparing Instructional Objectives* (Palo Alto, Calif.: Fearon Publishers, Inc., 1962).

a foreign map, and without the use of a ruler, the learner can estimate distances on the map by using the scale of miles found in the map legend." By including these important conditions the operation can be more clearly understood by the student and the evaluation is simplified.

THE OBJECTIVE IDENTIFIES PERFORMANCE STANDARDS. Ultimately, the student's performance must be evaluated. The complete objective statement will identify how the student will be evaluated by including some mention of performance standards, usually in terms of minimum accepted behavior. An example of setting a performance standard is to impose a time limit for acceptable behavior. Instead of simply expecting a fourth grader to calculate the multiplication facts, the teacher sets a standard of a maximum time of four minutes. A second technique is to specify the number of errors that will be accepted, that is, indicate conditions of acceptable performance. The fourth grader may be expected to calculate the multiplication facts in less than four minutes with fewer than three errors. Performance standards are value judgments; thus, criteria must be provided upon which evaluation can be derived.

These four characteristics of well-stated objectives are important guides to the entire planning operation. By satisfying these criteria a teacher's objectives for instruction and learning serve well the tasks of selecting the most appropriate teaching procedures and utilizing proper evaluative techniques.

Before concluding this section there are two other notes about stating objectives that seem worthy of mention. In terms of the first characteristic suggested here, the teacher must become acquainted with the kinds of words and symbols that add the least and those that add the most to communication. Objective statements that include such intentions as "to know; to understand; to appreciate; to believe" violate the efforts described here to make objectives communicative. These words can be interpreted in so many ways that it is virtually impossible to expect them to convey the writer's message accurately. Action words must be employed, such as, "to list; to identify; to recite; to contrast" so that communication is enhanced. The teacher has the responsibility of developing a facility with words and symbols of this more descriptive mode.

Second, the impression that an objective statement must be contained in one sentence is erroneous. The statement of objectives for a single goal may consist of several specific statements. If breaking down the objective statement helps it satisfy the characteristics discussed here, then by all means write as many sentences as are necessary.

A final remark about designing good objectives is that once the teacher has defined his objectives, then supplied his students with a copy, there may be little left for him to do.

SITUATION 6.3
Evaluating Objectives

An interesting way to check how well an objective is stated is to determine how adequately the objective can be evaluated. Consider the following objectives in terms of how precisely they can be evaluated. Identify an appropriate evaluative technique (method, instrument, and so on) and state your rationale for selecting this technique for each objective. Point out the strengths and limitations of the objectives.

1. Learners can identify the fifty states and their capitals on a blank outline map of the United States, with fewer than five errors and in less than ten minutes.
2. Learners can understand the process of multiplication with two-place multipliers.
3. Learners can write a creative story of two pages in less than fifteen minutes with fewer than eight grammatical or spelling errors.
4. Learners can appreciate the moral of the poem, "Tonight's Song," and relate this to the essay, "Jim's Bittersweet Trip."
5. Learners can cite seven influences upon their daily behavior that are the result of our Western culture and support their selection with the evidence presented in unit seven of the text.

A TEACHING UNIT PLAN PROBLEM

Because of the relative importance of unit teaching in the new elementary school, the remainder of this chapter is concerned with a more comprehensive examination of this process. The problem-centered approach presented here requires the reader to select a model teaching unit as a referent. This unit should represent a grade level the reader finds interesting and may be chosen from a host of sources. Resource units are available in most curriculum libraries, teaching units make up most elementary texts, and many curriculum guides are presented in unit form. The problem here will key on helping the reader develop a set of guidelines for planning a unit of instruction. These guides will be left for the reader to conclude for himself, but will be introduced here through the use of questions.

HOW DOES THE TEACHER SELECT A UNIT FOR STUDY? Quite often, there is really little freedom for the teacher to select the units he will teach. These are often required in the course of study or, because a certain text has been selected, must be taught in order to complete the text. The course of study may present options to various units that are appropriate for a grade level, or the prescribed text may contain more units than can be taught in one year. In either case, the following criteria for selection can be used:

1. The unit should contribute to the achievement of the objectives cited in the long-range plans.
2. The unit should deal with a significant area of study that allows opportunities for the development of a wide variety of educational objectives: cognitive, affective, and psychomotor.
3. The unit should relate to the children's past experiences and have potential for developing these experiences in depth and breadth, in a continuous fashion.
4. The unit should suggest instructional resources and learning experiences that can be modified to meet the full range of individual differences that persist in most classes.
5. The unit must satisfy the limitations of time and available instructional resources so that a reasonably in-depth study can be experienced.
6. The unit should make some provisions for evaluation. There should be evidence that the evaluative techniques suggested complement the stated objectives.
7. The unit should fit the educational backgrounds and growth characteristics of the teacher's unique set of learners.

Satisfying these criteria will reduce the chances of selecting an inappropriate unit. Even in this hypothetical situation, if the reader cannot be reasonably sure that his unit referent is satisfactory, another unit should be chosen before moving to the next question. Does the reader's unit measure up?

HOW DOES THE TEACHER PREPARE TO TEACH THE UNIT? The success of a unit will be more nearly assured when the teacher feels confident about his background of experience with the topic. Most units suggest a number of ways and references that the teacher can use to enrich his background, for example, other texts, periodicals, audio-visual materials, and materials suggested for the children. The resources that may be available for use as the unit develops should be checked, including the availability of resource people, study trip ideas, and audio-visual media. A collection of graphic materials, realia, and artifacts may be begun, enlisting the support of the children in the class. The unit may include an annotated bibliography of children's references, teacher's materials, and other media. Using these aids the teacher should begin preparing an outline of content, organized ideas, and activities. With this sort of background preparation assured, the teacher can now plan the introduction of the unit and feel better prepared to be involved in the student-teacher planning stage.

At this point the reader should review his preparation status in relation to his model unit. Do the suggestions cited above seem reasonable? Would the time demanded to satisfy these criteria be easy to justify?

HOW DOES THE TEACHER ORGANIZE THE OBJECTIVES? Another section of this chapter has been given to a comprehensive examination of organizing and stating objectives effectively. The reader is invited to challenge the objectives cited in his model unit by submitting them to the test defined by the characteristics of good objectives. If the objectives do not meet these criteria, would it be difficult to modify them so that they do? Is there any evidence that the unit objectives contribute to long-range objectives of any kind? Do the unit-objective statements make any provisions for breaking them down to more specific, daily-type plans?

HOW DOES THE TEACHER INTRODUCE THE UNIT? A very effective way to introduce a new unit is to plan it well in advance and make it an on-going study of the preceding unit, a rather natural evolution. This relationship can be aided through good questioning and by identifying problems that cause the students to be interested in learning experiences that the teacher knows are presented in the next unit. Instead of using this more subtle approach the teacher may simply suggest that the next logical unit be studied. By involving the students in a discussion about the appropriateness of the forthcoming unit, continuity and student satisfaction can be experienced.

The unit may lend itself to introduction by only a special event or a particular incident. If the event is seasonal or constrained by the calendar, the unit should be reserved for the more timely introduction. If the event or incident can be arranged, the teacher may plan accordingly. Other introductory techniques include an interesting pretest, followed by discussion designed to arouse motivation; reading a book that would create interest in a particular topic; using certain audio-visual materials that elicit interest in the subject; taking a study trip or using a resource visitor; or arranging the classroom environment to create interest in a particular area of study.

As the year progresses the dynamic teacher will use a variety of methods for introducing new units of study. The reader should begin to examine how extensive is his repertoire of ideas for this technique. Does the model unit suggest any other strategies for the introduction of this study? Does the reader recognize any modifications of the suggestions here that he could make to improve upon the implied directions for introducing his model unit? Can the reader explain how the introduction of a unit may be important to satisfying certain objectives selected for the unit by giving an example from his model unit?

HOW DOES THE TEACHER INVOLVE STUDENTS IN PLANNING THE UNIT? To begin with, the objectives cited for most units are prepared for a general audience of learners. The teacher can reveal these to his students and request their ideas for modifying the objectives to be more appropriate for their class. Some objectives may have already been attained, others may not be important, and some just not very imaginative. Depending upon the extent of involvement by the students in modifying the objectives, a more personal alliance with the unit can be achieved by including their ideas. Next, the students can be involved in selecting the procedures to be followed in studying the unit. Before embarking upon the study of some units the teacher may choose to let the students identify every conceivable procedure that could be used to engage in the study of the unit. After listing all the ideas, the students' attention could be directed to predicting the consequences of practicing each procedure submitted. After this exercise the teacher should be assured of an intelligent selection of workable procedures for the unit and, at the same time, have provided the students with a valuable exercise in decision making.

Now is the time to cooperatively determine the dimensions of evaluation for the unit. Student involvement is important since a clearer understanding about the evaluation of the unit should expedite a class's movement toward the objectives. The evaluation process is often the best-kept secret in the learning act, regularly causing an unnecessary level of apprehension on the part of learners. There is no excuse for this sort of behavior by a teacher. By involving the students in planning for the evaluation of the unit, objectives can be clarified, procedures kept in line, and evaluative techniques made instructional.

Reflecting upon his model unit, the reader can speculate about the possibilities for involving students in planning for the execution of the remaining unit experiences. Is a technique for organizing and directing this planning operation beginning to emerge in the reader's thoughts? Would it be difficult to guide the students in a cooperative planning venture so that the model unit's objectives could be met? Does the reader believe that a teacher can be "democratic" as he involves the students in planning the unit's objectives, procedures, and evaluative techniques? What particular skills will the reader have to develop in order to plan with students in an effective manner?

HOW DOES THE TEACHER INTERACT DURING THE ACTIVITY PERIOD? Action is the key word for the activity period; this is the *doing* part of the unit. Flexibility is another important concept to keep in mind as the action begins. "The best laid plans of mice and men" may work only in the minds of the planners, and as the plans demand modification during the activity period both the students and the teacher must be willing to adapt.

This is one important role the teacher must assume, that of mediator for change. The teacher will usually be the first to recognize that some plans will never be effected; thus he must anticipate the right moment to direct the students toward a more workable situation. This is not the time to dictate or become authoritative. Usually, by asking good questions or otherwise pointing out basic flaws in the plan the students will suggest necessary changes in the approach.

A well-prepared teacher is an excellent resource person during the activity period. Elementary students often impulsively leap into activities that soon leave them floundering for direction and guidance. The teacher's role is to help them resolve their own dilemma by providing the least "advice" possible. Students feel good about resolving their problems, even if the teacher did provide some clues through questions or analogies. The resource-person role is also extended to include having available pertinent bibliographies, media references, resource files, materials and supplies, school policies about study trips or resource guests, and mechanical aptitude to deal with the machinery that may be employed. The teacher may be nothing more than a sounding board for students' ideas about activities they would like to use.

Most teaching units contain a wealth of suggestions for student-centered activities. The teacher must provide whatever support is necessary for intelligent selection, meaningful employment, and maximum production of the activities chosen by his students and himself during their planning.

The reader should continue the on-going experience of evaluating his model unit according to the advice suggested here about interacting during the activity period. Can the reader identify certain problems that may persist during the activity period if some of the activities suggested in his model unit were selected? How could these have been prevented by modifying the activity? What are some problems that may be common to any activity period that is cooperatively planned by students and teacher? What are some principles that should govern a teacher's behavior during the activity period? Which of these does the reader feel are regularly violated by many teachers?

HOW DOES THE TEACHER PARTICIPATE DURING THE CULMINATING PERIOD? Since this period is often a more formal presentation of the activities that have been going on, the teacher's role may change very little. If this is the case, more formal evaluation is also likely at this time; thus, the teacher may wish to record some of his observations or systematize his data collection in some other manner. During the culminating period the students are attempting to pull together important relationships, organize and share information concerning significant objectives, and reveal ac-

This teacher is mentally comparing her plans with what is happening. (Photo courtesy Norman Public Schools.)

complished skills and changes in attitudes. These efforts can often be enhanced by the teacher's well-prepared participation. A skit may be missing its golden opportunity to reflect an important concept by only a slight misunderstanding that could be clarified by a leading question from the teacher. A gap in communication between a panel discussion team and the rest of the class might be closed by an alert teacher who is able to interject a lucid thought. A theatrical-like production can be modified to produce meaningful insights into important organized ideas by the patient prodding of a perceptive teacher. In each case the teacher cannot afford to submit to the temptations of personal recognition for his keen insights or cogent suggestions. He must stay in the background, be supportive, urge success upon his students, and take his reward from their enhanced self-development.

The reader must begin to recognize this guidance-oriented role of the elementary teacher by pointing out the potential for its development in his model unit. Can the reader predict occasions during the culminating period of his model unit when he might have the obligation to support his students? Can he differentiate his supportive role with a more imposing, self-rewarding role the teacher might assume? What would the consequences be, in terms of learner behavior and attitude, if the teacher chose to participate in culminating activities in a more dominating fashion? Why may it be more difficult to presume a more guidance-oriented demeanor?

HOW DOES THE TEACHER EVALUATE A UNIT? An over-simplification for an answer would be: continuously, comprehensively, and cooperatively. But this is true. The teacher is involved in evaluation since the preplanning of the unit and from that point through the culminating activities. The comprehensive nature of his evaluation was determined when the objectives were formalized, since the evaluation is committed to determining how well the whole set of objectives was satisfied. The cooperative aspect of evaluation was cared for during student-teacher planning and honored throughout the unit.

For the reader, a worthwhile experience would be to cite an appropriate evaluative technique for each of the objectives he has accepted for his model unit. Then, go back and list at least one other technique that could be used to determine whether each objective has been satisfied. Now, rationalize why either of these methods might be more reliable for a particular type of student. What is the point of such an exercise? Why should a teacher consider a variety of evaluative techniques for each unit he teaches? Why is student-teacher planning of evaluative measures of paramount importance?

SUMMARY

1. Planning forces the teacher to define his directions, determine his goals, select his teaching strategies, but first of all it provides him with a basis for making decisions. Effective planning is learned behavior.

2. The teacher plans because he wants to provide his students with the best educational experiences as he faces severe limitations in time, materials, facilities, energy, and professional support.

3. There are three types of plans about which the elementary teacher must be concerned; long-range, unit, and daily. Synchronizing and integrating these types assures thorough planning.

4. The teaching unit is the most common unifying learning experience that elementary teachers plan and is the intermediary device for assuring coordination between daily and long-range plans.

5. Plans are developed within prescribed time schedules. These constraints often present unique planning problems in terms of curricular priorities.

6. Ability to state learning objectives may be the heart of effective planning for instruction. Stating objectives in behavioral terms facilitates the selection of teaching techniques, clarifies expectations, and simplifies the search for sound evaluative procedures.

7. Good objectives communicate accurately, identify performance, describe learning conditions, and identify performance standards.

8. In using the most common teaching module, the unit, a teacher must be skillful in: selecting an appropriate unit; preparing himself with background information; organizing the objectives; introducing the unit; involving the students in planning; interacting during the activity period; participating during the culminating period; and evaluating the unit.

RECOMMENDED READINGS

Collier, Calhoun C., et al., *Teaching in the Modern Elementary School.* New York: Crowell-Collier and Macmillan, Inc., 1967. A chapter in this text presents the three basic types of plans—daily, short, and long-range—plus information about scheduling and unit planning.

Goodlad, John I., *Learning and the Teacher,* ASCD Yearbook, "The Teacher Selects, Plans, Organizes." Washington, D.C.: A.S.C.D.-N.E.A., 1959. This chapter cogently presents an analysis of the total act of planning for instruction, considering a number of variables that affect selection and organization plus suggesting some criteria that may be applied to planning.

Jarvis, Oscar T., and Lutian R. Wooton, *The Transitional Elementary School and its Curriculum.* Dubuque, Iowa: Wm. C. Brown Company, Publishers, 1966. The historical development and rationale for unit teaching are included in a chapter that thoroughly explains the teaching unit.

Mehl, Marie A., et al., *Teaching in Elementary School,* 3d ed. New York: The Ronald Press Company, 1965. The methods employed by the classroom teacher in planning, from daily plans to long-range objectives, are reviewed in Chapter 7. The worth of the daily plan to the teaching process is emphasized.

Nerbovig, Marcella H., and Herbert J. Klausmeier, *Teaching in the Elementary School,* 3d ed. New York: Harper & Row, Publishers, 1969. Chapter 4 presents the teacher's responsibilities for long- and short-range planning that systematically satisfies important curricular objectives. Unit teaching, daily-lesson planning, and teacher-pupil planning are emphasized.

Popham, W. James, and Eva L. Baker, *Establishing Instructional Goals.* Englewood Cliffs, N.J.: Prentice-Hall, Inc., 1970. A handbook that includes five self-instruction programs that are designed to teach the reader how to select goals, state them, and establish performance standards for the learners. Popham and Baker also have a handbook out on planning the instructional sequence that complements this book.

Ragan, William B., and Gene Shepherd, *Modern Elementary Curriculum*, 4th ed. New York: Holt, Rinehart and Winston, Inc., 1971. The many responsibilities of the classroom teacher in his planning role are defined comprehensively in this current text.

Waskin, Yvonne, and Louise Parrish, *Teacher-Pupil Planning for Better Classroom Learning*. New York: Pitman Publishing Corporation, 1967. A practical discussion of the techniques the authors used for teacher-pupil planning, offering a step-by-step description of ways to increase student participation. The methods are particularly appropriate to unit teaching.

Chapter 7

Utilizing Extra-Teacher Personnel

We are on the threshold of a new opportunity to recast the role of the public school teacher. The full utilization of teacher aides (extra-teacher personnel) is one of the most promising ventures in this direction. . . . supportive personnel such as teacher aides will help the creative teacher maximize his potential. Thus, the teacher becomes truly free to engage in inquiry, and the entire educational enterprise is likely to prosper.

Donald J. McCarty, in Jack Ferver (Ed.), *Teacher Aides* (Handbook for Instructors and Administrators) (Madison: University of Wisconsin, 1968), p. 8. Dr. McCarty is Dean of the School of Education, University of Wisconsin.

The teacher in the modern elementary school enjoys success in his role, at least in part, according to how effectively he takes advantage of the contributions of many other people in the school. A teacher no longer operates in complete isolation from others, and most teachers recognize that a growing number of supportive personnel is being made available, indeed thrust upon them. While the use of supportive personnel is not new, it is true that various persons have been added to most school staffs. Consequently, the role of the classroom teacher takes on this additional dimension of responsibility for utilizing the talents that others can bring to the learners.

The new elementary school is designed to satisfy ultimately those educational goals with which it is charged by society. A growing number of expectations are apparent, many of a more technical nature and others simply more time-consuming. Since the classroom teacher cannot be expected to be all things and because he is limited in time, the proper use of extra-teacher personnel becomes paramount. In fact, the utilization of persons who can lend support to the total school program is one of the most challenging and demanding tasks the teacher may face.

For presentation in this chapter the persons who are in some way or another connected with the elementary school and the total educational process will be assigned to two general categories: other professionals and other personnel.

OTHER PROFESSIONALS

The other professionals in the elementary school are those who accept the same general responsibility as the classroom teacher, have been specially educated for their work, and assume a supportive role to the teacher. While they are specialists and the classroom teacher is a generalist, these other professionals must not be viewed as subordinate to the teacher in any sense. In fact, it is indeed fortunate for any school to have the benefit of professional services that extra-teacher personnel can provide.

Teacher Specialists

Many new elementary schools are organized so that young learners may have the advantage of a teacher specialist, one whose academic preparation or teaching experience has provided him with a particular expertise. For example, it is not uncommon for an elementary school to have the services of a vocal music teacher who coordinates the school's music program and teaches music for many if not all of the teachers. In other cases, two or more schools may share the vocal music specialist, which may limit his availability and range of services.

Instrumental music, physical education, art, and foreign language specialists are commonly a part of elementary school faculties in various ways. These specialists can provide important experiences for young learners that could not be expected of the self-contained classroom teacher. Often, schools can organize in a number of ways to make the very best use of the talents and interests of their present faculties without adding specialists. For example, a teacher may wish to teach a special area for only part time and maintain his regular position the remainder of the day.

The teacher who has access to specialists must assume the responsibility for coordinating the various activities his students are experiencing.

The principal at Longfellow School, Oklahoma City, finds time to work with an individual pupil. (Photo courtesy Oklahoma City Public Schools.)

Teaching strategies are demonstrated by specialized personnel at the Developmental Learning Center, Oklahoma City. (Photo courtesy Oklahoma City Public Schools.)

Specialists should enhance the total school program, but this will be assured in direct relation to how well the classroom teacher and specialists communicate. Those parts of the long-range plans to which specialists can contribute something must be made available. Sufficient advance notice to the specialist is essential to effecting long-range, unit-type, or daily plans. Likewise, the specialist must advise the classroom teacher of his plans for activities that may involve some cooperation or support. There should be a scheduled planning and evaluation period, plus a common agreement to keep others informed when a change in plans could influence another's plans.

The School Principal

The one member of the total school team in whom the classroom teacher is most likely to place the most trust for support in improving his teaching is the principal. This is as it should be, since the most generally accepted definition of the principal's major responsibility is the improvement of instruction. Unfortunately, this is not the only obligation to which the principal can direct his attention and energy. Depending upon the school situation and, particularly, the number and nature of supportive personnel accessible to him, the principal carries out this primary task of supervising and encouraging positive changes in curriculum and instruction.

The classroom teacher must know when and how he can make the very best use of the time and talents of the principal. The principal, as well as other professionals who serve with the teacher, will appreciate and solidly support the requests for their services that are reasonable, but will soon resent overdependence, excessive or premature demands, and a lack of sensitivity to their constraints.

The elementary principal is many things to many people in the school system. He is charged by his superintendent to coordinate all of the activities that in any way involve his school, its personnel, and its educational program. He is responsible for the final reporting of a formidable number of records, both business and educational in nature. He is the key public relations agent for his school and gives no small amount of his time to fostering sound community relations. He is often seen as counselor, disciplinarian, substitute teacher, and secretary and is expected to wear each of these hats with patience and expertise.

Despite the heavy demands placed upon the principal by a host of other sources, he must not lose sight of his paramount concern, that of working with teachers to provide the best learning situation possible. Nor can the teacher fail to consider the ways he can best utilize the principal's time. For example, the teacher may wish to have some new materials or teaching aids for his classroom. By carefully specifying the nature of the materials, where they may be available, how they can be used for the total school program, the approximate cost in relation to budget suggestions, and how soon they are needed, the principal's task is simplified and the request will likely be attended to more quickly.

Any significant changes in the curriculum and/or strategies of instruction are effected through the principal's office. If a teacher should wish to depart from the use of a basic text in a subject, either by replacing this text with another or by de-emphasizing the adopted text, he should explain his rationale for this departure to the principal. If two or more teachers wish to experiment with team teaching or some other innovative instructional practice, they should confer with the principal early in the planning stages and keep him apprised of the development of the idea. If teachers wish to conduct some action research concerning their teaching or the curriculum they should involve the principal, requesting his advice and taking advantage of his expertise.

The Assistant Principal

At the present time it is uncommon to find a full-time assistant principal in most elementary schools, unless the school is unusually large or houses a special program. Most schools either employ a part-time assistant to the principal or the principal may designate a classroom teacher to assume responsibility for the building when he is out.

While there are few full-time assistant principals, there are fewer common definitions of his role in the elementary school. The responsibilities of the assistant are prescribed by the principal and typically reflect the duties accorded the administrative staff that the principal does not choose to spend his time doing. Maintaining an accurate pupil personnel accounting system; procuring and distributing materials and supplies; co-ordinating rooms, schedules, and teachers' activities; arranging for programs, study trips, and resource people; keeping texts, materials, and supplies inventories; making home visits; dealing with discipline problems; counseling with students and parents; evaluating materials and media; chairing faculty committees; and representing the school at various functions are some of the tasks that may fall to the assistant principal.

In many school systems, the position of assistant principal serves as a training ground for a later assignment as school principal. Thus, the experiences the assistant has should be comprehensive. The classroom teacher must be alert to the expectations that are assigned the assistant and learn to take advantage of his services whenever they can enhance the learning situation.

SITUATION 7.1

The Principal Supports Instruction

Remember that the primary general responsibility of the elementary school administrator(s) is to "improve instruction." Make several suggestions that point out how the self-contained classroom teacher can utilize the expertise of the principal and/or assistant principal to bring about the improvement of instruction. List several ways the classroom teacher can support the administrators of the school.

The School Psychologist–Guidance Counselor

The school psychologist represents the same person who may be called the school guidance counselor. The major difference between the two is generally the extent of training taken, with the school psychologist having typically taken an additional year of study beyond the usual master's degree demanded of the counselor.

That part of the school program administered by the school psychologist-counselor is generally defined as helping a pupil realize his personal and educational potential. To do this, the psychologist-counselor is equipped to interpret the relevant data from a number of sources that describe each learner accurately. For example, both group and individual intelligence and/or achievement tests are given to young learners. Aptitude tests, interest inventories, and projective techniques may be used. Structured interviews may be conducted with parents, teachers, and pupils. Health records and other information taken from the cumulative records may be called upon for analysis. It is the task of the school psychologist-counselor to make some sense of the wealth of information that can be available about every elementary youngster to which a referral is made.

Because school psychologist-counselors are not plentiful and one such person may serve up to 2000 pupils, it becomes the role of the psychologist-counselor to work with teachers and whole faculties of teachers for most of his time. He helps teachers understand how they can interpret test data, cumulative records, and other information. He may meet with groups of parents to inform them about the role of tests and testing in the schools. The psychologist-counselor often heads a team of educators in a particular building who are working on individual cases of the emotionally disturbed, slow or accelerated learners, and other learning problems. He may be involved in orientation programs for prekindergarten youngsters and their parents or in activities that introduce the sixth graders to the junior high school.

As the classroom teacher becomes more aware of the services that a school psychologist-counselor should provide, he can learn to make intelligent referrals for aid. The heavy demands placed upon the psychologist-counselor personify the teacher's role here. Each teacher must carefully select only those cases that fall within the domain of the psychologist-counselor and especially those that command his expertise.

The School Social Worker

The expanding role of the school, as the agency charged with more and more responsibility for the total welfare of children, includes several items that can best be handled by a school social worker. While the classroom teacher has probably performed most of these tasks in the past, his more carefully defined role as the professional educator will leave little time for social-worker functions.

The classroom teacher cannot be expected to go into the homes of his students to gather information of a sociological nature, not only because of the already too heavy commitments placed upon his time, but especially because he is not educated to do this. A proficient social worker can provide an invaluable service to the teacher by arranging home visits to gain information pertinent to a child's learning difficulties. The social worker can then observe the child in the classroom and assist the teacher in making decisions that are relevant. Information about children in the schools can be collected, interpreted, and made available to social agencies; home conditions can be evaluated; parents can be advised about the availability of community agencies; case conferences can be arranged and directed; cooperation with the school psychologist can be promoted; assistance with mental-health education can be given the teachers; an evaluation of the school community, its environment, and agencies can be conducted; and active membership on the total teaching team are some of the ways the school social worker can enhance a school's program and support the classroom teacher. These are professional responsibilities in their own right and should not be left to the classroom teacher.

SITUATION 7.2

The Teacher Uses Others

Both psychologist-counselor and the social worker provide important information to the classroom teacher. Briefly differentiate the nature of the information each of these agents would be called upon to provide the teacher. Cite one example of a learning difficulty toward which both of these professionals could probably contribute. Explain how their contributions complement each other.

The Speech and Hearing Clinician

Most classrooms of approximately thirty youngsters will contain one or two children with serious speech difficulties. Closely related to the speech deviation are those who have hearing deficiencies. An individual's inability to hear, understand, and speak properly, when given unfavorable attention, can create both personal and academic problems. Thus, the speech and hearing clinician is important to the teacher who desires a maximally effective learning situation.

Clinicians work with children both in small groups and individually when a child's defect is serious enough to merit this attention. Clinicians can help the teacher learn to hear children's speech accurately, to become conscious of the presence of defects, to recognize the symptoms of hearing loss, and to make intelligent referrals to the clinician. Because the clinician will have time to deal only with the more serious defects, the teacher may confer occasionally with the clinician about how he is handling other, less serious problems in the classroom. The teacher may also support the clinician by complementing the corrective program set up for children who are receiving treatment. Good speech behavior by the classroom teacher is essential to both the speech defective and the hard-of-hearing.

The Medical Personnel

Medical doctors and dentists usually serve the schools on a voluntary or part-time basis, making periodic minor examinations of elementary children to detect both dental and physical defects before they become serious. They are valuable resource persons for health instruction and are often willing to give considerable time to this cause. The teacher can best take advantage of these services by preparing children for the visit by the doctor or dentist, explaining the nature and reasons for such a visit, encouraging good questions, and providing the visitor with ample information concerning the objectives held by the class.

Nurses often serve each school on a much more regular basis, as a resource person for health instruction and providing an important link between home and school in dealing with health problems. The nurse may also be able to give additional insights into a child's learning situation from a medical standpoint and may be an important member of the diagnostic team of educators in the school. The nurse's additional training in child growth and development makes her an excellent resource person in the early identification and remediation of developmental lags and health problems in children who may be experiencing learning difficulties.

The Substitute Teacher

Teachers can seldom predict with any degree of accuracy when they are going to be ill or when other circumstances may force them to be absent from their classroom. All too often the teachers who are called upon to serve a classroom as substitute can attest to this fact, simply by experiencing the difficulties that are presented when a substitute teacher has not been expected. Perhaps a teacher should arrange his plans so that a substitute could use them effectively every day.

The substitute teacher is usually called to fill a position on very short notice and often arrives only minutes before the school day is to begin. To expedite the substitute's work the following suggestions may be worthy of consideration:

1. A file folder of important information for the substitute could be left in a conspicuous place.

2. The name and location of one teacher who is especially familiar with the teacher's routine could be given. This teacher could serve as the substitute's 'buddy' for the day.

3. A map of the building, pointing out rest rooms, the lounge, supply room, office, playground, etc., could be supplied.

4. The daily schedule, both the teacher's and the building's, must be available. Special note should be made of any particular responsibility the substitute may have.

5. A list of important school policies is to be accessible to the substitute. Also, any extensions of these policies as they apply to the particular classroom can be outlined.

6. Names of a small number of students upon whom the substitute can rely could prove helpful.

7. A seating chart for easy identification of the students is important and must be current.

8. Complete lesson plans are mandatory. The substitute will search to recognize the scope and sequence within which each lesson fits. The objectives for each lesson should be defined, suggested procedures outlined, and evaluative considerations explained.

9. The classroom teacher can include the information he expects from the substitute; that is, how the plans were followed or adjusted, what objectives were satisfied, an attendance report, and so forth.

Ultimately, the classroom teacher must attempt to prepare for a substitute so effectively that very little disruption in the normal routine of the learning situation is experienced by the pupils.

The School Librarian

An important trend in the new elementary school is the addition of a central library, often complete with a trained, certified school librarian. Many progressive schools have developed the library to include more comprehensively the total collection of all media that are available to the faculty. Appropriately designated the "media center," this educational concept is complemented by the services of a highly trained media-center director and is discussed in more detail in Chapter 9.

The school librarian, or media-center director, can provide helpful instruction to young learners about the use of reference materials, the development of research skills, the use of card catalogues and categorization systems such as the Dewey Decimal, and the organization of materials in libraries. Librarians are fine resource people to students who are working on independent or class research questions. They also supplement the teacher's work in academic areas by familiarizing the class with appropriate books.

SITUATION 7.3
Questioning Supportive Personnel

Choose any one or any number of these topics: Teaching Specialist; Speech and Hearing Clinician; Medical Personnel; Substitute Teacher; School Librarian. Design several questions you would raise with one or more of these professionals and tell how this would aid you as the teacher.

OTHER PERSONNEL

Many of the persons who assume significant responsibilities in the elementary school are not certified as professionals, but do provide services that are essential to the operation of the school. Each has a special skill that contributes to the education of children, and the master classroom teacher recognizes how these skills complement his own many roles.

Teacher Aides and Parent Volunteers

Perhaps the greatest hope for releasing the classroom teacher from non-professional activities that occupy so much of his time is the employment of teacher aides and parent volunteers. Also referred to as paraprofessionals, the teacher aides and parent volunteers are people who support the teacher in countless ways so that time can be gained for truly professional duties;

that is, planning lessons and personalizing instruction. Aides and volunteers often work without salary, but may occasionally receive some small remuneration for their services.

As much as one-fourth of a teacher's time is typically given to doing the kinds of things that could be handled quite well by aides. The following list is incomplete, but suggests many tasks that responsible teacher aides and parent volunteers can be employed to do:

1. Making charts, posters, and other graphic materials.
2. Cutting paper, sharpening pencils, preparing dittoes, distributing supplies, and other "secretarial" chores.
3. Checking papers and recording daily paper and test results.
4. Supervision of the playground, lunch room, library, study rooms, nurse's room, and halls.
5. Taking an inventory and making a record of the books, supplies, materials, and other media in the building.
6. Assisting the custodian.
7. Reading to individuals, or groups of children.
8. Listening to children as they practice oral reading.
9. Serving as a resource person.
10. Preparing equipment and materials for art, music, science, and physical education lessons and then caring for these things upon completion of the lessons.

The number and kind of supportive roles the aide can be expected to fulfill are limited only by the imagination of the classroom teacher.

As the list of duties for aides and volunteers continues to grow, care must be taken to assure that professional and legal standards are understood and observed. Schools would be well advised to use information bulletins that advise the aide-volunteer of his responsibilities, status, limitations, and the general expectations that are held for him. The information that is provided in writing should be made available to him through carefully planned orientation classes, with adequate time for thorough questioning by the aide.

A cautious generalization that may prove helpful to any teacher who contemplates using aides is that teacher and aide agree at the beginning of their work together that the aide will not perform any service in the classroom unless that act has been sanctioned beforehand by the teacher. The teacher must assume the final responsibility for the teaching in his classroom; thus he should be aware of the planned behavior by any other adult who shares the educational process. Teacher aides must never be allowed to assume the professional duties of the teacher, and only by open communication between teachers and aides can the proper use of aides be guaranteed.

Supportive personnel such as teacher aides are becoming more plentiful by virtue of federally supported projects as well as an upsurge of interest in the schools by citizen groups. Every classroom teacher may eventually have access to one or more teacher aides. Cooperative planning by both professional educators and aides will prove a wise investment for both parties as the ultimate objective of this activity is sought—the welfare of young learners.

Parents may volunteer to serve the room as a room mother and be responsible for organizing the recreation and collecting refreshments for one or two room parties. Parents may volunteer to represent the room on the PTA Council, attend one or more Board of Education meetings, be a member of parent-teacher committees, telephone other parents upon request by the teacher, provide transportation for study trips, construct equipment for physical education or science, check extra books from the public library, and even serve on busy intersections as traffic monitors. The number of ways parents can become involved in a service capacity to the classroom teacher is virtually limitless. One method for identifying and compiling a list of parent-volunteer service functions would be to involve a number of parents with a group of teachers and to charge them to cooperatively design such a list.

Once again, open and honest communication between classroom teacher and parent volunteer is essential to a productive volunteer program. The primary responsibility rests with the teacher for defining the expectations and limitations of the contributions parent volunteers can make. Parents wish to know what is expected of them when their services are requested, and they will hesitate to volunteer again if they have been left with nebulous, ill-defined directions. For the protection of the professional role of the teacher, parents must understand the standards of behavior that are demanded, as well as the limitations inherent in the task that has been suggested.

Surely the two general objectives of a parent-volunteer program, strengthened home-school relations and release of the teacher from subprofessional chores, are worthy of the time and energy that must be given to initiating such a plan. An established school-wide program could be self-perpetuating and helpful to all teachers. One final caution is that any program of this sort should be continuously evaluated by teachers and parents alike.

The School Secretary

The secretary often gives the first impression one will receive of the school. She receives guests of the school, answers the telephone, interviews parents for enrollment information, processes messages to and from the school, and may interpret school policies to the public. Time-consuming clerical work is assumed by the secretary to release teachers for teaching tasks.

Judicious delegation of authority to the secretary cannot be over-emphasized, and only those nonprofessional responsibilities she can expertly undertake should be assigned. A good secretary is aware of her prerogatives and never preempts the roles of the principal teachers. Teachers can support the secretary by planning their requests for her time as far in advance as possible and by being reasonable when a more immediate request must be honored. Good teacher-secretary relations contribute to the teacher's ability to satisfy important educational objectives.

The School Custodian

Probably no other person in the elementary school enjoys the visibility that is the custodian's. Almost by definition, he is the silent, active observer of what is going on throughout the building and has ready access to the classrooms before and after school hours. His major responsibility is to maintain the physical plant, but his influence on teachers and children generally extends beyond this domain. He knows a great deal about the total operation of the school. The proper use of this knowledge is essential to maintaining good faculty relationships.

The custodian is charged with two rather general responsibilities: the care of the school property and the protection of students while they are on the school grounds. He keeps the building, grounds, and school equipment clean and in good repair as judged by relatively high standards. The utmost standard by which he abides is the safety factor. Essentially, the building and grounds are maintained to be maximally functional, safe, and healthy. The classroom teacher must remain aware of these criteria as he interprets why the custodian may have insisted on some physical imposition for the classroom. The success with which a custodian carries out his responsibilities is largely determined by effective communication and a feeling of mutual respect.

The School Lunch Personnel

Most elementary schools must make some provisions for children to have their lunch at school. Many schools operate a hot lunch program, often supported by federal and state governmental agencies. The extent of the involvement of teachers in a school lunch program varies from little or no responsibility to the complete administration and supervision of the program. Fortunately, school cafeterias, directed by full- and part-time cafeteria personnel, are on the increase and teachers are being relieved of the direct responsibility involved in administering the school lunch program.

There are ways that classroom teachers can capitalize on the experiences young learners may have with the lunch program; for example, health units about a balanced meal, acceptable behavior while eating with others, estimating the cost of a meal, and other experiences. Mutual cooperation among teachers and school lunch personnel is important to everyone and will be enhanced by policies that have been determined by all those who are concerned.

SITUATION 7.4
Qualifications Criteria

The "other personnel" discussed here are not required to be formally certified and seldom experience very rigid qualifying standards. List several criteria that you believe are important to consider when employing these personnel. Explain why you think your criteria are important.

SUMMARY

1. The modern elementary teacher will have more opportunities to work with others in the schools, both professionals and paraprofessionals.

2. Many of the supportive personnel are specially educated, certified, and prepared to provide specialized services that must be coordinated with the total school curriculum.

3. The classroom teacher must be familiar with the contributions that other professionals in the school can make to his program and be willing to participate in this cooperative venture.

4. Availability of the nonacademic professionals will allow the teacher more time to devote to his responsibilities in the classroom.

5. Persons who can provide important nonprofessional services to the busy classroom teacher are becoming more plentiful, thus releasing the teacher to his professional role.

6. The work of the nonprofessional in and about the classroom must be carefully utilized to enhance the education of young learners.

7. Every person involved in the total school program deserves the full respect accorded any member of this team.

8. The teacher should have a "plan" that comprehensively designates how he will take advantage of the many contributions that others can make to his teaching.

RECOMMENDED READINGS

Byrd, Oliver E., *School Health Administration*. New York: W. B. Saunders Company, 1964. Two chapters are given to discussing the roles of the school physician and the school nurse.

Collier, Calhoun C., et al., *Teaching in the Modern Elementary School*. New York: Crowell-Collier and Macmillan, Inc., 1967. Chapter 5 presents data about a wide range of auxiliary teacher personnel, both professional and paraprofessional.

Dinkmeyer, Don C., *Guidance and Counseling in the Elementary School*. New York: Holt, Rinehart and Winston, Inc., 1968. A section of this reader is devoted to a perusal of the work of an elementary school counselor.

Faber, Charles F., and Gilbert F. Shearron, *Elementary School Administration*. New York: Holt, Rinehart and Winston, Inc., 1970. Chapter 9 is devoted to a thorough presentation about the elementary school principalship, especially the tasks involved with improving the curriculum.

Heinemann, F. E., "Defining Duties of Aides," *Minnesota Journal of Education*, Vol. 44, No. 19, November 1963. Does just what the title implies.

Jarvis, Oscar T., and Haskin R. Pounds, *Organizing, Supervising, and Administering the Elementary School*. West Nyack, N.Y.: Parker Publishing Co., Inc., 1969. A complete examination of the many roles of the elementary principal, plus information in Chapter 15 about several extra-teacher personnel.

Magary, James F., *School Psychological Services*. Englewood Cliffs, N.J.: Prentice-Hall, Inc., 1967. The function of the school psychologist is treated, especially as he relates with classroom teachers, principal, special-education teachers, school physician and nurse, social worker, and counselor.

National Elementary Principal, Vol. 46, No. 6, "Auxiliary School Personnel," May 1967. This entire issue of the *NEP* shares some interesting insights into the functions of extra-teacher personnel.

Wolf, William C., and Bradley M. Loomer, *The Elementary School: A Perspective*. Chicago: Rand McNally & Co., 1966. The second chapter discusses the "nature of an elementary school team" by analyzing the roles of a number of professionals and paraprofessionals in the elementary school.

Part III

CURRENT ISSUES AND PROBLEMS

Current Issues and Problems

Research in the Elementary School Subjects	Teaching Culturally Different Children
Instructional Technology	Creative Ways of Teaching and Learning

Part III deals with issues and problems that are currently receiving a great deal of attention by those who are concerned with the elementary school program. How to use available research to make the teaching of elementary school subjects more effective; how to make effective use of various types of instructional media; how to provide quality education for culturally different children; and how to promote creativity in elementary school children are the concerns selected for inclusion.

Chapter 8

Research in the Elementary School Subjects

Research is a way of dealing with ideas. It is nothing more than this, and it is nothing less.

Fred P. Barnes, *Research for the Practitioner in Education* (Washington, D.C.: Department of Elementary School Principals, N.E.A., 1964), p. 13.

Of all the sources of knowledge—intuition, divine revelation, tradition, and science—the last, science, is the one about which most agreement can be reached. The basic tenets of science invite others to replicate the experimental conditions to test the truth of the findings. Unlike other sources of knowledge, science is open and inspection of scientific findings is expected.

WHAT IS RESEARCH?

Research is a way of thinking. Unlike other sources of knowledge research has a relatively standardized procedure for seeking truth. Other texts provide a more definitive description of research, and the reader is encouraged to refer to them for a more detailed analysis of the research process. Suffice it for our present purposes to suggest that research is a progression of steps that leads from a general question to a specific finding that will contribute at least a partial answer to the original question.

Another way to answer the question "What is research?" is to examine what those engaged in research do. Educational researchers, in their quest for solutions to educational problems, collect, classify, organize, analyze and interpret data. Some research includes all of the above procedures. Other research, especially that dealing in areas that have just recently been explored, may include only the collection and classification steps.

Scientific research is the systematic quest for answers to specific questions. The validity of the obtained answers is a function of the amount of control the scientist or researcher exercises over the variables that could affect the results. The "hard sciences" have an advantage regarding control because they deal primarily with inanimate objects. The social sciences, however, including their educational researchers, deal almost exclusively with human beings, over whom, much to the dismay of researchers, little real control can be exercised.

If we assess what seems to be the general practice of "keeping school," it may safely be said that the most widely used source of knowledge has been tradition. Too frequently, in the authors' opinion, elementary school teachers justify their behavior solely on the grounds of, "That's the way it was done last year."

Educational research, more specifically research in elementary school subjects, holds the promise of being a common, verifiable source of information for teachers of the new elementary school. This is not to suggest that tradition, intuition, and even divine revelation have absolutely no place in school practices; but a shift toward research-based knowledge is called for in an effort to build upon that which has been done that is good and discard practices that have failed to yield what is desired.

LIMITATIONS OF RESEARCH

Social scientists use the physical scientist as their model for research. Some critics suggest that the degree of empiricism physical scientists can achieve with their sensitive scales and (usually) easily measured objects can never be achieved by the social scientist. For example, the distance between ten and twelve inches is exactly equal to the distance between two and four inches; whereas distance between, say, IQ scores of 130 and 150 is somehow not equal to the distance between IQ scores of 70 and 90. The social scientist has difficulty retaining complete objectivity; that is, he needs to guard against qualitative interference in his quantitative methods.

TWO KINDS OF THEORIES

There are two kinds of theoretical statements found in the writings related to school subjects. One kind includes words like "should" or "ought." Statements that admonish with "shoulds" or "oughts" are normative statements, and they reflect what is called normative theory. By definition, normative theory describes something that ought to be but is not yet happening.

Empirical statements contain the word "is." They describe what is happening, not necessarily what ought to or should happen. Empirical theories describe, explain, and predict what will happen in a given situation. When theories have withstood numerous tests and trials they become laws. The law of gravity was at one time an empirical theory.

The distinction between normative and empirical theory is made here to clarify the anti-intellectualism evidenced by many school people when they deride theory in contrast to practice. Many times, normative theory is made to sound like empirical theory, and when the "shoulds" and "oughts" are followed unsuccessfully by practitioners, all theory becomes suspect. "Nothing is more practical," said Lewin, "than a good theory." We do not have to jump from sixth-story windows to test a theory of gravitation. We have one. It works. Think of how much pain it saves us.

Whether or not theories of human behavior can ever be as simple and consistent as theories of the physical sciences may be an unanswerable question. The research in elementary school subjects is too diverse and inconclusive for anyone to judge whether any or all of it is futile. Humble beginnings and modest advances have been made in some areas. It would be premature to attempt to weave all the research into a theoretical fabric that covers the myriad aspects of elementary school subjects. It is in order, however, to select that which appears sound, briefly describe the research, and examine the generalizations as they may apply to teaching in the new elementary school.

READING

There were over 700 published research reports on reading in 1960, and by 1967 that number had more than doubled.[1] The *Encyclopedia of Educational Research* divides the topic into the following aspects: Sociological, Psychological, Physiological, and Teaching. Our concern will be with the research done in the area of teaching reading.

---

[1] Theodore L. Harris, in Robert L. Ebel (Ed.), *Encyclopedia of Educational Research*, 4th ed. (London: The Macmillan Company, 1969), pp. 1069–1104.

The research conducted in the teaching of reading, especially that done in recent years, exceeds by far the amount done in the other aspects of reading. It includes research related to aims of reading instruction, role of the teacher, school and classroom organization, and developmental reading practices. Because of the large number of studies in the teaching aspect of reading, we will only briefly mention those that are likely to have the most immediate bearing on beginning teachers.

Aims

Smith collected evidence that indicates the goals of reading instruction have shifted from a predominantly utilitarian base to the importance of reading as a source of personal development.[2] After reviewing the major historical-comparative studies, Harris suggests that the recent rapid growth of remedial reading facilities and special reading programs at the high school and college levels indicates the presence of a substantial percentage of underachieving readers.[3] He specifies the following conditions:

> [The underachievers] . . . have either (1) not learned to read well initially; or, (2) having learned to read well initially, have failed to develop the more advanced reading skills and abilities; or, (3) regardless of previous learning, have not retained and cannot transfer the necessary reading skills and abilities to the more complex reading tasks of later years.[4]

More attention may need to be paid to the preparation of prospective teachers' skills and abilities in teaching reading.

Teacher Role

Austin and others conducted a national survey of preservice programs for the preparation of teachers.[5] The college supervisors and cooperating teachers most frequently criticized student teachers for their general lack of understanding of phonetic principles, their inability to group children for reading instruction, and their inability to adapt to individual differences among the children. If preservice experiences for teaching reading are not adequate or even present, the responsibility of providing such experiences rests with the school districts and takes the form of in-service education.

[2] Nila B. Smith, *American Reading Instruction* (Newark, Del.: International Reading Association, 1965).

[3] Harris, pp. 1084–1085.

[4] Harris, p. 1085.

[5] Mary C. Austin and Coleman Morrison, *The First R: The Harvard Report on Reading in the Elementary Schools* (New York: Crowell-Collier and Macmillan, Inc., 1963).

The amount of time elementary teachers devote to basal reading instruction (that which uses a basal text as opposed to less-organized instruction) was studied by Brekke.[6] He surveyed grades 1–8 in over 1000 schools and found that the time spent in basal-reading instruction progressively decreased through the grades, but still accounted for more than one-half of the total reading instructional time. The optimum amount of time to spend on basal instruction was studied by Jarvis.[7] He found no difference in vocabulary and comprehension among students who received 60–78 versus 40–50 minutes of reading instruction in grades 4–6. Jarvis concluded that any more than fifty minutes of basal reading instruction per day was unwarranted and recommended that more time be spent on reading activities in other areas of the curriculum.

School and Classroom Organization

There are conflicting findings where school and classroom organizations have been studied.[8] Nongraded versus graded school organization and the effects on reading achievement frequently show no significant differences. The same obtains in studies of intra- versus interclass grouping for reading instruction. Even the relatively radical departure from the traditional basal-text approach, advocated by Veatch, and called "individualized reading," has yielded only minor improvements over the traditional practices.[9] The one area that usually reveals greatest positive difference, however, in both nongraded and individualized approaches is the attitudinal. Children tend to like the departures from tradition better than the traditional practices.[10] To what extent the positive attitude is associated solely with the fact of change and not the substance of it is unknown by the researchers.

Developmental Reading Practices

Research in developmental reading practices has centered around the improvement of word-attack skills, vocabulary, and comprehension. Word-attack skills include using contextual, structural, phonetic, and configurational clues to pronunciation and meaning. Phonics, the linking of sound values to letters and letter combinations that permit decoding written

[6] Gerald Brekke, "Actual and Recommended Allotments of Time for Reading," *Reading Teacher*, January 1963, pp. 234–237.

[7] Oscar T. Jarvis, "Time Allotment Relationships to Pupil Achievement," *Elementary English*, February 1965, pp. 201–204.

[8] Harris, pp. 1086–1087.

[9] Jeanette Veatch, *Individualizing Your Reading Program* (New York: G. P. Putnam's Sons, 1959).

[10] Harris, p. 1087.

messages into their spoken sound equivalents, has received most of the research attention. Clymer examined forty-five phonic generalizations derived from teachers' manuals of four basal texts and found only eighteen had utility value as high as 75 percent when applied to reading texts used at the same level.[11] The decision to teach a phonic generalization, however, cannot be made only on the utility percentage. Harris advises:

> Since virtually all phonics generalizations admit to some exceptions because of the conglomerate nature of English, their teaching must have relevance to the instructional materials being used and their application must necessarily be tentative and be considered in relation to other word-attack clues.[12]

Improving meaning vocabularies was studied in a review of research by Serra.[13] She found that there was a need for systematic attention to extending the scope and precision of meaningful vocabularies. This could be accomplished vicariously as well as directly. Eickholz and Barbe have more recently reported that self-instructional techniques were more effective than conventional teaching techniques in improving vocabulary among seventh graders.[14]

There is very little research in the area of comprehension. The effects of pretests and outlining and skimming skills on comprehension have been studied and found to be of little or no significance.[15] Covington reported, however, that emphasis upon certain aspects of critical reading can result in performances generally superior in terms of making inferences, sensitivity to discrepancies in fact, and asking questions.[16]

Shortly before his death, Gray, one of the most eminent reading scholars, summarized the research findings into four essential points that are still relevant today. The four points are:

1. The same method (of teaching reading) does not secure equally satisfactory results in all schools and classrooms. This indicates that other factors, such as the teacher, the pupils, and the materials used, exert a vital influence on progress in learning to read.
  2. Contrasting methods emphasize different aspects of reading. A phonic

---

[11] Theodore Clymer, "The Utility of Phonic Generalizations in Primary Grades," *Reading Teacher*, January 1963, pp. 252–260.

[12] Harris, p. 1091.

[13] Mary C. Serra, "The Concept Burden of Instructional Materials," *Elementary School Journal*, May 1953, pp. 508–512.

[14] G. Eickholz and R. Barbe, "An Experiment in Vocabulary Development," *Educational Research Bulletin*, January 1961, pp. 1–7, 28.

[15] Harris, p. 1091.

[16] Martin V. Covington, "Some Experimental Evidence on Teaching for Creative Understanding," *Reading Teacher*, February 1967, pp. 390–396.

method gives most emphasis initially to word recognition. A word method gives most emphasis from the beginning to the meaning of what is read.

3. Contrasting methods start pupils toward maturity in reading over different routes. Sooner or later any specialized method must be supplemented to insure growth in all essential aspects of reading.

4. Best results are secured when both meaning and word-recognition skills are emphasized from the beginning.[17]

In spite of the large number of studies in the field of reading there is still a great need for continued research. There is the problem of conflicting findings, poorly designed studies, and some areas virtually unstudied that require attention from educational researchers.

WRITING

Handwriting

Most schoolmen agree handwriting is a necessary tool. It is the means through which one can express himself in a personalized manner. Research in the area of handwriting has mostly been of the survey or descriptive type. Efforts have been made to find out how important handwriting is and what kinds of teaching methods are used.

Templin studied the handwriting of 1946 graduates of high schools on the Eastern seaboard.[18] He asked them to fill out and return a postcard that was used as a sample for their handwriting. A questionnaire was sent to 454 other adults to ascertain the volume of their handwriting and its type. The following findings were reported by Templin:

1. Professional workers used the most handwriting.
2. Men engaged in more handwriting than did women.
3. Pencils were most commonly used as writing tools.
4. Handwriting was deemed important to efficiency in the business and social worlds.

Handwriting apparently will remain an important tool for children to master or at least one in which some degree of proficiency should be obtained.

A review of the research in handwriting conducted between 1949 and 1959 revealed the following practices as prevalent in the schools.

---

[17] William S. Gray, "Current Reading Problems: A World View," *Elementary School Journal*, September 1955, pp. 11–17.

[18] E. M. Templin, "How Important Is Handwriting Today?" *Elementary School Journal*, December 1969, pp. 174–178.

1. The regular classroom teacher usually taught handwriting.

2. Most programs included instruction in both manuscript and cursive writing. The shift from manuscript to cursive writing was usually made between grades two and four.

3. Seventy-three percent of the schools surveyed began instruction in grade one; 88 percent had begun by the end of grade two.

4. Three-fourths of the schools had instruction through grade six; one-half through grade eight.

5. Modal length for handwriting periods was fifteen minutes, usually five times a week.

6. Most teachers relied on commercially prepared material.

7. The improvement and control of efficient motor patterns under the various conditions of handwriting depended more on the cognitive and perceptual processes than on the establishment of automatic behavior.[19]

Herrick reported other findings having to do more specifically with the handwriting act.[20] Some of his findings included:

1. There has been a trend toward simplicity in the formation of letters and numerals.

2. The letters r, e, and a are major troublemakers.

3. The most efficient angle of pursuit lies between 135° and 160°.

4. Cursive writing is a little faster than manuscript up to the junior high school period.

5. No simple single factor of handwriting distinguishes between samples of good and bad handwriting alone.

Finally, research findings not included in the above were reported by Harris in the *Encyclopedia of Educational Research*.[21] These include:

1. Copying in learning handwriting has long been established as a method preferable to tracing.

2. There is evidence that copying ability in children from six to nine years of age is itself a variable that develops rapidly until about age seven and more slowly thereafter.

3. Children of different ability levels may differ significantly in their perception of the handwriting task and in their ability to appraise their own handwriting as a basis for further improvement.

---

[19] Committee on Research in Basic Skills, *Ten Years of Research in Handwriting, 1949–1959* (Madison: Department of Education, University of Wisconsin), 26 pp., mimeographed.

[20] Virgil Herrick, "Handwriting and Children's Writing," *Elementary English*, February 1961, pp. 264–267.

[21] Theodore L. Harris, "Handwriting," in Chester E. W. Harris (Ed.), *Encyclopedia of Educational Research*, 3d ed. (New York: Crowell-Collier and Macmillan, Inc., 1960), pp. 616–624.

This last generalization seems most pertinent for teachers in the new elementary school because it supports the need for individualizing and personalizing instruction in handwriting skills.

Research dealing with the optimum time to change from manuscript to cursive writing, handwriting and left-handers, and improving handwriting skills has been conducted and is conveniently summarized in *Improving Language Arts Instruction Through Research*.[22] The reader interested in further information should consult this source.

Written Expression

In 1958 two research reports by Cahill suggested that creative writing cannot be taught and that the teacher can only act as a catalyst by helping the child with experiences, excitement, and tools.[23] A technique for fostering creative writing was offered by Kennedy.[24] It involves preparing a highly adventurous story developed around characters who are members of the class. Witty and Martin's research indicated the use of a silent movie as a powerful technique for fostering creative expression.[25]

Edmund reviewed limited research in creative writing and suggested the following topics about which most of the research is conducted:[26]

1. Writing as a way of identifying and motivating gifted children.
2. Experiences forming the bases for children's stories.
3. Pupil interest as related to the selection of writing topics.
4. Methods and materials appropriate for teaching writing.
5. Writing and total personal involvement.

Torrance, one of the more able scholars who has studied creativity, suggests the element of prestige as an important factor in fostering creativity.[27] Prestige is achieved by the student when he observes his teacher and peers valuing his ideas.

[22] Harold G. Shane and June Grant Mulry, *Improving Language Arts Instruction Through Research* (Washington, D.C.: Association for Supervision and Curriculum Development, 1963), pp. 54–60.

[23] Walter T. Cahill, "Can You Teach Creative Writing?" *Clearing House*, November 1958, pp. 163–165, and "Writing for Real," *Clearing House*, January 1958, pp. 304–305.

[24] D. Kennedy, "Technique that Fostered Creative Writing," *Elementary English*, March 1957, pp. 163–164.

[25] Paul A. Witty and William Martin, "An Analysis of Children's Compositions Written in Response to a Film," *Elementary English*, March 1957, pp. 158–163.

[26] Neal R. Edmund, "Writing in the Intermediate Grades," *Elementary English*, November 1959, pp. 491–501.

[27] Paul E. Torrance, "Creative Thinking Through Language Arts," *Educational Leadership*, October 1960, pp. 13–18.

May and Tabachnick compared three kinds of stimuli for their effectiveness in fostering creative writing.[28] Conflicting evidence regarding ordered and unordered stimuli was the basis for conducting their study. They provided 600 children with one of three different stimuli—ordered, unordered, and both—and compared the results in terms of creative expression. Their findings indicated no simple, single answer to the question, "Which kind of stimulus is best?" In general, when given a choice, the children selected the organized stimulus.

Approaches to functional writing, for example, letters, reports, and records, have been suggested by several authorities. Shane and Mulry provide an extended bibliography for further inquiry.[29]

Too little is yet known about the area of writing. Burns and others suggest caution when reading the admonitions of authorities. They advise:

> Some teachers apparently achieve some success with certain techniques, others are just as successful with other approaches. Consequently, providing "rules" for success in this area of the language arts is misleading and dangerous. Many of the statements found in print are merely suggestions and opinions which the reader should consider as such.[30]

The task of pulling together all the relevant research in written expression is unfinished, and until it is accomplished teachers must either rely on somewhat biased compilations or examine the original research reports themselves.

LISTENING

Interest in listening skills has grown in recent years. Taylor said, "Research has suggested that the average person will retain only 50 percent of what he hears, no matter how hard he concentrates, and that two months later he can be expected to recall only 25 percent of what was said."[31] Much of our everyday lives is spent listening, and our poor retention rate is sufficient need to focus on listening skills at the elementary level.

The most significant type of research in listening has been that which pursued the question, "Can listening skills be taught?" Lundsteen

[28] Frank B. May and H. Robert Tabachnick, "Three Stimuli for Creative Writing," *Elementary School Journal*, November 1966, pp. 88–94.

[29] Shane and Mulry, pp. 61–67.

[30] Paul C. Burns et al., *The Language Arts in Childhood Education* (Chicago: Rand McNally & Company, 1971), p. 193.

[31] Stanford E. Taylor, "Listening," *What Research Says to the Teacher*, No. 29 (Washington, D.C.: National Education Association, 1968), p. 4.

studied this question specifically to test the possibility that listening skills could be measured and improved.[32] She used six fifth-grade and six sixth-grade classes as control and experimental groups. Both groups were given pre- and post-tests to establish similarities, initially, and to test for differences in listening skills. The control group did not receive specific listening-skill instruction. The children who received special instruction in listening scored higher on the post-test of listening ability than the children in the control group.

The evidence supports and is supported by other research in the area. The implication of such findings is that listening skills can be measured and improved with instruction and practice.

SPELLING

A good example of the collecting and classifying activities of educational research is the classic study by Horn.[33] He surveyed letters written by professional people, excuses written to teachers by parents, minutes of organizational meetings, committee reports, books, magazines and newspapers, and other sources to ascertain the most basic words used in writing. He collected a total of 5 million running words and 36,000 different words. From this he selected the 10,000 most basic words according to these criteria:

1. The total frequency with which the word was used in writing.
2. The commonness with which the word was used by everyone regardless of sex, vocation, location, educational level, or economic status.
3. The spread of the word's use in different types of writing.
4. The cruciality of the word as evidenced by the severity of the penalty attached to its misspelling.
5. The probable permanency of the word's use.
6. The desirability of the word as determined by the quality of the writing in which it is used.

Lest some believe the language is so rapidly changing that his work would prove futile, Horn later reported, after studying the age of 5000 words of greatest frequency in the 10,000 words most commonly used in writing:

> Less than four percent of these words have come into the language since 1849, and less than 10 percent have come in since 1759. More of these

---

[32] Sara W. Lundsteen, "Teaching and Testing Critical Listening in the Fifth and Sixth Grades," *Elementary English*, November 1964, pp. 743–747.

[33] Ernest Horn, *A Basic Writing Vocabulary*, University of Iowa Monographs in Education, No. 41 (Iowa City, Ia.: University of Iowa Press, 1926).

words were in the language before 1099 than have come into the language since 1799.[34]

A breakdown of the percent of writing accounted for by Horn's words is presented by Burns et al. They note:

> 100 words: 55 to 60 percent of the total words used in an average person's writing;
> 500 words: 75 to 80 percent of the total words used in an average person's writing;
> 1000 words: 85 percent of the total words used in an average person's writing;
> 2000 words: 90 percent of the total words used in an average person's writing;
> 3000 words: 95 percent of the total words used in an average person's writing.[35]

Ames surveyed seven basic spelling text series with 1955–1960 copyright dates that purportedly subscribed to the social utility theory espoused by Horn.[36] He found the average number of words introduced was 3209, but the total for all seven series was 6043. There was agreement among the authors of the seven series on only 1283 words. Noting that the grade placement discrepancy was severe, Burns et al. observed:

> Thus it appears there is no great amount of agreement among authors of spelling textbooks with respect to spelling vocabulary or its placement.[37]

As logical as the social utility approach is, the textbook publishers still demonstrate their biases for other, usually some kind of phonetic, approach. Therefore, teachers should consult Horn's original list if they want to be assured of benefiting from his research.

It may be that computer-assisted instruction and programmed learning will play important roles in the teaching of spelling in the future. Wilson has commented on the use of programmed learning as follows[38]:

> "Programmed learning" is not really in the experimental category if one can judge by the increasing sales and uses of instructional materials of this

---

[34] Ernest Horn, "The Validity and Reliability of Adult Vocabulary Lists," *Elementary English Review*, April 1939, p. 134.

[35] Burns et al., p. 307.

[36] Wilbur S. Ames, "A Comparison of Spelling Textbooks," *Elementary English*, February 1965, pp. 146–152, 188.

[37] Burns et al., p. 308.

[38] L. Craig Wilson, *The Open Access Curriculum* (Boston: Allyn and Bacon, Inc., 1971), p. 255.

type. . . . Routinization and mechanization of the basic skill areas may or may not lead to self-teaching and improved communication. However, no one can deny that remarkable gains have been made in curriculum materials development. Similarly, there are few approaches which have had more success in making the purposes of the teacher more explicit and visible.

One solution to the problems encountered in teaching spelling would be a reform of the language itself. Since that is not very likely, educators will have to continue in their research efforts to help teachers who can help children learn to spell with the most efficacy.

SCIENCE

A survey of what children like in elementary science was conducted by Perrodin.[39] His procedure was to have the children complete sentence fragments about science topics and activities. He surveyed more than 500 children who were enrolled in urban and rural districts. Perrodin concluded health, safety, and the human body were the most popular topics, and the activities that were most desired were general participation and specific experimentation.

Involvement and participation of children in science activities are key elements of many of the national science curriculum study committees. After surveying the several national science projects, Ragan and Shepherd noted the similarities:

1. All of them emphasize that experiments are to be performed by children to find answers rather than their accepting "ready-made" answers.
2. All of them are concerned with helping children develop the ability to think.
3. All of them provide opportunities for the child to develop an understanding of the structure of the discipline.
4. All of them are designed to help the child broaden his understanding of the environment.
5. All of them expect school experiences to result in behavioral changes.[40]

The Science Curriculum Improvement Study is one such national program that has had some impact on teacher education. Wilson com-

[39] Alex F. Perrodin, "Children's Interest in Elementary School Science," *School and Mathematics*, No. 64, 1965, pp. 259–264.
[40] William B. Ragan and Gene D. Shepherd, *Modern Elementary Curriculum*, 4th ed. (New York: Holt, Rinehart and Winston, Inc., 1971), p. 372.

pared the frequency of pupil involvement in five essential science experiences taught by SCIS-educated teachers and the frequency of pupil involvement in classes taught by teachers not educated in the project's methods. The science experiences observed were: observation, measurement, experimentation, interpretation of data, and prediction. One of Wilson's conclusions was that the SCIS-educated teachers encouraged pupils to become involved in over twice as many of the essential science experiences as did the traditional science teachers.[41]

Renner and Stafford reviewed other studies of SCIS-educated teachers and noted:

> The results seem to suggest that the deviation from the traditional mode of teacher education and not the materials [in the teacher's classroom] is the significant factor in changing the teachers' instructional patterns.[42]

The quality of preparation of science teachers appears to be the significant ingredient in the SCIS-trained teachers.

Dilorenzo and Halliwell compared science achievement of elementary students who had special science teachers with students whose regular classroom teacher taught science.[43] Over 200 students were involved in the study. The investigators found no significant difference in science achievement between the children with special science teachers and children with regular classroom teachers.

Of all the elementary school subjects, one might expect science to be the most researched and best understood. But science educators, like mathematics and social studies educators—indeed all educators—have had to contend with myriad variables that are not amenable to precise control and assessment. No aspersions can be cast on science educators any more than on any other educational researcher because they all face the same dilemma of social scientists generally, and that is a lack of sophisticated and refined techniques for carrying out empirical research.

MATHEMATICS

Much of the folk wisdom suggests children dislike mathematics, and this is usually blamed on teachers' poor attitudes toward teaching it. Stright

---

[41] John H. Wilson, *Differences Between the Inquiry-Discovery and the Traditional Approaches to Teaching Science in Elementary Schools* (Norman, Okla.: University of Oklahoma, unpublished doctoral dissertation, 1967).

[42] J. W. Renner and D. G. Stafford, "Inquiry, Children and Teachers," *The Science Teacher*, April 1970, p. 1.

[43] Louis T. Dilorenzo and Joseph W. Halliwell, "A Comparison of the Science Achievement of 4th-grade Pupils Instructed by Regular Classroom and Special Science Teachers," *Science Education*, No. 47, 1963, pp. 202–205.

surveyed over 1000 elementary students and twenty-nine teachers to determine what their attitudes were toward mathematics.[44] An attitude scale was used and results were classified according to grade (third, fourth,

[44] Virginia M. Stright, "A Survey of the Attitudes Toward Arithmetic of Students and Teachers in the Third, Fourth, and Sixth Grades," *The Arithmetic Teacher*, October 1970, pp. 280–286.

Science and mathematics curricula are being tailored to children's abilities. (Photo courtesy Norman Public Schools.)

or sixth) and sex. The findings indicated that in all three grades over 75 percent of both boys and girls expressed a relatively strong liking for mathematics. Similarly, the majority of teachers liked teaching mathematics, irrespective of their educational level or years of teaching experience.

Studies of whether special mathematics teachers at the elementary level produced superior achievement when compared with regular classroom teachers were reviewed by Spitzer.[45] He concluded:

> Research studies of 10 to 15 years ago comparing the achievement of pupils in schools of departmental with schools of self-contained types of organization failed to show superiority in the departmental type of institution.[46]

The new mathematics, which had its genesis in the 1950s and greatest impact in the early and mid-1960s, emphasizes the structure of mathematics, whereas the traditional mathematics emphasized specific computational skills. Typically, before the new mathematics was implemented, structure was not taught until high school level when algebra (a generalized arithmetic) was taught. The new mathematics usually introduces some structure, for example, sets and principles, in the early elementary grades.

How effective the emphasis on structure is in teaching mathematics was a researchable question pursued by Gray.[47] He compared a method of teaching multiplication that emphasized the distributive principle with a method that emphasized multiplication as repeated additions and included practice, drill, and memorization. Twenty-two third-grade classes participated in the experiment.

The results indicated that the children who received the instruction emphasizing the distributive principle were better able to compute multiplication problems, transfer their abilities to untaught procedures, and give rational explanations of procedures. Gray concluded:

> Insofar as the distributive property is an element of the structure of mathematics, the findings tend to support the assumption that teaching for an understanding of structure can produce superior results in terms of pupil growth.[48]

More studies of this nature need to be made to provide empirical evidence justifying a change from one instructional emphasis to another.

[45] Herbert F. Spitzer, *Teaching Arithmetic: What Research Says to the Teacher* (Washington, D.C.: N.E.A., Association of Classroom Teachers, 1968).

[46] Spitzer, p. 18.

[47] Roland F. Gray, "An Experiment in Teaching of Introductory Multiplication," *The Arithmetic Teacher*, March 1965, pp. 198–203.

[48] Gray, p. 203.

SOCIAL STUDIES

The social studies encompass more disciplines than any other elementary school subject. For this reason social studies means different things to different people. Some consensus is achieved, however, when specific programs are compared. McLendon and Penix reviewed several investigations and surveys of what social studies programs consisted of and reported that:

> Objectives understandably vary little between elementary and secondary social studies, although actual approaches to attaining aims differ markedly at each level. Somewhat more emphasis on personal guidance, the nearby environment, and basic study skills characterizes the approach at the elementary level.[49]

That study skills are attached to social studies is curious. Whether they can be learned more effectively as a part of some other elementary subject has not been investigated.

A study that examined whether study skills are learned more effectively when taught explicitly as compared with incidental teaching was conducted by Schiller.[50] She used 296 seventh graders in her experiment. Half of them received specific instruction in how to use reference books, tables of content, indexes, graphs, and maps while the other half of the group received instruction in study skills only when it was needed to comprehend a particular lesson. Tests of study skills at the end of the experiment indicated that those children who received specific instruction scored significantly higher than the children who learned only incidentally.

The popularity of social studies as an elementary subject has been surveyed a number of times. The most recent study was Herman's, in which he polled 214 elementary boys and girls as to the school subject they liked best.[51] In addition, he included specific activities of each subject for ranking. His findings indicated that social studies was about the least liked subject of the children. Girls had even less interest in it than boys. Herman speculated that the reading problems of children may account for this dislike because frequently social studies is taught in such a manner that reading plays an important role. Also indicated was

---

[49] Jonathan C. McLendon and Findlay C. Penix, *Teaching the Social Studies: What Research Says to the Teacher* (Washington, D.C.: N.E.A., Association of Classroom Teachers, 1968), p. 4.

[50] Sister Philomene Schiller, "The Effects of the Functional Use of Certain Skills in Seventh Grade Social Studies," *Journal of Educational Research*, December 1963, pp. 201–203.

[51] Wayne L. Herman, Jr., "How Intermediate Children Rank the Subjects," *Journal of Educational Research*, April 1963, pp. 435–436.

the expanding environment approach that has been common to many social studies programs.[52]

There are several social studies programs currently in use that offer alternatives to the expanding horizons approach. Joyce presents an excellent review of various organizing concepts that have been devised for the elementary level.[53]

OTHER RESEARCH

Other aspects of schooling, for example, administration, curriculum, and general instruction, have received a good deal of research attention. Journals, textbooks, and general reference works contain reports of this research.

The authors have not intended to be comprehensive or even representative in the selection of studies reported in this chapter. If the student begins to get a taste of the variety of topics investigated and methods used in the research, it is our hope he or she will be more likely to read other research reports with some sophistication. Some of the more comprehensive books containing research reports and summaries and popular research journals are listed below for further reference.

Books

Alexander, Carter, and Arvid J. Burke, *How to Locate Educational Information and Data*, 4th ed. New York: Bureau of Publications, Teachers College, Columbia University, 1958. Provides the student with hundreds of sources for locating educational information.

Dissertation Abstracts. Ann Arbor, Mich.: University of Michigan, monthly. A collection of abstracts of all doctoral level dissertations and monographs, each of which can be ordered complete on microfilm or in printed form.

Ebel, Robert L. (Ed.), *Encyclopedia of Educational Research*, 4th ed. London: The Macmillan Company, 1969.

Education Index. New York: H. W. Wilson Company, monthly, 1929 to present. A guide (subject, author, and title) to articles originally appearing in education journals.

Gage, N. L. (Ed.), *Handbook of Research on Teaching*. Chicago:

---

[52] See, for example, Ronald O. Smith and Charles Cardinell, "Challenging the Expanding-Environment Theory," *Social Education*, March 1964, pp. 141–143.

[53] Bruce R. Joyce, *Strategies for Elementary Social Science Education* (Chicago: Science Research Associates, Inc., 1965); see also, Martin Feldman and Eli Seifman, *The Social Studies: Structure, Models, and Strategies* (Englewood Cliffs, N.J.: Prentice-Hall, Inc., 1969).

Rand McNally & Company, 1963. Contains a comprehensive treatment of 23 research areas related to the study of teaching.

Journals

American Educational Research Association, N.E.A., *American Educational Research Journal*. Washington, D.C., January 1964 to present. Published four times a year, this journal is an excellent source of contemporary research in education.

——, *Review of Educational Research*. Washington, D.C., 1931 to present. Published five times a year, this journal provides a comprehensive review of research in specific areas. Every three years each area is reviewed again.

Elementary School Journal. Chicago: University of Chicago Press. Provides articles and research reports dealing with elementary education.

Journal of Educational Research. Madison, Wis.: Dembar Publications, Inc. Provides reports of significant research carried out in many fields of education.

SUMMARY

1. Research is the systematic quest for answers to specific questions.
2. Research procedures include collecting, classifying, organizing, analyzing, and interpreting data.
3. The quality of research is a function of the control over variables involved in the study.
4. Educational research has the potential for providing the most reliable and valid information needed by teachers.
5. The limitations of research stem from the lack of sophisticated and refined techniques for studying human behavior.
6. Normative theory suggests what ought to or should be.
7. Empirical theory describes, explains, and predicts what is.
8. In spite of the increasing amount of research being done in all the subject areas and other areas of education, no overall theory has yet been established to account for what happens in the schools.

RECOMMENDED READINGS

Barnes, Fred P. *Research for the Practitioner in Education*. Washington, D.C.: Department of Elementary School Principals, N.E.A., 1964. A practical, nontechnical introduction and guide to research methods and problems in education.

Burns, Paul C., Betty L. Broman, and Alberta L. Lowe. *The Language Arts in Childhood Education*, 2d ed. Chicago: Rand McNally & Company, 1971. A comprehensive presentation of elementary language arts that includes references to pertinent research.

Dunfee, Maxine, *Elementary Science: A Guide to Current Research*. Washington, D.C.: Association for Supervision and Curriculum Development, 1968. A useful summary of research relating to elementary school science.

Feldman, Martin, and Eli Seifman (Eds.), *The Social Studies: Structure, Models, and Strategies*. Englewood Cliffs, N.J.: Prentice-Hall, Inc., 1969. A collection of readings in the various disciplines in social studies that provide background information for research.

Herman, Wayne L. (Ed.), *Current Research in Elementary School Social Studies*. London: The Macmillan Company, 1969. A compilation of research studies pertinent to elementary social studies.

Hyman, Ronald T. (Ed.), *Teaching: Vantage Points for Study*. Philadelphia: J. B. Lippincott Company, 1968. A collection of readings that present theoretical frameworks and general backdrops for study.

Johnston, A. Montgomery, and Paul C. Burns (Eds.), *Research in Elementary School Curriculum*. Boston: Allyn and Bacon, Inc., 1970. A collection of research reports in the elementary school subjects, administration, and general curriculum.

Joyce, William W., Robert G. Oana, and W. Robert Houston (Eds.), *Elementary Education in the Seventies*. New York: Holt, Rinehart and Winston, Inc., 1970. An in-depth look at the elementary subjects that includes research reports as well as theoretical articles.

Chapter 9

Instructional Technology

tech·nol·o·gy /-jē/ n [Gk technologia *systematic treatment of an art, fr.* techno- + -logia -logy] 1: *technical language* 2a: *applied science* b: *a technical method of achieving a practical purpose* 3: *the totality of the means employed to provide objects necessary for human sustenance and comfort.*

Webster's Seventh New Collegiate Dictionary (Springfield, Mass.: G. & C. Merriam Co., 1967), p. 905.

Many elementary teachers think of technology as meaning "machines," and instructional technology as adding up to "audio-visual equipment." While it is true that machines are a part of a technology, the literal meaning and spirit of "technology" goes much further. Historian Charles A. Beard, in discussing technology, noted that:

> Narrowly viewed, technology consists of the totality of existing laboratories, machines, and processes already developed, mastered, and in operation. But it is far more than mere objective realities. . . . Technology has a philosophy of nature and a method—an attitude toward materials and work—and hence is a subjective force of high tension.[1]

---

[1] Charles A. Beard, "Introduction to the American Edition," in J. B. Bury, *The Idea of Progress* (New York: Dover Publications, 1955 [first published as the American Edition by Macmillan in 1932]), p. 22.

The late James Finn, for many years a leading authority in the study of instructional technology, described it from the "more than machines" standpoint:

> . . . In addition to machinery, (instructional) technology includes processes, systems, management and control mechanisms both human and non-human, and above all . . . a way of looking at problems as to their interest and difficulty, the feasibility of technical solutions, and the economic values—broadly considered—of those solutions.[2]

Instructional technology may be seen, then, as a point of view toward instructional problems. This point of view does not seek to dehumanize or "mechanize" teaching and learning in schools, but rather to seek *optimal solutions* to instructional problems.

In an increasing number of universities, instructional technology has become the successor to "audio-visual instruction" as an area of study and university-wide service. As an outgrowth of the audio-visual field, instructional technology has grown from an equipment-oriented approach to instruction to a process-oriented approach, in which instruction is viewed from a technological—or "technical"—standpoint.

Many educators believe that this evolution has been in part caused by the impact of teaching machines and programmed instruction.

In the early 1950s "teaching machines" suddenly came to the fore as a revolutionary innovation, with *potential* for causing revolutionary changes in the structures and effectiveness of education. While practically all educators had opinions about them, teaching machines and programmed instructions tended to become a central concern of educational psychologists—those educators with the background and interest in the learning theories that spawned the machines—and audio-visual specialists—those concerned with instructional materials and equipment and its effective utilization. After a few years it became clear to practically everyone involved that the "teaching machines" themselves were much less important in most applications than the programs which they contained. It became obvious that a number of alternative ways exist to present programmed material. Instead of expensive teaching machines, either books or booklike formats were used, and conventional and inexpensive educational media like slide and filmstrip projectors and tape recorders were used to present programmed instruction sequences. The process of finding appropriate *media* for highly specified and highly developed instructional packages gradually became part of most "audio-visual" experts' background and interest. From then on the audio-visual field has never been the same. In

---

[2] James D. Finn, "Technology and the Instructional Process," AV *Communication Review*, Winter 1960, p. 10.

learning to work with the teaching machines, the audio-visualist became, by necessity, part learning psychologist and part instructional designer. And most recently, the innovations of educational simulations and computer-assisted instruction have added force to the trend of moving away from the traditional structures of audio-visual education to the broader and more process-oriented approach of instructional technology.

EDUCATION AND TECHNOLOGY

William Clark Trow points out that education is the last major human enterprise to be significantly influenced by technology.[3] To illustrate this, let us consider, for the moment, education as a *production* enterprise. The *input* may be seen at the start of the school year in the incoming class of children, teachers, physical plant, staff, materials, and equipment; the primary goal-oriented *process* is generally "day-to-day" teaching; and the *product* is children as changed by the year of school. This "input-process-product" view of school places the school in the perspective of being an *operating system*. There are three primary levels of technology at which systems commonly operate in modern societies: (1) the *small-batch* or single-unit technology, such as an artisan's work in making crafts, in which the pace at which the "system" produces is largely up to the individual producer—not only the pace of production, but the entire aspect of *control* of the production process is individual and often idiosyncratic; (2) the *assembly-line* technology—for which an auto assembly line is a classic example—in which some start-stop and slowdown may be found as being controlled by the individual worker, but is most characteristically a process in which the rate and nature of the production process itself is one that is controlled more by the provisions of the assembly line than by any originality on the worker's part; and (3) the continuous-process technology, as exemplified by the workings of an oil refinery, in which the system must be *very* precisely controlled, continuous in operation, and heavily dependent on feedback and nonhuman control due to the requirements for both precise and continuous control. It should be obvious what level of technology most nearly describes the workings of the typical elementary school. Education is moving, however, from the small-batch level to one more nearly resembling the assembly-line and continuous-process levels (the final chapter of this text gives attention to some possibilities for the elementary school of the future which may be the culmination of the technological shift now underway).

[3] William Clark Trow, *Teacher and Technology* (New York: Meredith Publishing Co., 1963), p. 5.

What does a technological revolution mean to the elementary teacher of today? First, the impact of changing technologies causes new strains and tensions on the educational system and on teachers themselves. For example, the early 1950s saw the introduction and popularization of programmed instruction, most popularly in the form of "teaching machines." As it became apparent that teaching machines could in fact help students learn without intervention of a teacher or anything else, a near panic developed among many teachers at the threat of being put out of a job by a machine. The teacher panic may be seen as having been caused by producers and promoters of the new product not wholly understanding (and/or honestly communicating) what their machines could and could not do, and teachers themselves not clearly perceiving their own functions in the system. At any rate, while the possibility of being replaced never was real, the fear, frustration, and anger at the perceived threat was definitely real. And while eliminating teachers has rarely been seriously considered as a potential side effect of massive use of teaching machines, a definite shift in teacher role *does* seem an inevitable outcome. Surely it is disconcerting to anyone who has taught for many years to conceive of the possibility of as drastic a change in role as might be called for by heavy and widespread use of automated instruction.

A second major implication of the technological revolution seems to be the potential for real and significant improvement in the *quality* of education. While we should understand that there are very serious drawbacks to conducting education on an "assembly line" basis, it is quite possible that the assembly-line level can be bypassed and that we may be moving to a level of operation most closely resembling the "continuous process" technology. There would seem to be reason enough for such a move in consideration of the fact that learning and human behavior rarely can be seen to exist in segmented "hour-long" periods in the real world. Human learning and development are continuous processes themselves, and each is closely related to the other. A major thrust of curriculum reformers since the beginning of this century has been that learning should be recognized as a continuous process. It now seems within our reach to make instructional provisions of such a nature as to enable truly "continuous" learning. Learning would be the result of instruction conducted in such a way that the exact material required by each learner is provided at the precise time at which the learner needs it based on precise multifactor continuous feedback and instructional control provision. Feedback and control will be achievable with a precision hitherto reserved to the physical sciences. Evaluation of the effect of such sophistication should be from the standpoint of human, not mechanistic, goals. To be considered successful, technology must help schools achieve the broad, human-centered purposes of education.

EDUCATIONAL MEDIA

Television

Most people think of television as that which they watch on the television set at home. Actually, there are at least three kinds of television: commercial, educational/public, and instructional.[4] To identify which of these types a given televised presentation would fit, its purpose and origin would have to be ascertained, for both factors have a hand in making this determination. For example, many programs of commercial origin—the kind of programs most people generally watch on the television set at home—have primarily educational goals. Documentaries, "specials" on current events, programs on art and serious music—all of these have at least as much informative value for most viewers as they do entertainment, and many commercial programs (including the news, weather, and sports) are basically informative. On the other hand, many programs broadcast via educational television facilities have entertainment as their goals; for example, a serialized melodrama, "The Forsyte Saga," was broadcast on the educational television network during the 1969–1970 season and, incidentally, had higher viewer ratings than commercial competition in many locales.

COMMERCIAL TELEVISION. The beginnings of broadcast television in this country were expansions of the commercial radio networks in existence at television's beginnings. Radio broadcasting began in 1895 when Guglielmo Marconi sent and received radio signals at his home in Bologna, Italy. In the United States, widespread public interest in broadcasting was first aroused in 1920 when the returns of the election of President Harding were broadcast. Industry sensed the interest, and in the next two years Westinghouse Manufacturing Company and American Telephone and Telegraph Company had opened radio broadcasting stations. The two companies manufactured radio sets, and the broadcasting was done in expectation of gaining revenue from the sale of radios. Years passed before advertising became the source of support for stations and networks.

Almost two decades after television had become a laboratory reality, a few NBC and CBS radio affiliates began transmitting television programs in addition to their regular radio programming. As television became widespread, the pattern of advertiser-support remained with it, despite independent networks' recurring attempts at "pay as you watch" television. The fact that commercial television is supported by advertisers is more

---

[4] Instructional television is considered by most authorities to be a form or type of educational television. The two are treated as they are here to facilitate a clearer exposition of each.

important than it may seem at first, and the implications of that fact may account for much of commercial television's characteristics as a medium.

The significance of advertiser support of all commercial television available in the United States is apparent when one considers that that portion of the electromagnetic spectrum in which radio and television broadcast frequencies lie is considered, like the air in which it coexists, *public domain*. It was very early in broadcasting history that the issues of public control and regulation, freedom of speech, protection of the ideals and interests of the people, and private financing became real ones at the federal level. In 1927 the Federal Radio Commission (now the Federal Communications Commission) was formed. Previous public-utility legislation had formed the conceptual basis for the regulation it would impose, and that basis was that the regulation imposed would lie in "public interest, convenience, or necessity." Licensing of broadcast stations was to become the means by which the public good was to be served. Before too long, a pattern had developed in the way in which the commission exercised its regulatory function—to set technical broadcast standards (technical quality parameters such as allowable distortion, power-level regulation, and maintenance of precise broadcast frequency) and to more or less automatically renew licenses to stations. These policies have generally encouraged the *growth* of the broadcasting media, but have not encouraged programming *quality* or represented the public interest in any way other than "protection" from such violation of public morality and standards as nudity and obscene language.

The programming on commercial network television represents what only a very small number of people with common commercial goals wish the public to see. While the news and public affairs services of the major networks seem to have somehow remained by and large above this serious bias, the television that we watch on NBC, CBS, and ABS is free but *not* public—it is commercial. Its purpose is only secondarily to entertain or inform; its primary purpose is to sell things.

Teachers who use commercial television programs (or parts of them) in school should understand this. While news and public affairs broadcasting may be reasonably free from specific bias imposed by the commercial orientation, the pressures to reflect such a bias *do* exist, and *can* from time to time show up in *any* program's content.

EDUCATIONAL AND PUBLIC TELEVISION. Educational and public television are those forms of television which are not commercially supported. For a number of years the American public had no television options. When a person watched television, it was commercial television. A few years later, many viewers had two options: to watch commercial TV or educational TV. However, the TV set in many homes was not able to receive an educational TV station, and there was no option. And in any event, the American who wanted television *entertainment* had no choice—commercially supported programming was all there was. So, while the viewer did have a choice as to whether the source of the program he was to watch would be public or commercial in its orientation, if he opted for public, he was *not* entertained (in the case of a large majority of early ETV programs, the "not" is *most* emphatic). However, in the past few years, the major educational television organization, National Educational Television (NET) has become increasingly "public television" oriented. More and more programming has been presented that was not originally produced with "educational" goals in mind—for example, plays, dramatic series, and musical performances. For years there has been a conflict of opinion as to what ETV programming should be at the national or network level. One set of proponents has held that ETV should appeal to as broad an audience as possible with "popular" programming. Others have argued that ETV can best function if it serves a smaller audience with "quality" programs. Because part of each position has clear merit, and because no single solution seems capable of satisfying the dilemma, the newer form of noncommercial television, public TV, is developing from within the existing ETV structures, notably, the National Educational Television network.

In an essay describing NET as the "fourth network," John F. White points out that NET's programming is devoted to the following three areas: public affairs, cultural programming, and programs for children.[5] While the commercial networks do put on some public affairs programs, NET's emphasis has been to bring out submerged issues, to trace relationships and evolutions of problems and issues not handled in depth by the commercial networks. A publicly supported programming source is in a good position to tackle controversy at an issue-oriented level, and may do it with somewhat more fearlessness than could a source supported by "nervous" sponsors. Cultural programming has included performances in drama, music, and dance, as well as programs on the humanities and sciences.

Children's programming, covering a wide range of topics in both educational and diversional domains, seems not to have made any significant impact on the lives of America's children until "Sesame Street." That series may have marked a turning point in the role and importance of educational television in the lives of American children.

"Sesame Street" was originally designed as a series of programs

[5] John F. White, "NET as the Fourth Network," in Allen E. Koenig and Ruane Hill (Eds.), *The Farther Vision, Educational Television Today* (Madison, Wis.: University of Wisconsin Press, 1967).

proving compensatory, "head-start" experiences for underprivileged minority-group children. The series' first year was financed by a Ford Foundation grant of $8 million. The series of thirty-two programs that resulted had such widespread appeal that the network literally was forced by public demand to renew the series, despite rather firm plans to the contrary. While its limited objectives have been the object of criticism, there can be no doubt that "Sesame Street" and other programs following its production philosophy are demonstrating that public and educational television *can* have large, loyal audiences—an issue which before "Sesame Street" was one of major concern. While money will not guarantee a successful production, a clear difference between "Sesame Street" and its less successful predecessors has been the amount of money provided. One might theorize that if youngsters are to view educational television programs voluntarily and attentively, those programs must be of a comparable level of production as the commercial programs which the child has become accustomed to viewing. As educators, we have been slow to accept the fact that such factors as originality, playfulness, and a general esthetic pleasure are valid ones in educational applications, especially with regard to television. Until recently, little if any proof has existed of the beneficial effects of such factors on learning. A problem with research studies that have viewed these "production" variables has been that the outcomes which the research has viewed have been primarily differences between short-term cognitive (intellectual) gains. We are finding—and "Sesame Street" has demonstrated this at a national level—that the *affective domain* is of considerable importance, and seems to be the area in which production-quality differences will show a difference in result. Achievement of such goals in the affective domain as "willingness to voluntarily attend or listen" and "valuing" has been clearly and uniquely demonstrated by ETV programming of the "Sesame Street" type.

Most critics of "Sesame Street" do not question that it has met or even exceeded its objectives. Their criticisms have been that the objectives themselves were too limited in scope to have been a profitable use of the time and money spent on the series. It should be noted, however, that the program's $8 million budget, when spread out among its 7 million regular viewers, worked out to less than a penny a day per child.

INSTRUCTIONAL TELEVISION. Instructional television (ITV) is one form of educational TV, its distinguishing characteristics being its *limits*. ITV is limited to either highly specific instructional goals or local use, and generally both. ITV often originates from within an individual school, and sometimes from a school district or regional ITV service. The following illustrations may help the reader to visualize the kind of work which ITV can perform. A teacher may wish to use television to present certain instructions and a demonstration to students working on individual projects. The same instructions need to be given to each child individually because the instructions are appropriate only when the student has reached a certain point in his individual work. In this situation, the teacher may make a videotape recording—a sort of tape recording that plays back through a television set and gives regular picture and sound television— to eliminate the repetitive task of communicating an identical set of instructions and demonstration thirty or so times (given the conventional class). With a team-teaching structure the recording could serve many more students. While the time required to make the video recording of the demonstration would be something more than just giving the demonstration to a child, once the recording has provided the instructions to three or four children, the teacher would be way ahead on time, and would have *more time to work with children* on whatever is unique about each child and his learning. In another situation, a group of teachers might wish to prepare and present a highly informative and motivating program to start their students off on a project or unit. Such a choice of television as the mode of information presentation might have been based on the capacity of television as a medium to *accept and integrate* many of the other more conventional media—films, slides, overhead projection, tapes, records, flat pictures, and so on—presenting the slides, films, and so on without the physical trouble and distraction of displaying each individual form. A videotape may combine the unique information and helpfulness of a wide. variety of other materials, mainly through the fact that a television camera can see just about anything put in front of it but *only* what it is pointed at. The camera sees the motion picture on the screen, not the projector and the person running it; the slide on the screen, not the slide projector; it can see only a chart if you wish, without the easel and background. The group of teachers might find that they can effectively present in one-half hour material that would take many class periods to present "live."

ITV EQUIPMENT. Considering what it can accomplish, most ITV equipment is simple to use and inexpensive. The television *camera* is functionally similar to any other camera—snapshot, home movie, and so on—in that it is a device to pick up images. A television camera "sees" through a lens at its front and translates what it sees into electrical current. Whereas a movie camera or snapshot camera puts what it sees onto film, a television camera puts what it sees into a small cable. That cable is typically connected to one of two things: a television monitor or a videotape recorder. A television monitor is merely a TV set that will accept a signal from either a TV camera or videotape recorder. Actually, any home TV set can be converted to a television monitor with the addition of a few small parts. Many uses of ITV require only connecting a television camera to a monitor. Then, whatever the camera is pointed at, the monitor (television set) will show. Shoplifter-detection systems are common examples of these simple camera chains. A television camera is pointed at a given area of a store—a back corner, for example. A cable may connect the camera to a monitor placed anywhere in the store, so that one can see what is going on in the area "covered" by the camera. It should be noted that such installations show what is happening at the moment—the installation is analogous to a microscope or telescope or binoculars. You may be able to see what you could not otherwise see, not because of any ability to store information, but solely because of a way of *transmitting* information (the word "information" is used here in a very broad sense). The ability to store images and sound is provided by the third common major component of an ITV system: the videotape recorder. The videotape recorder is, to put it without exaggeration, a device of fantastic potential. In principle, its operation is similar to an ordinary tape recorder. Everyone who has used a tape recorder knows that it is a simple matter to speak while the recorder is in "record" mode, to rewind the tape, and play back what was said, store the tape and play it over and over almost indefinitely, or to record something else over all or part of the old recording. A videotape recorder allows the user to do the same thing, except in addition to sound, what we see is recorded also. Like the ordinary tape recorder (audiotape recorder), a tape made on a videotape recorder needs no processing or development—it can be viewed as quickly as one can rewind the tape to the start. The camera-recorder-monitor chain's basic capability can be visualized using the following illustration. At least one ski school uses the videotape recorder to help beginning skiers apply good form.[6] The student is shown a basic element of skiing—a technique for turning and stopping for example. Then the student tries to apply the technique himself out on a nearby hill. In skiing, with many other skills, students often think they are doing something properly, but they cannot figure out why the suggested technique does not yield the predicted results. In such cases, the instructor turns on a videotape recorder, threads it with a blank tape, switches the recorder to "record," and points a television camera at the student attempting to turn and stop. When the student reaches the bottom of the hill, the instructor takes him over to the little shack where the camera, recorder, and monitor are housed, rewinds the tape, and starts the

[6] See Robert M. Benrey, "I Learned to Ski Electronically!" *Popular Science*, December, 1969, pp. 136–138.

"instant replay TV" of the student's attempt at turning and stopping. If there is some *visible* manifestation of improper technique, the instructor can point out to the student what he is doing wrong—while the student is standing there in the comfort of the little shack watching what he has done. If he misses it the first time, showings can be repeated as often as is needed. The videotape recorder can make picture and sound recordings as well as picture-only recordings. Simply connecting a microphone to the videotape recorder will provide for the sound-recording element.

Making a videotape recording is an extremely simple operation. In fact, the planning required for producing clear, cogent demonstrations and lectures is considerably more difficult than any feats of technical expertise required to merely "make a recording." Threading a machine with tape is more complicated than threading an ordinary tape recorder, but much less complicated than threading a sound motion picture projector, and in any event, can be learned by looking at the manufacturer's instructions provided with the machine—generally in the form of a threading diagram supplemented by a booklet. A new innovation in videotape machines is the cartridge (or cassette) versions. These models require no threading, and some models offer prerecorded programs in color. While the initial market impetus for the development of these easier-to-use recorders has been to capture a sizable home-user market, this development may become as big a boon to teachers as has the cassette tape recorder. To make a recording, most of the small, inexpensive video recorders require practically no adjustment. On some, only the camera aperture and focus is variable—all the rest is automatically taken care of by the machine itself. On practically all machines, recording levels are automatically controlled, making the machine easier to operate in one major dimension than many audiotape recorders.

Videotape recorders suitable for school use, complete with camera and monitor, can be purchased for approximately $1,500, which is only a little more than many sound motion picture projectors in common school use. Enough videotape to record for one hour costs about $40—less than one day's rental on many hour-long films. Extensive-use studies conducted at Stanford University and elsewhere have established conclusively that the smaller "one-half inch" units perform at least as well, if not better, than their larger and more expensive "one inch" counterparts. While little difference in picture or sound quality is generally the case, the smaller, less expensive units are generally much more durable and trouble-free, especially where mobile use is made of the machines. Some one-inch units have special capabilities and features not found on the smaller machines, but the additional price is justified only when the extra capabilities are needed.

ITV USES. The uses to which ITV may be put are legion. A few of the more common and generally helpful to elementary teachers are: front-row seat uses, effort storing, and feedback.

"Front-row seat" uses of ITV. Typically, a front-row seat use of ITV requires only a simple camera plus monitor chain. This application of television addresses itself to the problem of how to give every student in a class an optimum view of object or demonstration. Most commonly a television camera is situated above the teacher's desk, its lens pointing downward, aimed at the top of the desk. Although, unavoidably, many demonstrations must be accomplished on a flat desk (dissecting a frog, tying a knot, and applying a watercolor wash are a few of the many clear and obvious examples), this is about the worst place possible if everyone is to be able to see clearly what is going on. Typically, classes are too large to be accommodated standing around a single desk, so a device that would allow all pupils to see the demonstration from a preselected, ideal point of view would be a helpful provision. The television camera aimed at the teacher's desk is such a provision when connected to a monitor (or monitors) appropriately placed for student viewing. The camera can be placed to simulate looking over the teacher's shoulder, thereby giving a point of view identical to that of the person performing the demonstration. It might be well to note at this point that training research conducted during and shortly after World War II established that the "over the shoulder" point of view resulted in significantly greater student-learning achievement than did viewing the demonstration from other angles. Whether a camera located above a teacher's desk is used or not, the essential element in "front-row seat" TV applications is the giving to a student a view of something going on before him that it would be inconvenient or impossible for him to see otherwise.

"Effort-storing" uses of ITV. As all experienced teachers know, many hours are spent every year doing the same things that were done the year before. Often these yearly tasks are introductions to a skill or concept such as "sets" or "long division." Sometimes these instructional tasks are repeated a number of times during one school term, for example, when the readiness for the material to be covered varies widely from member to member of the class. In such cases, a good approach is to present the material to the child on an individual basis when he is ready. If the topic were "sets," the teacher might be presenting her twenty-five-minute lesson on "sets" thirty times during one term. Using a recorder, the basic lesson could be recorded on videotape. When the child is ready for the instruction, he would be referred to that specific tape. Far from replacing the teacher, the videotape recorder has placed him in a position to do what he can do best—work with the *individual* learning through *diagnosis* of readiness, *correction* of learning problems, *interaction* with

students as individual people, *guidance* of students through a program of activities, and *designing* programs of instruction and activity to meet educational goals. Releasing the teacher from the enervating aspects of teaching can provide more time and energy for those things that it takes the live presence of a skilled and dedicated human to perform.

The feasibility of elementary school teachers and students using videotape equipment has been established. The smaller and less complex half-inch-format equipment is clearly appropriate for use at this level. That cassette and cartridge television recorders are usable in the classroom by untrained users is also certain. With manual threading machines, children will have to be taught how to thread the machine, start, stop, and rewind. Children who have grown up with television (many with color television) will not be as intimidated by the machinery as their teacher might be. The automatic threading provided by cassettes and cartridge television makes any sort of training unnecessary—a demonstration should suffice. When a teacher wishes to produce a lecture or demonstration for videotaping, it is helpful if an instructional media specialist is available to ensure that the instructional plans take the greatest advantage of the characteristics of the recording medium used. While successful videotaped lessons can be made without such help, the odds of success are higher and the effort expended by the teacher to achieve desired results is often less when a person with some television production experience is there to help. If a *production facility* is available at the school or regional level, then production assistance is a necessity and will be provided. Lessons made in a television "studio" have the potential of higher quality in *technical details* such as picture sharpness and lighting (to ensure that glare and heavy shadows do not obscure or distract from the subject), and *production factors* such as ensuring that the general production design is appropriate to the *intent* of the lesson and providing visual pace to enhance or reinforce meanings in the lesson. It should be clear, however, that a full-scale television facility is *not* a necessity for producing television lessons for limited, local use. A facility can expedite, facilitate, and upgrade the quality of locally produced materials, but is not essential for production. At the individual school level, the space available for the television facility is smaller than most classrooms. In such cases, a mobile recording unit consisting of a recorder, cameras, and auxillary equipment can be mounted on a cart. Practically all of the equipment that a studio provides can be so mounted to allow high-quality productions "on location" in classrooms, libraries, and any other spaces accessible with a cart.

"Feedback" uses of ITV. Sometimes the capability of the videotape recorder to record picture and sound and immediately play back both is a capability with unique applications in teaching. The example outlined

previously of a ski school's use of television "instant replays" illustrates this unique capability offered by the videotape recorder. At the secondary level and in training situations, examples of the usefulness of instant replay feedback provision are easy to find. Learning any skill in which "form" is important, such as skiing, tennis, swimming, typing, or even driving, can benefit from information about how closely the proper form was approximated. Television replays can provide this information easily and immediately. For many learnings at the elementary level in which television replays might be helpful, the certainty with which we may predict helpfulness is low. For example, it *may* be of help to the learner to be provided with replays of his eye movements while reading aloud—he could see what his eyes were doing while hearing himself read the material. It seems possible that certain learning difficulties in reading could be attacked with this technique. Possibly a child could see what he was doing wrong in other skills such as penmanship, but whether replays in this and other applications of this sort would be of real value has not been established. It does seem, however, that the primary domain of videotape feedback usefulness at the elementary level will be in dealing with individual learning difficulties and dysfunctions. The major exception to this situation lies in physical education, in which videotaped instant replays are of clear and recognized value.

Another sort of feedback that videotape can provide or enhance is one that provides the learner with a display of the results or probable results of his actions or decisions. Many situations provide feedback of this sort without need for supplement. Games, for example, are characterized by having "winners" and "losers." In a game, the important result of one's actions is whether or not they contributed to winning. In a repair or assembly task, feedback in the form of successful results is generally immediate and clear-cut. Many of the more frustrating and difficult repair and system-correction jobs are those in which the results of one's efforts at correction are delayed or undependable, such as use of certain drugs and medications to correct "human system" malfunctions. For those situations in which immediate or clear knowledge of the results of one's actions is *not provided* by the situation itself, then a means can often be devised to provide the necessary feedback. Sometimes a videotape can provide the necessary information, such as a video recording of an audience's reaction to a message. The beginning speechmaker may not have the composure necessary to both give his speech and judge its impact. A video recording of the audience can let the speechmaker practice audience analysis under conditions better suited to reflective thought than those encountered during the presentation of the speech. Furthermore, groups may profit from seeing themselves in action, and individual group members can see clearly what the impact of their individual contributions may be.

SITUATION 9.1

*Problems and Issues Relating
to Educational Television*

1. What effects do you predict instructional television will have on the school curriculum? On commercial television? What effects will commercial television have on educational television now that the commercial side of the industry is heavily engaged in education—the major networks in particular?
2. What important things do children of today know at the age of six that were not known by the six-year-old fifty years ago? And vice versa.
3. Some maintain that children of today do not have firsthand experiences as rich as those enjoyed before we developed the secondhand experiences of radio, motion pictures, and television. Do you agree? Why or why not?
4. Have most schools and colleges quickly adopted and systematically used motion pictures, radio, and television in a planned curriculum? If not, what were some of the barriers to adoption and use?
5. Interaction and feedback characterize successful learning. But many of our modern media seem to be one-way systems with limited opportunity to talk back to writers, speakers, or film makers. How would you propose that consumers get into closer touch with the producers?
6. Since television is especially effective in presenting certain kinds of information, what does this do to the role of the teacher as a dispenser of information? What new role can the professional teacher take in such a situation?
7. It has been said that the audience does not select the television program, but that the program selects the audience. What does the statement mean to you? Is it sound?

See work by Edgar Dale in the Recommended Readings at the end of this chapter.

Motion Pictures

Motion pictures have played a part in our educational efforts for a number of years. Earliest uses of motion picture films were characterized by overstated claims, shortsighted predictions, technical problems, and a few real successes. Over the years, large production and distribution firms have come into being to serve the demand for educational films. ERPI, Coronet, and Britannica, to name a few of the larger companies, produced and distributed thousands of films to elementary and secondary schools throughout the nation.

Traditional rationales for use of films have emphasized their concreteness. Before television, film's ability to "bring the world into the classroom" was a claim of considerable significance. Today, however, most children routinely watch events from around the world on the evening news, and to have "the world" brought to them in any fashion is nothing to cause particular interest. Perhaps due to this competition and perhaps for reasons quite unrelated to the phenomenon of television, two developments in the motion picture field have given a new dimension and, hence, a new lease on life to classroom films.

Single-concept films. At a time when the potentials of independent study are beginning to be realized, film makers have begun to produce more and more films for use by individual students. These short films, sometimes referred to as "film loops," generally run for three to five minutes and have a very limited topic—a film might present a demonstration of a particular technique, a principle, or a small part of a basic skill or knowledge. By limiting the *scope* of what each film attempts to accomplish, it is highly probable that the film will achieve its objective successfully. Instead of the standard 16mm format, these short films are in an 8mm format (either "regular 8" or "Super 8"), until now used only for "home movies." 8mm projectors are smaller, lighter, quieter, and cheaper than their 16mm counterparts. Furthermore, self-loading cartridges are available for the 8mm formats, which makes it possible for even young students to use films on their own. Cartridged film loops dealing with very limited topics make some of our time-honored dictums for "good film utilization" obsolete. Whereas the 16mm classroom films were made for group viewing with a teacher's introduction and follow-up, the single-concept films are made for individual student use, and hence, are produced in such a fashion as to be independent of introductions and follow-ups in the traditional sense. One should realize, however, that good use of single-concept films requires that the individual student using a given film is ready for the material in the film. While it is possible that an "introduction" to the film may be the answer in some cases, more often the situation will be one in which the films that are chosen for the child are ones for which he is ready. In using single-concept films, the primary teacher's role shifts from "the giver of the introduction to the class" to "the person who keeps track of children's learning and ensures that they are working with appropriate materials."

Nontheatrical films. Over the past few years motion pictures have been produced that seem to defy the old classifications of film types. Neither are these films "Hollywood" entertainment films, nor are they strictly "educational" films. This new genre may well have had its roots in the classic documentary films of the 1930s and 1940s. Some of the better new films have been "underground" productions, others as "above ground" as the Ford Foundation, and Canadian National Film Board, large corporations, universities, and governmental branches.[7] These films, gen-

---

[7] The source of most "underground" films is not quite as sinister as the name implies. Generally films produced at an individual film maker's own expense are given that label.

erally produced in the 16mm format, are not generally found in catalogues of "educational" films, but many of them constitute the best educational films available. What has been learned by today's creative film makers is how to put across a message with control and power hitherto reserved to poetry. Short films are now being produced that can be shown to an elementary grade class with assurance on the teacher's part that a given *affective* goal (a given feeling, value, or value set) will be achieved in most of the viewers. It is in this capacity for motion pictures to not only communicate information but to communicate attiudes about it and the "what should be" dimension to the "what is" that is making 16mm films of unique value in schools.

These two developments in the motion picture field—single-concept films and nontheatrical or "experimental" films—add two important new tools to the already existing ones. In the first, single-concept films, the area to be covered is highly circumscribed. The very narrow topic is treated in a no-nonsense, efficient, and systematic fashion. Such films are generally produced in a highly "scientific" manner, in which the contributions of how people learn from the learning psychologists are taken note of and put to very practical use with a thoroughness that few classroom teachers would have the time or training to accomplish.

In the second development—nontheatrical films—an attempt is made by the film maker to communicate a "message" or statement—a position or feeling, an attitude or outlook—that is generally difficult or impossible to express any other way but by a film. In many ways similar to poetry, a topic is characteristically treated in an idiosyncratic, original, creative, and often brilliant manner. Whereas the single-concept film owes much to behavioral science for its effects, the nontheatrical film is an art form.

Between the two new types of film lies the traditional educational film—sometimes effective instruments, sometimes not—but generally undistinguished in any particular fashion. Hopefully, in the near future that undistinguished middle will become a higher third, comprised of the best of the science of learning and the art of film. There is good reason to believe that the "new educational film" will be a welcome contribution.

Other Instruments of Instruction

There is currently quite a wide variety of instructional media in addition to those previously discussed that are available for use by the elementary teacher. While the term "media" has come to refer simply to materials and equipment, irrespective of the way they are used, it is sometimes useful to characterize as "instructional media" only those equipment and materials which are being used as the *medium* through which instruction proceeds. Sometimes, for example, the real medium of instruction is the live teacher, interacting with his students as *aided* by various devices. A film may be either the medium for bringing about achievement of a given set of objectives, or the film could be used in such a way that it provides a *contribution* to the learning that takes place as part of a lesson conducted by the teacher. There is a place for both types of use, and certain "media" are capable of handling either role. There are, however, some instructional instruments that can*not* stand on their own—they are incapable of anything more than *helping* the teacher make a presentation or conduct a class more forcefully, clearly, dramatically, efficiently, colorfully, or conveniently. Such devices and materials include overhead projection, 2 × 2 transparencies, tape recordings and phonograph records, filmstrips, charts and posters, maps and globes, models, mock-ups, and realia.

Overhead projection. The most popular instructional instrument to come along since the chalkboard is the overhead projector. It can help the teacher do what he knows he needs to do with unprecedented ease. The characteristics of the overhead projector that make this possible are (1) it is operated from the front of the class rather than from the back; (2) the teacher can write on it much as one uses the chalkboard, but while facing the class; (3) the teacher can use prepared transparencies; and (4) room darkening is not needed due to the extremely bright image produced. Many educators deplore the use of the overhead projector as a substitute for the chalkboard, stating that such uses do not take advantage of what the machine can do, and therefore constitute misuse. It is our belief that no particular harm is done by this application, *if* the teacher realizes what he is doing. Under certain conditions it is advisable to work with the content or material under study in front of the students. For example, the process of writing a poem may take place in front of students as the teacher writes and rewrites and works with the structure and meaning of a poem. While some reasonable alternatives exist including use of the chalkboard and use of preprepared transparencies illustrating the poem-writing process, the use of the overhead projector in the manner described has advantages of immediacy for the student and ease for the instructor. There are other times, however, when it is a real loss not to take advantage of the power of preprepared overhead transparencies. Preprepared overhead transparencies can do much to help the teacher clarify complex subject material for students. By having material already on the transparency, many kinds of presentations may be made more efficient. The time spent before the class writing out material is eliminated —the teacher can move from one display to another by merely replacing one transparency with another. The teacher may develop a topic or concept through either, revealing only portions of a transparency at a time, using hinged cardboard masks, or by using "overlays." When overlays are used, only a portion of the material to be developed is on each of a number of sheets of transparency film. Each sheet is hinged to a mount so that a visual display may be built up a stage at a time. Such procedures as selec-

Carefully developed instructional sequences, variety, clarity, and impact are offered in filmstrips. New materials and viewing devices have created renewed interest in this valuable resource. (Photo courtesy Norman Public Schools.)

Children use audio materials that are part of an instructional system. (Photo courtesy Norman Public Schools.)

tive revelation and use of overlays can do much to aid the teacher in clarifying complex ideas and relationships.

2 × 2 transparencies. The growth in popularity of the 35mm camera with photographers, both amateur and professional, has produced over the years cameras, projectors, and film capable of producing full-color transparencies of extremely high technical quality using equipment and techniques that are simple and widely available. Anyone who has wanted to do so and who could afford it could, for many years now, document a vacation trip with a greater number of sharp, colorful, dazzling "slides" depicting the scenery along the way more extensively than most friends, neighbors, and relatives have wished had been the case. Using the same fine-grain films and processing that have been standard "snapshot" and "vacation slide" materials, it is possible to make graphic materials for classroom use of ultrahigh pictorial quality at a moderate cost. Not only can outdoor scenes, wildlife, indoor views, and people be photographed, but using the Single-Lens Reflex (SLR) type camera, copies of practically anything—books, magazine pictures, large charts, and postage stamps—can be shown on a slide. 35mm transparencies are generally returned from the processor in 2 × 2 cardboard mounts. Because of the popularity of the format, 2 × 2 slide projectors have become known popularly as "35mm projectors." The reason why the technically correct "2 × 2" terminology is to be preferred is because there are a few real applications of the projector that do not involve 35mm transparencies. The two most common are "Super Slides," which are the product of cameras using 127 film and which place a considerably larger transparency than does the 35mm type in the 2 × 2 mount, and transparencies made using the "Instamatic" camera that uses type 126 film cartridges. 2 × 2 slide projectors have virtually replaced the older 3¼ × 4 "Lantern Slide" projector for classroom use. While the ability of lantern slides to resolve the finest detail is unmatched by anything else, the excellent sharpness of which the 35mm format is capable makes the difference of no real consequence in practically any application. In addition to their capabilities, their relative ease of use and common availability have helped to make 2 × 2 transparencies common aids to instruction.

Filmstrips. Technically, a filmstrip is a continuous strip of film on which each individual frame is a transparency for still projection. Filmstrips can be made—and have been—in 70-, 35-, 16-, and even 8mm formats. By far the most common, however, is the 35mm filmstrip. A 35mm filmstrip is made on the same film stock as 35mm slides.[8] Filmstrips have a vertical frame arrangement, in which frames are above and below each other, whereas 35mm slides are located side by side on the film—

---

[8] A film format that was, incidentally, originally created as a motion picture film, and which is still the most common film on which Hollywood movies are made.

before being cut and mounted as individual transparencies. Two filmstrip frames take up the same amount of space on the film as does one "slide."[9] Filmstrips are somewhat less expensive to produce due to the fact that a given amount of film will produce twice as many filmstrip frames as it will slides, and to the fact that filmstrips do not require the materials and labor involved in mounting each frame as an individual slide. However, the equipment required to make filmstrips is not as widely available or inexpensive as is that involved in producing slides. A result of this situation is that while slide sets are often made up by the teacher for his own classroom use, the teacher wishing to use commercially prepared transparency series will more often find the series available in filmstrip form than in 35mm slide form. Another characteristic of filmstrips that makes them well suited to commercial productions in which the nature of the presentation has been carefully worked out and tested for its effectiveness is the fact that, unlike slides in a slide set, individual frames of a filmstrip can not be misplaced or improperly arranged.

A neglected form of filmstrip that could be of great value to classroom teachers is the 16mm filmstrip. While single 16mm frames projected on large screens are significantly less sharp and clear than 35mm, the increasing applications of media to individual study situations, in which a carrel is fitted with a slide or filmstrip viewer and a tape recorder, are ideal ones for the more compact and inexpensive 16mm format. A small 25-foot reel of 16mm film can house over 350 individual frames. The cost to reproduce this, in color, is less than $5.00. At this writing a stumbling block exists with regard to equipment availability for 16mm filmstrips. While a few 16mm filmstrip viewers do exist, they are generally so expensive that the potential cost benefits of using this material are lost in the purchase of the equipment.

Tape Recordings and Phonograph Records

Since the demise of educational radio in the 1940s and 1950s only two forms of audio materials are in common classroom use today: tape recordings and phonograph records. Tape recordings may be made by the teacher from practically any source of sound—lectures, radio, television, and even other tape recordings. Tape recorders are fairly simple to use, and with the advent and popularity of cassette recorders and automatic recording volume controls, the only areas which ever gave the neophyte much trouble (threading and properly setting up the recorder for recording) have been eliminated. While skillful use of the recorder can allow the user to take advantage of more of the potentials in recording, just to

---

[9] Readers who note a similarity between the filmstrip and the format of the "half-frame" 35mm camera are correct—they are the same.

make and play back recordings in ordinary settings requires no more dexterity or skill than that mustered by a first grader. A tape recorder can be used to present prerecorded material from commercial sources. Many of the new curriculum projects have developed instructional systems packages that include tape recordings to not only present material, but to provide a basic control for other media. Most slide and filmstrip projectors can be connected to an inexpensive coupling device that translates tones recorded onto a tape recording into advance signals for the projector. Thus, a tape recording can both present the material and control the visuals required, advancing to a new visual when it is needed. Such slide-tape combinations are also being made by individual teachers. The same coupling device during playback of slide-tape presentations is nearly always a dual purpose device which is also capable of generating the tones used for tape advance. Once a teacher has established points along a narration or musical sequence at which he would like to have visual changes, he connects a slide projector to a tape recorder using the "programmer" and goes through his slide set while recording both the subject material and the advance tones. The teacher can create self-instructional slide-tape programs in this manner and make them available for individual student use. Not only is a tape recorder useful as an information-storage device and a media-control device, but it also can be used in an "interactive mode" with students. Interactions between student and machine, which most people think can only be achieved by "teaching machines," are simple tasks for the ordinary tape recorder. For example, the tape recorder can be used by individual students as a sort of "teaching machine" for most facts and skills that require drill to learn. In the instance of spelling, a child with a list of words which he does not know how to spell may learn the list very quickly by: (1) recording the first spelling word on the list, (2) repeating the spelling of the word silently, very slowly, as the machine is still recording, and (3) repeating the spelling of the word aloud, thereby recording it after the silent pause. Each word on the list is recorded in this fashion—the word, a period of silence, and the correct spelling of the word. When the whole list has been recorded, the child can go back to the beginning and play back his recording. When he hears a word pronounced, he should attempt to spell it on his own. Immediately after his attempt, he will hear the correct spelling. This feedback will be gratifying to the child if he is correct, and it will provide immediate correction if he is wrong. The same techniques may be applied to other areas of learning, such as number facts, history facts, and foreign-language vocabulary. Subject material that is amenable to the "self-programmed" approach is the kind in which a large number of discrete learnings must be accomplished, rather than achievement of understandings of concepts or rules.

Phonograph records, while not so easily produced by the teacher, have unique advantages over tape. Storage and use of records are easier for most people because of both characteristics of the medium and the fact that most people are more familiar with records than they are with working with magnetic tape. Even when compared to the no-threading-required cassette recorder, a phonograph record is easier to use for certain applications. A record is by far easier to use when there is a need to skip portions of material, or return to a previously played selection. On a record it takes no longer to return to a selection which is thirty minutes away than it does to something adjacent to what the class is listening to. Furthermore, in many areas, especially music, prerecorded materials are by far more easily available on record than on tape. There is also some economic advantage to records when compared to prerecorded tapes. While tapes deteriorate with time, records do not. Thus, if a record is carefully and infrequently used, it can outlast a tape recording of the same material. A problem is that school use does not generally lend itself to the careful handling of delicate equipment necessary if records are to realize their potential long life. In certain applications, however, the advantages of records outweigh the problems and limitations and phonograph records become the medium of choice. In such instances, the teacher should do all he can to take proper care of the records, including doing what he can about assuring adequacy of playback equipment to the task of playing records in such a fashion as to not ruin them.

SITUATION 9.2

The Tape Recorder as an Aid to the Teacher

1. As a practice teacher or a teacher in service, plan for the actual use of the tape recorder in enriching learning opportunities in your subject area. Include a statement of objectives and a description of the recording activities you will use. Also describe the physical and mechanical arrangements for using the tape recorder.
2. Set up a tape recorder in any normal classroom situation. Later, in private, listen to the playback and ask yourself such questions as: Is my speech pleasant? Is my enunciation clear and understandable? Is my manner toward children pleasing? Can I learn anything from the children's responses to my questions and leadership?
3. As a teacher, anticipate the problems in language arts, music, or general learning that will arise next week, and make plans for handling them; use the tape recorder.
4. List the ways in which you feel that the use of a tape recorder may be important to your colleagues who are not now using one.

See Walter Arno Wittich and Charles Francis Schuller, *Audio-Visual Materials: Their Nature and Use*, 2d ed., New York: Harper & Row, Publishers, 1957, pp. 320–321.

MEDIA AND INSTRUCTION

The modern concept of the role of media in instruction has its roots in research and developmental experience in learning psychology, systems analysis, and educational media. As recently as ten years ago, educational media specialists tended to brand themselves as "film men" or "television men" or "graphics men." While there is still a need for specialists in these and other areas, the educational media "generalist" has lately come into his own. Media specialists have learned over the years that no one medium is "better" than any other. Additionally, some of the newer and more promising innovations in instruction have cut across specific media lines. Programmed instruction and simulations are prime examples of this development. These two areas will be used to illustrate the general thrust of developments in instructional innovations.

Programmed Instruction

As was noted early in this chapter, the advent of programmed instruction left an indelible mark on educational media and instruction. While many producers and distributors claim widespread usefulness for various teaching-machine designs, the real significance and value of most of them lie in the inherent potential of *all* autoinstructional programs—be they in machine formats or not. A highly respected authority in this area is A. A. Lumsdaine. He describes "autoinstructional devices" as instructional instruments that serve to present information and provide the student with a means to make responses to the material presented.[10] In assessing their potential contribution to education, he states that "autoinstructional methods may represent the most important innovation in education since the advent of the textbook."[11] He has stated also that:

> . . . the control of learner behavior and feedback which is provided by the continuous record of student responses from autoinstructional programs may afford the most promising vehicle yet developed for the analytic experimental study of variables affecting human learning (as well as for the incorporation of research findings in improved instruments).[12]

It should be recognized also that one of the primary advantages of any mediated instructional instrument to research and to day-to-day applica-

[10] A. A. Lumsdaine, "Instruments and Media of Instruction," in N. L. Gage (Ed.), *Handbook of Research on Teaching* (Chicago: Rand McNally & Co., 1963), p. 591.
[11] Lumsdaine, p. 592.
[12] Lumsdaine, p. 608.

tions lies in the fact that the instruction itself is reproducible. All experienced teachers know that, try as they may, they cannot "do the same thing twice" when it comes to repeating an instructional event. So many variables enter into the instructional act—word choice, emphasis, mood, and all the other differences that make one day different from the next. A motion picture film, however, does not have good and bad days. It may be received by classes in varying ways, but the variance is not caused by changes in the film, only by changes in the environment and the viewers. This eliminates a very troublesome variable from research and development in instruction. Systematic development and improvement of instructional instruments is obviously easier for those instruments that present a whole instructional event and can do it repeatedly without change. A slide-tape series, a sound filmstrip, a videotaped television lesson, and motion picture films can all present repeatable instructional events. The additional factor that autoinstructional devices present is that of producing data about the effects and effectiveness of the device or program by virtue of merely using it. Recording and analysis of students' responses as they use the program yield the data. In the case of most autoinstructional devices, the responses required of the student come at frequent-enough intervals to allow an analysis of not only how good a job the program is doing in teaching what it is supposed to teach, but also what parts of the program are working and what parts are not. The extent to which a programmed instruction sequence can be effective is quite high. The most common level of student achievement held to be acceptable by programmers for their products is that 90 percent of the students will retain at least 90 percent of the material. Many programs are written with a 100–100 percent criterion. If, in trial administrations to a large sample of students who meet the prior-knowledge prerequisites required by the program, the success criterion is not met, the program is revised and retested on another group, or it is discarded.

This procedure implies more than the technique involved in carrying it out. It includes, also, an *outlook* about the teaching-learning process. It holds, contrary to the viewpoint of some traditionalists, that when a student fails, it is the fault of the instruction, not the student. While the effects of conventional instruction may need to be viewed somewhere between the two extreme positions, the instructional programmer will blame the program every time—never the student. Either the design of the program will be found faulty, or the program's appropriateness for the student will be questioned. In any case, it is the *program*, not the student, which is held responsible.

It should be clear that the approach to teaching offered by programmed materials is more naturally suited to some education tasks than it is to others. Sensitivity to and awareness of other people, interpersonal interaction skills and processes, social responsibility, and a host of other areas of common concern to the elementary teacher seem clearly better suited to group work and interaction with people, rather than individualized, automated instruction. While realizing the truth of this, teachers need to take advantage of a contribution provided by the programmed instruction movement, and that is a realization of the extent to which an *analytical view* of the instructional process can be of help to that process, no matter what instruction is being contemplated. For example, while it is obvious that to increase interaction skills, one needs to interact, the goal of "increasing interaction skills" should be recognized as being a very broad one. An analysis of that goal might well turn up the fact that among the various alternatives open to the teacher in designing instruction to meet it, individual work with autoinstructional devices may well be the best approach for achievement of certain objectives along the way and other approaches more well suited to other objectives. The last section of this chapter, on multimedia instruction, presents a step-by-step procedure for instructional development which can help teachers design instruction in a systematic fashion using an analytical, problem-solving approach.

Simulations

Although simulation is not exactly new to education, widespread interest in many applications in elementary schools is. The famous Link Trainer, a flight simulator, was a significant factor in our being able to train the numbers of pilots needed in the short time available in the early stages of World War II. Automobile driving simulators, while expensive, have been extremely useful to driver education classes in those school systems able to afford the sizable initial burden of purchase. Simulation events and games have been in common use in disaster-training programs, medical schools, law and business schools throughout the nation for decades. It has only been in recent years, however, that the potential of simulators and simulation games to accomplish a wide variety of educational goals has been realized. A simulation may be defined as the dynamic representation of an ongoing system. All simulations of value in instruction have the additional characteristic of making provision for individuals or groups of students to either run the system or intervene in its running.

SIMULATORS. Sometimes a complex system may be represented by a mechanical device or program—these are simulators. It is possible to simulate human illness with a computer and let medical students attempt to diagnose and treat the "patient." Treatment may be either written instructions to the computer notifying it of the treatment, to which the computer-patient responds with a typewritten description of the effect on "him" of the treatment given. With more money, it is possible to achieve more realism in the simulation by tying the computer into an instrumented model of a person that can visibly react with simulated symptoms and reactions, as controlled by the computer. One computerized simulation in the field of counseling psychology involved programming a computer to react to statements fed to it (or to "converse," as it were) in the manner of a good Rogerian nondirective counselor. A sample of practicing counselors, when given transcripts of "counseling sessions" between clients and the computer along with transcripts of real counseling sessions, were unable to distinguish the real from the simulated sessions. Within certain limits, then, a computer may be programmed to simulate human behavior with some fidelity.

Not all simulations are this complex, nor are all simulators computer-controlled. The Red Cross, local hospitals, or public health agencies can often make available for school use a simulator called the "Resusa-Annie." Annie is a life-size doll, designed to react to efforts at artificial resuscitation in much the same manner as a victim of drowning or asphyxiation. For something to be a training simulator it must not only represent in some fashion the working relationships between parts of a system, as a working model might, but also provide for human intervention in the workings of the system. A motor-powered model airplane is no more than a "model-airplane," but if in some aspects controlling or flying that model is a valid representation of some aspect of flying a real airplane, then for those aspects the model is a simulator. In designing and making training simulators, three basic questions must be asked: (1) What learning objectives will be served by the simulator? (2) What process or system must the simulator represent to allow students to achieve the objectives? and (3) What degree of realism in the simulation will be necessary for the simulation to work?

SIMULATION GAMES.[13] The idea of simulation began to find widespread application by social scientists in the early 1960s. Social scientists can create working models of social systems, international relations, demography and many other processes by *symbolic* rather than physical representations. A social simulation may be "run" by a computer or in game fashion. In a simulation game, participants take roles in the process being simulated and interact as governed by the rules of the game. A number of simulation games have been devised for school use, some of them specifically designed for use at the elementary level.[14] Some sample titles

[13] This topic is also treated, from a somewhat different perspective, in Chapter 4. The reader may wish to refresh his memory by quickly rereading that section before proceeding further.

[14] See Sarane Boocock and E. O. Schild (Eds.), *Simulation Games in Learning* (Beverly Hills, Calif.: Sage Publications, Inc., 1968).

may indicate the range of topics available—Economy, Seal Hunting, Market, Bushman Hunting, and Sierra Leone.[15]

The research available on the effects of simulation games, while not conclusive in many respects, does seem to consistently reveal one strong advantage of simulation games: high effectiveness in creating *empathetic understanding*, that is, knowing "how it feels to be in the other guy's shoes." A number of instructional approaches are suitable for teaching children about, for example, how our government works, but to teach children *how it feels* to be in the position of a legislator when torn between the demands of his constituency and his personal values can be approached by a simulation (and quite possibly very little else but a simulation). The power of simulations to provide meaningful vicarious experiences for children may be one of the primary advantages of simulation for elementary school uses. Elementary teachers have created game situations as a matter of course for years. The creation of new *simulation* games, it seems, would be a natural contribution which elementary teachers can make to their classes and schools.

Implications

Both programmed instruction and simulations are exceedingly powerful tools. We should not underestimate the *potential* of these two innovative instructional approaches. With regard to potential, programmed instruction and simulations are, in a sense, illustrative of an important fact about educational media in general—they have a long way to go before their promise is realized. Two primary implications may be drawn from this. First, if something in its infancy is as powerful as media has become, the adult potential should be staggering. And second, our assessments of an innovation are not well-founded ones if they consider only the present levels of development. It has often been pointed out by social scientists that teachers are among the most conservative of groups with regard to the acceptance of change, and that our system of education is a highly conservative one, being "behind" practically all other areas of endeavor and social institutions in the nation. Whether the reader completely agrees with this or not, such assessments may point out to us that *at least* we teachers should make an active effort to search out, find, develop, and test promising new approaches to old teaching problems.

In the final analysis, it is the problem-oriented approach which instructional technology brings to teaching that seems to hold most promise for improvement of education, not the power of any specific medium or technique (powerful as either can be). The last portion of

[15] These simulation games were devised by Abt Associates, Inc., Cambridge, Mass.

this chapter will provide the reader with one framework for carrying out the task of finding optimal solutions to instructional problems.

MULTIMEDIA INSTRUCTION

The usefulness of a particular medium, such as motion picture film or television or even the printed word, is highest in certain types of applications. While some media *can* be used for practically any teaching-learning job encountered in schools, any medium is most *effectively* used when it is carefully selected and its use based on a rigorous analysis of instructional goals and alternative media and procedures for conducting instruction. A definable unit or course of instruction will be likely to contain a large number of specific objectives. The optimum way to go about achieving one objective may not be optimum for the others. As it turns out, the highly detailed and specific analyses made of instruction that are the product of multimedia instruction design efforts generally yield specifications that call for varying *combinations of media* for various objectives. Often the specifications call for more variety or media sophistication than can be afforded by the school. Systems analysis concepts such as cost effectiveness and subsystem optimization are brought into play at this point to attempt to find the best "fit" between resources (money, time, space, human talents, and so on) and optimum performance of the system. Decisions that produce "trade-offs" are often demanded, so that, for example, an economy in one area can enable something of crucial importance to be achieved in another.

There is no single, accepted step-by-step procedure for developing multimedia instruction. However, there are some threads of similarity running through many suggested approaches found in the literature of instructional design. The remainder of this chapter is devoted to the presentation of a *systems approach* to multimedia instructional design. This approach can be a useful one to the teacher who wishes to improve the teaching-learning processes for which he alone is responsible, or it may be used in large, committee-based efforts at curriculum and instructional improvement on a school- or school system–wide basis.

A Procedure for Developing Multimedia Instruction

A useful procedure for development of multimedia instruction is incorporated in the following steps: (1) identification of specific objectives, (2) analysis of the objectives for determination of type of learning involved, (3) preparation of media and method alternatives, (4) designing instructional approach, (5) implementation, (6) evaluation, and (7) refinement of the program.

Specific objectives are generally accepted to be those written in "behavioral" terms. Robert Mager's short and interesting programmed text in this area can provide any teacher with the skills and knowledge needed to be able to distinguish "good" from "poor" objectives and be able to write good behavioral objectives.[16] The skillful objective-writer can translate practically any cognitive or affective learning into the behavior one could expect to elicit from one who has achieved that learning. It is sometimes believed that only low-level learning can be behaviorally expressed, and often a disdain for "measurable" learning accompanies this belief. However, the more the teacher knows about behavioral objectives, the more he will find them to be appropriate to higher-level school work than he could previously have imagined. The *Taxonomy of Educational Objectives* is highly instructive in this regard.[17] In the cognitive domain, for example, sample behavioral objectives requiring such high-level mental processes as analysis and synthesis are provided.

Analysis of objectives for determination of type of learning can be accomplished in a number of ways. The primary goal of this phase is to figure out, as best one can, what sort of learning processes will be engaged to achieve the learning. One standpoint from which to work through this phase is that provided by Robert Gagné's eclectic compilation of "types of learning."[18] Rather than associate himself exclusively with one theoretical position about learning, Gagné has found that some aspects of some learning theories do a good job of describing some kinds (or types) of learning. Gagné has identified seven major types of learning: signal learning, stimulus-response learning, chaining, verbal association, concept learning, rule learning, and problem solving. Not only does Gagné identify and describe these varieties but he also presents the concept that for each type of learning there exists a unique set of conditions which optimize it. Learning can be more *reliably* achieved through matching appropriate methodology and media to the learning task at hand, and the learning is generally more *efficiently* achieved as a bonus. For example, a common type of learning required by school work is concept learning. Concept learning results in the ability to correctly place an object or quality into a class of objects or qualities. "Gothic architecture" is a concept, as is

[16] Robert Mager, *Preparing Instructional Objectives* (Palo Alto, Calif.: Fearon Publishers, 1962).

[17] See Benjamin Bloom (Ed.), *Taxonomy of Educational Objectives, The Classification of Educational Goals, Handbook I, The Cognitive Domain* (New York: Longmans Green & Company, 1956), and David Krathwohl (Ed.), *Taxonomy of Educational Objectives, The Classification of Educational Goals, Handbook II, The Affective Domain* (New York: David McKay Company, 1964).

[18] Robert Gagné, *The Conditions of Learning*, 2d ed. (New York: Holt, Rinehart and Winston, 1970), Chap. 2.

"yellow," "chair," "round," and so on. A critical condition for the learning of concepts is that the learner become able to distinguish the critical cues (cues may be characteristics, features, dimensions, and so on) from the irrelevant ones. In Gothic architecture, some design and construction aspects are critical to the structure in question, being "Gothic," and others make no difference. A learner, seeing a series of pictures of Gothic cathedrals, might erroneously conclude that any majestic, large church with elaborate decorations, tall towers, and generally ancient appearance is "Gothic." When the learner has in fact acquired this concept, he knows to look for such critical cues as ribbed vaults and flying buttresses. When both the *necessary and sufficient* discriminations can be made, the learner can be expected to have acquired the concept. This means, then, that media which help the learner in his task of identifying and discriminating cues will be the most helpful ones. For learning the concept of "Gothicness," we can see the clear-cut need for visual representation. It is interesting to note that in this example, as well as in a good proportion of school learning tasks, good line drawings may be even better than photographs, due to the fact that the drawings may present less irrelevant detail, thereby helping the learner make the first discriminations. Each type of learning, according to Gagné, has some unique quality to it which makes some forms of instruction preferable to other possible forms. Especially helpful to elementary teachers are his observations about the conditions required to bring about chaining, concept learning, and rule learning.

Preparation of media and method alternatives should be accomplished through making use of what one has learned from the analysis of objectives and from what one knows about the specifics of his school environment. Implementation of the results of analysis of objectives will help the teacher determine what media and methods would be most psychologically appropriate, but such an analysis does not tell him anything about the *feasibility* of this ideal approach. The feasibility of using most materials and equipment depends, in all but the most well-equipped schools, on what materials and equipment are available. While a few situations do exist in which a teacher may specify (and get) any instructional materials he wishes to use, most of us must make frequent compromises. An additional essential element in large-scale instructional development projects is the assignment of personnel roles. Here again, compromises often must be made between the desire to have all personnel be "perfect" for the job, and proposing to use personnel resources available that are less than perfect or complete. A key aspect of this step in the process is that of preparing *alternative* approaches to each task. Just as good problem-solving behavior generally includes a consideration of a number of reasonable alternatives before arriving at a decision or solution, so does good instructional planning involve proposing for consideration many reasonable ways to achieve each objective.

Designing the instructional approach will require that decisions be made between and among the available instructional alternatives as they fit with the conditions. Due to the fact that most goals that are the starting point for instructional development projects translate themselves into many behavioral objectives, and to the fact that these sets of objectives generally fall into more than one type of learning, a given lesson or project generally calls for more than one medium as the best approach to conducting instruction. One objective may be best served through a film, another through still pictures, and yet another through live demonstration and student practice with supervision. It is primarily in this way that we find our strongest needs for "multimedia" design. Sometimes (though not often) a number of simultaneous media may be helpful, but information transmission research suggests that this sort of "multimedia barrage" more often impedes than fosters learning.[19] To have instructional plans specify a number of different media, requiring that each medium be used where it is "strongest," is a major goal of most instructional design efforts. Design, of course, often involves more than selecting a good medium for each behavioral objective. Good instructional design includes consideration of the overall impact of various portions of the package when taken in sequence. Instructional strategies can be the product of reflecting upon the probable effects of various media/method combinations in various sequences. Sometimes a true synthesis of the available possibilities will be the result of such reflection, and that synthesis will be an original and uniquely effective approach to an instructional problem.

Implementation of an instructional system includes physical preparations as well as carrying out the instruction as specified by the instructional design. Preparations will often include obtaining the necessary materials through purchase, rent, or borrowing. Sometimes materials will be specified which must be locally made. The instructional design should include specifications for materials in enough detail so that the question "What is needed here?" is answered clearly and completely by the specifications themselves. The manner in which the instructional program is carried out is also specified by the design, so that scope and sequence, content and methodology, are well known by the teacher or teachers participating in the project. While no specific staff utilization pattern is common to all instructional development efforts, the "team-teaching" pattern seems to often be associated with them. The team-teaching pat-

---

[19] See Robert Travers, *Research and Theory Related to Audiovisual Information Transmission*, USOE Contract No. 3–20–003, 1967. Distributed by Western's Campus Bookstore, Western Michigan University, Kalamazoo, Michigan 47001.

tern is a natural one when many media are used to help carry out teaching because of the inherent flexibility of the team-teaching approach. Many of the media or instructional methods specified in an instructional design will be individual study–based approaches, and many other approaches specified in the design are well suited to large-group presentation for efficiency's sake. Team teaching can provide the designer with an implementation pattern that will provide the needed flexibility in student grouping.

Evaluation takes place under school roofs for a wide variety of purposes. Possibly the most common purposes of evaluation in our schools are those related to the student. In other words, the product of a measurement effort, like a test, is the evaluation of the student. The value or purpose of such evaluations is beyond the scope of "evaluation" as it is meant here. Here, evaluation is conceived of as a part of the instructional design process, and is a tool to find out something about the effectiveness of the instruction. The means by which this end is achieved is measurement of student learning, but the purpose is program evaluation (it is understood that one measurement effort can produce data that are useful to *both* the student and to the program, but the possibility of *program* evaluation independent of any judgments about the student should be realized). As noted earlier, programmed instruction has a special strength in this area, because data are produced about the effects and effectiveness of the program and each part of it as the program is being used. Often, when a program fails to produce hoped-for results in student learning, analysis of the record of student responses—as produced as each one proceeds through the program—will indicate what part or parts of the instruction are contributing most to the problem. Generally, a greater mass of data about student progress is found to be most useful. In many situations, information about how students *feel* about various aspects of a program will be as useful as anything else available. An otherwise inexplicable failure rate at some juncture may be found attributable to the fact that the students just "don't like it."

Refinement of an instructional system involves making use of the feedback information received through the evaluation of the system's effectiveness. Putting the feedback to use may involve redesign of parts or all of the system and implementing the system again in its revised form. Refinement should be continual for all but the most limited training tasks. In a training environment, once stringent goals for training effectiveness and efficiency have been met, the program may justifiably be reused in one form until changes in the "outside world" make the training goals obsolete, or new developments in instructional design make previously unattainable standards feasible. The task of "education," however, is different. Who can say he has done all there is to do for a child? One can only say he has done his best, and it is for this reason that instructional system refinement in elementary schools is an unending process.

SUMMARY

1. Instructional technology is seen as being, besides equipment, materials, and instructional development techniques, a way of looking at problems and tasks in education.

2. Education may someday become significantly changed for the better through widespread, intelligent application of the increased power that a high-level technology produces.

3. There are a number of kinds of television—commercial, educational, public, and instructional—all of which may be productively used in teaching. Educational television has been demonstrated to be capable of efficiently, reliably, inexpensively, and interestingly provide millions of children with the instruction they need to acquire important facts, skills, and concepts. Instructional television is characterized by usefulness in specific local applications.

4. For many years, films have provided inputs to classrooms that could not be provided otherwise, but with widespread and common application of television to the same problems, the roles in education which films will serve are changing.

5. The wide variety of other instructional instruments—overhead projectors, slide and filmstrip projectors, and tape recordings and phonograph records —can make various unique contributions to what a teacher may wish to accomplish, each instrument having its own characteristic effects and areas of usefulness.

6. Two examples of instructional design approaches—programmed instruction and simulation—not only serve to demonstrate what impact sophisticated instructional design is presently making in education, but also indicate what we may be able to do in schools in the foreseeable future.

7. A step-by-step "systems" approach to instructional development can be used by teachers as well as groups of educators to develop and improve the quality and effectiveness of educational programs to achieve specified goals.

RECOMMENDED READINGS

Boocock, Sarane S., and E. O. Schild (Eds.), *Simulation Games in Learning.* Beverly Hills, Calif.: Sage Publications, Inc., 1968. A comprehensive treatment of the rationale and status of simulation games in learning.

Brown, James W., Richard B. Lewis, and Fred F. Harcleroad, *AV Instruction: Media and Methods*, 3d ed. New York: McGraw-Hill Book Company, 1969. Presents a comprehensive overview of audiovisual production and utilization techniques.

Bushnell, Don D., and Dwight W. Allen (Eds.), *The Computer in American Education.* New York: John Wiley and Sons, Inc., 1967. Provides the reader with an excellent grounding in the scope of computer applications in both providing instruction and managing the education enterprise.

Dale, Edgar, *Audiovisual Methods in Teaching,* 3d ed. Hinsdale, Ill.: The Dryden Press, Inc., 1969. Like Brown, Lewis, and Harcleroad, above, this text is a good basic resource of audiovisual materials and equipment production and use.

Espich, James E., and Bill Williams, *Developing Programmed Instructional Materials, A Handbook for Program Writers.* Palo Alto, Calif.: Fearon Publishers, 1967. An excellent "how to" book, with procedures clearly outlined for writing a number of different styles of programmed instruction. Places program construction within the framework of system development.

Gagné, Robert, *The Conditions of Learning,* 2d ed. New York: Holt, Rinehart and Winston, Inc., 1970. Synthesizes the work of learning psychologists from many different orientations to arrive at a taxonomy of types of learning. Analysis of objectives to determine type of learning required has clear implications for instructional design—implications that the second edition makes explicit.

Kemp, Jerrold E., *Planning and Producing Audiovisual Materials,* 2d ed. San Francisco: Chandler Publishing Company, 1968. A comprehensive textbook and reference manual for materials production techniques. This book also contains sections on photography, motion picture production, and television production.

Knirk, Frederick G., and John W. Childs, *Instructional Technology, A Book of Readings.* New York: Holt, Rinehart and Winston, 1968. A highly informative book that provides a good overview of the newer ways of looking at instruction and its improvement through systems, programming, use of media, school-plant design, and analysis of psychological factors in learning.

Koenig, Allen E., and Ruane Hill (Eds.), *The Farther Vision, Educational Television Today.* Madison, Wis.: University of Wisconsin Press, 1967. A number of distinguished contributors present informative essays on the structure, functions, problems, and future of ETV.

Lumsdaine, A. A., "Instruments and Media of Instruction," in N. L. Gage (Ed.), *Handbook of Research on Teaching.* Chicago: Rand McNally & Company, 1963. This chapter represents a most thorough and scholarly review of the research in educational media. The framework under which the author has organized his review is a particularly enlightening one, as are his suggestions for further research.

Mager, Robert F., *Preparing Instructional Objectives.* Palo Alto, Calif.: Fearon Publishers, 1962. This is an easy-to-read, delightfully written, programmed text that has as its primary goal enabling the reader to write "behavioral objectives" and to distinguish properly written behavioral objectives from those that are not properly written.

Minor, Ed, and Harvey R. Frye, *Techniques for Producing Visual Instructional Media*. New York: McGraw-Hill Book Company, 1970. A media production text, strong in its clear presentation of a large number of different techniques relating to strong visual media.

Nelms, Henning, *Thinking With a Pencil*. New York: Barnes and Noble, 1964. An exceptionally thorough treatment of the fundamentals and many other topics and techniques relating to drawing for communication.

Pipe, Peter, *Practical Programming*. New York: Holt, Rinehart and Winston, Inc., 1966. This short, concise paperback manual presents techniques and procedures for creating programmed instruction. Most of the material in this book is useful to classroom teachers wishing to use systematic procedures to increase effectiveness of instruction on specific topics or skills.

Trow, William Clark, *Teacher and Technology*. New York: Appleton-Century-Crofts, 1963. This book presents an interesting, often original account of the interplay between teachers' jobs and the work potential of educational technology.

Chapter 10

Teaching Culturally Different Children

Cultural disadvantage is an all-purpose phrase, and a somewhat self-conscious one. It refers of course to the variety of social, economic, and ethnic-interracial factors which impede full freedom of choice and which destroy the individual's right to maximum opportunity.

B. McKendall, Jr., "Breaking the Barriers of Cultural Disadvantage and Curriculum Imbalance," *Phi Delta Kappan*, Vol. 46, No. 5 (1965), p. 307.

Children in middle- and upper-class homes listen to the spoken word at an early age, are encouraged to speak at an early age, and have many experiences that stimulate the development of concepts. Children who grow up in rural or urban slums are different in their language patterns and in their rate of mental development; they have not ordinarily had a great variety of experiences that stimulate mental activity. These children are called culturally deprived, culturally disadvantaged, or culturally different.

A combination of environmental factors may cause these children to enter school with differences in language, dress, behavior, and readiness for learning school subjects. These factors frequently include poverty, low educational level of parents, and a defeatist attitude on the part of parents in relation to the life chances of their children. Unless the school makes special efforts to meet the needs of these children, they are not likely to experience equality of educational opportunity.

IDENTIFICATION OF THE CULTURALLY DIFFERENT

If teachers who belong primarily to the middle class are to work effectively with culturally different children, they must gain insight into the sub-cultures to which the children have been exposed. Deciding who are the culturally different is more complicated than may appear. Fantini and Weinstein have stated:

> The disadvantaged cannot be defined by race, residence, jobs, or be-havior alone. Although we tend to think first of such districts as Harlem, the disadvantaged are to be found also in small towns, in the rural slums of backwoods Appalachia, in the Spanish barrios of El Paso, on American Indian reservations—or on the fashionable streets of Scarsdale. They are black, white, red, and yellow; with or without parents; hungry or overfed; they are the children of the jobless, the migrant worker, or the employed.[1]

Perhaps the characteristic that most culturally different children have in common is that they do not have sufficient opportunity for the full development of their human potential: to develop a feeling of personal worth, and to be recognized by others as worthy human beings.

How They Live

SLUM DWELLERS. At least two-thirds of the residents of the inner city are Negroes, Puerto Ricans, Mexican-Americans, or members of some other minority group; 70 percent of the Negro population lives in the inner city. Ragan and Henderson have characterized *old city, middle-aged city,* and *new city.* Old city, which is sometimes referred to as "inner city," is described in part as follows:

> The majority of old-city residents live in dilapidated, insect- and rodent-infested multiple-family dwellings; streets are congested and parking space is insufficient; school and recreation facilities are inadequate. This area is occupied by predominantly low-income whites and nonwhites, with the majority being nonwhite.[2]

These families lack money to buy adequate food, shelter, or clothing; minimum physical comfort and security are unknown to them. Many poor

---

[1] Mario D. Fantini and Gerald Weinstein, *The Disadvantaged: Challenge to Education* (New York: Harper & Row, Publishers, 1968), p. 5.

[2] William B. Ragan and George Henderson, *Foundations of American Education* (New York: Harper & Row, Publishers, 1970), p. 177.

children live in tenements or ramshackle apartments. No matter where they live they seldom have adequate garbage collection, an adequate water supply, or functioning sewers. Poverty separates the slum dweller from the rest of society and forces the family to live in low-rent areas where the landlords are not motivated to keep their buildings in good repair.

Because of poverty and ignorance there is a high rate of illness among slum dwellers. The poor nutritional state of the mother, resulting from improper prenatal care, leads to a situation in which many babies suffer from anemias and physical disabilities. Once a baby is delivered, a physician is seldom called except in an emergency. One of the health hazards faced by children in the urban ghetto is lead poisoning. Lead-based paint is not used in modern buildings, but many old apartments in the slums still have the toxic paint on crumbling walls, ceilings, and window frames. Young children often pick up pieces of the paint and put them in their mouths. If they digest these paint chips, they may contract lead poisoning. Seven hundred cases of lead poisoning were detected by Chicago public-health officials in 1968. Few mothers in slum areas take advantage of free health services to have their children immunized; symptoms of disease or illness are frequently ignored. The poor generally resort first to self-medication, then to help from friends and relatives, and then to paraprofessionals such as druggists. It is only when all these fail that a medical doctor is consulted. Hunter has stated:

> In a city where slums represent about 20 percent of the residential area as much as 50 percent of the disease will be in that area. The Hough section of Cleveland is such an area. There the death rate from influenza and pneumonia is 44.7 per 100,000 population as against a rate of 29.7 for the city as a whole. Stillbirths are at the rate of 28.7 per 1000 live births, compared with a city rate of 17.9. The accident rate is among the highest in the city. These are health problems related to poverty.[3]

The extended family is a familiar phenomenon in the slums. It exists when the basic family and other adult relatives live under the same roof. When both parents are working, aunts, uncles, grandmothers, or grandfathers can take care of young children in the family. Frequently the income of the family can be supplemented by adult relatives. These advantages, however, are generally offset by overcrowding and lack of privacy for members of the basic family. When overcrowding exists privacy is missing, family clashes are fostered, normal parent-child relationships become difficult, and a sense of shame smothers family loyalty. It is difficult to estimate the harm that can come to children as a result of overcrowding in the home. It makes it difficult for children to develop a

[3] David R. Hunter, *The Slums: Challenge and Response* (New York: The Free Press, 1968), p. 77.

sense of self-sufficiency and individuality, to build identification with parents, and to do any school work at home.

The father is frequently uneducated, unskilled, and unemployed. The black worker is generally the last to be employed and the first to be laid off the job. It is not unusual on a weekday morning to find unemployed adults lingering on the street corners. Even when the father does have work the child sees him engaged in menial tasks such as dishwashing, garbage collecting, or street sweeping. The black child, especially, is likely to see his father employed at tasks that keep him in dirty work clothing while the white people he sees are more likely to be clean, well dressed, and generally prosperous. This situation tends to cause the child to develop a negative self-image and to begin to doubt his life chances.

MOTHER-CENTERED HOMES. The general disorganization of family life caused by frequent divorces, desertions, and common-law marriages is psychologically damaging to children who live in the slums. One study of a slum area indicated that fathers were permanently absent from the homes of more than half the youths responding to questions. There was a tendency for stepfathers or other father surrogates to be present. The mother was generally perceived as the boss in these homes. The position of the mother is indicated by the following statement:

> From the interviews it was clear that in subcommunities where there are proportionately more broken homes and illegitimate children than in other sections of the city, derogatory statements about a youth's mother are crushing blows at not only the *most* significant other person in his home but, often, the *only* significant other person in the home.[4]

There is considerable evidence that boys who grow up surrounded and dominated by women develop a sense of role confusion, have problems in handling aggression and accepting responsibility, and find decision making difficult. The elementary school should provide both black and white male teachers to serve as role models for culturally disadvantaged boys; develop resource units dealing with differences in role expectations for boys and for girls in our society; and use parent-teacher conferences to emphasize the importance of encouraging boys to assume responsibilities in the home.

Characteristics of Slum Schools

Schools in slum areas, which should be better than schools in other areas because of the lack of educational opportunities in the homes, are substandard in many respects.

1. There are fewer facilities for both education and recreation.

[4] Ragan and Henderson, pp. 198–199.

2. The buildings are generally older than those in other areas.

3. The schools are less likely to provide remedial facilities and programs than are schools in higher-income areas.

4. Substitute teachers provide a greater proportion of the instruction than in schools in other areas.

5. The high rate of teacher turnover in slum schools and the reluctance of more experienced teachers to remain in these schools mean that children in the slums are generally taught by the less experienced teachers. Indeed, public school teachers in the large cities generally begin their teaching careers in slum schools.

6. Teachers in slum schools frequently devote almost as much time to discipline as they do to instruction.

School Characteristics and Pupil Achievement

There is evidence that the achievement of minority pupils is influenced more by the characteristics of the schools they attend than is that of majority pupils.[5]

1. Twenty percent of the achievement of Negroes in the South is associated with the particular schools they go to, whereas only 10 percent of the achievement of whites in the South is.

2. Among the facilities (science laboratories, for example) that show some relationship to achievement are several for which schools attended primarily by minority pupils are less well equipped than are white schools.

3. Improving the school attended by a minority pupil will increase his achievement more than will improving the school of a white child increase his.

4. The quality of teachers shows a strong relationship to pupil achievement; it has more influence on the achievement of minority pupils than it does on that of majority pupils.

5. It appears that pupil achievement is strongly related to the educational backgrounds and aspirations of other pupils in the school. The effect is less for white pupils than for any minority group other than Orientals.

These findings argue strongly for providing schools for minority groups with excellent equipment, outstanding teachers, and contact with other pupils who have excellent achievement records and high-level educational aspirations.

It is a widely accepted belief that the ghetto school cannot be improved substantially without the understanding and support of parents

[5] U.S. Office of Education, *Equality of Educational Opportunity* (OE-38000) (Washington, D.C.: U.S. Department of Health, Education, and Welfare, 1966), pp. 20–22.

and other members of the neighborhood. The public schools of Chicago began a project in 1960 that was based on the premise that ghetto schools could not treat the problems of children effectively without working with the parents. The goals of the project were to plan cooperative programs with the parents to increase school attendance, to raise the levels of school achievement, and to increase vocational competence. Later, programs were added to upgrade the quality of family life and to encourage community participation. Staff members, in addition to regular classroom teachers, included a social worker, a home economist, a youth counselor, and a parent-education counselor. The project was successful in getting parents more interested and involved in the activities of the home, school, and community and in helping them learn techniques of working together toward the same goals. Unless parents are involved in school-improvement projects they are likely to resent efforts of teachers and social workers to improve conditions in the home and neighborhood. One social worker reported:

> The first thing people think when they learn you are a social worker is that you are nosy. The second thing they think is that you are middle class and that is another reason for them to resent you or mistrust you or dislike you.[6]

Disadvantages Suffered by Low-Income Children

It is perhaps not possible to enumerate all the effects of living in poverty in the home and of attending a substandard school. The differences in home environments seem to account for many of the disadvantages suffered by lower-class children as compared to middle-class children.

1. The inferior quality of the language used in the home and the poor speech habits limit language development before the child enters school and restrict the number and variety of words that the child recognizes. As the child's oral vocabulary is an important factor in learning to read, the child from the lower-class home is at a disadvantage in this respect.

2. Families in the slums have less time, opportunity, and desire to take their children on trips to zoos, museums, stores of different neighborhoods. The children also have fewer experiences with books, pictures, films, and music.

3. Children have fewer opportunities for solving problems or for thinking about a variety of issues as compared with other children in more stimulating environments.

---

[6] Louise Daugherty, "Working with Disadvantaged Parents," N.E.A. Journal, 52, December 1963, pp. 18–20.

4. Parents spend little time in conversation with children and do not encourage children to ask questions or express their thoughts or feelings.

5. Discipline in the disadvantaged home tends to be harsh and authoritarian—the "good" child is the one who remains quiet and out of the way. The child brings this experience to school with him, and this makes it difficult to get him to express his ideas in language.

6. A positive view of self is generally recognized as a prerequisite for success in school. The child gains his view of self from others, particularly from others who are regarded by him as important. The child from a low-income family may not be able to dress as attractively as others, his language does not conform to that used by the majority, and he does not achieve as well in school subjects as others. Consequently, he develops a feeling that he is disliked, unwanted, and unworthy. One of the most important responsibilities of the teacher is, therefore, to help the culturally disadvantaged child to develop a favorable image of self. Establishing schools that draw pupils from various ethnic, racial, and socioeconomic groups sometimes provides a means for enhancing self-images for low-income children. Developing and understanding by all pupils of the contributions of different cultural groups, providing opportunities for pupils to experience success in less academic tasks, capitalizing as far as possible on the disadvantaged pupil's special abilities, and providing opportunities for the pupil who is less able academically to assume leadership and responsibility for certain routine school tasks may prove useful.

SITUATION 10.1

American Indians in Slums

Not all slums exist in large cities. The El Paso (Texas) *Times* for July 12, 1970, carried an article on page 1-B titled "First Americans Residents of Vast Slum Areas." The article described conditions of living on an Indian reservation in the United States that were not too much different from those in city slums.

1. Thirty percent of the households did not have indoor toilets.
2. Twenty percent of the homes did not have running water.
3. Thin walls allowed daylight to come through a thousand tiny openings.
4. Roughly 30 percent of the people are receiving some form of public assistance, and it is estimated that that many more should be but have not asked.
5. Most Indian children come out of public school hating white people because of their condescending attitude.

   Find out from the Bureau of Indian Affairs or from other sources what is being done to improve living conditions and schools for Indian children.

Children enrich their experience when they work with
other children who differ from themselves. (Photo
courtesy Oklahoma City Public Schools.)

Tutorial service is provided for pupils who have been
deprived of a stimulating environment before they entered
school. (Photo courtesy Oklahoma City Public Schools.)

APPALACHIA: A FEEDER OF URBAN SLUMS. Poverty in the United States, particularly as it existed in the city slums, received a great deal of study during the decade of the 1960s. Franklin Parker has called attention to another depressed area that has not received so much attention. He wrote:

> Crucial inner city problems were examined and alleviatory programs were started. But less was known about the great feeders of urban slums— the poor rural areas where automation had squeezed people out of farming, mining, and manufacturing. Migrating to the cities for work and finding themselves ill-suited for urban life, they swelled the ranks of the jobless and swamped the welfare rolls.[7]

According to Parker, Appalachia has an area of approximately 175,000 square miles, contains sections of 13 states from New York to Alabama and Georgia, has 397 counties, and has a population of 18 million people— almost one-tenth of that of the United States. He says that this region has the nation's greatest concentration of deprived people.

The people of this region have a culture that differs from that of other minority groups. They have strong family and kinship ties; there is a harsh, authoritarian relationship between the father and the children; and they are slow to change their traditional ways when they move to a new environment. These and other characteristics of Appalachian people must be considered by teachers and curriculum planners.

QUALITY EDUCATION FOR THE CULTURALLY DIFFERENT

It will be both difficult and costly to provide high quality educational programs for all our culturally different children. There are, however, several compelling reasons for making determined efforts to do so. The first reason lies in the fact that our nation can ill afford the waste of human talent that is a natural consequence of substandard schools in slum areas. It has been said that when we consider all forms of wasted talent ". . . the one that must lie heaviest on our conscience is our disadvantaged minorities."[8] Second, providing quality education ranks high on the list of priorities when plans for rebuilding the inner cities and checking urban blight are discussed. What is needed in the slum areas is not just schools that are as good as those in other parts of the city; these schools must be better than those in other parts of the city to make up for the influence of deprivation in the homes and neighborhoods.

The dingy, antiquated school buildings in slum areas will need to

---

[7] Franklin Parker, "Appalachia: Education in a Depressed Area," *Phi Kappa Phi Journal*, Fall 1970, pp. 27–38.

[8] The Rockefeller Panel Reports, *Prospects for America* (Garden City, N.Y.: Doubleday & Company, Inc., 1958), p. 5.

be replaced with modern buildings that provide adequate space for modern teaching strategies. Much smaller classes, teachers with special preparation for working with culturally different children, more remedial programs, more adequate recreational facilities, and resource centers that contain an ample supply of books plus the most useful products of instructional technology will be needed.

SITUATION 10.2

Compensatory Education

Studies of conditions in slum-area homes reveal (1) that non-standard English is learned in the home, (2) that there is very little communication between parents and children, and (3) that there are few books, pictures, toys, or other objects to stimulate communication in these homes. Find out and discuss in class how compensatory education programs help children overcome these deprivations.

A survey of educational opportunity conducted by the United States Office of Education showed that when children from poor homes were placed in schools with children from middle-class homes they did better work than did the children who remained in schools attended primarily by children from poor homes.[9] The schools in New York City have been busing thousands of children from the ghettos to predominantly white schools for many years. The children who have been bused seem to have developed better attitudes toward themselves, their school, and their white classmates than they had in the beginning. While the children who were bused did read better than their counterparts who remained in the ghetto schools, 46 percent of the fifth graders and 51 percent of the sixth graders were reading one year below the standard for the grade.[10]

A third compelling reason for providing excellent schools for slum areas arises from one of our most cherished ideals—equality of opportunity. It is equality of opportunity, rather than equality of possessions or achievement, that is the essence of democracy. James Truslow Adams said, "But there has been also the American dream, that dream of a land in which life should be better and richer and fuller for every man, with opportunities for each according to his ability or achievement."[11]

[9] Harold Howe II, "Blueprint for Education," *Parents Magazine*, Vol. 41, No. 59, October 1966.

[10] E. G. Sherburne (Ed.), "Help and No Help for Ghetto Children," *Science News*, Vol. 92, No. 488, December 9, 1967.

[11] James Truslow Adams, *The Epic of America* (Boston: Little, Brown & Company, 1931), p. 404.

It will obviously cost many billions of dollars to provide the quality of education needed for culturally different children not only in the slums of the great cities but in the rural slums of Appalachia, on American Indian reservations, and elsewhere. There is, however, no other expedient that has a chance of ensuring a decent America in the future. Cities and states cannot raise anything like the amount of money needed. The leaders in our federal government will, therefore, need to begin thinking in terms of many billions of dollars for this purpose instead of a billion or so. The Elementary and Secondary Education Act passed by Congress in 1965 provided $1.5 billion in aid for disadvantaged children. The United States Office of Education reported in 1968 that only 8 million of the nation's 16.8 million children who need compensatory education actually participated in programs financed from this source.[12]

Another effort to improve the quality of education for culturally different children as well as to provide better programs for all children and youth is the educational park. School district boundaries are altered so that the resources of the entire metropolitan area are available for developing better school programs. The larger school attendance unit—sometimes enrolling 20,000 or more students—permits the school to provide a greater variety as well as a greater quantity of services and equipment than would be economically feasible for a smaller school unit. The educational park extends the neighborhood school concept to embrace an entire metropolitan area. Consultants from many leading universities are helping cities throughout the nation to plan educational parks.

Most educators realize that only a small beginning has been made toward providing quality education for culturally different children. School districts have been unable to replace old, decrepit buildings with modern school plants; remedial programs, recreational facilities, instructional resources, and specialized personnel have not kept pace with the need; and funds appropriated by the federal government for compensatory education have provided programs for less than half the children needing these programs. Compensatory education programs such as "Head Start" have helped children make gains in achievement, but these gains are soon lost when the children enter a substandard school. In the final analysis, therefore, the solution lies primarily in providing superior schools for depressed areas. This would include (1) services for children under six years of age; (2) specialized school personnel such as socal workers, guidance specialists, remedial reading teachers, and school psychologists; (3) a curriculum that recognizes the special problems involved in teaching culturally different children; (4) teachers who have had special preparation for working with low-income children; (5) an organization or setting for learning that elimi-

[12] U.S. Office of Education, *Education for the Disadvantaged—An Evaluative Report on Title I for the Year 1968* (Washington, D.C.: Government Printing Office, 1968).

nates the lock-step and provides for continuous progress and the individualization of instruction; and (6) a modern school building that provides large, open spaces for a variety of learning activities and for full utilization of learning resources.

Methods and Materials for the Culturally Different

Every facet of teaching that is treated in this book is involved in teaching the culturally different child: individualizing and personalizing teaching, making discipline educative, developing useful skills, developing more effective teaching strategies, organizing to maximize learning, and using modern procedures for evaluating pupil progress. The teacher who works with culturally different children needs to be familiar with recent research and successful innovations in these and other phases of teaching.

Although space is not available in this chapter to discuss problems of teaching the various elementary school subjects to culturally different children, a few generalizations that characterize approaches that have been relatively successful may be useful. The following list was taken from a paper written by Miriam L. Goldberg:[13]

1. Each pupil's status in each learning area has to be ascertained. Teaching has to begin where the pupil is, and materials must be appropriate to his present level. No assumptions can be made about the child's prior knowledge derived from home or neighborhood experiences.

2. Each pupil merits respect as a person, appreciation for his efforts, and understanding of his problems. The teacher must not show by word, look, or gesture that the child's inability to perform adequately or his lack of comprehension of even the most rudimentary concepts is shocking or disturbing.

3. All procedures need to be paced in accordance with the pupil's speed of learning. No assumption should be made that a child has grasped what he has been taught until he is able to demonstrate his grasp over and over again in a variety of contexts.

4. The learning situation needs to have a high degree of structure and consistency so that the child knows what is expected of him at all times and is neither confused nor tempted to test the limits through inappropriate behavior.

5. The learning situation should provide a maximum of positive reinforcement and a minimum of negative reinforcement. Self-teaching ma-

---

[13] Miriam L. Goldberg, "Methods and Materials for Educationally Disadvantaged Youth," in A. Harry Passow, Miriam Goldberg, and Abraham J. Tannenbaum (Eds.), *Education of the Disadvantaged* (New York: Holt, Rinehart and Winston, 1967), pp. 395–396.

terials, as well as the teacher, should confront the learner with as few tasks as possible in which there is a high probability of error.

6. The classroom, as well as afterschool learning activities, should provide as much one-to-one teacher-pupil contact as possible.

7. Materials should be related to the world of the learner but not limited to his immediate environment. Stories about cowboys and rockets may prove more exciting and thus a better learning medium than those about the local firehouse or the sanitation truck.

8. One additional proposition needs to be stated, derived not from evidence but from the basic values underlying education in a democracy. Although the school must start with the learner where he is, its responsibility is to enable him to move as far as he can go—which is often much further than he himself regards as his limits.

SITUATION 10.3
Methods and Materials

From your reading and from discussion with experienced teachers extend the above list of generalizations about methods and materials to use with the culturally different.

TEACHERS FOR THE CULTURALLY DIFFERENT

Recruiting an adequate supply of understanding and skilled teachers for. culturally different children is a difficult task. Providing in-service education programs for these teachers is another difficult undertaking. The preparation of teachers for children in slum areas has been a neglected area in teacher education. Most city school systems find it necessary to assign most of their beginning teachers to schools in low-income areas is order to meet regulations relating to the ratio of black to white teachers. Many of these teachers have had little contact with life in the slums. It has been estimated that 95 percent of the teachers in the United States are middle-class in their orientation. When these teachers are assigned to schools in the slums, they generally regard the assignment as a form of punishment and look forward to the first opportunity to be transferred to another school where the environment is more congenial.

Successful Teachers of Culturally Different Pupils

Many valuable suggestions relating to the qualities of successful teachers of the culturally different can be gleaned from the Recommended Readings listed at the end of this chapter. Only a few of these qualities can be mentioned here. The student should understand that successful teachers of the culturally different are not all cast in the same mold. Although these teachers may be similar in respect to many traits, perceptions, and behaviors, they may differ greatly with respect to a few. The creative teacher is not one who follows blindly the methods he learned in college; he is capable of developing his own unique methods to meet the demands of changing situations and of students whose needs vary over a wide range. Combs has stated the situation as follows:

> We may define the effective teacher formally as a unique human being who has learned to use himself effectively and efficiently to carry out his own and society's purposes in the education of others.[14]

1. The successful teacher of the culturally different child understands the image that the child has of himself, his school, his teacher, and his chances for success. Many studies have found that children from low-income families generally have a negative self-image. The successful teacher helps the child develop a more positive self-image.

2. The successful teacher of culturally different children understands that the language that the child uses is not the standard English that the school expects, but that it is the only kind the child has had an opportunity to learn in his home and neighborhood and that it has been functional in these situations. The teacher knows that the children must learn to speak the standard dialect of the larger community fluently in order to become successful. The children do not, however, have to give up the dialect that they have learned in the home in order to learn a second one. After all, most of us have a more formal dialect that we use on occasion and a less formal one that we use on other occasions. Since teachers have little difficulty in teaching a second language to elementary school children, they should be able to teach them a second dialect.

3. The successful teacher respects the culturally different children, understands why they seem to make little effort to learn, and why they look upon the school as the agent of an alien society. The teacher does not condone aggressive, hostile behavior; rather, the teacher uses his knowledge about the children to help them acquire knowledge and skills that will open doors of opportunity to them. He rewards each tiny success of a pupil, uses every opportunity for deserved praise, and withholds harsh criticisms when progress is slow. But, above all, he is honest; he doesn't pretend that a pupil's work is good when it isn't.

4. Successful teachers realize that culturally different children have not learned how to listen to adults talk. There is very limited conversation

---

[14] Arthur W. Combs, *The Professional Education of Teachers* (Boston: Allyn and Bacon, Inc., 1965), p. 9.

between children and adults in the home. In fact, children do not have their meals with their parents in many homes. Much is learned in school by listening to the teacher, to other pupils, and to films and recordings. Learning how to listen, therefore, becomes as much a part of the curriculum as learning how to read.

5. The successful teacher is consistent. Riessman has stated:

> Teaching deprived children does not consist of gimmicks or tricks. Much more decisive are certain basic attitudes. Effective teachers use different techniques—there is not just one right approach, although there are many *wrong* approaches. For example, toughness and brutality are most ineffective. Perhaps the best overall principle is to be consistent. These children want a teacher on whom they can depend. If she tells them to stop chewing gum one day, she cannot permit them to do it the next.[15]

6. Successful teachers realize that often children in slum areas have had limited opportunities to observe successful people in many different occupations. They cannot be expected to want to prepare for an occupation that they know nothing about. The school, therefore, has a responsibility to increase their awareness of a wide range of occupations. Sometimes this is done by taking pupils in the upper grades on trips to see people at work and sometimes it is done by bringing successful people from various occupations into the classroom to explain their work to the children.

SITUATION 10.4
*Schools for the Poor and Schools
for the More Affluent*

Visit at least one classroom in a poor section of a city, and then visit at least one in the most prosperous section. What procedures would you use to close the gap between the building, facilities, instructional materials, and quality of instruction in the two schools? Here are some questions to guide your observations and to help you arrive at solutions:
1. What differences do you observe in the amount of time teachers must spend on discipline?
2. In what ways would reducing class size to 15 or 20 pupils help?
3. What chores could be performed by a school volunteer that would give the teacher more time to work with individuals?
4. Summarize the resources available in one school that are not available in the other.

[15] Frank Riessman, *The Culturally Deprived Child* (New York: Harper & Row, Publishers, 1962), p. 81.

Teacher Preparation Programs

Although much of the preservice preparation of the teacher of the culturally different is likely to be somewhat the same as that provided for prospective teachers of other children, some adaptations have been reported.

1. Early and continuous contact with children and adults in disadvantaged areas in a variety of school- and nonschool-related activities.

2. Intensive involvement of behavioral and social scientists, who are asked to apply research and theory from their disciplines to the specific needs and problems of disadvantaged populations.

3. Intensive involvement of successful school practitioners—classroom teachers, principals, counselors, and others—working cooperatively with the teacher-education faculty in planning, supervising, and evaluating experiences.

4. Opportunities for preservice experiences with community agencies whose range allows for more insight into the life styles of disadvantaged students and, consequently, greater empathy with their difficulties.

5. More frequent exposure to diagnostic and remedial procedures, to methods and materials for individualizing instruction, to strategies for classroom control and management, and to material resources tailored to the disadvantaged population.

6. The establishment of internships and other means of continuing supervisory relationships between the college and the in-service teacher.[16]

SUMMARY

1. Children who grow up in rural or urban slums do not ordinarily have the advantage of experiences that stimulate the use of language and the development of concepts—they are disadvantaged when they enter school.

2. If teachers who are generally middle-class in their orientation are to work effectively with culturally different children, they must gain an understanding of the subcultures in which the children have grown up.

3. Culturally different children have not had sufficient opportunities to develop their human potential, to acquire a feeling of personal worth, and to be recognized by others as worthy human beings.

4. Decent housing and adequate health services are two of the greatest needs of slum dwellers.

5. School buildings in slum areas are generally older than those in other sections of the city; the schools provide poorer facilities for either education or recreation, have fewer remedial programs, have more substitute teachers and

[16] A. Harry Passow, pp. 463–464.

a higher teacher turnover, and the teachers spend more of their time on discipline than do other teachers.

6. School achievement of culturally different children is related to the type of schools they attend, the amount of equipment available, the backgrounds and aspirations of other pupils in the school, and the quality of teaching.

7. Disadvantages suffered by most children from low-income families include: limited language development during the preschool period; limited travel experiences to zoos, museums, and other places, and fewer experiences with books, pictures, films, and music; limited opportunities to ask questions or to express their feelings without harsh discipline that encourages the child to remain quiet; and a feeling that they are unworthy, unwanted, and disliked.

8. Rebuilding the inner cities requires excellent schools—better than those in the rest of the city. This means modern physical plants, effective teaching strategies, much smaller classes, more remedial programs, teachers with special preparation, resource centers, and an adequate supply of books and the products of instructional technology.

9. The successful teacher of the culturally different child understands the image that the child has of himself, his school, his teacher, and his chances for success; the difficulty that he has in learning to use standard English; why he looks upon school as an alien institution; why he has to learn to listen; and why he needs to come into contact with successful people from various occupations.

10. Modern programs for the preparation of teachers for the culturally different emphasize early contact with children in disadvantaged areas; contact with successful school personnel and community agencies; and exposure to remedial procedures, individualized instruction, and material resources that are tailored to the needs of the disadvantaged.

RECOMMENDED READINGS

Cheyney, Arnold B., *Teaching Culturally Disadvantaged Children in the Elementary School*. Columbus, Ohio: Charles E. Merrill Books, Inc., 1967. Section 1 deals with the characteristics of culturally disadvantaged children; Section 2 provides suggestions for teaching language to the culturally disadvantaged.

Fantini, Mario D., and Gerald Weinstein, *The Disadvantaged: Challenge to Education*. New York: Harper & Row, Publishers, 1968. Chapter 11 suggests appropriate classroom methods for making contact with disadvantaged learners.

Havighurst, Robert J., *Education in Metropolitan Areas*. Boston: Allyn and Bacon, Inc., 1966. Chapter 6 deals with the problem of urbanization of Negroes; Chapter 7 reports on the status of teachers in metropolitan schools.

Hunter, David R., *The Slums: Challenge and Response*. New York: The Free

Press, 1968. Examines living conditions in the slums and suggests educational implications.

Keach, Everett T., Robert Fulton, and William E. Gardner (Eds.), *Education and Social Crisis: Perspectives on Teaching Disadvantaged Youth.* New York: John Wiley & Sons, 1967. Part II explains some problems facing disadvantaged youth in schools; Part III describes some programs designed to meet the needs of disadvantaged youth.

Miller, Harry L. (Ed.), *Education for the Disadvantaged.* New York: The Free Press, 1967. Chapter 4 presents the problem of preparing teachers for the disadvantaged.

Miller, Harry L., and Marjorie B. Smiley (Eds.), *Education in the Metropolis.* New York: The Free Press, 1967. Explains problems facing the alienated learner; presents a teaching strategy for use with culturally deprived pupils.

Passow, A. Harry, Miriam Goldberg, and Abraham J. Tannenbaum (Eds.), *Education of the Disadvantaged: A Book of Readings.* New York: Holt, Rinehart and Winston, Inc., 1967. Part IV presents many suggestions for educating the disadvantaged.

Ragan, William B., and George Henderson, *Foundations of American Education.* New York: Harper & Row, Publishers, 1970. Chapter 13 reports on a study of the perceptions of youth relating to parents, neighborhoods, schools, and job opportunities. The study was made in the slum area of Detroit.

Riessman, Frank, *The Culturally Deprived Child.* New York: Harper & Row, Publishers, 1962. Examines the culture of the underprivileged, the significance of the family, the effective teacher, and other aspects of teaching culturally disadvantaged children.

Webster, Staten W. (Ed.), *The Disadvantaged Learner: Knowing, Understanding, Educating.* San Francisco: Chandler Publishing Company, 1966. Explains the characteristics of different types of culturally disadvantaged learners and suggests procedures for educating the culturally disadvantaged. Articles dealing with teaching the language arts, science, mathematics, and social studies to culturally disadvantaged learners are particularly valuable.

Chapter 11

Creative Ways of Teaching and Learning

It requires a person who is creative in his teaching to help children be creative in their learning. Then how can we know when we have been successful? Only by looking at the results. Do the children express their ideas more freely; will they try something new and different? Do they have more initiative, more self-confidence and self-respect? Are they more likely to question, to wonder, to explore?

J. Murray Lee and Dorris May Lee, *The Child and His Curriculum*, 3d ed. (New York: Appleton-Century-Crofts, 1960), p. 511.

We live in an age when creative ability is needed in a wide variety of human enterprises. The schools are challenged as never before to foster inquiry, originality, initiative, flexibility, and adaptability to change. Science and technology have been so successful in producing an abundance of material goods that we seem to be in danger of being dominated by machines unless ways can be found to use our inventive genius to nurture humane values. The schools are in danger of becoming standardized, mechanized, and dehumanized unless more emphasis is placed upon creative teaching and learning.

Normal schools were established in this country during the nineteenth century to *train* teachers in the use of specific methods of teaching; supervisors were employed to see that the approved methods were used; and teaching became a process of following cut-and-dried procedures.

Teaching has since become widely recognized as a creative process; teachers are expected to have a broad understanding of the forces that influence teaching and learning so that they can create procedures, select materials, and devise evaluation techniques to fit each unique situation. They do not have to depend upon rigid procedures that have been worked out by others. Teaching then becomes a creative rather than a patterned process; the teacher becomes a helper, and someone who provides encouragement, rather than a taskmaster; and learning becomes an activity in which pupils are actively involved in investigation, discovery, and self-teaching.

SITUATION 11.1
Training versus Educating

One frequently hears the expression *teacher training* used. Explain why *teacher education* or *teacher preparation* is more appropriate in view of the above discussion. Talk with a teacher who is employed in the elementary schools. Find out the extent to which she is expected to use methods and materials prepared by others. What evidence do you find that teachers create their own procedures in terms of the specific situations in which they teach?

THE MEANING OF CREATIVITY

People define creativity in many ways; one definition may emphasize one facet of creativity while another definition may emphasize another. It has been defined in terms of a process, a product, a personality, a form of behavior, and an environmental condition. It has been called a response that is unique to the creator, thinking and doing according to self-imposed tests, and an activity that involves initiative and conscious effort. A product is regarded as creative if it is new to the individual, whether others have previously created the same thing; if it bears the impress of the individual; and if it grows out of the experience of the individual himself. The following statement by Torrance indicates the wide application of the concept:

> Creativity is sometimes contrasted to conformity and is defined as the contribution of original ideas, a different point of view, or a new way of looking at problems; whereas conformity is defined as doing what is expected without disturbing or causing trouble for others. Creativity has also been defined as a successful step into the unknown, getting away from the main track, breaking out of the mold, being open to experience and permitting one thing to lead to another, recombining ideas or seeing new relationships among ideas, and so on. Such concepts as curiosity,

imagination, discovery, innovation, and invention are also prominent in discussions of creativity, and sometimes one or the other is equated with creativity.[1]

SITUATION 11.2

Opposition to Original Ideas

It has been said that the conformist is generally assured of popular approval while the person who has original ideas is feared, ridiculed, and persecuted. Discuss the extent to which this is true for innovative teachers. Why is the teacher who breaks out of the mold sometimes unpopular with other teachers? What responsibility does this situation suggest for administrators?

Creativity is not limited to highly talented artists, musicians, and inventors. In fact, it is now generally recognized that everyone has creative potentialities and that every school subject offers creative possibilities. Caswell and Foshay presented a broad view of creativity when they stated that the child can apply creative art abilities in decorating the classroom, in redecorating his own room at home, in landscaping the school grounds, in buying a dress or choosing a tie, in selecting a movie, in taking a snapshot, or in evaluating magazine illustrations.[2] It is well to realize that the child's need for creative activities cannot be met merely by adding to the length of the periods set aside for art and music—creativity can be an integral phase of every curriculum area.

CHARACTERISTICS OF HIGHLY CREATIVE CHILDREN

The school, of course, has the responsibility for helping each pupil develop his creative potential to the greatest extent possible, whether this be great or small. The school, however, has the additional responsibility of identifying those pupils who have high potential for success at tasks requiring creative ability. The summary that follows is designed to offer some assistance relating to this responsibility.

1. Most children seek to acquire skills and attributes that allow them to be different in some ways from peers and siblings. This delight in certain kinds of uniqueness seems to be related to creativity. Shulman

---

[1] E. Paul Torrance, *What Research Says to the Teacher: Creativity* (Washington, D.C.: Association of Classroom Teachers, N.E.A., 1968), p. 4.

[2] H. L. Caswell and A. W. Foshay, *Education in the Elementary School*, 2d ed. (New York: American Book Company, 1950), p. 192.

and Keislar cite evidence from a study of creative architects and mathematicians that ". . . a salient difference between the creative and non-creative professional is the desire of the former group to be creative, to be different from their peers."[3]

2. A high level of creative ability is generally accompanied by a high level of intellectual ability. However, high intelligence alone does not guarantee creativity; to produce creative work, the child must be stimulated, his urge to create nurtured, and his talents developed. Many individuals with both high intelligence and special talents have created nothing.

3. The highly creative child has built-in motivating power that makes unnecessary the application of external pressure in the form of rewards and punishments. Torrance and Myers have stated that research in social psychology has shown that almost any kind of human functioning can usually be improved by increasing or decreasing motivation in the form of rewards and punishments. They note, however, that such improvements are generally temporary in nature. They have reported as follows:

> We have observed that many children are almost totally unresponsive to external pressure, whether in the form of reward or punishment. In fact, it seems that the more they are rewarded the worse they behave and the less they learn, and likewise the more we punish them the worse they behave and the less they learn. . . . The inner stimulation and involvement from creative ways of learning make the reapplication of rewards and punishments unnecessary.[4]

4. The highly creative child persists in a self-selected task in spite of difficulties and frustrations; he works for the love of his idea rather than for an external reward; and he is not easily turned aside by what may be going on around him.

5. The highly creative child is characterized by the novelty of his ideas; he does not desire a "ready-made" pattern to which he can conform; he expects to learn by doing; and he wants to judge his products in terms of the values he sought to project.

6. The highly creative child is likely to be sensitive to problems and want to solve them. Whereas most pupils will abandon a toy when it fails to function, the creative pupil feels challenged to find out why it does not work; he is really more interested in finding the source of the difficulty than he is in playing with the toy.

7. Physical health and a high energy level contribute to creative achievement. The creative individual works tirelessly, hour after hour, to

---

[3] Lee S. Shulman and Evan R. Keislar, *Learning by Discovery: A Critical Appraisal* (Chicago: Rand McNally & Company, 1966), pp. 154–155.

[4] E. Paul Torrance and R. E. Myers, *Creative Learning & Teaching* (New York: Dodd, Mead & Company, 1970), pp. 49–50.

express his ideas; his energy is focused on one task rather than being spread over many.

8. The highly creative child does not always rank near the top of the class in school marks. The pupil who finds it difficult to conform to established patterns, who has a new idea to try out, frequently suffers when marks are reported. There is a difference, however, between the creative individual and the professional nonconformist. The former departs from the conventional because he has a new idea to try out; the latter departs just because he wants to be a troublemaker.

9. It is evident that the highly creative child cannot be identified by intelligence tests alone; many sources of information must be utilized— sources that will reveal the status of his health, intelligence, personal-social development, emotional maturity, achievement in school subjects, interests and hobbies, special abilities, and out-of-school activities. This information may come from tests and inventories, rating scales, observation by teachers and parents, conferences with school and community personnel, and from interviews with pupils and parents.

SITUATION 11.3
Concern for the Needs of Every Pupil

A visit to Mrs. Cowan's fifth-grade room revealed a concern for releasing the potential of every pupil. Five or six pupils were working on a mural to be displayed when parents visited school—the mural to give parents some idea of what the pupils were learning. Another group was arranging a bulletin-board display of the work of all the pupils—not just the "best" work. Another group was working at a table on plans for visitors' day. Two boys were putting together a crystal set, using materials provided by the school. Each pupil was working on his own project, seeking to express some idea that was significant to him.

What principles of creative learning are present in this illustration? What objections might a teacher raise to undertaking this type of activity? Summarize the advantages that this kind of learning situation has for pupils.

EFFECTS OF CREATIVE TEACHING ON PUPILS

Teachers are interested in finding out what difference creative teaching makes in the achievement and behavior of pupils. There are an increasing number of studies that support the contention that creative teaching does make a difference in the achievement and behavior of pupils. Although the authors recognize that it is difficult for the researcher to separate the influence of a teacher's approach from other factors that bring about

This child is being stimulated to think and discover through creative teaching. (Photo courtesy Norman Public Schools.)

changes in boys and girls, it seems worthwhile to present some research findings as well as some conclusions based only on observation by competent persons relating to the effects of creative teaching on pupils.

1. Spaulding conducted a study of teacher-pupil transactions in a sample of fourth- and sixth-grade classrooms. He found significant positive correlation between height of self-concept on the part of pupils and the degree to which teachers were calm, acceptant, supportive, and facilitating. He also found that pupils made significantly fewer gains in reading and performed less well on tests of originality when teachers were dominating and threatening.[5]

2. Pines made a survey of the leading programs for teaching primary children to read. The most successful programs have one thing in common —they all elicit the child's creativity by letting him make up his own words and stories.[6]

3. Torrance and Myers report on the results of a project in which

[5] Robert L. Spaulding, "Achievement, Creativity, and Self-Concept Correlates of Teacher-Pupil Transactions in Elementary Schools" (Urbana: University of Illinois, manuscript), 1962.

[6] M. Pines, *Revolution in Learning* (New York: Harper & Row, Publishers, 1967).

students in a class at a university were asked to recall instances in which they allowed pupils in their classes to become involved creatively and then observed the differences that the experience made in achievement and behavior. The 135 respondents mentioned "from nonreader to reader" as the change observed most frequently. Other changes observed include:

a. from destructive behavior to constructive behavior,
b. from troublemaker to star learner and teacher,
c. from estrangement and retardation to adjustment and achievement,
d. from bitter sarcasm and hostility to kindness and success,
e. from fighting and uncommunicativeness to improved speech,
f. from unloving and unloved to a loving and loved child.

Creativity is encouraged when pupils receive recognition by the teacher for their efforts. (Photo courtesy Oklahoma City Public Schools.)

The same report mentioned the following as some of the precedures that made the differences mentioned above:

a. permitting children to work alone and in their own way,
b. making curricular variations for different children,
c. creating a responsive, nonpunitive environment,
d. changing the perception that the group may have of a particular child.[7]

SITUATION 11.4

Opportunities for Creative Experience

Observe children during a period set aside for art experiences. Evaluate the extent to which learning is creative. Are the pupils free enough and self-confident enough so that they can really express their own thoughts and feelings in their own way? Are pupils using several media to express their ideas? Collect samples of children's art at different grade levels. To what extent do pupils seem to be developing new understandings and new relationships as they progress from one grade to another?

Each pupil achieves a number of values as a result of being guided into creative learning experiences. One reference mentions the following values:

1. *Self-discovery.* The individual comes to know his own abilities and his own strength through trying them out. He becomes an individual through expressing himself, his ideas, and his conceptions. Incidentally, he also reveals his own misconceptions so that the teacher can take note of these misconceptions and help him correct them.

2. *Self-reliance.* Creative achievement increases courage, self-confidence, and satisfaction. It frees the individual from damaging inhibitions, timidity, and self-consciousness. It brings the feeling of power and mastery.

3. *Persistence.* The development of intense purpose, the habit of hard work, and the ability to stay with a task are values that generally accompany creative efforts.

4. *Enthusiasm.* The creative person simultaneously loses himself and finds himself in his effort to produce; he adjusts himself to changing situations with courage, and lives fully and satisfyingly.

5. *Intellectual honesty.* Opportunities for creative expression bring intellectual sincerity. Things are valued for their true worth as revealed in experience. The creative student works for the love of his idea rather than for a grade or some other extraneous symbol.

[7] Torrance and Myers, pp. 24–43.

6. *Intellectual adventurousness.* The creative person is constantly lured to new interests and new ideas; he develops new purposes and is compelled to meet new hungers. He knows how to have fun with his own mind; his whole life is crammed with the joys of discovering and doing. He knows how to escape boredom.

7. *Constructive use of leisure.* Creativeness is the only avenue of escape from letting increased leisure become a bore to the individual and a danger to society. It alone can check the submergence of the coming generation in an ocean of passivity and commercial exploitation.[8]

HOW TEACHERS PROMOTE CREATIVITY

It is not feasible, of course, to set forth in a small space all the ways that teachers promote creativity. Indeed, it has been suggested that each teacher's way of teaching is a unique invention. It is, therefore, more realistic to speak of becoming a more creative teacher than it is to speak of becoming an "ideal" teacher. Creative teaching is not a mysterious kind of activity in which only a genius can hope to succeed; all teachers have many opportunities for trying something different, for breaking away from patterned procedures, and for using their own unique capabilities to make teaching and learning more creative. There is space here to mention only a few of the many ways that this can be done.

1. *Establish a creative teacher-pupil relationship.* The creative teacher sees his relationship to pupils as a helping or facilitating one. The pupil's thinking processes are uninhibited because the relationship is an open, nonthreatening one. Getzels and Jackson have explained that:

> If we wish to foster intellectual inventiveness, we may have to risk granting the creative student greater autonomy, and perhaps even to reward behavior that fails to comply with what we were prepared to reward.[9]

2. *Provide a rich experience background.* To create does not mean making something out of nothing. There can be no expression without there being first an impression. Unfortunately, pupils have sometimes been asked to express their feelings about things with which they have had little experience. Also, children are sometimes insensitive to things that are right around them. A pupil whose home and school both faced San Francisco's Golden Gate told his teacher that he had not seen very

---

[8] Adapted from John A. Hockett and E. W. Jacobsen, *Modern Practices in the Elementary School,* new ed. (Boston: Ginn and Company, 1943), pp. 167–168.

[9] Jacob W. Getzels and Philip W. Jackson, in Ronald Gross and Judith Murphy (Eds.), *The Revolution in the Schools* (New York: Harcourt Brace Jovanovich, Inc., 1964), p. 177.

many sunsets! The teacher must, therefore, be constantly alert to encourage sensitivity to beauty in the worlds of nature, prose, poetry, music, and art. Time must be found to talk about interesting places the child has been and interesting experiences the child has had, and the child must be encouraged to help plan ways of expressing his ideas and feelings in a variety of media.

3. *Provide recognition for creative efforts.* The pupil should feel that when he makes an honest effort his product will be noticed and appreciated. This need for recognition by his classmates and his teachers was evident in the case of a totally blind boy who, with his teacher and his classmates, had taken a trip to an orange grove and had written a story based on his experiences on the trip. After he had read his story, he asked a number of times, "What did you think of my story?" Ways of recognizing creative efforts include verbal approval by the teacher and by other pupils, display of the pupil's work, and the sending of samples of his work home with favorable comments by the teacher.

4. *Help pupils develop skills needed for creative learning.* The development of creative abilities depends upon the development of skills: skill in reading, spelling, computation, and other basic subjects required for any type of learning. Learning in creative ways requires skills of investigation, problem solving, and research. The problem of developing useful skills will be treated in greater detail in Chapter 12.

5. *Free young children from the threat of evaluation.* Evaluation tends to reduce the ability of young children to think beyond the obvious, the safe, and the familiar. Some authorities believe that no marks should be given to children who are in the kindergarten and primary grades. Torrance found that unevaluated practice compared with evaluated practice is followed by a more creative performance in similar tasks requiring creative thinking. "By the fourth grade, children are apparently so accustomed to being evaluated on everything that the instructions freeing them from the threat of evaluation had little effect."[10]

6. *Involve pupils in creative tasks.* The teacher who understands the value of involving pupils in creative learning recognizes the value of the ideas contributed by each pupil; provides materials that are interesting, stimulating, and exciting; and structures the activity so that pupils have a chance to learn on their own.

CREATIVITY IN THE SCHOOL PROGRAM

The school is expected to play an important role in reversing undesirable trends toward conformity in our society. It must become a place where originality, initiative, and individual deviations are cherished and en-

[10] Torrance and Myers, pp. 105–106.

couraged. Emphasis on group work, group conformity, and group judgment must not be allowed to deprive any child of opportunities to develop his special talents to the limit of his capacity. This does not mean that group work has no place in the program of the elementary school; it means, rather, that individuals be allowed to achieve self-realization through their unique contributions to group enterprises; it means also that schools must maintain a balance between group experiences and individual activities.

COOPERATIVE PLANNING BY THE SCHOOL STAFF. The teacher is the major influence in providing creative experiences for pupils. His day-to-day contacts with pupils provide opportunities for recognizing creative potentials and for encouraging originality in many ways. However, the quality of educational leadership provided by the school principal and the extent to which the entire staff of the school participates in cooperative planning of school programs are significant factors in providing an environment that is conducive to creative teaching and learning.

CREATIVE LEADERSHIP. Anyone who has taught in an elementary school realizes that the school principal can stimulate growth, encourage initiative, and release the creative potentials of teachers, or he can discourage initiative and reduce individual effort to a mere routine of conforming to imposed patterns. School principals who crave status and power over teachers, who are disturbed when teachers exercise initiative and self-direction, who are insecure in coping with change, are in serious need of creative reeducation. Fortunately, there is evidence that not all principals are cast in such a rigid mold, that many of them have a modern conception of their role as educational leaders, and have the confidence needed to break away from set patterns of action.

CREATIVE OPPORTUNITIES FOR ALL CHILDREN. Respect for the worth of each child and opportunities for each to develop his talents to the maximum are basic tenets of democracy. The potential for creative expression is a distinctive human characteristic. To maintain that the majority of children should be taught merely to conform is to deny them the opportunity to learn to live as a human being can and should live. The only kind of education that is consistent with the facts of human growth and development is the one that accepts each pupil for what he is and for what he is capable of becoming. Emphasis on creativity is consistent with our need to cop with the decreasing work week and problems of worthy use of leisure. Greater stress on creativity in school may well decrease some of the effects of alienation on children, and many of the frustrations of children that are reflected in the drug problem might be reduced by a blend of creativeness and humaneness in the elementary school.

SUMMARY

1. Schools are challenged as never before to foster inquiry, initiative, originality, flexibility, and adaptability to change.

2. Unless more emphasis is placed on creative teaching and learning, our schools will become increasingly standardized, mechanized, and dehumanized.

3. Teachers are now expected to have a broad understanding of the factors that influence teaching and learning so that they can create new procedures to fit different situations—so that each can invent his own way of teaching.

4. Creativity may be regarded as the contribution of original ideas, a different point of view, or a new way of looking at problems.

5. Curiosity, imagination, discovery, innovation, and invention are closely associated with creativity.

6. A high level of creative ability is generally associated with a delight in being unique; and with a high level of intelligence, sensitivity to problems, physical health and a high energy level, a reluctance to conform, and an urge to try out new ideas.

7. Values of creative experience include an improvement in the child's self-concept, more rapid gains in reading, an improvement in the behavior of the pupil, self-discovery, self-reliance, persistence, enthusiasm, intellectual honesty, intellectual adventurousness, and constructive use of leisure.

8. Teachers promote creativity by establishing a creative teacher-pupil relationship, providing a rich experience background, providing recognition for creative efforts, helping pupils develop skills, freeing children from the threat of evaluation, and involving pupils in creative tasks.

9. Participating in group work may limit opportunities for creative experiences unless arrangements are made permitting the individual to achieve self-realization by contributing his unique talents to group enterprises.

10. The principal of a school can discourage initiative and reduce individual efforts of teachers to a mere routine of conforming to imposed patterns, or he can stimulate initiative and encourage self-direction.

RECOMMENDED READINGS

Getzels, Jacob W., and Philip W. Jackson, "Education for Creativity," in Ronald Gross and Judith Murphy (Eds.), *The Revolution in the Schools.* New York: Harcourt Brace Jovanovich, Inc., 1964, pp. 170–183. Reports the findings of some research relating to the nature of creativity.

Glasser, W., *Schools Without Failure.* New York: Harper & Row, Publishers, 1969. Explains methods of directing class discussions in disadvantaged schools, drawing upon his experience in the field of psychotherapy.

Inlow, Gail, *The Emergent in Curriculum.* New York: John Wiley & Sons,

1966. Chapter 5 explains education's role in developing creative individuals.

Lee, J. Murray, and Dorris M. Lee, *The Child and His Curriculum*, 3d ed. New York: Appleton-Century-Crofts, 1960. Chapter 14 presents many useful suggestions for fostering creativity.

Pines, M., *Revolution in Learning*. New York: Harper & Row, Publishers, 1967. After surveying the leading programs for teaching preprimary children to read, Maya Pines concludes that the most successful ones have one thing in common—they all elicit the child's creativity by letting him make up his own words and stories almost from the beginning.

Shulman, Lee S., and Evan R. Keislar (Eds.), *Learning.by Discovery: A Critical Appraisal*. Chicago: Rand McNally & Company, 1966. Cites several studies dealing with creativity.

Shumsky, A., *Creative Teaching in the Elementary School*. New York: Appleton-Century-Crofts, 1965. One of the many recent books that describes creative teaching.

Smith, J. A., *Setting Conditions for Creative Teaching in the Elementary School*. Boston: Allyn and Bacon, 1966. Describes the environment that stimulates creative activity.

Suchman, R. J., *The Elementary School Training Program in Scientific Inquiry*. Urbana, Ill.: School of Education, University of Illinois, 1962. Suchman has developed and tested materials for teaching better inquiry skills.

Torrance, E. Paul, *What Research Says to the Teacher: Creativity*. Washington, D.C.: Association of Classroom Teachers, N.E.A., 1968. Explains how creativity is manifested at different educational levels, how it is measured, and what teachers can do to foster it.

———, and R. E. Myers, *Creative Learning & Teaching*. New York: Dodd, Mead & Company, 1970. Explains what it means to be a creative teacher and how to teach children to think creatively. Practical illustrations are found throughout the book.

NEW APPROACHES TO FAMILIAR TASKS

**Effective Mastery
of Skills**

**Individualizing
and Personalizing
Teaching**

**Classroom Management
—Discipline**

**Evaluating
and Reporting
Pupil Performance**

Schools for Tomorrow

*Part IV presents new ways of dealing with tasks that have
confronted elementary school teachers for many years. An effort
has been made to help the student understand how teachers in
the new elementary school approach these familiar tasks with
greater insight than has been true in the past. The final chapter
summarizes the findings of several studies of what life may be
like in our society and in our schools for a reasonable period ahead.*

240

Chapter 12

Effective Mastery of Skills

All too often we are giving our young people cut flowers when we should be teaching them to grow their own plants.

John W. Gardner, *Self-Renewal: The Individual and the Innovative Society* (New York: Harper & Row, Publishers, 1964), p. 21.

The opening chapter of this book has documented the fact that immense changes are taking place in this world. That our schools have not kept pace hardly needs documenting, for nearly all of us have firsthand evidence that they have not. Goodlad has estimated that the schools are ill suited to meet the needs of at least 30 percent of their clientele. This includes large numbers of children from minority groups, those with mental, physical, and emotional handicaps, and the few with rare intellectual gifts that separate them sharply from their peers. He has speculated that there is a lack of a reasonably satisfying relationship between the schools and 50 percent of their students.[1]

[1] John I. Goodlad, "The Schools vs. Education," *Saturday Review*, April 19, 1969, p. 61.

Part of the dissatisfaction students experience in school lies with the institution's reluctance to accept the children as natural learners. All too frequently the eager, curious five- and six-year-olds evolve into placid, indifferent nine- and ten-year-olds. Crary evidences the kind of faith more school people should share:

> Too often the school slanders its pupils. It judges them lazy, weary, or inattentive; it acts as though these were natural characteristics of learners. On the contrary, these are protective poses of people who are unwilling to invest themselves in adventures not their own. When the school helps students to discover the mountains they want to climb it also discovers their energies and capacities.[2]

Stendler supports the suggestion children should be the point of departure for planning school activities when she says, "The child must want something, notice something, do something, and get something in order for learning to take place."[3]

In spite of all the good our public schools have done in answering the plea for mass education, we would be remiss in our professional obligation if we ignored the shortcomings. The teaching of basic skills in the elementary school has been replete with such shortcomings. Misinterpretation, misdirection, and mistakes have plagued the elementary school teacher in the teaching of basic skills for generations. Let us see how the new elementary school can handle the problem of achieving effective mastery of basic skills.

In this rapidly changing world the phrase "basic skills" is something of an anachronism. It has a static ring. Its typical connotation is more absolute than relative. When we speculate about what the future holds for us, the only thing we can be certain of is more change. It would be inconsistent, if not presumptuous, for us to imply we know what the basic skills will be in the year 2000. No one does. The best we can do is assess what seems to be needed now, what has been done in the past, and hazard an educated guess about what will be needed in the future. The spirit is tentative. A social institution should serve the people, not vice versa, and when the basic skills embraced by schools are irrelevant they should be changed.

A BROADER VIEW OF SKILLS

Conventionally, the phrase "basic skills" has evoked a mental picture similar to the following:

[2] Ryland W. Crary, *Humanizing the School: Curriculum Development and Theory* (New York: Alfred A. Knopf, Inc., 1969), p. 114.

[3] Celia B. Stendler, *Teaching in the Elementary School* (New York: Harcourt Brace Jovanovich, Inc., 1958), p. 104.

SITUATION 12.1
Yesterday's Basic Skill Work

A room 30′ × 25′ filled with five rows of six desks each, all facing the front and occupied by twenty-five to thirty children listening, at least overtly, to a teacher who is either telling something or directing an activity. Their real attention is something less than intense, but, for all practical purposes, they are engaged in "basic skill" work—either hearing the rules or practicing them. ("Practice" is a euphemism for drill. Often the rhetoric has been the only change made in elementary schools.)

Indeed, a few would say the new elementary school should be geared to something other than basic skills, and that the concern for basic skills has been the corrupting influence in all educational innovations of the past. All too frequently basic skills have been synonymous with the required, or obligatory, and therefore unpleasant aspects of schooling. The charge cannot be denied. How then will effective mastery of basic skills be different in the new elementary school?

First, basic skills will be more than the reading, writing, and arithmetic of old. They will include skills related to human organizations: getting along well with others; sharing, cooperating, feeling for, and, in the largest sense of the word, simply being. Rubin lists the following as primary skills:

> The ability to manage one's emotions, to take advantage of one's creative potential, to cope with difficult problems, to spend one's leisure wisely, to think rationally, [and] to know one's self. . . .[4]

The basic skills of the new elementary school however go beyond the long neglected affective domain. If the rare, child-centered schools of the progressive movement erred, it was in their concern for the affective at the expense of the cognitive. The new elementary school will not neglect the cognitive aspects of development. It will operate on the premise that all human beings naturally desire to make sense of their environment. Satisfying curiosity and understanding oneself and one's surroundings are, like symbol making, natural activities of children. The new elementary school will respect these natural drives and, when appropriate, bring them to fruition.

Respecting the natural inclination to learn means structuring school environments that reinforce this inclination. Too much structure will thwart genuine curiosity, while too little will suppress and negate it in shy and reticent children. But achieving some kind of utopian structure will not

---

[4] Louis J. Rubin (Ed.), *Life Skills in School and Society* (Washington, D.C.: Association for Supervision and Curriculum Development, N.E.A., 1969), p. 9.

be as important as the toleration—or better, encouragement—of diverse learning styles and interests. No one structure will be optimum for all children. The teacher's primary concern should be with managing a plurality of structures appropriate for all children.

Perhaps the most significant difference between the old and the new elementary school lies in the concern for children mastering basic skills—whatever they may be—at specific stages in their school career. The old school was preoccupied with grade standards and expected the children to master certain skills before moving to the next grade. Nongradedness promised to avoid this lock-step approach to education but usually substituted a larger number of levels to replace the grades. Again, a change in terms but not practice. The new elementary school is distinctive in that mastery of basic skills will be encouraged throughout a child's elementary school career but not at arbitrary intervals as they were with graded and nongraded systems. If basic skills are really basic, children will master them when they are ready, and no amount of prodding or punishment will hasten the accomplishment. This does not mean teachers will cease to care whether children master basic skills, but it does mean less anxiety will transfer to the children from teachers who are over-concerned with mastery. It means so-called homogeneous groups—based on intelligence and achievement that automatically generate poor self-concepts to members of the "low" groups and frequently lead to self-fulfilling prophecies—will have no place in the new school.

Effective mastery of basic skills has other ambiguous qualities. Being able to spell is a basic skill. But will those children who have "effectively mastered" spelling never make a mistake in spelling? Hardly. Is "effective" synonymous with "reasonable"? What is reasonable?

Knowing the multiplication table is a basic skill. Knowing it in base ten, that is. Knowing multiplication in base two, the number system computers use, is seldom thought of as a basic skill. Bringing meaning to words on a page is a basic skill. What about concern for bringing meaning to facial expressions, gestures, and dance? Deciding what are the basic skills, and what effective mastery of them is, has involved somewhat arbitrary decisions. Schoolmen must decide what factors need to be considered in determining what skills will be basic and what effective mastery means.

It may be useful to consider effective mastery to be the degree to which a child can use a skill without dysfunctional consequences. Dysfunctional can mean either that the skill is not being used correctly or that the use of it creates more problems than it solves.

BASIC SKILLS OF THE NEW ELEMENTARY SCHOOL

In at least a general fashion, the basic skills for the new elementary school are known. Broadly speaking, the new elementary school will embrace four types of skills. Each type is important and related to the others. No hierarchy is implied in the following list, though some readers may wish to establish one. The division here is arbitrary. Understanding one's self and being creative in regard to problems one faces constitute one skill which will characterize the new elementary school. It's a life skill and one that may never be completely mastered.

Problem solving and research are involved in another of the new elementary school's skills. Effective and efficient communication is another skill the new elementary school will endeavor to promote. And the specific skills related to the typical school subjects constitute the final category of skills.

Self-Understanding and Creativity

Admonishing elementary teachers to help children understand themselves and be creative in solving their problems is one thing; specifically recommending how these goals can be achieved is another. Teachers need to realize that understanding one's self and being creative are, like many of the other skills of the new elementary school, lifetime endeavors. No one ever fully understands himself; and creativity, by definition, involves a kind of rebirth that can take place any time in one's life. When teachers fully grasp the fact that what matters to children is what *they* perceive, not necessarily what their teachers think *is*, they will be on their way to helping children better understand themselves.

> SITUATION 12.2
> *Working with Perceptions*
>
> A seven-year-old girl who confidently understands the beginning sounds of many words sees and hears her teacher matter-of-factly write and spell the word *once*. What was at least a temporary understanding for the child was smashed by the teacher and consequently so was her confidence in being able to make sense out of the world. Had the teacher prefaced her writing and spelling with a note about the absurdity of our language and its rules, the child would have been spared the trauma of trying to rebuild her universe of meanings.[5]

Teachers need to plumb the depths of their students' understandings in order to assess the levels at which they are functioning. Providing opportunities for children to think and talk about what they know, and how they know it, is a teaching skill that should be consistently developed.

[5] John Holt, *How Children Fail* (New York: Dell Publishing Co., Inc., 1964), p. 105.

Children can only move from where they are, not from where they are "supposed" to be. If teachers are using more than half of the talking time in a typical day, chances are the children in the class are not being given enough opportunity to reveal their levels of understanding.

Because it would never be possible for a teacher or any other adult to fully understand the world as the child sees it, it is important to have children share, with one another and in the group, the kinds of feelings they have about themselves and their world. Such sharing will help the children to realize they are not alone in their partial understanding with its concomitant doubt and anxiety. Teachers need not be passive and withdrawn for such sharing to be optimal. The classroom atmosphere is set by the teacher and, though she will not likely be aggressive during a discussion, she will frequently initiate a discussion of topics and feelings in an effort to draw the children into a feeling of group cohesiveness. Although the goal will be to achieve some degree of group unity, it will be characterized as more open than closed. A relatively open group is one in which the members have established bonds of trust with one another and are not reluctant to share their feelings.

Creativity is more likely to flourish in an atmosphere that allows and encourages divergent thinking. The old elementary school was characterized as being a place where convergent thinking was the predominate mode. Convergent-type questions are those that require one right answer. Postman and Weingartner, for instance, suggested one of the first skills children learn in school is to play the "right answer game" with teachers.[6] When children "psych out" a teacher in terms of discovering what it is she wants or what she considers right and correct and then behave accordingly, they are playing the "right answer game." So ingrained is the convergent thinking in schools, that even today college students plaintively ask their professors what it is *they*, the professors, want, and give little or no value to their own intuitive ideas.

Providing an atmosphere in which one may think divergently and still feel comfortable and confident—not just tolerated—means teachers of the new elementary school will have to rebuild their mental picture of an ideal classroom. Too few new teachers have experienced the encouragement of divergent thinking in their own school careers, and their propensity, therefore, is to perpetuate that which they have known.

Problem-Solving Skills

A classroom that is open and one in which divergent thinking is encouraged will be an especially fertile environment in which to promote the

---

[6] Neil Postman and Charles Weingartner, *Teaching as a Subversive Activity* (New York: Delacorte Press, 1969), p. 20.

problem-solving skills of children. Generally, problem solving involves inductive thinking. A problem is perceived, several hypotheses about its solution are generated, tests or inquiries are made, and one or more of the hypotheses are supported. Divergent thinking is indispensable to problem solving because seldom is there one and only one correct way to arrive at an answer and seldom is there only one best answer.

The inquiry-discovery methodology lends itself well to developing problem-solving skills. It capitalizes on Rubin's admonishment that ". . . the development of skills is essentially a matter of process rather than of content. It is the 'doing acts' of schooling which produce the greatest good." [7] The purpose of the inquiry approach to teaching has been best summarized by Postman and Weingartner as ". . . to help learners increase their competence *as learners*. It hopes to accomplish this by having students *do* what effective learners do." [8]

Lest beginning teachers think all discovery must be truly uncovering new knowledge, we remind them here that it can include all forms of obtaining knowledge or insight for oneself by oneself.[9] A child need not discover better devices than lines of longitude and latitude as reference points, if, when solving a problem related to a make-believe (or real) travel experience, he discovers such lines as being useful. *The* problem that confronts everyone, directly or indirectly, is making sense out of the world. Making sense means bringing meaning to things, events, and processes that surround the individual.

People who most effectively make sense of their environment are those who perceive a real need to do so. If a child can see no other reason for solving a problem than pleasing the teacher, he is less likely to be as concerned with the kind of sense (meaning) he brings to the situation.

Research Skills

Research skills range from asking an authority for an answer to discovering an answer for oneself. Although asking an authority is the quickest and usually easiest way to find an answer, it has several noteworthy shortcomings. Our society is such that one authority's views on a subject may clash violently with another's. We need many informed points of view before we are willing to make a decision. Because of the multiplicity and frequent contradiction of informed views, a good deal of emphasis needs to be placed on cultivating the skill of weighing and considering diverse opinions. Another shortcoming in seeking an authority for an answer is in

---

[7] Rubin, p. 31.
[8] Postman and Weingartner, p. 31.
[9] John W. Renner and William B. Ragan, *Teaching Science in the Elementary School* (New York: Harper & Row, Publishers, 1968), p. 111.

the message inherent in the process itself. That is, children soon learn that the way to learn is to ask an authority. (Most elementary children perceive their parents and their teachers as authorities, regardless of their qualifications.) The process induces and reinforces dependency, which augurs poorly for promoting self-directed learners. Authorities are indispensable in today's complex world, but they need not be the only source of information.

Research skills in the new elementary school will include: observing, questioning, gathering data, and forming judgments. All of these skills are used by children in their daily lives, but seldom is much attention given to them individually. Observing is a good example of a skill that is frequently taken for granted. Much more than physiology is involved when one "sees" something. Indeed, perception actually takes place in the brain, not the eye, so one's psychological set is a most important determinant for what one observes. Numerous studies have supported the generalization that perception is a function of experience and expectations.

Reality, then, is not something "out there" for all to see. On the contrary, reality is a phenomenon of each individual. When a teacher wants children to observe something she should try to be as specific as possible, unless, of course, she wants to encourage diverse impressions within her group.

Question asking is a natural activity that, like observing, can be improved if teachers consciously work at it. Probably the most obvious dimension of questioning that can be observed in school settings is whether the question leads to one or more than one answer. Many questions naturally lead to other questions. If a questioner can be satisfied with one answer, we say he has asked a convergent question. If more than one answer is needed, or another question is created, then the original question is said to be divergent. Most questions having to do with real-life situations require many answers. It seems that only in schools do we find a preponderance of single answers that satisfy questions. Unfortunately, children learn this quickly and mimic their teachers by asking more and more convergent questions.

The question-asking skill that needs to be developed most in the new elementary school is framing a question that requires divergence in thought and action. Naturally, teachers can best develop this skill by acting as models and reducing the number of convergent questions they ask—both orally and on tests.

Data gathering is an indispensable research skill needed in the new elementary school. The multiplicity of sources of information is so great that some order needs to be brought to the mass of information available to elementary-age children. As with the other skills, however, caution is urged in regard to simply teaching the skills as independent activities that are good to have for their own sake. Effective mastery of data gathering, and, for that matter, organizing and presenting, can best be obtained when the children perceive a need for it. How many adults cringe when faced with an outlining task that recalls for them the tedious practice of having to outline a chapter in order to "learn" the skill of outlining? Being able to abstract the major and minor topics from a chapter or other source of information is an important skill, but its value to children can be readily negated if pursued as an isolated activity—removed from any real need or desire of students to utilize it.

Reading is not to be neglected, but the emphasis in the new elementary school need not be only on reading to gather data. Children today, and even more, tomorrow, are literally bombarded by other forms of communication that carry all kinds of information. During school hours children can gather information from films, listening to tapes, listening to the teacher tell or read a story, performing an experiment, going on field trips, viewing pictures, slides, filmstrips, and reading. Outside of school other adults and acquaintances provide information as well as television, radio, newspapers, phonograph records and films, all of which constitute an almost endless supply of information.[10]

Forming judgments is a skill that is used regardless of intentions. It reflects a value or number of values of the individual. Even if judgment is suspended the decision to suspend it involved a judgment. Children can learn to minimize the effect of personal bias on a judgment by observing the teacher as a model of a good judge or decision maker. Teachers of the new elementary school need to emphasize the importance of gathering as much pertinent data as possible before judgments are formed. With the abundance of information children must learn to sift the relevant from the irrelevant in order to have a good foundation on which to base their judgments.

There is no perfect model for conducting research. There are generalizable kinds of activities that are typically performed, but variation in these is not uncommon. Similarly, the amount of time involved in doing research may vary. Hanna and others have advised:

> The time that children will need depends on the difficulty of the materials, the number of questions, the maturation and abilities of the children, and the amount of practice they have had. Some research will be completed in a short time. In upper grades, several days, a week, or even longer may be devoted to problems of concern to the group.[11]

[10] Neil Postman, "The Politics of Reading," *Harvard Educational Review*, Vol. 40, No. 2, May 1970, pp. 244–252, and Aldous Huxley, "Education on the Nonverbal Level," *Daedalus*, Spring 1962, pp. 279–293.

[11] Lavone A. Hanna et al., *Unit Teaching in the Elementary School* (New York: Holt, Rinehart and Winston, Inc., 1965), p. 242.

Teachers in the new elementary school will approach their students with a flexible time schedule and not be inordinately concerned with having too little time for their activities.

Communication Skills

Effective and efficient communication transcends all the skills and activities of children. No accident explains the connection between the words community and communication. Dewey knew this and further observed:

> Society not only continues to exist *by* transmission, *by* communication, but it may fairly be said to exist *in* transmission, *in* communication. . . . Men live in a community in virtue of the things which they have in common; and communication is the way in which they come to possess things in common.[12]

If our very quality of life is a function of our ability to communicate, it is incumbent upon teachers to do all they can to improve the communication skills of children. A more detailed discussion of communication as part of the language arts will be presented later. Two guiding principles for effective mastery of communication skills require discussion now.

Communication relies heavily on symbols that are manmade and consequently ever changing. Therefore there is something arbitrary and tentative in all symbols. How we communicate can be better understood if we are cognizant of the lack of absoluteness associated with the meaning of any symbol. The arbitrary and tentative nature of symbols gives rise to another principle of communication—consensus.

When individual A gives a signal and understands its meaning and individual B receives the signal and associates the same meaning with the signal, then consensus has been achieved. Communication depends on consensus. Effective communication entails the use of the most appropriate signal or symbol for the meaning that is to be communicated, with the understanding that the receiving individual will agree to such appropriateness. Such agreement will only occur when both the sender and the receiver apply the same meaning to a symbol. That the symbols themselves have no meaning is what teachers have to keep in mind.

Before we look at the separate school subjects and the skills they require, we can summarize most of the aforementioned basic skills in the form of an outline.

1. Skills in Group Processes
   a. Understands and assumes various roles in the formal group work
   b. Participates in discussions

[12] John Dewey, *Democracy and Education* (New York: Crowell-Collier and Macmillan, Inc., 1916), p. 5.

  c. Understands the need for group process rules and abides by them
  d. Helps clarify group aims
  e. Accepts group decisions
  f. Expresses opinions freely and listens while others express theirs
  g. Participates in planning, producing, and evaluating group activities
  h. Offers constructive criticism
  i. Reacts favorably to constructive criticism
  j. Shares materials
2. Skills in Problem Solving
  a. Recognizes a problem when it is confronted
  b. Plans how to approach a problem
  c. Finds information from all available sources
  d. Evaluates information
  e. Organizes information for presentation
  f. Arrives at conclusions
3. Locating and Gathering Information
  a. Knows which references to use and where located
  b. Finds the call number of a book from card catalog
  c. Knows that summary of an article is located in the first paragraph
  d. Knows the difference between call letters of fiction and non-fiction
  e. Selects news items related to class activities
  f. Uses the newspaper throughout the week
  g. Familiarizes himself with different types of magazines
  h. Utilizes interviews effectively
4. Organizing and Evaluating Information
  a. Discriminates among conflicting facts
  b. Arranges in logical order of sequence
  c. Organizes accounts of concrete experiences
  d. Distinguishes between fact and opinion; recognizes and evaluates propaganda
  e. Organizes information about time and chronology[13]

Traditionally, elementary schools have embraced various skills deemed necessary to the complete development of young children. Many skills are inherent in the school subjects of language arts, mathematics, social studies, science, the arts, and physical education. Because many of the skills listed above overlap with school-subject skills, special emphasis will be given to the school-subject skills not mentioned above. The purpose of this section of skill discussion is to give prospective teachers some familiarity with what most schools are engaged in now.

[13] Recommendations of the State Social Studies Committee of the Oklahoma Curriculum Improvement Commission, *The Improvement of Instruction in Geography, History, Political Science, Economics, and Related Areas*, Oklahoma State Department of Education, 1966, pp. 14–15.

Language-Arts Skills

A large number of the skills elementary age children use have been broadly classified as the language arts. These include four basic activities, which overlap one another as well as some of the aforementioned skills. Generally, we can abstract listening, speaking, reading, and writing from the total language arts and rest assured we have included the basic language-arts skills.

LISTENING. Listening is the foundation of all language-arts skills.It is more than hearing and it needs to be taught. Listening involves abstracting from the myriad noises that surround an individual. The rules for abstracting will vary with the purpose of the listening. Essentially, individuals listen for information and pleasure. How well they listen, that is, how much information or pleasure is obtained, depends on the amount of concentration. Though the degree of concentration can be affected by the setting, the purpose of listening comes from within the individual. When a child perceives a need to listen, he will, and no amount of prodding or baiting will help him. Effective mastery of listening can be worked toward by building purposeful listening experiences and controlling the setting enough to permit a high degree of concentration.

SPEAKING. Speaking is as natural as listening and is usually learned by imitation. The varieties of speech are a function of the purpose for which one speaks. Speaking can be entertaining, informative, inspirational, or all three, but an emphasis would be accorded one of the varieties in light of the purpose.

The mechanics of speaking, pronunciation and enunciation, are basic skills that need to be mastered in order for one to be an effective speaker. Experiences in school that call for speaking should be varied enough to allow students opportunities to refine and add to the skills they already have.

READING. Reading involves bringing meaning to symbols and includes such ancillary skills as remembering, ordering, and summarizing. Purposes of reading vary from critical to pleasureful, but all reading activities require the basic skill of recognizing symbols. Having an appropriate repertoire of meanings is required for success in reading. Visual acuity is necessary for symbol recognition. Such acuity can be improved by practice, especially when a purpose for practice is perceived by the young learner. Building repertoires of meaning is a function of experience. Rich and varied experiencing should be the rule, not the exception, to early childhood education.

There is probably more specificity of skills in reading than in any other school subject. Entire books have been written to list and illustrate the myriad skills. For further detail in reading skills one can consult such references.[14]

WRITING. There are at least two aspects to the writing of young children. Mechanically, writing needs to be legible. Whether writing cursively or in manuscript, the symbols must be easily discernible by the reader. The second aspect to writing has to do with purpose. One can write creatively for enjoyment, at which time some conventions may be disregarded, or one can write for expository reasons and follow the conventions closely to minimize obfuscation. And there can be blended purposes. Friendly letters can be entertaining as well as informational. The epitome of this kind of blend of purposes is the "novel as history and history as a novel" which is becoming more popular today.

Spelling and appropriate usage necessarily emerge as subskills of writing. Whether teachers use a standardized list of spelling words, or the child's previous errors, the teaching of spelling should proceed from near to where the child is and help create a more independent speller who values correct spelling as an aid to writing more clearly. Usage is no longer proper or improper, but simply appropriate or inappropriate. As with other writing conventions, usage is dictated by the purpose for writing.

SITUATION 12.3
Finding a Need for Language Arts Skills

A classmate is suffering an illness that prevents him from attending school. The children decide to share their classroom experiences with him. Some of the children decide to record messages on audiotapes, thus needing to polish their speaking skills. The children listen critically to the tapes before they are sent. The other children write either expository reports of what the class has done or creative pieces to lift the spirits of their friend.

Mathematics Skills

In order for children to think quantitatively, the primary goal of mathematics programs, it is necessary that a large set of subskills be mastered. The salient feature of the subskills is that they require bringing appropriate meanings to specific symbols. Mathematics is not unlike reading, and proficiency in both depends on recognizing symbols and applying the

[14] See John J. DeBoer and Martha Dallmann, *The Teaching of Reading* (New York: Holt, Rinehart and Winston, Inc., 1970); and Miles A. Tinker and Constance M. McCullough, *Teaching Elementary Reading* (New York: Appleton-Century-Crofts, Inc., 1962).

proper meanings from one's repertoire of meaning. The basic skills of a mathematics program include learning facts, developing concepts, and drawing generalizations.

It has been the authors' experience that mathematics, more than any other school subject, has been taught almost exclusively from a textbook. The new elementary school will assuredly have mathematics textbooks, but the teachers will teach for effective mastery of skills in ways other than simply presenting a concept and assigning twenty practice exercises from the text or a workbook.

Increased use will be made of materials, both commercial and teacher-made, that children can sort, count, measure with, and generally manipulate in quantitative ways. Teachers will create situations that maximize children's interaction with things, working toward inductive approaches to concepts and generalizations. When drill or practice is necessary, as it will be with some of the lower-order facts, it will be done only after the children perceive a need for it.

SITUATION 12.4

A Need for Mathematics Skills

Some upper elementary boys decide they want to lay out a football field that is at least close to regulation size. They accept the teacher's challenge to set it up without direct use of a measuring tape. Each boy counts the number of paces he takes to cover a measured fifty feet. Through division of fifty into 300 and multiplication of that quotient by his number of paces, he arrives at an approximation of the proper length. Actual measurement with a tape follows to see who came the closest.

The efficiency and effectiveness of mathematics instruction, like many other basic skill areas, has been increased through programmed instruction techniques. (Photo courtesy Norman Public Schools.)

Science Skills

The skills necessary for science parallel the general research skills discussed above. Renner and Ragan list them as:

> Isolating interesting problems, planning their solutions, carrying out those plans, and interpreting the data from experiments. . . .[15]

These general skills subsume ". . . the rational power of imagination, analysis, synthesis, classification, comparison, and inference."[16] According to Renner and Ragan, effective mastery of science skills can best be achieved when we ". . . confront the children in our classes with direct experiences involving phenomena from their environment which are at their intellectual level."[17]

What should become apparent to the reader at this time is that science education, as described above, is simply an inquiry/discovery methodology focused on science. Earlier in this chapter it was suggested that the inquiry/discovery approach to teaching was a general method appropriate for all children and skills. Here we find it specifically applied to science in order to help children develop their scientific frames of reference. Craig recommends some of the kinds of experiences children can have in science. They include: space, time, change, adaptation, variety, interrelationship, equilibrium, and balance.[18] The following situation is an example of a lesson in variety.

SITUATION 12.5
Developing Science Skills

In order for children to recognize that the material of an object may remain the same, even though the object's appearance changes, and that two objects may appear to be different but are still made of the same material, sugar cubes and rock candy are distributed to small groups of children who are equipped with magnifiers, mortars, and pestles. The children are asked to examine the objects, then to break them down separately in the mortar with the aid of the pestle. Each object is examined after decomposition, and the children are encouraged to generalize about the makeup of each as well as the original form.[19]

---

[15] Renner and Ragan, p. 231.
[16] Renner and Ragan, p. 237.
[17] Renner and Ragan, p. 240.
[18] Gerald S. Craig, *Science for the Elementary School Teacher*, rev. ed. (Boston: Ginn and Company, 1962), pp. 93–101.
[19] Science Curriculum Improvement Study, *Material Objects* (Teachers Guide), prelim. ed. (Boston, Mass.: D. C. Heath & Company, 1966), p. 54–55.

Not only concepts, but ways of working with things and ideas, are at issue in science. These "thinking skills" are becoming increasingly important in a complex, technological world. (Photo courtesy Norman Public Schools.)

Social Studies Skills

The social studies are comprised of a wide variety of disciplines. Elements of geography, history, psychology, philosophy, anthropology, sociology, and economics are frequently found in the kinds of activities children perform under the generic heading of social studies. The skills of each of the constituent parts of the social studies would require more space to list than our present purposes permit. Suffice it to say that teachers in the new elementary school can select from any of the disciplines when appropriate. Preston set the stage for skill development when he indicated the role of the social studies in the elementary school.

> The role of social studies in elementary education is to aid the child from kindergarten or first grade through sixth grade, to understand the concepts that describe and explain human society, and to develop the insight and skills required by democratic citizenship.[20]

Many of the skills required by democratic citizenship have been discussed earlier, in other contexts. Listening well (courteously and critically) and speaking fluently can be considered social studies as well as language arts skills. Other social skills, such as empathy, respect for property, and the ability to work with others, may be more indigenous to social studies, but the classification is admittedly arbitrary. Effective mastery of social skills is best acquired through example and situations that create a need for them.

[20] Ralph C. Preston, "The Role of Social Studies in Elementary Education," in Nelson Henry (Ed.). *Social Studies in the Elementary School*, Fifty-sixth Yearbook, Part II, National Society for the Study of Education (Chicago: University of Chicago Press, 1957), p. 4.

> SITUATION 12.6
> *Teaching Social Skills*
>
> A teacher can indicate to a popular child that she might send a valentine to one who would probably not otherwise receive one, to suggest to an athletic boy, always chosen as captain, that he select as a team member a boy continually left out of games.[21]

Substantively, history and geography have contributed the most to elementary social studies. To the extent that the skills of history and geography are perceived to fulfill a need of elementary children, they should be part of the new elementary school curriculum. Achieving an historical perspective is a skill that children need to better understand the present and to think about the future.

Constructing a time line is an activity that has been used successfully by teachers to help children obtain both sequences and relationships of historical events. Historical novels and biographies are sources of history that have wide appeal to the varied interests of children. And teachers who couch their comments in historical terms can serve as excellent models of the informed citizen of a democracy.

Map and globe skills have been frequently found in the elementary schools. One wonders if their amenability to teaching has outweighed their relevance to children. But if they are to be included as essential social studies skills, they too can be most effectively mastered when children are confronted with real problems that call for their use.

Creative Arts Skills

Music and art skills can be considered as having two dimensions: performing and appreciating. This abstracted dichotomy is useful for discussion but is dysfunctional for the arts. The distinction is one of degree of proficiency in the skill. In the first place, everyone has some degree of proficiency in both. Everybody has some degree of creativity. Whether it is nurtured or neglected is a function of one's environment. Likewise, appreciation is the foundation of the arts and, though varying degrees of sophistication are possible, everyone has the potential for deriving pleasure from the visual and aural arts.

---

[21] William B. Ragan and John D. McAulay, *Social Studies for Today's Children* (New York: Appleton-Century-Crofts, 1964), p. 231.

There are a host of subskills connected with art education, but the essential skill, if it can be called a skill, is creativity. Mastery of a skill, whether one paints or sculpts, draws or shapes, is less important than the surrounding atmosphere and the feeling that one is doing his best at creating something of his own. Appreciation for unique and skillful work is a natural result of one's own experience in creative endeavors.

Young children respond spontaneously to music. The skill is there to be developed. When children participate in musical activities they not only improve their skill in responding to but increase their appreciation of music. Unless one participates in the activity, the chances for effective mastery are reduced.

> SITUATION 12.7
> *Utilizing Art and Music*
>
> The entire class wants to show its appreciation for an elementary teacher who plans to retire in May. The children set about organizing a presentation of songs and art work. The practice is perceived as important because they all want to do their very best. The art skills for drawings, paintings, and wood blocks are applied to program announcements, invitations, and stage decorations.

Physical Education Skills

Physical education skills span exercise, recreation, and good sportsmanship. The teaching and practice of exercise skills are usually accomplished through demonstration and imitation. Incidental exercise is achieved in any physical activity, but systematic practice is most effectively mastered by some form of calisthenics.

The most necessary recreational skills are locomotion and object handling. Although specific attention may be focused on these skills apart from an activity that requires their integration, their effective mastery is dependent on the desire to perfect them. Such desire is created when children sense their usefulness in an activity.

Good sportsmanship, like the other social skills, is best learned by example. Physical education activities provide a rich setting for developing rules of good conduct both on and off the field of play. The context of a game with its explicit rules is often more conducive to learning the skills of good sportsmanship than other social settings where the rules are usually implicit.

There is no formula for ensuring effective mastery of a skill, but if we have learned anything from our experiences in school it is that effective mastery of any skill can best be achieved when the learner senses a need for it and practices it at a level at which he can experience some success.

SUMMARY

1. There is a general dissatisfaction with the school's ability or inability to reasonably satisfy a large portion of today's children and youth.

2. Schools have traditionally operated as if the learners were passive and indifferent about their education.

3. Basic skills are relative to the needs and interests of the children and society and should be changed whenever they are no longer relevant.

4. The basic skills transcend the 3 R's. There is a greater need now for skills in interhuman relationships.

5. Teachers in the new elementary school will assume children to be natural learners, striving to make sense of the world.

6. Proficiency in many basic skills is a lifelong endeavor. Arbitrary levels of proficiency are as useless as they are meaningless.

7. Understanding one's self and creatively confronting the problems one faces are two intrapersonal basic skills.

8. Problem solving, research, and effective communication are skills that will help the learner better understand his world and the people in it.

9. The typical school subjects of language arts, mathematics, science, social studies, the arts, and physical education subsume many intra- and interpersonal relationship skills as well as some indigenous to themselves.

10. Effective mastery of basic skills can be achieved when children perceive a need for the skills and engage in them at their level of understanding.

RECOMMENDED READINGS

Beauchamp, George A., *The Curriculum of the Elementary School*. Boston: Allyn and Bacon, Inc., 1966. A description of the typical school subjects' objectives and skills is preceded by a general consideration of curriculum in American public schools.

Crary, Ryland W., *Humanizing the School: Curriculum Development and Theory*. New York: Alfred A Knopf, 1969. A general view of America's efforts and shortcomings in providing humanistic education for all children. Chapters 1 and 2 provide an excellent background for skill development in the schools.

Hanna, Lavone A., Gladys L. Potter, and Neva Hagaman, *Unit Teaching in the Elementary School*. New York: Holt, Rinehart and Winston, Inc., 1963. The framework and organization of teaching units and their relationship to learning experiences are presented, as well as examples of units for teaching.

McKim, Margaret G., Carl W. Hansen, and William L. Carter, *Learning to Teach in the Elementary School*. New York: Crowell-Collier and Macmillan, Inc., 1959. A good book for beginning teachers faced with having to adjust to a new setting.

Postman, Neil, and Charles Weingartner, *Teaching as a Subversive Activity*. New York: Delacorte Press, 1969. A fresh approach to the problem of relevance in education. Excellent background laced with practical suggestions makes this book truly unique in the field.

Ragan, William B., and John D. McAulay, *Social Studies for Today's Children*. New York: Appleton-Century-Crofts, 1964. A broad overview of social studies education. Part III deals with problems and methods of teaching the basic skills of social studies.

Renner, John W., and William B. Ragan, *Teaching Science in the Elementary School*. New York: Harper & Row, Publishers, 1968. The application of the discovery method of teaching to elementary school science with specific examples of science experiences for children.

Rubin, Louis J. (Ed.), *Life Skills in School and Society*. Washington, D.C.: Association for Supervision and Curriculum Development, N.E.A., 1969. A collection of readings organized around current social and cultural problems. The first and last chapters, by Rubin, are most relevant to a broader understanding of basic skills.

Stendler, Celia B., *Teaching in the Elementary School*. New York: Harcourt Brace Jovanovich, Inc., 1958. A general elementary methods text with an especially good section on teaching the basic skills in Part II.

Chapter 13

Individualizing and Personalizing Teaching

Do not let us seek to persuade ourselves that an education of the masses is possible: that is a contradiction in terms. What is educable is only an individual, or more exactly a person.

Gabriel Marcel, *Man Against Mass Society* (Chicago: Henry Regnery Company, 1962), p. 11.

When lists of trends in elementary education are formulated or when needed improvements in teaching are mentioned, individualizing teaching almost always heads the list. Since this theme has been so prominent in educational writing, it is surprising that more examples of individualized teaching are not found in actual practice. Personalizing teaching means that a new dimension has been added. It is possible, of course, to require all pupils to study the same content and use the same materials, and still individualize teaching by permitting pupils to master the content at different rates. Personalizing instruction, however, means that different materials are used to correspond to the needs, interests, and abilities of different pupils. There are some materials that all pupils must learn in order to make progress through the school program. There are other materials, however, that only a few pupils can learn, want to learn, or need to learn. Teachers in the new elementary school are not content merely to individualize teaching; they want also to personalize teaching.

EIGHT DIMENSIONS OF SCHOOLING

There are at least eight dimensions of any schooling situation, and it will serve our purposes here to discuss them as they relate to individualized and personalized instruction. They include purposes, rules, learning styles, content, time, space, participation, and evaluation. By elaborating on each of these dimensions we can make more complete our definition of individualized and personalized teaching.

THE PURPOSE OF SCHOOL. Regardless of the school activity in which a child is engaged, some purpose is being served. One purpose frequently served in yesterday's schools, though teachers seldom seemed to be aware of it, was fostering dependence, on the child's part, on the various structures the school and teacher provided. Oftentimes the only reason a child could cite for engaging in a task was the teacher's request that it be done. The implicit message in such activities was that one learns by carrying out the orders of the teacher.

If helping to develop independent thought and action is a purpose teachers wish to serve, then they need to be sensitive to the child's perception of why he is engaged in an activity. If the child can see some relevance in an activity in reference to his needs and/or specific interests, the work will more likely have lasting meaning for him as he grows toward independence. The chances for achieving this ideal are enhanced when teachers individualize and personalize their teaching. That is, teachers must begin to treat the members of the classroom as individuals and reduce to a minimum the times when all children are expected to carry out the same activity.

RULES. All schools have some kinds of rules, and in many classrooms a great deal of time is devoted to creating, enforcing, and observing rules. There are at least two aspects of rules that bear discussing here. One aspect that students must contend with is their sheer number. Any group of individuals having to function within the confines of myriad rules will soon find its members inordinately concerned with staying within bounds and only slightly concerned with achieving tasks. There is a point of no return when creating rules for a group. When the number of rules increases to the point of making all of them dysfunctional, the teacher and children need to rethink and replan more effective ways of functioning. Attention might be directed to the nature of activities and relationships that require so many rules. There are important qualitative aspects of rules that need to be considered, too.

The relevancy of rules can determine how well they are observed. A rule is most relevant when it makes sense to students and, preferably, when the students have had a voice in its creation. Basic or fundamental rules require no equivocation. Health and safety must be secured in a group, and rules such as no running and no interfering with or disturbing others are as sensible as they are common. Many times groups will routinize their activities in such a way that the rules for such behavior will naturally emerge and be taken for granted as implicit rules.

LEARNING STYLES. There are probably as many different learning styles as there are children. Of course, many are similar enough not to warrant differentiation, but everybody is to some extent unique in the way in which he learns most effectively. A schooling situation that provides for diverse learning styles is one that is moving in the direction of individualized and personalized teaching.

Nearly all of the present schools that boast of having an individualized instructional program point with pride to their learning or resource centers that house various kinds of instructional hardware and software. The collection of such media is an effort to accommodate the varying learning styles of children. Hardware and software need not be the only alternatives for children, however. Other means of problem solving and data gathering can be provided by the creative teacher. Children can learn from conducting interviews and surveys, by observing and participating in community activities, and by an infinite number of methods if they have some choice in determining how they will learn.

CONTENT. Another dimension of a schooling situation is the content or substantive matter with which the child deals. Virtually all schools, even those purporting to embrace the ideal of individualization, reserve for the adults the decision regarding what content will be studied. When children have no choice about what they will be involved with, they are, in effect, losing a degree of freedom from their individualization and personalization.

Many subject areas and topics are broad enough to permit the teacher to provide children some latitude in deciding what it is they wish to study. Teachers in the new elementary school will select content that can be presented in such a way that each child can make a decision regarding the specific topic or area he wishes or needs to investigate. Stahl and Anzalone support differentiation in learning style and content:

> To ask all children at a given age or in a given grade to learn the same way or to do the same work in spelling, English, arithmetic, or any other subject is as unrealistic as asking them all to wear the same size clothing.[1]

[1] Dona Kofod Stahl and Patricia Murphy Anzalone, *Individualized Teaching in the Elementary School* (West Nyack, N.Y.: Parker Publishing Co., Inc., 1970), p. 19.

Permitting and encouraging different learning styles and content would be a definite step toward individualized and personalized teaching because it would demonstrate to the child that the teacher recognizes and respects his integrity as a person.

TIME. How time is used in a schooling situation plays an important part in helping to determine to what extent a program is geared to individual and personal needs.

The artificiality and arbitrariness of breaking learning into specified time segments have worked against most attempts at individualization in schools that retained class periods of designated lengths. Secondary schools have been more guilty of time regimentation than elementary, but even teachers of self-contained elementary classrooms have been slaves to the clock.

Modifications of curricular routines such as modular scheduling at the secondary level and variations of team-teaching approaches at the elementary level have been designed to make learning activities more flexible at both levels. Whatever the time organization is called in the new elementary school, it will be characterized as being as natural as possible to the way children learn. That is, though some time scheduling will be inevitable, the frequency of interruptions and distractions due to time-schedule requirements will be reduced to a minimum.

A corollary to the problem of an imposed time schedule is the individual child's need for time to carry out school activities. Teachers in the new elementary school will have to be sensitive to the various needs each of the children will have about how much time is necessary for completing an activity. The less uniformity teachers expect in terms of the time different children need, the more individualized and personalized their teaching will be.

SPACE. The sixth dimension of a schooling situation is space. Planned or expected learning has frequently been confined within the four walls of the classroom and, at most, within the school's walls. The new elementary school will be typified by an expanding of this parochial view of learning and will have learning experiences planned for many and varied locations.

Teachers will capitalize on the opportunities for learning that all children experience when they are at home or en route to and from school. Many teachers in the past have tried to shut off or shut out those experiences that were not indigenous to the school's or teacher's plan. This attitude and behavior helped widen the gap between school and the real world of children, a gap the new elementary school must bridge if schools are to justify their existence.

Where can learning take place besides in the classroom? The question might better be, "Where can't learning take place?" Within the

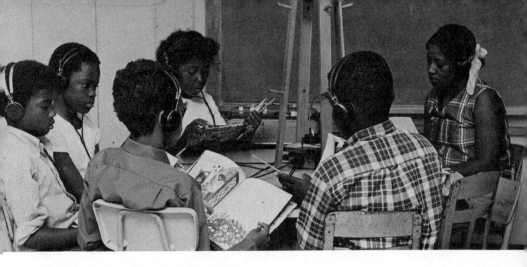

The use of tape recorders and earphones helps to individualize instruction. (Photo courtesy Oklahoma City Public Schools.)

province of the teacher's plan there are many places where learning experiences can be encountered. The media center of the school would be an obvious location. There the child would go to research problems, availing himself of the various hardware and software resources. Field trips planned for the entire class or small groups can be rich sources for learning experiences. From watching a sunrise to visiting businesses, shops, plants, community buildings, and farms, children can learn much more than if they are confined to a classroom or building during school hours.

PARTICIPATION. Compulsory school-attendance laws preclude a completely individualized and personalized teaching approach, and, because the repeal or modification of such laws is unlikely, we can only focus our concern for participation after the fact of attendance. Upon reflection it is really quite reasonable for an individual to opt occasionally for noninvolvement. Naturally, a teacher would be concerned if a child's primary mode of behavior were noninvolvement, but the teacher in the new elementary school will accept and respect as natural the personal desire a child may have not to engage in an activity.

Whenever one activity is presented to a group, a fair number of individuals turn off or tune out with such deftness most teachers may be deceived. Cutts and Moseley proclaim:

Teaching a whole class as a single group would be the most efficient form of instruction if it were not for individual differences. But it is in fact the most wasteful.[2]

[2] Norma E. Cutts and Nicholas Moseley, *Providing for Individual Differences in the Elementary School* (Englewood Cliffs, N.J.: Prentice-Hall, Inc., 1960), p. 36.

With occasional exceptions, presenting a single activity to a group in which everyone is expected to engage himself maximally is a futile endeavor and one that teachers in the new elementary school should avoid.

EVALUATION. Assessing growth in terms of how it was affected by the activities carried out under the auspices of the teacher or school is a form of evaluation. Evaluation is usually a summative and terminal activity, but there are other functions evaluation can serve and other times in a schooling situation when it can be applied.

Placement, formative, and diagnostic evaluation are as important as summative evaluation.[3] Placement evaluation is any attempt to place students in a schooling situation in light of data gathered from them. It typically occurs before students and teachers convene. Formative evaluation is that which helps the teacher better provide the setting for learning experiences for the children. It takes place during the time when teacher and children are together and serves essentially as feedback information for both teacher and child. Diagnostic evaluation may occur anytime. It is aimed at revealing psychological, physical, or environmental symptoms

[3] George F. Madaus and Peter W. Airasian, "Placement, Formative, Diagnostic and Summative Evaluation of Classroom Learning," Paper Presented to the Annual Meeting of the American Educational Research Association, Minneapolis, Minnesota, March 1970.

The multimedia approach to learning makes it possible for small groups of pupils to work on projects in which they are particularly interested. Personalized learning is facilitated. (Photo courtesy Oklahoma City Public Schools.)

manifested by children suffering from recurrent learning and/or classroom problems.

PREPARING FOR INDIVIDUALIZED AND PERSONALIZED TEACHING

Assuming the eight aforementioned dimensions of schooling are salient features of any teaching situation, we can discuss how one prepares for individualizing and personalizing one's teaching approach by reexamining them more specifically.

Experience would indicate the best preparation for the new elementary teacher would be a school career, including the teacher-education program, that was characterized by a great deal of individualization and personalization. One is likely to teach the way one was taught, and it will take concerted effort to teach differently. Having little or no control over that, however, we will assume a traditionally prepared teacher has decided to move in the direction of individualized and personalized teaching. What needs to be done to facilitate the move?

SELF-DIRECTION AS A PURPOSE. There is some evidence to suggest schools exist for purposes other than instilling self-direction in students. Indeed, there have been indictments that indicate schools consciously discourage self-direction and independence, not to mention creativity and imagination, in a effort to achieve predictable, modal behavior.[4] If a teacher is committed to self-direction as a goal, it is incumbent upon her to behave in ways that will reinforce and encourage each child in becoming an independent and viable member of society. Membership in society requires respect for laws and other rules of the group. We are suggesting self-direction and independence are reconcilable with social expectations. It is only because schools in the past have so frequently denied individuality that we deem it necessary to state an otherwise obvious consideration.

By keeping self-direction as a purpose clearly in mind, the teacher of the new elementary school will be less likely to violate children's rights and responsibilities. She can readily put any planned activity to the test of whether or not it encourages self-direction, both in terms of short- and long-range consequences. The specific goals should be consistent with

---

[4] See, for example, John Holt, "School is Bad for Children," *Saturday Evening Post*, February 8, 1969; Edgar Z. Friedenberg, "Curriculum as Educational Process: The Middle Class Against Itself," in Norman V. Overly (Ed.), *The Unstudied Curriculum* (Washington, D.C.: Association for Supervision and Curriculum Development, N.E.A., 1970); Ivan Illich, "The False Ideology of Schooling," *Saturday Review*, October 17, 1970, pp. 56–68; and Everett Reimer, *An Essay on Alternatives in Education* (Cuernavaca, Mor., Mexico: CIDOC Cuaderno No. 1005, 1970).

the general ones. Teachers should be cautioned not to associate one activity with one goal or purpose. Stahl and Anzalone note:

> Your goal in planning for instruction is not that of finding a direction in which to point the whole class. You must find a variety of directions in which to point a variety of individuals or small groups of pupils.[5]

DEVELOPING RULES. The quantity and quality of rules children experience are important factors in facilitating a move toward individualized and personalized teaching. Rules basic to preserving the health and safety of children need to be established and enforced whenever and wherever children interact with their environment. Before a teacher meets the children she should have a clear idea of what health and safety rules the group will need. These, of course, need to be clearly explained to the children before much activity takes place.

SITUATION 13.1
Making Rules Relevant

A teacher created a rule for the order in which children would hang up and retrieve their overcoats from the cloakroom. In spite of the rule the children were generally noisy and disorderly whenever they went to the cloakroom. Sensing the rule was doing little good, he abolished it. The children then became even more disorderly in the cloakroom. Then the teacher suggested the children make their own rules for solving the chaotic problem. They made all kinds of rules bordering on the absurd; for example, having the initials of their names determine when they would get their coats.

The result of the exercise, which took only a few days, was that the children realized *for themselves* that some kind of rule was necessary and that it would be in this case even somewhat arbitrary. The final rule was agreed upon and followed with no objection, and the hanging of overcoats was thereafter much less chaotic.[6]

Other rules, those primarily concerned with convenience and expediency, should be cooperatively developed and, generally, kept to a minimum.

"It is more important for children to appreciate and practice self-control than to be controlled by an adult."[7] As the children begin to engage themselves in various activities, or while they anticipate such activities, they can be guided by the teacher in establishing other rules.

---

[5] Stahl and Anzalone, p. 22.

[6] Herbert Kohl, "Rules of the Game," *Grade Teacher*, October 1970, p. 6.

[7] Stahl and Anzalone, p. 24.

PLANNING FOR VARIOUS LEARNING STYLES. Anticipating that the children of a class will have diverse learning styles, the teacher of the new elementary school will arrange to have a variety of devices and resources near at hand to accommodate them. Common hardware materials include 16mm film projectors, single-concept 8mm film loops and projectors, slide and filmstrip projectors, and overhead and opaque projectors. Other hardware needed would be cassette and reel-type tape recorders, phonograph record players, self-instructional machines, radio, and television. Software resources include books, periodicals, newspapers; and the tapes, films, and self-instructional programs for the machines.

SITUATION 13.2
Planning for Diverse Learning Styles

A frontal approach to determining learning styles would be to poll the children. Make a list of questions for the students beginning with, "Which helps you more . . . ?" "When do you learn more . . . ?" or "When do you try harder . . . ?" and complete them with some of your teaching behaviors. For example:
. . . When I give you one long assignment, or several short ones?
. . . When we practice together or you practice by yourself?
. . . When I tell you what to do or let you figure it out yourself?
. . . When I decide which project you should do first or let you make the choice?[8]

Teachers need to plan for other learning activities as well. Opportunities to observe and interview people outside the school should be arranged when appropriate. Participation in what traditionally have been called extracurricular activities should be encouraged and, whenever possible, integrated into the regular classroom activities.

PLANNING FOR CHOICE OF CONTENT. When the teacher selects the content that will be used during the school year, she needs to keep it on a sufficiently general level to permit the children some choice in determining specific topics. Some examples of individualizing and personalizing teaching of the traditional school subjects will be discussed in another section of this chapter. Suffice it to say here that every effort should be made to return the decision of what to study to the child.

FLEXIBLE SCHEDULING OF TIME. Teachers of the new elementary school will avoid strict adherence to a time schedule. Rather, large blocks of time,

[8] Madeline Hunter, "Tailor Your Teaching to Individualized Instruction," *Instructor*, Vol. 79, March 1970, p. 60.

from one to two hours, will be reserved for the kinds of activities that would otherwise suffer if arbitrarily broken into fifteen- or fifty-minute periods. General research projects that involve creating researchable questions, generating hypotheses, gathering data, and making judgments can be carried out with more efficacy if a relatively long period of time is set aside for them.

Other occasions with specific time limits, such as testing situations, story times, guest speakers, and other time-limited types of activities, will need to be planned for and scheduled by the teacher and children cooperatively. Preferably, such short-duration activities should occur during the same time of day as frequently as possible in order that the children begin expecting them. Such limited regularity lends an aura of ritual to the group that augurs well for group cohesion and security.

Two ways of looking at time in school are by the day and by all the years that make up a school career. Times of the day have typically been associated with certain subjects or activities, as well as points of time in a school career. Such scheduled times should not be considered sacred. There's no support for the notion that 9:30 A.M. is the optimum time to teach reading, or that the fourth grade is the best time to teach the muliplication table.

UTILIZING SPACE. Anticipating instructional activities, the teacher ought to concern herself with the utilization of space outside her regular classroom. If a resource center is available in the school, she needs to arrange with the director or building principal the times it would be possible to have her children avail themselves of it. Using other possible centers, such as libraries, audio-visual and multipurpose rooms, may require similar planning activities by the teacher. Conventional field-trip destinations should be contacted to determine convenient visiting times, hours, and other restrictions. Many school systems have a guidebook listing interesting places to visit with the various restrictions or recommendations concerning such visits.

A corollary activity of arranging for other spaces is meeting with some parents who are willing to serve as aides in supervising individuals or small groups of children when they need to leave the classroom. Many times such volunteer help is overlooked simply because teachers never initiate the request.

PLANNING FOR CHOICE OF PARTICIPATION. All of us experience times when we just do not feel like doing something, even though we may know it is expected that we do it. Children are no different in this regard. It is about time school people overcame the myth that "idle hands are the devil's workshop." Too many schools of the past operated on the premise that if you simply keep children busy, your behavior problems will diminish. Children in the new elementary school will have the right to opt for inactivity without feeling guilty about not being busy.

If teachers provide a wide variety of recreational materials, such as puzzles, chess boards, and other nonacademic devices, the children will probably engage in these when they feel like taking a break, rather than not do anything at all. Assuming a respite is natural, the teacher need not concern herself with occasional idleness or other nonacademic activity. She must decide, however, when such behavior is symptomatic of a problem that may warrant her investigation and subsequent guidance.

PLANNING FOR DIFFERENTIATED EVALUATION. If teaching is to be individualized and personalized, the evaluation should be too. Schools of the past emphasized summative evaluation that was usually applied for the purpose of assigning a grade or mark to some level of performance. Moreover, there was usually an implicit group comparison involved in the evaluation. The types of evaluation employed in the new elementary school will include the aforementioned placement, formative and diagnostic as well as summative. No longer will there be an inordinate concern for the summative type of evaluation.

Keeping track of twenty-five or thirty youngsters' progress in their various school endeavors can be a formidable task. Fortunately, many children will be able to make daily corrections and keep cumulative records of their work. Those who are not so responsible will need the teacher's assistance in providing them with immediate feedback.

SITUATION 13.3
Keeping Children's Records

The teacher's records should be simple and easily maintained. They should include this information: What has the student accomplished? Is he floundering, or is the task so easy he does not need to exert learning effort?

Devices can vary from checklists and anecdotal file cards to teacher-made tests and observations. It is important to have all the information you need, but on the other hand not to waste time collecting useless or obsolete data. Keep only those data that are indispensable.[9]

[9] Hunter, p. 63.

ANOTHER LOOK AT THE SCHOOL SUBJECTS

Although considering as exclusive the traditional school subjects of language arts, mathematics, science, social studies, creative arts, and physical education has frequently been cited as too narrow an approach in the past, we will consider them below for two reasons. First, the narrowness of the school subjects is a function of how the teacher uses them with children. If any indictments of yesterday's schools are valid, it would surely be the singular approach to the content areas that typified most schooling. We submit that the subject areas can be approached in a number of ways that permit individual choice-making by students. The second justification is that school people are most familiar with the school subjects as content. Because it is much easier to move within familiar ground than to leap to some unknown, leaving behind the security that enables one to try something new, we will begin with the familiar.

LANGUAGE ARTS. It was noted in the previous chapter that the language arts are comprised of listening, speaking, reading, and writing. There will be inter- as well as intrapersonal differences in these skill areas. One of the first tasks for the teacher, then, is to assess each child's skill level in each of these subareas as soon as possible. This information will help her provide and guide appropriate learning situations for each of the children.

Most of the language skills are also social skills. By creating social settings that call for as many of the skills as possible, the teacher will be providing real needs for children to practice and improve their language skills. Herrick recommends this kind of structuring:

> . . . individual differences are best provided for when the teacher starts with the social situation, which gives purpose and meaning to learning, and then relates the appropriate media and mechanics [of language] to the situation, rather than reversing the process.[10]

The social situation needs to be complex enough to accommodate the range of skill levels of all the students in order to avoid embarrassing some and boring others.

Other activities, such as experience-stories, biographies, and dramatizations, can provide for a wide range of interest and ability levels in each of the language-arts skill areas.

Language at the elementary level is primarily a conveyer of other content areas. Therefore, the children should have opportunities to develop their language skills in the content areas as well. Reporting, recording,

[10] Virgil E. Herrick, "The Language Arts," in Cutts and Moseley, p. 129.

discussing, and debating within other subject areas can provide such opportunities.

MATHEMATICS. The skills of learning facts, developing concepts, and drawing generalizations, like the language-arts skills, will vary from child to child as well as within each individual. Mathematics is the best example of two important dimensions of learning: easy-to-difficult and simple-to-complex. The easy-to-difficult continuum begins with serial ordering, adding, subtracting, multiplying, dividing, fractions, and beyond, while the simple-to-complex spans recognizing, recalling, understanding, applying, problem solving, analyzing, synthesizing, and evaluating.[11]

The learning situations the children confront should afford opportunities for children to be successful and contributive at any or all of the various levels along the two dimensions. Assignments and practice exercises should be appropriate in terms of length, difficulty, and complexity. Individual record-keeping works well with mathematics because there are so many standardized tests against which students can plot their progress. Commercial, individually prescribed instructional programs are also available in mathematics.

SCIENCE. In the previous chapter we indicated the basic skills of science were research skills: specifically, imagination, analysis, classification, comparison, and inference. Because these skills transcend subject matter, it is possible to learn and practice them with different experiences. Sheckles suggests:

> Since learning the same facts is not needed to achieve our objectives [similar to those above], it is no longer necessary to provide the same experiences for all children of a given age or in any given classroom.[12]

The suggestion, however, does not mean science activities should be random and not planned.

There are several general frameworks teachers can utilize in planning the kinds of science activities the children will experience. Sheckles suggests the seven basic science patterns of the universe: time, space, change, adaptation, interrelationships, variety, and energy.[13] Each of these patterns can be utilized in observing and analyzing scientific phenomena. Specific topics for inquiry can be decided by each student. The teacher's responsibility would be to guide the child in his study vis-à-vis the seven patterns.

---

[11] Hunter, p. 55.
[12] Mary E. Sheckles, "Science," in Cutts and Moseley, p. 183.
[13] Sheckles, p. 184.

Another general framework is suggested by Slawson. It includes the study of man's environment in terms of matter, change, energy, and man's control and use of his environment.[14]

SOCIAL STUDIES. The social studies area of the new elementary school curriculum provides the teacher with many opportunities to help children develop lifelong habits of good citizenship. Chambers admonishes that teachers of social studies:

> . . . must adapt materials to levels of ability, note individual rates of progress in the learning of skills, give special help at points of weakness, enrich learning and make it significant, build on interests and experiences, and encourage self-direction and initiative.[15]

None of these things can be accomplished if teachers require all children to read from the same text or participate in identical activities.

SITUATION 13.4
Individualizing and Personalizing Social Studies

At the beginning of any unit or when a new topic is scheduled by the course of study, the teacher can present an overview of the content to be studied and ask the children to list pertinent topics they would particularly like to learn about. This helps the teacher be sure he is not ignoring a strong interest. It gives him an opportunity to increase the pupils' purpose in learning. And it may indicate a basis for setting up small groups of children who have common interests that they can pursue together.[16]

A distinctive feature of the social studies as a content area is its concern for social skills of children. Many opportunities for developing social skills can be found in social studies activities. Groups of children or even the whole classroom can be involved in making plans, observing culminating activities of a unit, and taking field trips.[17] Such involvement helps children realize the necessity of working together courteously, sharing, taking responsibility, and meeting a deadline.

CREATIVE ARTS. The creative arts, which include at least art and music, and may embrace drama, dance, and writing, ought to require the most in-

---

[14] Wilber S. Slawson, "Bases of Science Curriculum Development in the Future," in William W. Joyce, Robert G. Oana, and W. Robert Houston (Eds.), *Elementary Education in the Seventies* (New York: Holt, Rinehart and Winston, Inc., 1970), p. 226.

[15] J. Richard Chambers, "The Social Studies," in Cutts and Moseley, p. 152.

[16] Chambers, p. 156.

[17] Chambers, p. 157.

dividualization and personalization because they tap the creative abilities of each child. In the past there was some deference paid to differentiating instruction in the creative arts, but most instruction was geared to the likenesses of the children of a group. Mattil warns:

> When the art program of the classroom is geared to the likenesses of children and tends to ignore the differences, there is little possibility that it will rise above mediocrity or that it will yield the rich results in child growth that should be the outcome of any creative experience.[18]

An art lesson in sculpturing, for example, need not have but one medium for the children to sculpt. Indeed, both additive and subtractive sculpturing could be encouraged when different media are used.

The musical experiences are just as amenable to individualization and personalization as those in the art program. Nye suggests:

> The [music] program should include opportunities to experiment with aspects of music that interest the individual and musical experiences undertaken as an outgrowth of other areas of the curriculum or as a contribution to them. In every case there should be provision for participation by the children in planning, directing and evaluating music activities.[19]

Singing is not the only legitimate musical behavior of elementary-age children. There are other rhythmic responses—playing bells, the autoharp, musical flutes, percussion instruments, and learning about music recorded on tapes and records—that are just as valid an indication of musical skill, interest, and appreciation.

Five points that should be kept in mind when planning for individualized and personalized creative arts are suggested by Mattil:

> 1. At each level the program should have a broad base in order to accommodate children at various levels of development;
> 2. The program should be based upon intense experiences, whether real or vicarious;
> 3. No single material or medium can satisfy the needs of all children;
> 4. Each child should have a record or portfolio of his progress and work; and
> 5. Teachers must respect differences as normal and expect them to increase, not decrease.[20]

PHYSICAL EDUCATION. The movement skills of elementary children can be improved in an individualized and personalized program of physical edu-

---

[18] Edward L. Mattil, "Art," in Cutts and Moseley, p. 79.
[19] Robert E. Nye, "Music," in Cutts and Moseley, pp. 106–107.
[20] Mattil, p. 99.

cation. The skills children use when expressing feeling or demonstrating knowledge and ability include speaking, writing, jumping, dancing, playing ball, and performing on a musical instrument. Each skill is learned by building increasingly complex and automatic movement patterns. Hunter suggests a series of questions to be asked to determine what each child has already accomplished and what he is now ready to learn:

> 1. Has the learner perceived what he is to do? You can waste much time trying to teach a skill when the student has not focused on the critical elements of the task.
> 2. Has he a "set" to perform the skill? Does he understand what part of his body is involved, and does he know what to do with it?
> 3. Has his performance been guided physically (placing his arms for him) or verbally ("Hold your arms this way") so he will know what is expected of him?
> 4. Has he "mechanized" the response—can he perform without stopping to think what comes next?
> 5. Has the skill become an automatic, complex response to the appropriate stimulus?[21]

Just as in the other subject areas, the children in an individualized and personalized physical education program will be working at different stages of development and at different tasks.

SITUATION 13.5
Physical Education in the New Elementary School

The teacher will be teaching some students how to use their bodies properly in throwing, catching, running, or balancing. Students who have mastered the basics will be given the more advanced task of practicing throwing and catching to automate their responses. Still others will be automatically using their skills in a fast ball game, in a complex type of race, or in advanced gymnastics.[22]

As in the other curricular areas, differences in physical-education skills should be considered normal and desirable.

USING CLASSROOM AIDES

One of the reasons yesterday's teachers did not individualize and personalize their teaching was their inability to manage a number of different and

---

[21] Hunter, p. 57.
[22] Hunter, p. 57.

simultaneous activities. The teachers of the new elementary school are no different, except perhaps in their confidence that a pluralistic approach is more appropriate than a singular method, and in their knowledge that there are many untapped resources waiting to be utilized as supplementary classroom and school aides. Identifying these resources people and describing how they can be used will be discussed below.

PARAPROFESSIONALS. School districts that can afford the cost employ part- or full-time teacher aides. Because some college training is frequently required of such aides they are referred to as paraprofessionals. They represent a step toward staff differentiation, an arrangement in which teachers are differentiated on the basis of responsibility, training, and salary. College and university towns usually have an abundant supply of unemployed but college-trained people who could serve well in the capacity of paraprofessionals.

How paraprofessionals, or any teacher aides, are used should depend upon what it is the teacher needs most adult help in performing. Some may work with individuals or small groups of children in the classroom or in another room of the schol. Others may be most helpful by assisting the teacher in her supervision of a large group of children engaged in different activities. And others may be most effective working behind the scene, duplicating materials, correcting exercises, and performing other clerical tasks. Whatever role the aide plays, it should be the teacher's choice and one in which the aide can feel comfortable.

ADULT VOLUNTEERS. When budgetary tightness precludes the hiring of aides, the teachers may want to enlist parents or other adults to assist in the school on a volunteer basis. The most likely to volunteer would be the parents of the children involved. They should be surveyed as to whether they would be interested, the times they could be available, and any special hobbies they have or trips they have taken that could be shared with large or small groups of children.

If there is an active parent-teacher association in the school, the organizing and administrative detail can be worked out by one of its members. Otherwise, a teacher, or the principal, may have to initiate the program with the understanding that one of the volunteers will eventually take it over. Teachers and administrators must bear in mind, however, that volunteer aid is not going to relish carrying out the duties paid professionals dislike. Supervising cafeterias and playgrounds and doing clerical work are all jobs that volunteers are not likely to stay with for long.

CHILDREN VOLUNTEERS. Some school districts have cooperating arrangements between their elementary and secondary schools whereby secondary school students have released time to serve as aides in the elementary schools. Upper-grade children, even in the same elementary school, can provide a kind of help that adults frequently cannot. That is, the establishment of rapport between, say, a nine-year-old and a twelve-year-old can be much easier than between a child and an adult. Children from the same classroom can help one another and the teacher when she needs that third hand or extra pair of ears.

Classroom aides represent at least a tentative answer to the question, "How can I manage a variety of activities at one time?" They are a frequently neglected resource that needs to be tapped to help teachers individualize and personalize their teaching.

SUMMARY

1. The purpose of school ought to be consistent with our values of independent thought and action.

2. Rules should be perceived by children and teachers as reasonable and relevant.

3. Learning styles differ and teachers ought to accommodate and encourage the differences.

4. Children should have some part in the decision of what content they will study.

5. Time schedules that are unnecessarily arbitrary and artificial do not facilitate learning.

6. Learning should be encouraged in places and spaces other than the school and classroom.

7. Children should have some voice in deciding the activities in which they will participate.

8. Evaluation should be individual and not necessarily competitive with the group.

9. The school subjects are broad enough to permit individualized and personalized instruction.

10. Teachers can more easily individualize and personalize their teaching with the assistance of classroom aides.

RECOMMENDED READINGS

Cutts, Norma E., and Nicholas Moseley (Eds.), *Providing for Individual Differences in the Elementary School*. Englewood Cliffs, N.J.: Prentice-Hall, Inc., 1960. Some general principles of individual differences and specific suggestions for accommodating them are presented in addition to like treatments of the various school subjects.

Dennison, George, *The Lives of Children*. New York: Random House, 1969.

A description of the First Street School in which individualized and personalized teaching was the first principle. Written in a practical style with suggestions for teachers at any level.

Doll, Ronald C. (Ed.), *Individualizing Instruction*. Washington, D.C.: Association for Supervision and Curriculum Development, 1964. A collection of papers that present a theoretical case for individualizing instruction. Especially noteworthy is Chapter 2, which examines the assumptions made about children when we individualize our teaching.

Henry, Nelson B. (Ed.), *Individualizing Instruction*. The Sixty-first Yearbook of the National Society for the Study of Education, Chicago: University of Chicago Press, 1962. A classical collection of papers addressed to all aspects of individualized instruction—from biological differences to community implications.

Joyce, William W., Robert G. Oana, and W. Robert Houston (Eds.), *Elementary Education in the Seventies*. New York: Holt, Rinehart and Winston, Inc., 1970. A thorough collection of writings in the traditional school subjects that includes methods and innovations, as well as different conceptual approaches and their critiques.

Kohl, Herbert R., *The Open Classroom*. A New York Review Book, 1969. The subtitle is "A Practical Guide to a New Way of Teaching," which this little book is. Kohl suggests some very practical ways to break away from the traditional authoritarian model of teaching.

Neill, A. S., *Summerhill*. New York: Hart Publishing Company, 1960. Subtitled "A Radical Approach to Child Rearing," this book is ranked as a classic in modern educational philosophy and method. Neill's approach to education is the best model to which educational innovators may point with pride.

Stahl, Dona Kofod, and Patricia Murphy Anzalone, *Individualizing Teaching in the Elementary School*. West Nyack, N.Y.: Parker Publishing Company, Inc., 1970. A practical treatment of individualizing and personalizing teaching in the elementary school. Contains a good description of the changing role of the teacher.

Chapter 14

Classroom Management– Discipline

*Children cannot develop the discipline for freedom by being
held under the complete domination of the teacher day after day
and month after month; neither can it be achieved by "taking
the lid off" and allowing children to do as they please. It can be
achieved only by living in the classroom from day to day in
accordance with the ways of democracy under the guidance of a
teacher who understands how human behavior develops and
who, in his daily activities both in school and in the community,
practices the discipline of a free man.*

William B. Ragan, *Modern Elementary Curriculum*, 3d ed.
(New York: Holt, Rinehart and Winston, Inc., 1966),
pp. 200–201.

If asked to predict those aspects of teaching that will most likely present
beginning teachers with serious difficulties, a more experienced teacher
will quite regularly place at the very top of the list, "discipline." Once
the prospective teacher has gained even incidental experience with a
roomful of young learners, he can be expected to recognize classroom
management problems worthy of a great deal of attention. The issue of
arranging and maintaining a comfortable and productive classroom-learning environment, whether it is called discipline, management, order, or
whatever, persists as a concern with no equal for virtually all teachers. In
fact, there is probably no other topic about which teachers, administrators,
and parents will become involved with more emotional overtones than the
matter of how youngsters are managed in the learning situation.

With the present perspective about discipline in the classroom as it is, the stage is set for the inexperienced teacher to begin establishing a kind of "mind set" on how he is going to maintain his classroom. While it may be understandable to begin entertaining ideas about how one should establish discipline and organize his learning environment before he faces his own first class, it is premature to have determined precisely how this will be done. An inexperienced teacher cannot "know'" in advance how he will deal with classroom management. There are too many considerations, about which he is totally unfamiliar, and only experience will provide the familiarity necessary to make these important decisions about management style.

This is not to say that discipline and classroom management should not be studied, only "experienced," but an important implication is that one who studies such an issue without tempering his study with experience must take care in drawing final conclusions. Keeping this caution in mind, this chapter will consider the relevant and emotionally charged topic of managing the classroom—discipline as an open point of view—with the suggestion that the reader personalize what is found herein. A further charge is that each idea should be challenged to ascertain its applicability and validity for young learners; alternatives must be entertained, with consequences considered, and at least some tentative positions established for review.

SITUATION 14.1
Staging a "Model" Class

Consider a particular grade level of elementary youngsters; mentally establish the "type" of class they represent; determine a logical physical setting for this class; and outline other conditions that characterize this 'model' group. Now, as you read further in this chapter, take specific notes and raise questions about the stance presented here in relation to your mythical class and how you feel you will want to manage this class—handle discipline—so that the very best learning situation is assured. Be prepared to challenge the position taken here in open, reasoned discussion.

WHAT IS DISCIPLINE?

What does discipline have to do with managing the classroom so that maximum learning can transpire? The intent of classroom management is to assure the most productive and enjoyable learning environment for all of the students. Discipline seems to imply a negative connotation toward an otherwise positive situation. A further examination of the meaning of discipline reveals at least four choices of definitions for the concept and suggests that any negative connotation that may be applied to discipline has to have been learned, probably through each individual's unique experiences.

Redl, a pioneer in the study of classroom discipline, submits three entirely different meanings for discipline:

1. Discipline as synonymous with "order." This suggests the discipline we *have*, or the extent of order that is maintained in the learning situation.

2. Discipline as a means of education. This definition refers to the *kind* of discipline a teacher *uses*. The methods or techniques employed are considered here.

3. The verb "to discipline"—actually the punishment—or that which the teacher inflicted upon the child when he misbehaved.[1]

These three interpretations of discipline are all teacher-centered or teacher-initiated acts, imposed upon the learner to maintain control or order. A fourth definition of discipline would shift the impetus for behavior *to the child* and be considered self-control or self-discipline. As we entertain the various concepts of discipline, a guiding concern should be the question, "For what do we want discipline in the classroom?" Is our goal "order," a "method," forms of "punishment," or a kind of "reasoned behavior"?

What about Goals for Discipline?

One has only to examine the alternatives to a classroom that is effectively organized with self-fulfilling disciplinary techniques and procedures to understand why there must be discipline. In general, discipline must be practiced so that planned learning can take place in the most expeditious and productive manner. Discipline must be practiced so that young learners, grouped in the school as a social body, can have a model to pattern their behavior as they interact in other groups that function for a variety of reasons. Discipline must be employed so that sound mental health, engendered by a healthy psychological climate, can be developed and approved. Discipline must persist so that others who are affected by the behavior of any group or individual can enjoy the rights and privileges that are theirs. Discipline must be indulged so that learners can experience the fact that only through disciplined behavior can people ever reach the "good life" that abounds in our society. Discipline, it may be recognized, personifies the notion that "reason is mightier than force."

Thus, we begin by recognizing that *discipline must always be goal directed*. The teacher establishes and maintains order, organizes and manages the classroom environment, and extends punishment and rewards

---

[1] George V. Sheviakov and Fritz Redl, *Discipline for Today's Children and Youth* (Washington, D.C.: A.S.C.D.-N.E.A., 1966).

for behavior according to the purposes he has accepted for the learning situation. An analysis of the techniques used by the teacher to manage his classroom environment will reveal the objectives he values. For example, the teacher who imposes a rather strict set of rules for class discussion apparently values "orderly" behavior more than "spontaneous" interaction. The teacher who constructs lines of boys and girls and marches the lines single file to and from points in the school building values moving expeditiously more than he values giving the children the responsibility to learn self-control by choosing their own mode of travel.

Upon visiting a number of elementary classrooms throughout the country one can quickly conclude that there are no *commonly* held goals, at least as evidenced by the wide variety of management and disciplinary techniques that are being practiced. From this point on this chapter will take the position that such a condition should not exist and there should, indeed, be evidenced in the schools of our country a type of learning environment, conditioned by discipline, that adheres to and promotes common goals for elementary learners.

SITUATION 14.2
Management for Specific Goals

As suggested here, the classroom is always managed in whatever way it is for definite reasons. Teachers have goals in mind when they select management techniques, whether these objectives are overtly apparent or not. For what reasons will you practice the management strategies (discipline) that you intend to employ? Cite at least five goals that you can support for effecting sound management of the classroom. Continue to examine these goals as you study further about discipline and classroom management.

SOME CONSIDERATIONS

It can no longer be assumed that the elementary school curriculum should be designed to prepare young children for interaction in society *when* they become adults. All of the experiences that students have in the school—the curriculum—must represent actual living experiences the child is having day by day within the contemporary conditions of his world. The school should be an accurate representation of life in a democratic setting, keeping in sight the ideals toward which our society strives as well as the difficulties and problems that beset us. The learners confronted with such a curriculum should have the opportunities to develop, *by experience*, the knowledge, attitudes, and skills that are demanded of an enlightened citizen.

Education must accept, as an overarching goal, the responsibility for helping every individual realize his potential to the fullest extent. This is a joint obligation that the schools accept along with the home and other institutions, but it is one that must be realized if the democratic way of life in America is to be perpetuated. The classroom must be managed so that this basic principle is complemented, and no disciplinary technique can be in evidence that derogates this proud notion.

No one is isolated unto himself as he enjoys his self-realization, and, as our world seemingly grows smaller, each one is likely to confront greater numbers of others in his life span. A truism in our society is that one's freedom to express himself ends when his behavior infringes upon this same right held by another individual or group. If the classroom is an experiment in living, then care must be taken to help the learner understand his responsibility to the welfare of others. The individual must experience independent self-fulfillment within the confines of group living.

Inherent in the democratic process is the notion that problems can best be solved through the practice of rational thinking. Problem solving should involve all of those who are in any way affected by the problem and its eventual solution. Analytical, critical, and creative thinking skills are necessary and can only be developed through practice, especially when dealing with a real situation. The implication here is that any teacher who accepts this responsibility to develop the rational powers of his students must take advantage of the daily opportunities presented in his class to solve management problems by democratic means.

Because, in a democratic setting, every individual has the right to be different, there must exist a variety of both goals and procedures. The maturity and development of a person largely determine the goals that are suitable for him in his quest for self-discipline. The elementary child develops and moves toward maturity according to the experiences that are his, both past and present. The nature, complexity, and incidence of objectives cited for each learner must result after taking these things into consideration. Just as important are the procedures used by the director of instruction to manifest the desired results. The teacher can be sure that every child will react just a little differently to the techniques he has chosen to effect the management of the learning situations. While it may not be possible to always individualize instruction, taking into account how different children perceive a single method will give the teacher some advantage.

To further complicate the differences that persist in goal setting and selecting appropriate procedures, consideration must be allowed for the behavior of a child acting independently as opposed to his behavior in a group situation. Certain liberties an individual in isolation may practice could quite possibly be destructive to a group setting. In addition to this variable there are many different environments that require a change in expectations. For example, playground behavior differs significantly from classroom behavior, both of which are different when guests are present, when there are interclass activities, or when the class is taking a study trip.

These considerations are submitted in order to question the rather tenuous practice of advising about good or poor management without fully considering the total picture of the learning environment. The ideas presented point up the considerable difficulty that persists with trying to design a "cookbook" approach to the issue of classroom management—discipline.

SITUATION 14.3
The Influence of Teacher Behavior

There are six rather generalized considerations submitted here, each to be expanded throughout the chapter. To build upon the 'model' class defined in Situation 14.1, cite analogies showing how you could interact with your class to violate each of these considerations, thus hampering your likelihood for successful classroom management.

Let us operate further with the proposition that at least five thematic strands must be dealt with while developing a system of classroom management. First, this system must be developmental; just as learners are experiencing various levels of development, the plan accounts for this. Second, the system must adhere to basic democratic principles of organization and behavior. Third, the system must be personalized and made flexible enough for both the individual differences that persist and the situations that arise. Fourth, the classroom must be managed so that the learner can experience, on a daily basis, the same kind of life for which our society stands. Fifth, the system must help participants gain the facilities that are necessary to satisfy the ultimate objective of discipline—self-discipline. Something has been said about each of these strands already, but the remainder of the chapter will define these characteristics in more depth.

The System Must Be Developmental[2]

By taking a look at the way children could be raised in a mature society, in ideal conditions, we can define basic developmental stages through which these children should progress to mature, adult status. The stages are not pronounced in their separation so that one suddenly leaves one stage to

[2] Sheviakov and Redl.

enter the next, just as progress along the continuum is often spasmodic and uncertain. Essentially, the child would be expected to move from a point characterized by egocentricity and self-love to the stage where his behavior evidences sincere and compassionate concern for others. Six developmental stages are differentiated here.

1. This stage depicts the world of the baby, who typically evidences almost total self-concern. With limited perceptions and experiences, the baby behaves according to his basic needs with no one or nothing else quite worthy of his attention or energies.

2. During this stage the love for mother is slowly emerging and developing, initially with rather selfish overtones, but eventually the child gives a little of himself in favor of the mother. The child's affection, at first directed only to the mother, is soon enjoyed by the father and others who are in close contact with the child. The degree and speed of the extension of his affection for others is largely determined by how happy a child's early childhood has been. Trust and love develop as a result of positive experiences.

3. Just as a child's physical boundaries are extended, so are his psychological and social limits. Strong affiliation with members of small groups or "gangs" often emerges with such strong loyalties that the home is virtually forgotten for short periods of time. Membership in these groups is important and is usually limited to friends of the same sex and about the same age. Gradual transition through this stage is common to most youngsters in the middle and upper elementary grades.

4. A further broadening of friendships to include members of the opposite sex marks the next developmental stage. Groups comprising members of both sexes with limited membership attract the adolescent, broaden his social world, and create personal problems that approach a yet undeveloped concern for the social problems that face adults. While much of the behavior exemplified by the adolescent resembles the behavior practiced by a more mature adult, emotionally this young person is still quite self-centered and reluctant to assume the responsibilities he is beginning to identify.

5. This stage is usually descriptive of the young adult, married only a short time, with young children, and a member of several social institutions. A close and abiding attachment to his spouse, their children, and his institutional ties remains stronger than the emerging concern he feels for local and national issues. If pressed to define his value system, the young adult will usually reveal a preponderance of rather selfish concerns.

6. This final stage may never be fully realized by many persons. Perhaps even more mature adults are "becoming" associated with the credentials cited here. This person advances his domain of loyalties completely beyond his more immediate personnal needs and desires. He is

willing to sacrifice self for higher ideals such as the welfare and dignity of every individual, justice, tolerance, and civil rights. The realization of human values takes precedence for his energies above the time he might give to personal satisfaction gained for selfish reasons. Ultimately, this individual is willing to relinquish personal friendship and group acceptance, even jeopardize the position he holds in his family, for a principle or an ideal he feels he must defend.

These developmental stages suggest an important consideration the teacher must take into account as he designs a system of classroom management and discipline. No system will work that does not assume the importance of knowing at which stage of development each child is operating. The classroom environment must be planned to take advantage of the children's readiness levels and admit to the limitations of a group of learners' intellectual, social, physical, and emotional development. Recognition of the behavioral expectations that can reasonably be demanded of youngsters of different ages is vital to the learning climate the teacher may create. These expectations intimate the impropriety of some control measures that are in common evidence in classrooms and homes alike. The ultimate goals of social development are essential to the teacher as guiding principles toward which even the youngest learners can be moved.

The System Must Be Democratic

An embarrassing charge commonly leveled at the American public elementary school is that this institution is the place one would be least likely to find democracy in action. The truthfulness of such a charge cannot be settled here, but even the consideration that this condition exists is unacceptable. If young learners are to ever comprehend the complicated abstraction, democracy, they must have firsthand experience with it. This experience must not be limited to "lessons about democracy" or short periods of time that democracy is "practiced." Indeed, democracy must be the way of life of the class for the entire school year.

Democracy has been ill defined as a kind of ethos or spirit, the rights of the majority, an "everyone is a leader" concept, permissiveness, and a host of other misnomers. Such interpretations of democracy create classroom situations that reflect the inadequacy of the definitions, just as they have been detrimental to the future employment of democratic practices. First of all, democracy is not a product, it is an organizational process, a set of human-relations experiences that honor the welfare of each and every human being. Democracy is operational, not something achieved, and functions in any situation that involves the interaction of people. In the elementary classroom, democracy is the process by which the classroom is managed and through which discipline is experienced.

The children in a classroom that values the democratic process will recognize the teacher's honest respect for them as individual, unique personalities. They will be guided and encouraged to become increasingly self-directing by a wealth of activities that allow them the opportunity to express themselves meaningfully. This faith in children the teacher exudes complements the value and dignity of each human being as an end, not a means.

Democratic practices in the classroom present learners with opportunities and freedom to experiment as well as experimentation with freedom. Students are encouraged to identify problems and work out solutions on their own by experimenting with alternatives that they, too, have defined. Guidance by the teacher is not forced upon the students, nor are solutions judged by an authority with finality. A number of hypotheses may be tested and tentative conclusions drawn only after the learner has entertained a satisfactory number of alternatives. The child must feel free from threat to try his ideas, test his notions, inject his opinions, question others—including the teacher—work out his own solutions to problems, and be willing to live with the consequences of this type of behavior.

While testing this freedom to experiment, the student may indeed be experimenting with the very nature of freedom. Hopefully, every elementary school child will learn to appreciate the responsibility that is attached to every freedom and be gaining the skills and understanding that are necessary to deserve more freedom. Freedom is an achievement that can be earned only by experience and careful, directed evaluation of the experiences by the learner, usually under the guidance of the teacher. Ultimately the child will learn that in a democratic setting the choice for one's behavior is not between freedom and control. In truth, the person who is finally free is a carefully self-controlled, self-disciplined individual.

Those who employ the democratic process in the classroom also have faith in the ability of individuals in a group to work cooperatively for the group's welfare. Selfish, socially immature persons are antithetical to the democratic idea. Mutual respect, trust and confidence in others, loyalty to a common cause, and cooperation are essential to democratic living. These latter traits flourish when children understand the role they play in group living and experience the warmth and satisfaction that come from working together. Competition in the classroom, whether between the teacher and the class or among members of the class, seldom enhances the cooperative spirit the democratic process embraces. While some competition may be advisable, learning the skills that are involved in cooperation must be accentuated if we value democratic practices.

A high level of participation and involvement in the affairs of the classroom persists in a democratic environment. Any action to be taken should involve all of those who may be affected by the decisions that will be reached. Planned, meaningful participation will assure growth in a child's ability to interact intelligently in democratic group processes. The trust that is held for the rational approach to solving problems is built upon the notion that vigorous participation by sizable portions of a group will lead to the most acceptable solution of conflicts. This, of course, is dependent upon the degree of human intelligence that is applied.

Therefore the classroom that is managed and disciplined in democratic fashion is concerned with the ongoing process of the daily routine. There is exemplified in this routine a deep mutual respect among members of the class, including the teacher, for the individuality, creativeness, and dignity of every person. Children are free to try their ideas and feelings as they learn about freedom, experientially. Cooperation is more important than competition, just as involvement and participation in the affairs of the class are rewarded instead of excluded. Problems of individuals and the class are approached rationally, with confidence that reason is a more profitable approach than coercion.

SITUATION 14.4
Socialization and Freedom

Thus far, the teacher is encouraged to make his management system "democratic" yet allow for the development of young learners from a natural state of egocentricity. Is there a problem inherent here? Can selfish youngsters handle the freedom experienced in a democratic setting? Wrestle with this problem, especially as it relates to your 'model' class, and take a position about whether a dichotomy really exists here.

The System Must Be Personalized

Any system designed for classroom management and discipline is complete only when it includes a set of exceptions, the personalizing element. Great care must be taken when one accepts and practices the command, "Be consistent," as applied to any list of principles suggested for managing the classroom and dealing with discipline. Absolutely consistent, predictable behavior by the teacher when reacting to a management problem that involves various children in the class will very likely refute the omnipresent condition of individual differences.

Every child behaves a little differently in any situation, perceives each teacher or other student act according to his experiences, interprets another's behavior in terms of his own feelings, reacts within given circumstances because of the conditions bearing upon him, and judges his behavior always in relation to the values he honors. Therefore the teacher who applies any systematic approach to managing the classroom that does not consider this highly personalized data is begging for conflict.

Structuring a classroom-learning environment that is comfortable to all of the learners in any single classroom is a formidable challenge. Children are more or less acceptant toward an environment that resembles one in which they have interacted successfully before. Change, especially one of significance, is threatening to children just as it may be to the teacher. Perhaps this threat prevents many teachers from trying any management routine that is different from those they experienced as learners. Nonetheless, the teacher has the task of creating a management system that takes advantage of the differences that persist in his class, never losing sight of the fact that personal interpretations are being made of every act that transpires in his classroom.

An especially relevant aspect of managing the classroom that must be personalized concerns both rewards and punishment for a child's behavior. Once again, the teacher who employs a rigid set of reward and/or punishment practices to all members of a group of two or more is sure to have failed in individualizing his system. We know that basic personal, social, psychological, and emotional differences abound in youngsters, and we must honor this, or, by turning our backs, create additional problems.

The System Must Be Life Itself

The experiences the child has while he is in school must closely resemble the life he should be enjoying while he is not in school. The learning environment should be managed in such a fashion that the experiences gained in school have direct relevance to the learner's daily life. Children have time for independent activities, interact in small groups, and participate in some rather large group situations when they are removed from the classroom, and it is a major responsibility of the school to provide the education for how to do these things best.

Whenever any lesson is planned within the domain of any subject area, the management of the learners is a vital concern. How can the children, the materials, and the teacher be organized to ensure the very best use of time and talent? What transfer value will both the content and the experiences gained from the lesson have for the child's everyday living? If any lesson is planned without these concerns in mind, or, in planning the teacher discovers the irrelevance of a lesson, changes must be made. More important than the teacher's satisfaction that the criteria for everyday relevance are met in his planning and execution, there rests the demand that members of the class fully understand how the lessons, environment, and process contribute meaningfully to their life problem. The test is that each child can identify why and how the learning situation was structured and managed to contribute to his self-realization.

It is not a limitation that the experiences children have in school are not all-encompassing and as inclusive as life itself. The classroom experiences are planned and the interaction is managed to represent a system of selected activities for particular reasons. Hopefully, children who are raised in a democratic setting will recognize the outstanding merits of such an approach to life and they will internalize these attributes with such fervor that they will insist that their lives are managed in this manner. A system of managing the classroom that promotes democratic ideals as they relate to everyday living in each child's experience is designed to expose the child to his responsibilities as a citizen. And, ultimately, those youngsters who begin to acquire the understandings, skills, and attitudes essential to productive living in a democratic setting will contribute to individual and group living.

SITUATION 14.5
Making Management Personal and Relevant

The demand to personalize the manner in which the classroom is managed and to make the learning situation relevant to each child's life outside the classroom is a responsibility fraught with problems. Identify three practices that may be common in elementary classrooms that refute these two considerations—for example, the teacher's own time-honored poster of rules for classroom behavior.

The System Must Promote Self-Discipline

Obviously, the vast majority of times that a youngster needs control will be presented when there is no one around to impose these limits upon his behavior. But all too regularly, one can observe management conditions in elementary classrooms that ensure order only when the teacher or some other authority is present. The child who learns to manage his behavior without being free of an external control factor can hardly be expected to become self-directing. Children who constantly interact in groups that are supervised and controlled by an official of the school will be forced to learn about mature group behavior in extra-school situations.

An effective system for managing the classroom must intentionally have situations and opportunities for the children to experience the demand for self-direction. Such activities are designed to force the young learner to become a decision maker about the way he is going to use his time. Accompanying this freedom to inject his desires as to how he will be involved in classroom activities is the important element of responsibility. The child can learn that every freedom that he will enjoy must presume an obligation on his part, and he can learn this only by experience. The teacher who lets his children drink from the fountain in the hall as often as they wish must also help them understand that others in the room or the school may be disturbed by unbecoming behavior. A student who has the freedom to select an independent activity in lieu of group work must learn to indulge in his work without distracting others.

Younger children are ready for less sophisticated levels of self-direction and often are actually uncomfortable with too little structure in the classroom. Teachers are well advised to keep in mind the developmental characteristic of the socialization process. Every child should be permitted to experiment with self-directing experiences that are commensurate with his level of social development, though, and care must be taken not to underestimate a child's readiness. As noted above, the system must be designed to account for these individual differences.

Upper-grade youngsters should be enjoying a wealth of experiences that will move them toward successful self-disciplined behavior. These students can more adequately intellectualize the rather abstract concepts freedom, responsibility, and democracy. They can be held accountable for most of the decisions they accept after the teacher has taken care to discuss the issues—their scope, alternatives, and consequences. Just as much caution should be used to not overestimate the thinking and reasoning facilities of upper-grade students. The goal remains the same for all elementary school children: challenging each one to become comfortable and successful in managing his own behavior through the experiences he gains on a daily basis in the classroom.

SOME COMMON MANAGEMENT PROBLEMS

Almost all discipline or management problems are viewed in the context of a classroom or group situation. Very few management cases in the school are reduced strictly to an individual and how he relates to himself, without accounting for his relationship to others. This section is included to consider common management problems, created by the individual(s) that are the result of forces working in a group setting. Six factors, explained in more detail in another source,[3] are presented here for consideration. Obviously, these factors, manifested through the behavior of the group, are evidenced in the actions of individuals. Nonetheless, these psychological factors persist especially and, often, only when the individual is involved in group activity.

An Unacceptable Learning Climate

Within every group of learners is a rather common *feeling* that members of the group experience in their interactions with the others. This is a

[3] Sheviakov and Redl.

Effective classroom management does not mean rigid
control. As this picture indicates, learning activities can
take place under a variety of circumstances.
(Photo courtesy Oklahoma City Public Schools.)

kind of "ethos" that persists, made up of the emotional attachments that
members of the group assign to their peers, the teacher, other school
officials, and the everyday life of the group. Teachers must continuously
analyze and assess the learning climate as it affects every member of his
class simply because of the immeasurable impact the climate renders upon
the group's potential for success. This is difficult but mandatory. The
following climate characterizations suggest some of the symptoms that may
be in evidence and that cause learning climate problems that lead to
management disturbances.

THE REPRESSIVE CLIMATE. A sure characteristic of this climate is a rigid set
of solely teacher-designed rules and regulations for behavior, order, organization, and procedures. Punishment meted out for violation of this
code is severe enough to be rarely administered—the threat is adequate.
The fear of being embarrassed before peers, punished by acceptable cor-
poral means, shamed in public, or tongue-lashed, even in private, guarantees an outwardly orderly class. The pressure remains predictably present
and harsh so that students learn to expect either complete acceptance or
rejection in direct relation to their adherence with the teacher's standards.

The morale of the group will be destroyed by a number of forces that are created in such an atmosphere. First, the membership of the class is likely to be split into two camps: a submissive group that openly sides with the teacher, generally demanding that they compromise their tenuously developing principles; and, a group of rebels, those who give their greatest energies to undermining the work of the teacher. Identification with either camp alienates the student from those in the other group. Second, the hypocritical behavior practiced by those who try to please both the teacher and their peers will weaken a child's self-concept and create frustrations. Third, the demise of mutual respect between pupils and teacher will harm the learning situation.

A repressive climate encourages rebellious behavior on the grounds that it is justified and supported by those with the same motivation, but less courage. Unfortunately, a child's natural inclination for fairness is misrepresented by one he has been taught to respect. Instead of learning the joy that should come from honest self-expression, children in this kind of climate learn deceit and pretension.

THE SELF-DEPRECATING CLIMATE. Similar to the repressive climate, this atmosphere is camouflaged by a teacher who bombards children with assurances of his love for them. Meanwhile, he designs the climate that assures his acceptance will be enjoyed by only those "good" children who practice approved behavior. Rivalry for the teacher's approval is developed so that those who are simply ignored have found cause to subject themselves to rigorous periods of guilt feelings. A high degree of emotional dependence upon the teacher is engendered. Consequently, punishment is replaced by self-accusation and self-deprecating feelings that are not relieved by the teacher. Growth toward independence is hampered by this type of climate, often experienced by students later in their lives.

THE EXCESSIVE COMPETITION CLIMATE. A healthy degree of competition in an elementary classroom can be productive to learners, both personally and academically. By the same token, a healthy degree of cooperation is just as important, perhaps more so. When the climate reflects an imbalance toward competitiveness, problems are likely to arise. Competition is an emotional experience and, improperly channeled, can cause hatefulness.

With too much competition and too high stakes the losers may become outcasts, shamed by their performance and characterized as millstones. The feeling of competition may influence virtually every activity of the class, and friendship and cooperation may become the casualties. Snobbish behavior by those who find it easy to win and gain praise will only divide the class and deter the hope for more democratic self-management.

THE "ESPRIT DE CORPS" CLIMATE. This climate should not be confused with the class that enjoys a healthy level of pride in accomplishment. Once again a matter of extremes, the group that is overly conscious of class achievements may produce a few self-styled judges who ostracize anyone who detracts from the class image. Such a feeling of vanity and deceit can build up that emotions run rampant when members of a group behave in substandard form, for whatever reason. The victims of such a climate are those who suffer the wrath of the group under the guise of righteous group indignation.

SITUATION 14.6
Diagnosing the Emotional Climate

Even the most experienced teacher will have difficulty recognizing the true causes of an unhealthy emotional climate. A less experienced teacher must be alert to the symptoms that betray an unacceptable learning climate. Study the types of climates characterized here and make a list of behavioral clues that would be helpful in guiding the teacher toward diagnosis of learning-climate problems.

Organizational or Personal Management Problems

Many teachers evidence successful command of an enviable number of professional characteristics and facilities in the classroom and still experience a great deal of difficulty in management and discipline. The problem often lies in how they deal with group interaction: leadership, followership, feedback, and personalities. A few particularly important examples of problem sources are cited here. Some of these may be viewed as mistakes in organization and others are more accurately described as personal mistakes.

Another "happy medium" situation is that desired degree of satisfaction children earn from not-too-much adult leadership, but enough to assure security. Learners who are ready for more independent expression should not be organized in only teacher-dominated activities with no opportunities for self-rewarding behavior. The other extreme, when teachers impose too many responsibilities on the children without preparing them gradually, is just as damaging. Disciplining oneself to organize a preponderance of his learning experiences without adult support is possible only when the expectations have been cumulative in nature.

The organization of experiences and responsibilities must account for the developmental maturity—physical, emotional, and educational—of members of the group. Schools serving patrons that represent a variety of socioeconomic or ethnic groups, for example, present an additional challenge to the teachers to design group organization that focuses on the needs of the students.

Occasionally, group-management problems are simply a matter of too much or too little organization of children's activities. A rule for every act may stifle creative behavior, and growth toward independence while "playing it by ear" causes anxiety because children do not know what to expect. The same concern should be held for a reasonable definition of expectations for group behavior. Expectations set so high that failure is common breed feelings of defeatism and often incite youngsters to strike out in retaliation. But when expectations are too simple the challenge is missing, the sense of accomplishment is dimmed, and boredom may result. Obviously, most organizational problems concern striking the happy medium, staying clear of the extremes.

There are other elements of a more personal nature that the teacher must learn to control. For example, teachers must learn that respect is commanded because it is mutual. The amount of tact demanded of learners should be defined by the measure of tact used by the teacher when he communicates with the learners. This notion is also applicable when considering how sensitive one should be when he encounters the other's little idiosyncrasies. Tolerance is a monumental characteristic that is developed mostly by model behavior.

An improper association of a child's act to the teacher, personally, may move a teacher to demand vengeance. This misinterpretation can be brought on by an overly sensitive reaction to an otherwise innocent situation, often caused by a child operating with a different value system. Gaining revenge for a child's act can only assure the teacher loss of face before his class.

A teacher is well advised to take particular care when he considers the use of promises and/or threats, punishments and/or rewards. Being consistent, a common discipline principle, is misleading. Slavishly administering uncompromising promises, threats, rewards, or punishments derogates the notion of individual differences. Learners will be much more interested in how thoughtfully the teacher planned these actions and how considerate and humane he was when modifications were obviously in order. Here again the child's adherence to the fairness principle is paramount.

How the teacher supports the "why" of his use of certain teaching strategies, evaluative techniques, and educational procedures is important to children. A good cause, when poorly defended or explained, may agitate enough disenchantment to create an unnecessary problem. Upon being challenged, the teacher who replies, "because I told you to," deserves further inquiry by the children. The child, whose time and energy is being expended, deserves the courtesy of some explanation about the rationale for the teacher's approach. This should be an educationally sound use of time by the teacher.

Curriculum Implementation Problems

With unequivocal boldness the students in our schools are insisting upon an assessment of the curriculum and the instructional practices being employed. While older students are evidencing their concern for more "relevance" in their educational experience with loud, often well-organized, protestations, the younger students in the elementary school quite regularly become management problems. Poor teaching and inadequate organization of the curriculum are prime causes of discipline problems because they induce boredom, negate motivation, and misrepresent the essence of learning for enjoyment. To suggest that these are the only causes of problems in classroom management would be to oversimplify, but they are significant concerns.

The objectives the teacher selects for his learners must be in congruence with the readiness level that each child has attained. Frustration is sure to be experienced by youngsters who encounter subject matter that is above their level of comprehension. Others may have disconcerting experiences with subject matter or skills goals that are too simple and without challenge. In either case the children's reactions will vary from reticence to aggression, but will represent a problem in behavior.

Other considerations the teacher should evaluate include: the communication gap that may exist because of vocabulary, use of analogies, slang, and so on; unreasonably difficult assignments; inadequate and unfair evaluative techniques, especially when they were not carefully explained; poor selection of teaching strategies for the subject being taught; learning experiences that do not satisfy the social, emotional, and physical developmental needs of learners because they are too accelerated or too elementary; an imbalance in the selection and distribution of verbal versus motor activities; and, poor choice of time during the day for certain subjects.

Children who are not satisfied with the experiences they are having in the classroom will usually not tolerate these circumstances for long. Disenchantment breeds boredom and causes fatigue, ensuring problems in management. A close examination of the manner in which the curriculum is being implemented should be continuous and accountable.

Stressful Interpersonal Relations

The school is an organized experience in living and should allow for and take advantage of every aspect of the child's being. The child is not just an academic component to be manipulated in whatever fashion will produce the greatest intellectual achievement. Of far more importance is the fact that he is also a social, emotional, and physical character with the general need to gain command of all of his facilities so that he can handle the life situation competently. A major responsibility of the school is to aid the socialization process, and conflicts such as those exemplified and discussed below are likely contributors to problems in management.

Children's relations to each other in terms of best friends or worst enemies change continuously and in most unpredictable fashion. Whether the children are trying to protect and maintain a strong friendship or increase the animosity that exists between enemies, any intrusion by the teacher is apt to cause resentment. For example, a teacher may innocently group his charges in such a way that friends are separated or enemies are placed together; thus, a problem is created that may affect the whole class's learning.

The teacher must also be aware of the little cliques of children that form in every classroom. These affect the morale of both the members of the subgroups and those who have been ostracized from the groups. Often, competition for leadership within a group is just as keen as the strife experienced by those who want to break into the group. Many management problems can be traced to the tensions that are created by the workings of cliques. When the subgroups are formed because of social, racial, or ethnic differences an additional dimension complicates the teacher's task.

Tensions and friction also develop between the teacher and certain students, often for reasons that are very difficult to define or identify. On occasion a conflict between the teacher and a child can be traced to some difficulty at home, that is, the child may project his hostile feelings for a parent to the teacher because of the similarities in the roles both teachers and parents play. The teacher may innocently misinterpret the effect his facetious interaction with the students has and be building tensions with no awareness of this. Despite the teacher's most noble efforts to hide his true feelings toward the youngsters, each child seems to know. Deceitful or pretentious behavior by the teacher can be expected to create friction and produce undesirable behavior. While it may not be terribly difficult to know *when* the children are not identifying positively with the teacher it is usually a real problem to know *why* there is conflict. Often created by unconscious acts and experienced with little awareness, these tensions must be resolved between the teacher and learns to diminish the management problems.

Grouping and Group Membership

To begin with, the large group—the whole class—must be carefully analyzed to reveal the differences among members of the class that could create problems. An obvious example concerns the socioeconomic, ethnic, or racial backgrounds of the children. Students are the products of their homes, and their behavior will predictably reflect the attitudes and values esteemed by their parents. These cultural differences must be understood by the teacher to prevent management problems that would result from improper subgrouping practices. Much can be learned from others who operate within differing value systems, but certain times are more opportune than others for mixing students to gain these experiences.

Other criteria that define the personal, social, and educational characteristics of members of a single class are worthy of consideration when assigning small and large group memberships. The maturity level of youngsters, both physical and social, is a factor that will affect group cohesiveness. The degree of independence from adult supervision that different children have begun to practice should be considered. The interaction of bold students with those who are shy may foster learning for both or could be harmful. How bright and/or knowledgeable some students are will render some influence upon the group, just as will the level of interest for assigned work. The differing abilities of students for organization and planning, how acceptant children can be to peer leadership, simple physical coordination differences, and the enjoyment experienced through school activities are all important criteria when the teacher arranges and changes the learning groups. Many discipline problems can be traced to the composition of membership in group situations. A continuous analysis of why children behave so differently in a variety of group situations is a must for managing the classroom effectively and will provide invaluable information relevant to learning.

Continuous Change and Emotional Stress

Changes in the physical, psychological, emotional, and educational climate of the classroom occur constantly if anything is happening at all. The reaction to changes accounts for a surprisingly large number of management problems; therefore, understanding the likelihood of disorder upon making changes should give the teacher some advantage in dealing with the problems.

A few examples of the kinds of changes that occur with regularity in the elementary classroom will remind the reader of the pervasiveness of this problem. Rearranging seating within the room for different activities causes noise, confusion, physical contact, and demands some order. Darkening the room to show a film invariably initiates behavior changes by some students. Changing the teaching strategy from exposition by the teacher to inquiry or discussion will cause some unrest and behavior modification. Imposing a new class leader such as a substitute teacher, special teacher, or lunchroom monitor usually causes a change in behavior by some children. Conducting some class periods in an autocratic manner and others somewhat democratically will assure some disorder due to misunderstanding which role to play at the proper time. The point is, no matter how informal the change, if the teacher has not prepared the students for it adequately there is likely to be some unseemly behavior.

The emotional stress mentioned here can be a result of the changes suggested above, but is not limited to this one consideration. Anxious, often fearful, behavior generally results from misunderstandings about what the teacher has done or is about to do. A classic example is the period of systemwide testing, using either achievement or mental maturity tests, when teachers have not properly explained the testing exercises. Children often "panic" upon being tested, and the emotional stress experienced in the classroom is sure to create management problems.

Special events in the community, holidays and celebrations, national affairs such as the cold war happenings, school-sponsored affairs, or culminating activities for an important unit of study can prompt strong emotional feelings that have a significant influence on group and individual behavior. At the other extreme is the classroom where absolutely nothing happens, and the boredom that results has a deleterious effect on the children, usually in the form of frustration and irritability. These children can be counted upon to strike back with disruptive behavior.

Once again, the answer is to find the happy medium both for encouraging change in the classroom and for dealing with the emotional stress that accompanies normal classroom activities. Change cannot be prevented or emotional stress eliminated, but intelligent planning for their occurrence and sensitive handling of the resulting behavior are demanded.

SITUATION 14.7
Techniques To Assure Awareness

The last five sets of conditions that lead to management problems can be dealt with effectively only by a teacher who remains "aware" of the persistence of these negative conditions. The teacher's "awareness" is more nearly assured when he has developed techniques for gathering and processing the data provided through the behavior of his students. Some teachers use personal interviews with students; others incorporate "creative writing" for feedback; and still others use the information gathered from parent-teacher conferences. Start a file of strategies you feel would be effective as data sources to help you deal with these group psychological conditions that will affect your classroom climate for learning.

Some Suggestions

Perhaps the most pressing and important charge leveled at the classroom teacher is to *know his students*, both as individuals and as participants in group situations. Without a sensitive and perceptive acquaintance with the learner the teacher's task is virtually impossible. Success with management problems will bear a direct positive relationship to the accuracy with which a teacher views his students.

Another concern is to not be misled by the first impression of a management problem. Often, the symptoms of the behavior problem misrepresent the true source. A system for analyzing a problem can be helpful to prevent wasting energy solving the wrong difficulty. Try categorizing the primary source of the problem as (1) physical, (2) educational, (3) emotional, or (4) social. Then question the child's behavior to further isolate the possible causes. Challenge the psychological factors reviewed above about groups. Introduce all of the information available that may shed some light, especially concerning the "why" of the child's or group's behavior. Then consider the alternatives a teacher may choose to deal with the problem, select the likeliest, and put into practice an organized plan of both remediation and future prevention.

Teachers must learn to take advantage of all of the resources available to them for support. The professional quest for help from other teachers is imperative. Talk with others, explore each other's strategies, challenge each other's ideas, try each other's techniques, and share your experiences —the good and the not-so-good. Use every aspect of the cumulative folders that report about the children. Carefully interpret the relevant data from these records and utilize the information for planning as well as problem solving. Call upon the principal, the school psychologist, the school nurse, the doctor, and other professionals who may have some expertise to share. Involve the home when it becomes important to the child's welfare. Parents, often the last to know, can usually provide keen insights about a child's behavior that may simplify a difficult problem.

Take a look at yourself. The personality of the teacher plays no small part in the successful management of an elementary classroom. Only a small number of important personal characteristics will be mentioned here, but this is not to be considered a complete list nor does this intimate any small concern for the importance of teacher personality. One such characteristic is a good sense of humor, perhaps the most important single attribute. Another is best defined as a lack of pretension. Children have a sort of "puppy-dog" sense of knowing when they are liked, appreciated, or just tolerated, and they very naturally are offended by dishonesty. Enthusiasm, understanding, patience, creativeness, and empathy are all admirable characteristics. In short, while the teacher is searching for the cause of management problems, he must always consider the possibility of his own personality.

SUMMARY

1. Those about to enter the teaching profession must begin establishing an ordered way of thinking about how they plan to manage their classroom and be prepared to temper this with actual teaching experience.

2. Management of the classroom must be directed to satisfy defensible goals for education in a democratic setting.

3. There is no recipe for managing and/or disciplining a class of young learners. At best, the teacher can only be cognizant of the many considerations that determine proper action.

4. When developing his system of classroom management, a teacher may be well advised to make his system (1) developmental, (2) democratic, (3) personal, (4) lifelike, and (5) promoting self-discipline.

5. Most management problems occur in and are a result of the group. Common group circumstances that create problems include (a) an unacceptable learning climate, (b) organizational or personal management problems, (c) curriculum implementation problems, (d) stressful interpersonal relations, (e) grouping and group membership, and (f) continuous change and emotional stress.

6. The teacher must know his students, have a scheme for diagnosing behavior problems, learn to use all of the resources available, and perceive himself accurately in order to successfully manage his classroom to maximize learning.

RECOMMENDED READINGS

Beckwith, Mary, *The Effective Elementary School Teacher*. West Nyack, N.Y.: Parker Publishing Co., Inc., 1968. A set of basic guidelines about managing the classroom is submitted in one chapter while another chapter is designed to show how the neophyte teacher can help youngsters develop responsibility and self-management.

Cutts, Norma E., and Nicholas Moseley, *Providing for Individual Differences in the Elementary School*. Englewood Cliffs, N.J.: Prentice-Hall, Inc., 1960. Chapter 12 discusses the teacher's role in helping children become well-adjusted, integrated people who are capable of fulfilling their best selves. Self-discipline is recognized as an essential characteristic of learners who operate well in a democratic classroom setting.

Elsbree, Willard S., Harold J. McNally, and Richard Wynn, *Elementary School Administration and Supervision*. New York: American Book Company, 3d ed., 1967. An interesting treatment of discipline "as end and as means" takes one full chapter in this text. Central to the authors' goals for classroom management is the notion that teacher behavior should be directed toward making children self-directing.

Gnagney, William J., *Psychology of Discipline in the Classroom*. New York: Crowell-Collier and Macmillan, Inc., 1968. Current research about discipline in the classroom is reported. Situations and incidents that have happened in classrooms are examined in light of this research.

Kelner, Bernard G., *How to Teach in the Elementary School*. New York: McGraw-Hill Book Company, Inc., 1958. Book includes a chapter about developing class spirit where the correlation between freedom and responsibility is considered. The highest level of freedom, self-discipline, is accentuated, and suggestions for moving young learners toward this goal are included.

Kounin, Jacob, *Discipline and Group Management in Classrooms*. New York: Holt, Rinehart and Winston, Inc., 1971. A report of a twelve-year research study about the techniques teachers use to manage children's behavior. The author accentuates concrete teacher behaviors. The group-management strategies have been found to be effective in a variety of learning situations and apply to both boys and girls. Most of the data were taken from day-long videotapes of naturally occurring elementary classroom situations.

Leeper, Sarah Hammond, et al., *Good Schools for Young Children*. New York: Crowell-Collier and Macmillan, Inc., 1968. In the chapter on guiding behavior of young children, the importance of helping learners become self-directing individuals is stressed. Knowledge of the child, environmental influence, and teaching techniques are discussed.

Mehl, Marie, et al., *Teaching in Elementary Schools*. New York: The Ronald Press Company, 1965. Chapter 9, "Group Living and Social Adjustment," explores some of the characteristics of group practices that seem useful in facilitating learning, both academic and social. Self-control is accentuated. Also, some common behavior problems, possible causes, and ways of dealing with them are considered.

Sheviakov, George V., and Fritz Redl, *Discipline for Today's Children and Youth*. Washington, D.C.: A.S.C.D.-N.E.A., 1966. An excellent small booklet that succinctly presents principles and practices of classroom management that complement a democratic classroom environment. This volume should probably be in the library of every elementary teacher and provides an especially practical orientation to classroom management for teacher trainees.

Webster, Staten W., *Discipline in the Classroom*. San Francisco: Chandler Publishing Co., 1968. Common classroom management problems are discussed in a cause-and-effect framework with some theoretical considerations suggested. Several case studies, complete with analysis by experienced teachers, make up the second part of the book.

Chapter 15

Evaluating and Reporting Pupil Performance

The experience of having his progress evaluated represents one of the most influential factors in the child's development. It determines to a great extent whether he will strive for real understanding or be content with memorizing answers; whether he decides that honesty is the best policy or that cheating will improve his marks; whether he learns to cooperate for the common good or to take advantage of his classmates; and whether he forms the habit of evaluating his own progress or of depending upon others to tell him whether he has passed or failed.

William B. Ragan, *Modern Elementary Curriculum*, 3d ed. (New York: Holt, Rinehart and Winston, Inc., 1966), p. 451.

There is no other single factor among the many experiences that every learner has in school that will have the impact upon his development of the evaluation and reporting of his performance in learning. The very personal nature of being "judged" by another person for one's performance is almost antithetical to basic democratic principles for which the public school stands. Students' reactions to the evaluation and reporting practices employed by the teacher will significantly influence their attitude and behavior toward the school's objectives, the teacher's goals for instruction, parent-child relations concerning school, relationships with other students, future educational experiences and plans, the developing appraisal of self-worth, and the continuous quest for identity. Any attempt to recognize the relative importance of pupil evaluation and reporting when analyzing the overall role of the elementary teacher would probably be inadequate.

EVALUATION DEFINED

Evaluation is the total effort extended by the teacher to acquire and process every accessible bit of reliable information about the learner's behavior in relation to the educational objectives. This important process is not to be confused with testing, interviewing orally, assigning marks, observing, recording data, conferring, and/or analyzing behavior, while it may include any or all of these tasks. Evaluation can never be reduced to a single, simple act because of its very comprehensive nature. A host of artificially independent, teacher-directed activities must be carefully synthesized and lucidly interpreted to represent the essence of evaluation.

The Complementary Nature of Objectives, Teaching Strategies, and Evaluative Techniques

Obviously, evaluation cannot be understood unless one places it in perspective with the rest of the teaching-learning act. Expectations for educational experiences are cited as the *objectives*. The means by which these objectives will be satisfied are defined as teaching strategies or *procedures*. These two factors make up two parts of a teaching-learning triangle, a representation of the teaching-learning act, but must be joined by the third factor, *evaluation*, before learning is assured. By this interpretation, evaluation is the process by which the teacher determines whether the educational objectives have been satisfied through the use of certain teaching procedures.

Further use of this scheme has been implied in the statement about the fourth goal for evaluation, but should be clarified here. The teaching-learning triangle is a cross-checking device that points up the charge of evaluation as a check on both the teacher's objectives and his teaching strategies or techniques. But the triangle is a continuum that runs in both directions; thus, the evaluation system itself may be subjected to scrutiny. For example, it may be found that both the objectives and the procedures were satisfactory as integral parts of the teaching-learning act, but the evaluative techniques were not appropriate. A teacher may be striving to help a youngster change his attitude about culturally different people (objective), using role-playing and role-reversal activities (procedures), but selects a paper-and-pencil test as his evaluation of how well the child has learned. The choice of such an evaluation as this refutes the complementary nature of the objectives, procedures, and evaluation components of the teaching-learning triangle.

No matter how incidental or major the teaching-learning act a teacher plans to effect, a reference scheme such as the teaching-learning triangle will increase the likelihood of success in the classroom. Elementary students can learn the merits of such a device as they plan for leadership roles in their daily lives.

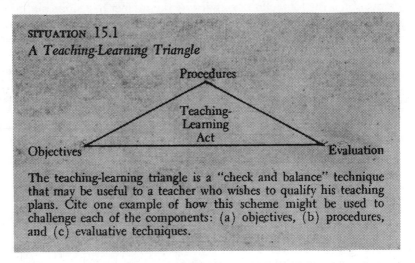

SITUATION 15.1

A Teaching-Learning Triangle

Procedures

Teaching-
Learning
Act

Objectives   Evaluation

The teaching-learning triangle is a "check and balance" technique that may be useful to a teacher who wishes to qualify his teaching plans. Cite one example of how this scheme might be used to challenge each of the components: (a) objectives, (b) procedures, and (c) evaluative techniques.

THE GOALS FOR EVALUATION

The goals for evaluation are determined by the uniqueness of objectives that are cited for each planned educational experience. Evaluative techniques are always chosen because of their likelihood to assess appropriately how well a learner has satisfied the stated objectives. With this caution in mind, a rather general set of goals for evaluation can be identified for further consideration here.

The very most important goal for evaluation is that the experiences that are involved in some way help the child understand himself more accurately. A major task of formal education is learner self-understanding and realization, and no part of the educational process is more compatible to this need than is evaluation. As a result of the evaluative procedures planned and executed by the teacher, each child should become just a little better acquainted with himself.

A second, and nearly as important, goal for evaluation is that the student's involvement with evaluative activities should equip him with greater facility in self-evaluation. Those charged with the responsibility of evaluating young learners must keep in mind that some day these students must face this important task of judging their own behavior, and they alone will be held accountable for the consequences. It is only fair to elementary youngsters that teachers employ evaluative techniques that have a built-in feature of self-evaluation development.

Evaluation should provide meaningful feedback to the teacher concerning his selection of instructional methods or teaching techniques. The degree of success experienced by the student in meeting the objectives of a lesson or unit of study can often be explained by the appropriateness of the teaching methods. Only by formally considering the influence of the techniques can the teacher hope to improve his instruction with future lessons.

A fourth goal for evaluation is that it can provide a basis for improvement of the curriculum. All aspects of the curriculum deserve to be continuously evaluated so that the needs of the learners can be more nearly assured. Curriculum guides, texts, workbooks, A-V media, enrichment materials, resource units, and all other aspects of the curriculum must be made accountable when the results of evaluation are processed.

Evaluation should supply the teacher with information that will make subsequent decisions about the student's total welfare more accurate. The data collected through the use of various evaluative measures and techniques can give a more complete picture of a child's mental maturity, academic achievement, personal-social development, special skills, and limitations. Satisfactory interpretation of this information for guidance purposes may mean the difference between a well-adjusted, interested, and happy student and one who finds school oppressive, boring, and irrelevant.

Another goal for evaluation concerns the way a teacher uses this information to organize his classroom, to allow for individual differences, determine grouping practices, identify slower and faster learners in the various subjects, locate the social isolates, and suggest seating arrangements. A well-organized classroom that is prepared to take advantage of the unique characteristics that each class guarantees is a result of the careful dissemination of evaluation data. Through the use of the appropriate instruments and procedures that are available for the collection of such data the alert teacher organizes the most productive learning environment.

A seventh goal for evaluation information is the more impersonal need for data to aid in administrative decisions. These data are collected and processed by downtown, as well as local, school administrators to make school- and system-wide curriculum, personnel, and school-plant decisions, usually in terms of economic efficiency.

The final goal to be cited here for evaluation is the important need to let the parents and other members of the local community know what the school is striving to accomplish, and to what extent these objectives are being met. Citizens who are contributing to the continuance of their schools deserve an occasional performance report and a sound evaluation system will make provisions for this at the classroom, individual-school, and school-system levels. The best school program cannot continue to succeed unless it assures public understanding and commands the earnest support of school patrons.

Each of these goals, in one small way or another, contributes to the general purpose of a teacher's evaluation practices in the elementary classroom—that is, to enable him to present those educational experiences for which the student is ready, is interested, and is in concert with his developmental needs.

SITUATION 15.2

Evaluation and Objectives

As an experienced learner, the reader has had many occasions to be evaluated. Recalling some of these experiences, consider how some of the techniques employed by the teachers may have complemented the goals for evaluation cited here. Report several specific examples of evaluative methods that would satisfy any of these goals. Was the reader made aware of the objectives held for the evaluation experiences? Do you believe this knowledge is important to a learner? Why?

TECHNIQUES AND METHODS FOR EVALUATING

The teacher spends very little time in the classroom when he is not evaluating his pupils, either formally or informally. An observer might not be aware of the teacher's concern for the collection of evaluative data, but every teacher who operates with long-range to daily objectives is also operating with data collection. Effective teachers have an extensive repertoire of techniques and methods for evaluating the wide array of educational objectives.

Observation

Probably the most generally used technique for gathering evidence that would satisfy most of the goals for evaluation is teacher observation. Primarily a method that is used to discern personal and social growth, observation can help the teacher recognize changes in health and physical characteristics, developing interests, ever-changing attitudes, and positive work-study habits. Creative self-expression, critical and analytical thinking, can also be noted by planned observations.

Observing a child behave in relation to stated objectives is not simply a matter of watching him perform. Listening to his interactions with others in the class, encouraging his questions, noting his nonverbal communications, raising relevant questions for his responses, and creating situations that force his attention are a few ways observation can be enhanced as an evaluative technique. In addition, the teacher must arrange some systematic method of recording the information collected by these observations for later reference. While this method may appear somewhat casual, observation is a time-consuming and demanding way to acquire data of an evaluative nature.

Testing

Testing, in its many forms, is an important evaluative technique. Basically, there are two kinds of tests used in the elementary school—standardized and teacher-made. Standardized instruments are prepared to test widely agreed upon objectives, and the results of these tests can then be used to compare students with a large, often national, population. While they would probably not be as useful in determining how well the more specific aspects of a particular local program are being handled, the standardized test is usually more technically prepared, easy to administer and interpret, and dependable in terms of reliable comparisons.

The most common and, perhaps, the most useful standardized test is the achievement test. One particular strength of this type of test is its usefulness as a diagnostic tool to aid the teacher in isolating a child's weaknesses in the academic areas. Limitations in the total curriculum of the school can often be spotted by carefully analyzing the results of standardized achievement tests, just as these data can help the teacher understand ways to improve his instruction. Achievement tests serve their greatest potential as a *single source* of guidance for the total evaluation responsibility and must never be used as the sole basis for passing or failure, comparing teachers or schools, to mold the local curriculum, or indiscriminately to compare one child with another.

A second prominent standardized test is the intelligence test. More recently this instrument may be referred to as a "survey of mental maturity," but the intent of the test has changed very little—to determine the ability level of elementary students so that intelligent decisions can be made about their educational, social, and personal experiences. *How* the results of these tests are used is of vital importance, not *whether* they are used. There is little argument worth examining about the need for testing a child's mental maturity. Obviously, if the teacher is to be equipped to make the very best educational decisions about a child, he must have access to a storehouse of information, not the least of which are the data gleaned from a reliable intelligence test.

The results of intelligence tests are not used for purposes of admission or selection in the elementary school; they are used to determine the educational experiences that will profit each child the most. The results are used to facilitate instruction for individual differences, to guide the teacher in grouping practices, to select appropriate materials for a child's readiness level, and, in general, to identify more adequately those aspects of the elementary curriculum that will allow each child his full measure of academic, social, emotional, and physical success. The information collected through intelligence tests serves as just one more important source in the teacher's quest for a complete picture of the learner.

An intelligence quotient (IQ) is usually reported as the symbol denoting a child's performance on an intelligence test. This quotient is derived by dividing the mental age (MA) as determined by the intelligence test, by the chronological age (CA) of the child, expressed in number of months. This figure is then multiplied by one hundred to give the IQ score. For example, if a child is ten years old (120 months) and scores a mental age of eleven years, six months (138 months), you would divide 138 by 120 and multiply that figure by 100 (138 [MA] divided by 120 [CA] equals 1.15 and when multiplied by 100 will equal 115, the child's IQ). Another child may be the same age, but score a mental age of nine (108 months). In this case you would divide 108 by 120 and multiply that figure by 100. (108 divided by 120 equals .9 and when multiplied by 100 equals 90, the child's IQ.)

A final comment about intelligence tests concerns the fact that they can be given to individuals or in group testing situations. While it is far more common to find testing done in groups, one should remember that individually administered tests, given by a trained person, are much more reliable. The expense incurred by giving individual tests to all children prevents most school systems from using this more acceptable method of testing.

Other standardized tests are available to help teachers evaluate additional factors that are essential in the total evaluation program. Attitude scales can be used to glean information about children's attitude development or to isolate problems the child may be experiencing. Tests have been designed to diagnose problems of work-study skills. Other instruments can be helpful in determining a child's analytical and critical thinking power or his creative self-expression level.

Much more common to the experiences that children have with testing is the teacher-made test. Too often, testing in the elementary classroom is an unpleasant experience. While virtually all teachers give tests, a very few teachers have had any special education to aid them in effectively designing, administering, and using tests. This brief introduction to teacher-made tests will not attempt to treat the subject in comprehensive detail, but the reader is encouraged to search further so that he will not be guilty of misusing his own testing energies. Note the references at the end of this chapter.

Teacher-made tests may be used for several reasons, such as: (1) pretesting may present clues about where you should begin in your instruction; help identify those in need of remedial work; suggest a basis for grouping certain academic areas; and, when compared with later testing, inform you about how much learning has transpired; (2) periodic testing may serve as a guide for the selection of appropriate teaching strategies; (3) testing may provide opportunities for the teacher to give much-needed praise or an excuse to hold a personal conference with the children; (4) test results may be useful when holding parent-teacher conferences; and, (5) tests may serve as a basis for a child's self-assessment or as a source of motivation.

There seem to be certain basic criteria to observe when making a test for elementary learners. First, will the test really tell you whether you have satisfied the objectives you are trying to evaluate? Is the child given a fair chance to show how well he has learned? Second, does the test allow for the individual differences that persist in any class? Are there test items that only a verbal child can answer adequately? Are there opportunities for the slower learner to experience some success and for the faster learner to enjoy a challenge? Third, does the test go beyond the lower levels of cognitive development, recognition, and recall? Does it allow for some speculation on the part of the respondent, yet remain reasonably easy to score and interpret? Fourth, could the test be considered a valid teaching technique and not just an exercise in "fool the students"? Did the test teach and further the cause of desirable study habits? Fifth, did the test help the learners become a little more independent? Was the behavior demanded by the test the kind that would reward the child for his developing more independent learning skills, or would the test cause him to be even more dependent upon the teacher? Last, did the test contribute anything toward engendering wholesome teacher-pupil relations? Did the experience leave the students with good feelings about the teacher's intentions, and would they anticipate the next such evaluative experience positively? A teacher-made test with these criteria in mind will surely satisfy many worthy objectives held for the elementary classroom.

SITUATION 15.3
Processing Evaluative Feedback

While taking advantage of the feedback that can be gleaned from both of these important evaluative techniques, observation and testing, the teacher should practice well-planned behavior. For example, in processing both techniques, he should enter the results of the evaluation into the cumulative records and review the nature of these data regularly. The information gathered from each source should be compared; with inconsistencies checked, supportive data corroborated, and redundant reporting eliminated. Reexamine the objectives suggested here for observation and testing and identify several other ways these techniques complement each other as the teacher processes them.

Daily Work

Perhaps the most reliable, at least the most persistent, method of evaluating children's progress is the continuous collection of daily written and oral work. Every day the child is in attendance he provides a wealth of evaluative data for the teacher's perusal. In fact, the record-keeping that is demanded to maintain an orderly set of this information is enough to discourage some teachers from staying in the profession. Daily performance feedback from the students is useful in direct relation to its interpretability as a measure of meeting objectives. Incidental unplanned information may prove of some value to the teacher's evaluative task, but the most minute data that speak to a stated objective can be depended upon to serve well. Daily work can be used to evaluate a child's achievement in various academic areas, his personal and social adjustment, work-study skills, self-expression, analytical and critical thinking, and his personal as well as scholarly attitude.

Checklists

A method for evaluating that has potential for both the teacher and the student is the checklist. These helpful chartlike lists of objectives can be cooperatively developed by the group, specially designed by the teacher for his particular needs, or prepared by individual students who want to strive for improvement in certain ways. Checklists are very useful in evaluating many aspects of social learning, skill development, interests, attitude changes, and concept acquisition. One characteristic of the checklist is that it demands periodic use by the evaluator, thus forcing a rather continuous examination of one's progress toward the stated objectives. A notable limitation of the checklist is that it must be almost perfectly objective, according to precisely designed categories.

Anecdotal Records

Similar to the checklist, but somewhat less structured, is the anecdotal record that many teachers prefer as an evaluative device. This is a systematic record of relatively short, concise statements about the student's behavior, activities, interactions with others, conversations with the teacher, contact with parents, and any other events that may have some bearing on the evaluation of the student. It is well to remember that a teacher's memory is only valid for a reasonable length of time, and a written, factual account of a child's behavior will aid this memory for more of the related information than the teacher may have stored. Each entry to the anecdotal record is a normative account of the situation that is being reported. If the teacher wishes to add his interpretations and recommendations, they should be recorded on a separate part of the report and treated as personal feelings. Each anecdote is assigned perspective by describing the time, setting, and circumstances of the event. Over a period of time, the records may be reviewed and should provide some interesting insights about any child's behavior development. Quite often, entries on the anecdotal record that seem unimportant at the time will either contribute to another incident or become important in their own right because of another event that was reported.

Elementary children should be encouraged to keep anecdotal records of their own, especially if the teacher believes such a record would help the children become more aware of certain habits or traits they practice. Otherwise, an anecdotal record should help anyone see himself more accurately, or as someone else may be viewing him.

As the teacher evaluates the anecdotal records he may find them particularly revealing about the personality of his students, and they may direct his attention toward each student as a unique individual. They encourage a teacher to become interested in phases of student growth other than the achievement in the academic areas of the curriculum. In addition, anecdotal records provide important information about students to new teachers, whether at a new grade level or when the child is being transferred to a new school.

Cumulative Record

A method or source of evaluation information that is used in virtually every elementary school is the cumulative record. This is the record that is usually housed in the principal's office, accessible only to the teacher and other members of the professional staff, and noted for its comprehensive collection of vital information. The "cum record" contains both facts and opinions, for the period of time since the child first enrolled in school. Standardized test data, academic reports, health records, actuarial data, teachers' comments, samples of the student's work, contributions by school specialists, parent conference forms; teacher, parent, and student checklists; evidence of honors, and statements about the student's potential all are things likely to be found in the cumulative record. This is the one source that any teacher who recognizes the importance of knowing his students well must make his "bible" early in the school year.

Sociogram

Sociometry is the technique whereby teachers may study the relationships that exist in their class as a social group. The sociogram is a diagram of these social relationships within the group of students and can serve as a useful tool as the teacher groups the students for academic or social activities, identifies social isolates, recognizes class leaders, and keeps abreast of the changing structure of the class. A sociogram is a technique reserved for professional use by the teacher and must not be employed indiscriminately. Only that information that will be used to help individuals gain status in the class should be taken through sociometric devices. Once a sociogram has been plotted for a class the teacher will recognize the need to keep the information about the interrelationships current. Elementary children's feelings for each other change rather quickly; new leaders for the class are likely to emerge for apparently insignificant reasons, and some children can become socially isolated practically overnight. The teacher who is interested in the social dynamics of his class will want to use the sociogram on a regular basis.

To construct a sociogram, first have a good reason, since contriving a reason for the collection of sociometric data is often resented by the students. Perhaps the teacher wishes to group the class in small committees for a social study activity. In this case he would ask the students to write the name of the one person they would most like to work with on a committee assignment. A second and third choice should be noted also. The teacher then tabulates these choices on a large form so that the incidence of choice for the committee work is easy to discriminate. Some of the students will appear socially isolated and others will show strong leadership potential. This information should be helpful to the teacher who is concerned about his group's social relationships and aware of each child's need for acceptance by his peers. Once again, this technique is a single source that provides data that must be supplemented by other sources before it can contribute significantly to the total evaluation program.

SITUATION 15.4
Techniques That Personalize

These last five techniques and methods for evaluating (Daily Work, Checklists, Anecdotal Records, Cumulative Records, and Sociogram) serve the teacher well in many ways. One rather general goal for these devices might be called "personalizing the instruction." List one or two ways each of these methods could be used by a teacher to make the instructional program more personal for a group of elementary learners.

SOME GUIDING PRINCIPLES FOR EVALUATION

Evaluation without a guiding philosophy is wasteful, punitive, and meaningless with regard to action programs for children in a democratic society.

Too frequently in the past, evaluation has been regarded as an end in itself; the highest values have been placed on scientific objectivity; and the importance of that which is to be evaluated has been overlooked. Traditional teaching procedures were based on the theory that learning consisted of the acquisition of knowledge and skills; thus, evaluation was often reduced to paper-and-pencil tests. Modern teaching procedures have grown out of a psychology of learning that emphasizes behavioral changes, continuous growth; multiple learnings in the cognitive, affective, and psycho-motor skills domains; and rational insight. In harmony with this concept of learning, evaluation is now charged with the responsibility of providing feedback about many factors other than academic achievement. The following list of principles is a brief summarizing outline of theoretical foundations of the modern approach to evaluation.

1. Evaluation is a continuing process of studying the growth and development of students both as they are influenced by the formal program of the school and by the cultural forces that bombard them outside the school.

2. When evaluation is regarded as a continuing process, as an integral part of the teaching-learning act, the complementary nature of objectives, teaching procedures, and evaluative techniques must be considered in total.

3. No single testing device can play more than a very small part in a comprehensive program of evaluation.

4. Measuring isolated aspects of student growth, although necessary as a first step, neglects the difficult task of synthesizing these separate measures into a composite picture of a functioning individual.

5. When a teacher depends too heavily upon evaluation instruments brought to him by outside experts, he has abdicated his professional responsibility and has sacrificed his own values to the values held by others.

6. Student performance and progress should be evaluated in terms of the educational objectives developed cooperatively by all who are concerned with the student's education.

7. Evaluation of pupil progress should be comprehensive. This means that evidence must be obtained not only in regard to academic achievement, but in regard to physical development, work-study skills, personal-social adjustment, interests and attitudes, analytical and critical thinking ability, creative self-expression, special aptitudes, and home and community backgrounds.

8. A wide variety of evaluation instruments and procedures must be used if the teacher is to do the best job possible in guiding the wholesome growth of children and preparing them for effective living in a democracy.

9. Students should be encouraged to engage in self-evaluation. The teacher who fails to develop in students both the desire and ability to evaluate their own progress, under the guidance of the teacher, is robbing the pupil of an important phase of his education.

10. Evaluation is carried on in a variety of situations. The concept of evaluation as "something that takes place after teaching has been completed" is outmoded. Every phase of the school program provides opportunities for obtaining evidence concerning student growth.

There is no single program of evaluation that is right for every teacher. It is the duty and challenge of each teacher to examine thoroughly the alternatives that are at his fingertips and to select those components that will serve him best in his efforts to personalize an evaluation program for his unique set of elementary learners.

REPORTING THE CHILD'S PERFORMANCE

Although there is actually nothing in the laws of any of our states that requires a report from the schools to parents about a child's performance, every school makes such a report, usually in a variety of ways. The most common techniques for reporting are examined in this section, including some speculation about future practices in reporting.

The Report Card

The traditional report card continues to be the most popular reporting device being implemented in elementary schools today. The reference to "popular" here is strictly in terms of quantitative usage. Report cards have a long history of unpopularity with both students and teachers and seem to be continued almost solely because of the demand by parents. But this may not be fair either, since parents do not demand report cards specifically, only some appraisal of their children's development in school.

The report card is such an attempt by the school to inform parents about a child's performance in school. As with any reporting device, report cards carry the assumption that those who make them can convey mutual understanding about a child's performance through the use of a few arbitrary symbols. Those who read the symbols, including the student being marked, presume to enjoy this high level of understanding being transmitted by the evaluator. When accurate communication fails, the cause can often be traced to the inadequacy of the marking symbols. More often than not, a great deal is presumed in the message carried by a "B" for a student's performance over a period of nine weeks in a very general academic area like social studies, but this is often the only information cited on a report card except that a "B" denotes above average performance.

Whether the marking symbols used on the standard report card are A, B, C, D, and F; E for exemplary, S for satisfactory, and U for unacceptable; a reporting scale using percentiles; or whatever, the symbols must be accompanied by a comprehensive explanation of their meaning, or communication between school and home will fail. For example, it is of little value to know that a "B" represents above-average performance unless one knows what the performance is being compared with. Did the learner perform in an above-average manner in comparison to other members of his class (which may be made up of accelerated students), other members of his grade level in the entire school or school system, or even all students at his grade level across the nation (a national norm)?

To further complicate the ability of report cards to indicate something interpretable to parents, there is a question of whether they report a child's performance or his progress. Informal surveys of teachers, parents, and students by the authors are convincing in the evidence that the same reporting device is understood to do both, an impossibility with a single symbol. For example, a fairly bright student may be performing at a level that easily earns a "B" for above-average achievement, but be realizing absolutely no progress over the period of time evaluation took place. Another student, somewhat slow, may be progressing well above average for his ability level, but performing at a "D" or below-average level when compared with others who make up his norm group. What mark do you assign him? Strictly performance-based marking systems are especially punitive to the self-concept development of slower students, while systems that use progress as the standard provide little in their reports that is useful in comparing a child's work with a standardized norm. Dual methods of reporting pupil progress and performance on the same report card are often confusing, misunderstood by the students, and interpreted by parents according to how they choose to read the report card.

Perhaps the major bone of contention about report cards is that they attempt too much with too little. Many school systems that use report cards are making good use of supplemental reporting procedures. An example of how the "B" for social studies could be explained more completely would be a supplemental form that listed the major objectives for social studies instruction during that reporting period and a performance according to the continuum for each objective. Then the student's level of performance according to the continuum could be recorded for each objective. If one objective is "Asks good questions," the performance continuum could be represented as ( ) never asks questions; ( ) asks some questions, but often not related to social studies; ( ) asks questions that meet lower-level social studies objectives; ( ) regularly questions during social studies period; ( ) asks analytical questions that reflect keen insights about social studies concepts and skills. This sort of supplementary form would provide an opportunity for meaningful communication to the parents and the students. A similar performance continuum for the major objectives selected for each academic area would surely enhance the significance of this reporting device. Some form of the report card is probably here to stay, but the present form that is limited to arbitrary symbols, with often meaningless definitions, must undergo some changes.

SITUATION 15.5

Supplementing the Marking System

In a recent article attacking the marking system, Melby makes some of the following charges about using marks to report students' performance in school[1]: ". . . marks say nothing meaningful about a pupil"; ". . . marks tell us a little about what the pupil has done to the subject he studies but nothing about what his study of the subject has done to him"; ". . . the marking system is irrelevant, mischievous, destructive, and destroys the self-concepts of millions of children every year"; ". . . all children are injured . . . because they are induced to seek the wrong goals"; ". . . unless we abandon our crude and destructive marking system, nothing else we do will have much value." What are your reactions to Melby's accusations about marks and the marking system? Consider each charge cited above in relation to your own experiences with marks, especially if elementary school marks can be recalled. Begin thinking about some ways a teacher can improve upon or supplement the marking system he may be asked to administer.

SITUATION 15.6

Evaluating a Report Card

Select a report card for elementary students. Interpret the card from the parent's vantage point and answer the following questions: (1) Does the form report the child's *performance* or his *progress*? How is this made apparent? (2) Is the child being compared with some sort of norm group? How can the parent discern this? (3) Is the mark assigned for a particular academic area (math) explained further in some manner—for example, by using another mark for major objectives? (4) Would the report form be adequate as the only evaluative source to parents for a reporting period? List three advantages of this report form. List three limitations to this form.

Written Report

The written report to parents takes many forms, from a blank sheet appraisal of the student's behavior and performance that the teacher composes from scratch to a highly structured report that demands a written statement by the teacher about very specific categories. The better written reports allow the teacher considerable freedom to report in detail

[1] Ernest O. Melby, "It's Time for Schools to Abolish the Marking System," *Nation's Schools*, Vol. 77, No. 5, May 1966.

those aspects of the curriculum that the child performs well or is experiencing difficulty in accomplishing.

An immediate reaction by those who may consider using the written report concerns the amount of time that such a device must take. By the time a teacher accumulates the necessary information to write a meaningful narrative, composes the essential message, and puts it on paper an average of an hour per report would probably be a minimum. The teacher must weigh this expenditure of time with the effects such a venture would have on the child, his parents, and the teacher's own future relationships with each student.

The written report presents an opportunity to inform the parents about the personal contacts the teacher has with each student; the accomplishments and the difficulties they have shared; the child's performance and his progress in relation to the teacher's expectations; the long-range objectives for the school year and how the student is accomplishing these; and gives carefully worded suggestions about how the teacher and the parents can work together for the child's welfare.

There is no assurance that a written report about a student's work in school will be any more communicative than a report card unless unusual care is taken to relate the information in understandable terms. While having more assurance that the report is communicating a teacher's intentions, a second objective fostered by this device can be satisfied. The student whose performance is being reported is naturally concerned about the message contained in any reporting technique. To relieve these apprehensions, to increase the communication level between teacher and student, to provide essential feedback to the learner about his achievement, and to encourage more positive student-teacher relationships, the teacher should spend some time in conference with the student, revealing the contents of the report. At this time the student can help clarify whether the report is written in such a fashion that the parents will fully understand its intentions.

Those who are forced to use a report card to inform parents of a student's work may want to consider the written report as a supplementary method of reporting more than the grade card can. The written report could be used as a form of communication between the teacher and his students, or it could be an important addition to each child's cumulative folder. Whether it is ever adopted as a replacement for the report card, this form of reporting has its place in a comprehensive program of evaluation in the elementary school.

PARENT-TEACHER CONFERENCES

If there was ever a light on the horizon for the improvement of evaluation and reporting practices it must emanate from the continuing thrust for parent-teacher conferences. Face-to-face meetings between those who largely determine a child's educational experiences, these conferences are held with large groups of parents, small interest groups, or a single parent or set of parents and the teacher. The general purpose of the conference is to explain, discuss, share, and raise questions in an effort to report about a child's school experiences. A secondary purpose for the teacher is to gather additional information about the student so that student-teacher relations can be strengthened and a more appropriate learning environment can be planned.

The Group Conference

Early in the school year, often at the first PTA meeting, many teachers arrange to meet with all of their parents in a large group. This gives the parents a time to meet the teacher, take a look at their child's academic environment, peruse the physical facilities of the school, and gain important information about the rather mechanical operation of the school. Schedules are discussed, monies are appropriated or conferred about, "extracurricular" opportunities are indicated, school regulations are reviewed, school board policies are distributed, transportation and lunch program information is exchanged, and the rest of the "nitty-gritty" of a school's operation is discussed by the teacher for the parents' benefit.

More important than this information, which can usually be cared for with a well-prepared school bulletin, is the opportunity presented by the group conference for the teacher to discuss the school program he has planned for the year. The objectives that will be sought in each academic area can be briefly reviewed, with parents given time for questions about the expectations. The organization of the class as a method of enhancing instruction can be explained. Study trips, use of resource people, special events, school convocations, and other affairs that may involve the parents can be revealed at this time. Requests for volunteer aid from the parents are admissible during this meeting. A quick look at the formal evaluative techniques that will be used during the year can be taken. This is an excellent time to clarify a teacher's personal interpretations of the evaluation program that is employed in the local system. In general, the group conference is designed to set the stage for future parent-teacher meetings by introducing the objectives the teacher holds and providing the parents with an occasion to raise questions about the role the school will play in their children's lives for this new school year with a new teacher.

The Small Group Conference

During the course of the school year, some teachers suggest regular meetings with "mothers' groups" or small groups of parents who have indicated a special interest in something the teacher is doing with his class. For example, a teacher may wish to organize a group of volunteer mothers who will assist in the school program in some fashion. Readers, secretaries, paper graders, errand runners, telephone dispatchers are all roles that parents can play to support the teacher. A regular meeting of these volunteers may provide an excellent source of information that is earmarked for evaluation. A regularly scheduled coffee with mothers can be a feedback source for the teacher who has learned to ask good questions and listen attentively. Usually rather informal, the "small group conference" with parents can be organized as an important evaluation and reporting technique.

The Individual Conference

When talking about parent-teacher conferences, one will most likely be referring to the conference that is formally scheduled between the teacher and either one or both parents. Typically, this conference comes near the end of the first formal reporting period for the year and often replaces the report card as the reporting device. The individual conference is planned well in advance, often at first with the rest of the faculty to assure some consistency, and then with considerable care by each teacher. The parents will come to the school for the conference at a time mutually agreed upon, with approximately twenty minutes arranged for the visit.

PREPARING FOR THE CONFERENCE. The degree of success experienced from the conference will depend largely upon the amount of time and effort spent in preparation for each child's conference. Consideration should be given for this preparation at the very beginning of the school year. The successful conference will be enhanced by planning and preparation not only by the teacher, but also by the principal and the student's parents.

THE PRINCIPAL SHARES. The principal's first obligation concerning the parent-teacher conference is to outline the school system's policies to the members of his staff. Most superintendents will have issued bulletins about the way conferences should be conducted. This administrative bulletin will usually give an overview of policy and leave the interpretation for the principal and his faculty to adapt to their particular school's needs.

A faculty meeting could profitably be spent discussing these policies and the way the principal would like to see the conferences carried out in his building. Care should be given to ensure a consistent manner of presentation. This is the time for the principal to discuss with the faculty some of the dos and don'ts that would strengthen their school's use of the conferences.

There are other services that can be provided the teachers by the principal's office. These include letters of introduction and explanation concerning the parent-teacher conferences; a descriptive bulletin explaining the general philosophy of the conference, with suggestions for parents; and schedule sheets for setting up the interview times. The scheduling should be designed to help the teachers coordinate visits by parents who have more than one student in the building. Parents appreciate this extra courtesy.

A final contribution by the principal would be to issue an interview guide or check sheet, similar to the one shown below. Teachers may or may not choose to use the guide, but often some sort of structure is necessary to assure more closely the coverage of important ideas the teacher has planned to discuss. The teacher may wish to prepare a carbon copy of the guide so that the parent can have a copy to take home, particularly when one parent was not able to attend the conference. Notes can be made in advance on the guide, to which the teacher can refer as he makes his comments. Leaving the carbon sheet in during the conference, the teacher can note any significant comments made by the parent, so that both parties can have a record of the major ideas aired during the visit.

PARENT-TEACHER CONFERENCE GUIDE AND CHECK SHEET

Child's Name _____ Date _____

School _____ Grade _____ Teacher _____

A. Development—Physical, Social, Emotional
B. Study Habits
C. Home and School Problems That May Affect the Child
D. Strengths, Weaknesses, Special Interests
E. Recommendations or Suggestions
F. Scholastic Achievement Now (Teacher's Comment)

	Arith.	Lang.	Reading	Spelling	S.S.	Science
Above Grade Level						
At Grade Level						
Below Grade Level						

Additional Comments

THE TEACHER PREPARES. The teacher's preparation must begin with the first day of school. One practical suggestion would be to start a personal file for every child in the class. The file should include short personal notes concerning observations the teacher makes throughout the year. The child's personal file could include information, taken from the cumulative record, that it is advisable to have readily available; a continuing sample of work from all subject areas; information gleaned from special teachers; and a copy of all correspondence with the parents.

The teacher is well advised not to schedule too many conferences in succession. The professional demeanor of a teacher is important to the conference, and meetings with parents after a day of teaching can be mentally and physically exhausting. Three or four conferences a day would normally be a maximum for even the most energetic and the stoutest of character.

When scheduling the conferences the teacher should allow a brief period of time preceding the meeting for a review of the information about the child. Evidence of a ready grasp of significant data about a student is impressive to the parent and also gives the teacher confidence. This last-minute review of information is no more important than a brief quiet time immediately following each conference. Now the teacher must note, perhaps in the same shorthand fashion, the immediate impressions he has about the conference: the parent's attitude, new information from home, reactions to planned questions, agreement or disagreement in ideas, questions raised by the parent, and other insights that were gleaned. A time to reflect upon the conference, immediately following, is imperative.

THE PARENTS DO THEIR PART. It is the school's responsibility to inform the parents of their obligation to come to the conference prepared to take an active part. When parents understand that the conference is a mutual responsibility that is designed so that both the home and the school cooperate to benefit the learner, they will add to the conference. An informative bulletin to the home, well in advance of the conference, will enhance parental involvement and assure a more productive meeting. Often the children can be involved in the preparation of such a notice about conferences. This tact would give the teacher an opportunity to help both the children and the parents understand the real function of the conference.

CONDUCTING THE CONFERENCE. Within the framework of planning that the teacher sets up in anticipation of the meeting with parents, he must try to perceive how all of this information is going to be presented and how it will be received. He must take into account his own ability to communicate with the parents. He must remember that it is impossible to expect a favorable reception of his presentation unless he is able to see the child through the parent's eyes and to recognize how the parent may be viewing him, the teacher. These are vague phenomena, but the effective teacher will reflect upon them as he plans for this kind of interaction.

Part of the suggestion here is that the teacher convey his message in a manner easily comprehended by lay people. The temptation to employ pedagogical phraseology must be stifled. The use of concrete examples of a child's work will be remembered, not a laborious attempt to explain a percentile rank on a standardized achievement test. A practical example of how test results may be useful will be more meaningful than the "statistical inferences one might draw from a variation in achievement test and mental maturity test results." The information contributed by special personnel should be related in as simple terms as possible without losing its real essence.

The selection of a likely environment for the conference will make the exchange of information more comfortable. If the classroom is deemed the meeting place, the teacher must not sit behind his desk for the conference. A little time and imagination can make some part of the room attractive, less austere and academic, and more conducive to informal visiting. Good lighting, ventilation, and comfortable seating are requisites. A corner of the room, made more attractive by some work of the children, may be quite appropriate.

The teacher should be prepared to initiate the interview with something personal and casual, icebreaker-fashion, before taking up the more formal part of the conference. If the teacher chooses to make his observations about the child first, it would be advisable to stop occasionally to ask for questions, or at least to imply that questions or comments are in order and expected. It is the teacher's responsibility to stay with the subject of reporting, without being discourteous. The maximum use of the limited time is assured not only by careful planning but often by tenacious execution. The teacher also faces the task of closing the conference in a tactful manner. Some schools arrange to have bells rung to note the beginning and ending of conference times that have been commonly arranged, but most teachers must design their own technique for concluding the conference.

On occasion, the need for another conference may become apparent so that a child's situation can be more comprehensively pursued. This is a good time to schedule the next meeting, while the parent is available. Upon concluding a conference, parents should be made to feel welcome to visit the classroom and, if they wish, schedule another conference. The teacher's presentation of the school as a friendly, cooperative institution is invaluable for good public relations. A feeling of sincere interest in her child should be extended to every parent.

THE CONFERENCE FOLLOW-UP. Far too many teacher file cabinets enclose a wealth of evaluative material, including information gleaned from teacher conferences, that has been religiously and laboriously gathered only to lie idle and never be used. What happens after the conference is of prime importance.

First, there should be some permanent record made of the interview and what transpired during its course. Time should be taken to rewrite the hastily taken notes so that a more elaborate record of the conference could be entered in the file. A more formal rewrite of the conference should cause the teacher to pull together his thoughts about the child as he reflects upon the notes he made before the meeting with the parents, the conversation during the conference, and the summarizing notes he made immediately after the conference.

After all of the conferences have been concluded the teacher can then spend considerable time reviewing the conferences as a source of information and insights that were gained in an effort to improve the curriculum, his instruction, student relationships, and home-school ties. Viewing the class with this enlightened perspective will surely be productive to the concerned teacher.

SITUATION 15.7
The Parent–Teacher Conference

Parent-teacher conferences represent a potential for evaluation that many teachers report is seldom realized. In reviewing the mutual responsibility of parents and teachers for making the conference productive, identify those aspects of this method that may demand the most professional skill by the teacher.

STUDENT INVOLVEMENT

Implied throughout this chapter is the cooperative nature of the evaluation and reporting process. Without the active and serious involvement of the elementary learner in the entire process of evaluating and reporting his performance, evaluation is a sham. The product of an effective evaluation and reporting system is a learner who is more knowledgeable about his strengths, limitations, aptitudes, interests, and human potential.

The goals for evaluation may be recalled here. They include student self-understanding, skill in student self-evaluation, improvement of teacher instruction, improved student-teacher relations, improved classroom organization, and improved school-community relations. All of these goals are enhanced by more actively involving the students in the evaluation process. A few suggestions for the inclusion of students follow:

1. Spend quite a lot of time at the first of the school year discussing the "why" of students' school experiences. As the questions are pursued of why the school exists, why certain subjects are important, why school time is distributed the way it is, and others, understanding begets cooperation.

2. Discuss the goals and objectives of each academic area with the students. Enlist their suggestions for goals they may wish to satisfy. Encourage them to question the objectives that may be cited in curriculum guides, teacher's editions, or other sources, including the teacher's own ideas.

3. Talk about the different roles that are expected of teachers, students, the principal, teacher specialists, and other school personnel. Help students understand how their changes to appropriate roles will be evaluated and why this is important.

4. Explain the criteria that are employed to discriminate between marks that are used on report forms or on daily work. As a class, try to reveal ways the system can be improved, either by modification or avoidance. In critically examining the marking system, communication is improved; the threatening nature of the marks may be relieved somewhat, and accurate interpretation may be enhanced.

5. Involve the students in the preparation for parent-teacher conferences, from the beginning of the school year. Invite questions about the conferences; consider the use of parent-teacher-student conferences; consider an "open file," whereby the students have access to the file of materials that will be used in their parent-teacher conference; role-play a parent-teacher conference with each student, with him acting as he would expect his parents to react to an evaluation of his performance in school.

6. By all means hold an individual conference with each student before each reporting period to assure clarification of your report's intent. Encourage questions and challenges.

7. Use supplementary report forms whenever they seem appropriate and explain these to the students. Enlist the ideas of the students for ways reporting can be made clearer. Encourage them to design their own evaluation and reporting devices.

SUMMARY

1. The evaluation and reporting of a student's performance in school may be the single most important factor in a teacher's relations with a student.

2. Evaluation is the total effort extended by the teacher to acquire and process every accessible bit of reliable information about the learner's behavior in relation to the educational objectives.

3. The goals for evaluation include student self-understanding, skill in

student self-evaluation, improvement of teacher instruction, improved student-teacher relations, improved classroom organization, and improved school relations.

4. Evaluation is part of a teaching-learning triangle that includes objectives, procedures, and evaluative techniques.

5. The teacher engages in evaluation most of the time. Some techniques include observation, testing, daily work, checklists, anecdotal records, the cumulative record, and the sociogram.

6. Evaluation is guided by certain principles, including the notions that it is a continuous integrative process, multifaceted and comprehensive; a professional responsibility of every teacher; demanding of a wide variety of instruments; bent toward student self-evaluation; and unique to each teacher.

7. The results of evaluation are reported in many ways. Some of these are the report card, written reports, and the parent-teacher conference.

8. Parent-teacher conferences seem most appropriate as a technique for reporting student performance, but they demand a great deal of preparation by teachers and parents alike.

9. The entire evaluation process is strengthened by a high level of student involvement. Without this involvement, any evaluation system is inadequate.

RECOMMENDED READINGS

Association for Supervision and Curriculum Development, *Evaluation as Feedback and Guide*. Washington, D.C.: A.S.C.D.-N.E.A., the 1967 Yearbook. The traditional system of marking and reporting must be replaced by the more humane system introduced in this book, so say the members of this yearbook committee. An excellent comprehensive study of evaluation.

Beauchamp, George A., *The Curriculum of the Elementary School*. Boston: Allyn and Bacon, Inc., 1964. Chapter 18 discusses the basic nature of evaluation and its usefulness in keeping the curriculum alive to meet the needs of students. Many devices appropriate to the evaluation process are reported.

Gronlund, Norman E., *Measurement and Evaluation in Teaching*. New York: Crowell-Collier and Macmillan, Inc., 1965. Considers the role of evaluation in teaching, explores the relation of evaluation to objectives, and suggests ways to contruct classroom tests and use standardized tests. Also clarifies methods of reporting evaluative data.

Hedges, William D., *Evaluation in the Elementary School*. New York: Holt, Rinehart and Winston, Inc., 1969. This handbook presents the whole of evaluation in the elementary classroom; teacher-made and standardized tests, observation strategies, and other techniques are included. A "Bill of Rights" for children included in this volume is a fascinating document, entirely relevant to the topic of discipline.

Mehl, Marie A., et al., *Teaching in Elementary School*, 3d ed. New York: The

Ronald Press Company, 1965. This book contains one of the more complete discussions of the entire process of evaluating and reporting pupil performance. Also included is a rather detailed treatment of the parent-teacher conference as a reporting technique.

Michaelis, John U., *Social Studies for Children in a Democracy*, 4th ed. Englewood Cliffs, N.J.: Prentice-Hall, Inc., 1968. Chapter 17 presents a thorough and easy-to-read definition of evaluation, including many evaluative techniques, suggestions for making and using tests, and other practical aids for a complete evaluation program.

Nerbovig, Marcella H., and Herbert J. Klausmeier, *Teaching in the Elementary School*, 3d ed. New York: Harper & Row, Publishers, 1969. Includes a section that comprehensively discusses evaluation, giving many practical suggestions from a theoretical framework that is useful.

Remmers, H. H., N. L. Gage, and J. Francis Rummel, *A Practical Introduction to Measurement and Evaluation*. New York: Harper & Row, Publishers, 1965. Practicality and simplicity, while maintaining subject integrity, are assets of this book. This is a fine introduction to evaluation.

Sawin, Enoch I., *Evaluation and the Work of the Teacher*. Belmont, Calif.: Wadsworth Publishing Company, Inc., 1969. A systematic treatment of evaluation, including scope and function of educational evaluation, development and use of evaluative instruments, selection of instruments and procedures for particular evaluation purposes, and the interpretation and use of evaluation results.

Shuster, Albert H., and Milton E. Ploghoft, *The Emerging Elementary Curriculum*. Columbus, Ohio: Charles E. Merrill Books, Inc., 1963. A rather complete coverage of many facets of the evaluation process.

Wittrock, M. C., and David E. Wiley (Eds.), *The Evaluation of Instruction, Issues and Problems*. New York: Holt, Rinehart and Winston, Inc., 1970. A fine coverage of the essential topics concerning evaluation, but presented in a theoretical context that may prove a little heavy for teacher trainees.

Chapter 16

Schools for Tomorrow

The quality of living that students experience today determines in large part their tomorrows and the tomorrows of our country.

Rodney Tillman in Marion Nesbitt, A *Public School for Tomorrow*, rev. ed. (New York: Dell Publishing Company, 1967), p. xi.

The study of the future has become a special study; it is called futurism, and those who specialize in studying the future are called *futurists*. The number of publications containing estimates of possible futures having a bearing on education increased from a mere trickle in 1940 to something like a torrent by 1970. Long-range studies have been concerned with estimating conditions several decades from now; relatively short-term studies have looked ahead only five or ten years. Both types serve useful purposes. Not only have publications dealing with possible futures increased in number, they also have been using increasingly more sophisticated methods.

When judged by current standards, most of the older studies represented mere speculation or educated guesses, although subsequent events proved that some of them were surprisingly accurate. The older forecasts visualized the future in a linear fashion, stretching out in a single straight line like a highway running across a desert. More recent forecasts present a number of alternative futures and explain how decisions that are made now will likely influence life in the future. Kahn and Wiener have commented on these differences:

> What makes the present studies, therefore, so completely different from those of the past is that they are oriented to specific social-policy purposes; and along with this new dimension, they are fashioned, self-consciously, by a new methodology that gives the promise of providing a more reliable foundation for realistic alternatives and choices, if not exact predictions.[1]

PROSPECTS FOR THE FUTURE

It is not possible, of course, to predict in detail the kind of environment in which the people of the United States will be living ten years from now, much less what life will be like in the twenty-first century. We can be certain that tremendous changes will occur and that any estimates we make are likely to turn out to be too conservative. Aldous Huxley stated in 1962, "When I wrote *Brave New World* in 1932, I had no idea how soon so much of it would come true."[2] There can be no intelligent planning of school programs for the future unless current trends are examined to find what conditions are most likely to prevail in the future.

SITUATION 16.1

Consequences of Improper Uses of Power

Leonard (Chapter 12) says that with the help of science and technology we are destroying much of what is beautiful and valuable on this planet. Give examples of this destruction. Suggest some things that could be done about it. How can the schools help in this effort?

Exciting Prospects and Grave Threats

Forecasts of the future, which have been coming to us in increasing volume, cover a wide range of possibilities. They range from new products

---

[1] Herman Kahn and Anthony J. Wiener, *The Year 2000: A Framework for Speculation on the Next Thirty-Three Years* (New York: Crowell-Collier and Macmillan, Inc., 1967), p. xxv.

[2] George B. Leonard, *Education and Ecstacy* (New York: Delacorte Press, 1968), p. 226.

that will reduce the drudgery and increase the comforts of home life to advances in behavioral technology that will give man more control over the social forces that influence our daily lives and our relations with the rest of the world. If we can assume that our progress in the area of human relations will be sufficient to discover ways to abolish war, poverty, prejudice, and pollution and hold the increase in population within reasonable bounds, then the prospects for those who will be living ten, twenty, and a hundred years from now are indeed exciting.

It is not to be expected that a single chapter can touch upon more than a few aspects of the future that have been treated in other publications. The discussion that follows is, therefore, illustrative rather than comprehensive.

HOUSEHOLD AUTOMATION. The twenty-five-year period following the end of World War II witnessed many spectacular developments: placing men on the moon, transplanting human organs, releasing nuclear energy, and so forth. Equally dramatic changes took place in the American home during this period, and still more exciting developments seem certain to occur in the next few decades. It is likely that a majority of the appliances that will be common in homes in 1980 have not yet been invented and that few of the kinds of foods we now have on the dining room table will be there in 1980. It has been predicted that a new electroluminescent glass wall panel will heat and cool a room instantly, and the color of the wall will vary in response to the movement of a dial to the color desired. It will be possible to have cold packaged anywhere in the house, eliminating the need for a refrigerator. Clothes will be cleaned by ultrasonic waves while they hang in the closet overnight; and radio and television will be built into the wall to be tapped on and off like a wall switch.[3]

Kahn and Wiener have called attention to the possibility that by the year 2000 we could have a moderately priced robot that would completely eliminate the drudgery involved in housekeeping. The robot would be programmed to carry out standard operations such as sweeping and dusting, laying tables, making beds, and scrubbing floors. It would operate other specialized machines such as the vacuum clearner and the clothes-washing machine.[4] This, of course, is a prediction that is difficult to accept—perhaps no more difficult than a prediction made thirty or forty years ago that men would walk on the moon by 1969.

---

[3] For additional predictions see William B. Ragan and Gene D. Shepherd, *Modern Elementary Curriculum*, 4th ed. (New York: Holt, Rinehart and Winston, Inc., 1971), p. 484.

[4] Kahn and Wiener, p. 94.

SITUATION 16.2

Educational Implications of the Automated Home

Think of other devices in the home that relieve the drudgery of housekeeping and provide more leisure for the housewife. As this trend continues, what possibilities will this open up for mothers to serve as volunteer workers in schools? Mention other ways that this development will influence the program of the school.

THE LASER. The concentrated ray of light called a laser was developed in 1960. It promises to achieve as much success and recognition during the 1970s as the computer did in the 1960s. Lasers are used in communication, as range-finders by the military, as detection devices to assure safety in the air and under water, in surgery, and for many other purposes. In fact, more than one hundred possible applications are being investigated. It is expected that almost every corporation and university will obtain a laser within the decade of the 1970s. Kahn and Wiener called attention to experiments with lasers at the Massachusetts Institute of Technology. They have stated:

> The experiments suggest that lasers can weaken rock controllably, permitting convenient-sized pieces to be removed in sequence. If it turns out to be practical, laser rock-crumblers are likely to be used in the near future to make tunnels for highways, railroads, and water distribution, and might make it economical to build tunnels for high-speed, underground intercity transportation.[5]

BIOLOGICAL ADVANCEMENTS. Developments in biology, medicine, and chemistry that seem certain to take place in the next few decades are exciting to contemplate. Oceanography has become an interesting field of study. It seems certain that men will increasingly explore the ocean as a source of food; farming the sea will become increasingly important. The use of domesticated animals as a source of food will decline because plants can convert solar energy into food much more efficiently.

An article in *Changing Times* for January 1968 stated, "Medicine is poised at the threshold of magnificent new achievements."[6] We can expect that new drugs, new treatments, new uses of chemicals and elec-

---

[5] Kahn and Wiener, p. 99.

[6] "What the 1970s Will Bring," *Changing Times: The Kiplinger Magazine,* January 1968, p. 13.

tronics will come into general use during the 1970s. The article summarizes the victories that lie ahead as follows:

> In the 70s diseases that today cripple or kill will be well on the way to extinction or control. Vaccines will have practically eliminated mumps and measles. Great progress will have been made toward blotting out TB and controlling some of the more common viruses. Cancer will not be conquered, barring a miraculous breakthrough in pinpointing its causes. But some forms of cancer, particularly leukemia, may come under control. And tremendous strides can be expected in the use of drugs, chemicals, radiation, and surgery in treating cancer victims.
>
> The art of transplanting organs will come much closer to perfection in the next decade. Another development will be improvement in the use of artificial hearts, artificial kidneys, and other man-made substitute organs. These advances will be accompanied by agonizing questions: Which life should be prolonged, which allowed to go nature's way? How can terribly expensive therapy be made available to all?
>
> The aging process will come under better control in the next 10 or 15 years. Based on what's being learned now about the DNA molecule and about such proteins as hormones, enzymes, and antibodies, Dr. Augustus B. Kinzel, former president of the Salk Institute, predicts that by 1980 "the man of 65 to 75 years of age . . . will have that health and vigor necessary to productivity which he had at 45 to 55 years of age, assuming that he had then been healthy."[7]

A great many medical achievements that can be expected during the 1970s have not been mentioned in the summary listed above. One notable omission is the number-one killer in the United States—heart disease. This killer has been responsible for 55 percent of all deaths in the United States in recent years—525,000 Americans annually. Kahn and Wiener have reported many significant developments relating to the prevention of heart disease and the treatment of its victims:[8]

1. Improved drugs that reduce blood pressure.
2. Intensive care "which by itself may cut heart attack deaths in the United States by fifty thousand a year or so."
3. Artificial pacemakers installed in the chest and air-driven pumps to take over a part of the work of the left ventricle expected to come into general use.
4. Rejoining blood vessels—"About fifty thousand people are now using blood vessels made of nylon and dacron."
5. Completely artificial hearts made of silicone or natural rubber, with a synthetic valve system, are expected to be available by about 1980.

---

[7] "What the 1970s Will Bring," p. 13.
[8] Kahn and Wiener, pp. 106–107.

The elementary school building of the future will reflect
the best that is known about learning. It will be designed
as an example of beauty as well as utility. (Photo courtesy
Oklahoma City Public Schools.)

Kahn and Wiener state:

> It seems reasonable to expect that many or most of [these] predictions
> of artificial substitutes for human parts will be realized before the year
> 2000, particularly after 1975–80 when new materials and success with
> some artificial organs will stimulate doctors and engineers to become
> even bolder.[9]

NUCLEAR ENERGY. Stuart Chase has pointed out that, when energy becomes
abundant and cheap, a material Utopia is not an impossible dream. Following is a list of what he says we can reasonably expect from nuclear
energy, directed to peaceful purposes and intelligently managed:

1. It can industrialize the low-energy world, two-thirds of mankind, and
virtually equalize living standards everywhere. Poverty can be obliterated—
provided, of course, that population control goes along with it.

[9] Kahn and Wiener, pp. 106–107.

2. It can help to reduce economic rivalries between nations by making abundant resources available to all. The struggle for scarce materials will be muted; every nation will be a Have nation. Belligerent nationalism will also be undermined by the necessity of joint action in drilling through the earth's crust, capturing ferric satellites, exploiting the seas and Antarctica.

3. Nuclear energy will make it possible to put cities, towns, and communities anywhere on the map, and facilitate a more flexible distribution of population.

4. It can solve much of the fresh-water shortage that is now threatening us, and even irrigate and reclaim deserts. If water is to be pumped a reasonable distance inland, the same plant that desalts the sea water can furnish power for the job.

5. It will be invaluable for rebuilding Megalopolis, a project demanding . . . great blocks of both inanimate and human energy.

6. It will give industry lower costs for power, and thus help pay for necessary antipollution installations.

7. It will make practical the exploitation of minerals now buried in the earth's crust and at sea bottom.

8. It will make practical the reclaiming of minerals by grinding up common rocks and by applying electrolysis to ocean salts.

9. At some point on the trend curve, energy will be abundant enough to synthesize any element we desire. I doubt if we will desire gold—except a little for dentistry and medicine.[10]

[10] Stuart Chase, *The Most Probable World* (New York: Harper & Row, Publishers, 1968), pp. 97–98.

Classroom furniture in the elementary school of the future will be flexible enough to accommodate a variety of activities. (Photo courtesy Oklahoma City Public Schools.)

A NEW KIND OF ELEMENTARY SCHOOL

Thus far in this chapter an effort has been made to document the thesis that we are entering an era that will be characterized by continued and accelerated change in many segments of our society. It is to be expected that such an era will also witness significant changes in the elementary school. Indeed, one does not have to search very long to find evidence that a new kind of elementary school is emerging. One writer has predicted that the elementary school three decades from now will be almost completely unlike the one we know today.[11]

One thick volume would hardly suffice to cover adequately all facets of elementary education that are undergoing significant changes and in which really new programs and procedures are being developed. The remainder of this chapter will be concerned with a few segments of the new elementary school for the next two or three decades. Instructors will, no doubt, want to suggest other segments for examination, and inquiring students will want to explore on their own some phases of the elementary school for tomorrow.

Accelerated Change

Changes in elementary school programs will, no doubt, come more rapidly in the next few decades than has been the case in the past. Many have been surprised by the enthusiasm with which innovative programs have been received by teachers and parents. The principal of Nova, an experimental educational complex at Fort Lauderdale, Florida, has been quoted as saying, "If there is a better method, we can scrap the one we're using and try it. We're dedicated to change, to innovation. That's the beauty of Nova."[12]

Shane, who has suggested general directions for educational changes through *future*-planning, has expressed optimism about what can be accomplished. The rapidity with which changes have already been taking place has made people more willing to accept additional changes and to begin the task of making adjustments to new ways of thinking and behaving. Changes that have been unprecedented in rate, extent, and importance have increased man's belief in what man can accomplish.[13]

---

[11] William D. Hedges, "Will We Recognize Tomorrow's Elementary School?" *N.E.A. Journal*, December 1967, p. 9.

[12] Joan Beck, "Nova Report: The Leading Edge of Education," *Insight* (Chicago, Ill.), Winter 1966, p. 1.

[13] Harold G. Shane, "*Future*-Planning as a Means of Shaping Educational Change," in National Society for the Study of Education, *The Curriculum: Retrospect and Prospect* (Chicago: University of Chicago Press, 1971), p. 194.

Enduring Concerns

A type of elementary school that differs in important respects from the type we have known in the past is already in operation in many communities throughout the United States.[14] This new type of elementary school has emerged from an intense desire of professional educators and laymen alike to make greater provision for quality, equality, individualization, and relevancy in school experiences of children. These and other concerns may in the next few decades give rise to educational programs, materials, teaching strategies, and evaluation procedures that are unknown today.

QUALITY. There is increasing evidence that taxpayers are going to demand a higher quality of product in return for increased expenditures on schools. This demand may in some cases be based on a narrow concept of what constitutes quality education, but the demand is there nonetheless. Suggestions for improving the quality of education have been presented in previous chapters of this book: effective development of skills, more effective teaching strategies, the use of more effective learning resources, organizing to promote effective teaching, and so forth. There are those who believe that we are on the threshold of a tremendous breakthrough that may completely remake the elementary school. They count heavily on the application of systems analysis and the entry of technology via big business into education.[15]

EQUALITY. Equality of educational opportunity is a basic tenet of democracy. Minority groups in particular are the victims of discrimination relating to quality of schools and chances for jobs. Efforts to remedy this situation have been discussed in Chapter 10. A beginning was made in the Elementary and Secondary Education Act of 1965 that made more than a billion dollars of federal funds available for schools, most of it earmarked for compensatory education programs for the culturally disadvantaged. Chase expressed optimism relating to this problem when he looked ahead to the year 2001:

> Nearly every child on earth receives all the education his genes permit. He grows up an independent thinker, informed by the scientific attitude. This has gone far to heal race relations but no final solution can yet be announced.[16]

INDIVIDUALIZATION. Efforts to individualize and personalize instruction, as Chapter 13 has suggested, have been under way for many years. Most of these efforts consisted of the development of new plans for grouping

14 Nancy Faber, "Ten Top Elementary Schools," *Ladies Home Journal*, September 1968, pp. 72–74.

15 Hedges, p. 11.

16 Chase, p. 229.

children for instruction. The children were expected to use the same materials, but various grouping plans allowed them to progress through these materials at different rates. Only rarely have the plans included providing differentiated materials or curriculum alterations.

Instructional technology has already come to the aid of the teacher in the matter of providing for individual differences. The use of a tape recorder and earphones can, for example, enable the teacher to teach one group of pupils certain materials suited to their level of development while two or three other groups are being instructed in other materials through the use of the tape recorder and earphones. Hedges has predicted that the computer will enable the teacher to go much farther toward complete individualization of instruction:

> The computer promises to help the teacher accomplish what he has always desired and dreamed of but has too rarely been able to bring about—virtually complete individualization of instruction according to the child's rate of learning, his interests, and his approach to learning (his style). We face the possibility that we can humanize the process of learning for the many rather than the few.[17]

RELEVANCY. Educators have always been faced with the difficult task of keeping the school program in line with current conditions and problems of living. Far too much of what is learned in school has no relation to life outside the school. The need to introduce children to the real world in which they are growing up will become even more crucial in the era of accelerated change into which we are entering.

SITUATION 16.3
School Volunteers as Aids to Individualization

It has been estimated that as much as 26 percent of the time of some teachers is taken up with nonteaching chores—supervising lunchrooms, taking up money for various purposes, making out reports, taking attendance, preparing instructional materials, distributing supplies, and so on. School volunteers can perform many of these chores, leaving more time for the teacher to provide individualized instruction. Over 1000 University of California students served as volunteers in 1966; Seattle schools used 1100 volunteers in 1968. Community college students, university students, and capable parents can provide a pool of eager and able workers in almost every community. Explain why the volunteer program should be directed by a full-time employee of the school system. What should be included in a bulletin that defines the role of the volunteer? List some things that volunteers can ordinarily do to help the teacher.

[17] Hedges, p. 11.

School Buildings Designed for Learning

The elementary school building of the next few decades will bear little resemblance to the "eggcrate" type of building that has been so common in the past. Classrooms will give way to large instructional areas to permit a more flexible use of space. Instead of going to the library, pupils will be able to use materials that are provided by a learning-resource center located in the center of the large instructional area. The school architect of the future will realize that he is not just planning a building; rather, he is designing space that will facilitate rich and varied learning experiences for children.

The "space for learning" concept was incorporated in the new building that was opened in September 1968 at John F. Kennedy School in Norman, Oklahoma. There was originally one large instructional area, without partitions, with approximately 16,000 square feet of floor space. More than 400 pupils received all their instruction there except for music and physical education; this area also included the resource center. Ordinarily, this amount of space would be divided into about fourteen classrooms in each of which one teacher would work with a group of pupils in almost complete isolation from other teachers in the building. This is only one of several bold new ventures in the use of space for learning that provide a glimpse of the future.

Greater Use of Technological Media

There can be little doubt that one of the most significant developments in the elementary school during the next few decades will be a tremendous increase in the use of technological media to (1) teach subject matter more efficiently, (2) relieve the teacher of nonteaching chores and free him for more creative tasks of a truly professional nature, and (3) enable pupils to work more independently of the teacher. Although many types of technological media are in use in the schools, most authorities are convinced that our schools are using only a fraction of the potential of these media.

The use of technological media in instruction has aroused a great deal of controversy. Some regard it as a means for bringing about a new era in elementary education; others fear that it will dehumanize the school program. Engler has presented convincing arguments to the effect that the supposed conflict between the humanistic curriculum and instructional technology rests upon false assumptions. He contends (1) that instructional technology is essentially a tool that can be used to implement any curriculum decision, (2) that there can be no curriculum without an instructional technology—conventional methods and materials represent an instructional technology, (3) that the current problem is how to devise an instructional technology that will further humanize the curriculum, and (4) that our present strategies and instruments of instruction are not adequate to accomplish what is expected of our schools.[18]

Many well-informed educators expect to see extensive use of computers in elementary and secondary school in the near future. They expect to see the computer used to assist in the teaching of reading, arithmetic, and language in elementary schools, as well as in the fine arts. Most computer-based instructional programs employ the same basic methods: (1) the learner is presented with a stimulus that gives him information, requires a response, or does both; (2) there is a continual necessity for the learner to utilize this information in making some response or decision; and (3) after responding, the learner is presented with feedback information that enables him to judge the appropriateness of his response. The immediate feedback gives the student motivation for continuing the process. Computer-based instruction is not expected to reduce the number of teachers needed, but to lead to a significant gain in the quality of education provided. Perhaps teachers will soon be using computer-based terminals in the same way in which they now use textbooks and other conventional media.

The Curriculum of the New Elementary School

There are many indications that the curriculum of the elementary school will undergo significant changes in the next few decades—perhaps what children study will carry entirely different titles than those with which we are familiar. The curriculum will change more rapidly in the future than it has in the past because new tools for gathering data upon which to base decisions will be available and new agencies for disseminating innovative curriculum designs among schools will be in use.

A comprehensive treatment of impending changes in the elementary school curriculum is beyond the space available in this section. However, it is feasible to call attention to a few of the key concepts that will give direction to curriculum change in elementary schools.

CREATIVITY. If we can judge by the experimentation and writing that is currently directed to creativity, we can conclude that the new elementary curriculum will place a high priority on fostering creative thinking. The new curriculum will provide for experiences that enhance "divergent" or innovative thought rather than "convergent" thought based on acceptance of authority. It will employ the "open" method that stimulates discussion

[18] David Engler, "Instructional Technology and the Curriculum," *Phi Delta Kappan,* March 1970, pp. 379–381.

and original thinking rather than the "closed" method that concentrates on the right answers—the answers of the book or the teacher.

PROCESSES OF INQUIRY. The curriculum of the new elementary school is not likely to neglect the basic subjects. Since knowledge will be increasing too rapidly to expect to teach everything that is known about any subject, increasing emphasis will be placed on teaching children how to learn, on the processes or modes of inquiry. When the curriculum emphasizes process as well as content, children will develop the intellectual tools needed for a lifetime of learning. The practice of providing teachers with suggestions for fostering the processes of inquiry will become more common. Some curriculum guides have already followed this practice.[19]

KEY CONCEPTS. Another practice, arising in part from the explosion of knowledge, is that of listing curriculum content in terms of key concepts to be learned. These concepts help the pupil to understand the interrelatedness of knowledge and provide him with a scheme for organizing bits of information into a meaningful whole. Concept learning, which has already been given consideration in Chapter 2, is likely to be given greater emphasis in the curriculum of the new elementary school.

NEW RESOURCES. The future seems to be destined to bring both promises and threats in relation to new instructional materials. There can be little doubt that schools, during the next few decades, will have available an abundance of exciting new instructional resources that will help to speed up learning, assist in providing for individual differences, and leave more of the teacher's time free for truly professional work. At the same time professional workers will be challenged to resist high-pressure salesmanship on behalf of sure-cure, largely untested and unsound programs that may produce marvelous results for a limited segment of the instructional program at the expense of a balanced offering. Drummond, who has recognized these dangers, suggests a means of countering them:

> Truly competent curriculum development staffs will be standard in every major city and in every state department of education—and they will be given the time and the resources to study new products, new packages, new proposals. They will, in turn, recommend adaptations of commercially produced curriculum materials, create programs of their own which will utilize commercially produced and locally produced materials and techniques, and continually attempt to seek ways of providing better

---

[19] See, for example, James M. Becker, in Dorothy M. Fraser (Ed.), *Social Studies Curriculum Development: Prospects and Problems* (Washington, D.C.: National Council for the Social Studies, 1969), Chap. 3.

balance—something which the special interest groups will not and cannot do. Teachers will serve in such positions for a year or two, and then return to teaching posts with new insights.[20]

Teachers for the New Elementary School

Frazier has expressed the view that the functions ascribed to the new teacher will be defined more precisely and fully than in the past and that ". . . we shall need to have much in mind how best to prepare the new teacher and how better to support and serve him on the job."[21]

The next few decades seem likely to witness the development of programs for the preparation of elementary school teachers that will differ in important respects from those we have known in the past. These programs are likely to place less emphasis on courses and regularly scheduled classes and more emphasis on individual study, small group discussion, seminars, and working with children. Teachers in the new elementary school will need scholarship, but they will also need imagination and creativity; they must not only select content from a wide variety of sources, but they must also be able to help children internalize this richness so that it becomes their very own. Prototypes of future programs for the preparation of elementary school teachers can be found today in programs that are already in operation and in models that have been developed and offered for adoption.

The Syracuse University Model

Pursuant to a contract with the Office of Education, U. S. Department of Health, Education, and Welfare, specifications were developed at Syracuse University for a comprehensive undergraduate and in-service teacher education program for elementary teachers. The final report was published in two large volumes in October 1968.[22]

RATIONALE OF THE MODEL. The rationale of the model-building staff is explained in detail in Volume I of the final report. The following excerpt provides an insight into the view of the staff in regard to the model:

[20] Harold D. Drummond, in Alexander Frazier (Ed.), *A Curriculum for Children* (Washington, D.C.: Association for Supervision and Curriculum Development, 1969), p. 34.

[21] Frazier, p. 96.

[22] Syracuse University, *Specifications for a Comprehensive Undergraduate and In-service Teacher Education Program for Elementary Teachers*, Volumes I and II (Washington, D.C.: Office of Education, U.S. Department of Health, Education, and Welfare, October 31, 1968).

The program is seen as evolving, and capable of fostering its own "revolutions." The fundamental model is a process model as the basic design of the program will reveal. The working position of the staff has been a pluralistic one, that is, recognizing the inevitability of differences in teacher education and the potential value of such differences for the generation of new knowledge, feelings, skills, and professional practices. We view the program as an open "system" capable of drawing energy from its environment and utilizing that energy within itself to generate new creations and adaptations. Indeed, the proposed program is conceived as being as much a generator of new purposes, new actions, and new practices, as it is a description of objectives, learning experiences, assessment practices, and organizational structures.[23]

Additional insight into the rationale which guided the staff is contained in the following statement:

> To recapitulate, the model program is designed to meet the challenges of change in education by developing elementary teachers who have: (a) a positive self-concept, (b) a congruent professional value system, (c) a sensitivity to other people and a capability of enhancing others' potential, (d) a commitment to the welfare of those with whom they work, and (e) a flexibility that would allow them to be highly receptive to change. The model program is firmly grounded in the realities of behavioral objectives, real instructional situations, and behavioral criteria for the assessment of performance.[24]

COMPONENTS OF THE MODEL PROGRAM. The seven components of the model program are diverse in nature and character. The report states, however, that they are integrated into the basic design of the total program. They are: (1) Liberal Education, (2) Methods and Curriculum, (3) Child Development, (4) Teaching Theory and Practice, (5) Professional Sensitivity Training, (6) Social-Cultural Foundations, and (7) a Self-Directed Component. Volume I of the final report devotes an entire chapter to an explanation of each of these components.

The University of Florida Program

The University of Florida has a new program for the preparation of elementary school teachers that is based on the principle that teaching is a helping relationship rather than a command relationship. During the last two years of his program, the student takes no courses and attends no regularly scheduled classes; the program consists of three parts: the seminar, the substantive panel, and field experience.

[23] Syracuse University, *Specifications* . . . , p. 12.
[24] Syracuse University, *Specifications* . . . , p. 11.

THE SEMINAR. Blume has pointed out that the seminar is the heart of the program.[25] The student has the same seminar leader during the entire time that he is in the professional sequence. Thirty students are assigned to each of three seminar leaders; these thirty students are divided into two groups of fifteen students each and each small group meets for two hours every week to (1) discuss anything relating to education that comes to the minds of the students and their leader, and (2) discover personal meanings for the information and experiences that students are encountering in other facets of the program. The seminar leader serves as adviser to each of the thirty students in his group. He keeps the records for the group and conducts evaluation activities.

THE SUBSTANTIVE PANEL. Faculty members who would normally teach courses in curriculum, methods, and foundation courses are members of the panel. "The faculty member distributes lists of competencies for students to complete and hand in, or to discuss at the faculty-student conference."[26] Students are given a great deal of freedom in selecting substantive panels to attend and in signing up for small-group discussion sessions.

FIELD EXPERIENCE. Level one of the field experience consists of tutoring a child for an entire quarter and observing classrooms, usually about ten one-hour observations. The student serves as teacher assistant in level two, doing whatever needs to be done. He serves as teacher associate in level three, accepting responsibility for planning and teaching lessons to certain groups. Level two requires six hours per week in the classroom and level three requires two hours of teaching per day. Level four requires teaching full time for five weeks.

One of the most commendable features of this program is the participation of students in decision making relating to various phases of the program. Student membership on various faculty-student committees gives the student a sense of being involved and a sense of responsibility. Several student-initiated changes have already been made in the program.[27]

What Educators Believe May Happen in the Schools

Shane and Nelson have reported what 333 educators believe may happen in the schools by the year 2000. The respondents to queries relating to

25 Robert Blume, "Humanizing Teacher Education," *Phi Delta Kappan*, March 1971, p. 413.

26 Blume, p. 413.

27 For more information about this program, see A. W. Combs et al., *Florida Studies in the Helping Professions*, Monograph No. 37 (Gainesville, Fla.: University of Florida Press, 1969).

forty-one possible educational futures included seventy-two school administrators, forty-two subject-matter specialists, thirty-seven professors of curriculum, eighty-seven doctoral students, and ninety-five public school
teachers selected at random. The writers state that these beliefs, if widely
held, could "perceptibly influence future developments in education." [28]
The findings of the survey included the items listed below.

1. Almost all the educators believed that the multimedia approach to
learning resources (instead of the monopoly that the textbook has enjoyed)
would become prevalent between 1975 and 1985. Ninety-six percent of the
respondents agreed that the multimedia approach was desirable.

2. Over half the respondents were convinced that work in the expressive
arts would double its present time allotment in the curriculum within ten to
fifteen years.

3. Over 90 percent of the respondents believed that before 1980 instruction in the social studies would come to grips with controversial topics (activist
movements, discrimination, and so on), and 84 percent believed that our
schools will be open for 12 months each year.

4. Three quarters of the replies favored the enrollment in school at three
years of age and the provision of health services for babies no later than at
age two.

5. The average respondent opposed the idea of corporation management
of school systems, but 10 percent believed that the purchase of instruction
from corporations will be far more widespread as soon as four years from now.

6. Ninety-two percent believed that teacher education will be drastically
modified to prepare teachers to work in teams, to individualize instruction,
and to make greater use of educational technology. Sensitivity training as a
phase of teacher education was forecast by 64 percent of the respondents.

SUMMARY

1. The number of publications containing estimates of probable futures
increased rapidly between 1940 and 1970.

2. We can be certain that almost any estimate we make about changes
in the future will be too conservative.

3. If we can find ways to abolish war and reduce poverty, prejudice, and
pollution the prospects for those who will be living ten, twenty, and a hundred
years from now are indeed exciting.

4. Household automation, the uses of the laser, biological advancements,
and intelligent management of nuclear energy promise to make life in the
future safer and more enjoyable.

5. A new kind of elementary school, almost completely unlike the one
we know today, is likely to emerge.

[28] Harold G. Shane and Owen N. Nelson, "What Will the Schools Become?"
Phi Delta Kappan, June 1971, pp. 596–598.

6. Changes that have already taken place in our society and in the school have inspired new confidence in what man can accomplish.

7. The new elementary school will emphasize quality, equality, individualization, and relevancy.

8. An "open space" arrangement will replace the "eggcrate" arrangement in elementary school buildings.

9. New technological media will be used more extensively in the future to (a) speed up learning, (b) relieve the teacher of nonteaching chores, and (c) enable pupils to work more independently of the teacher.

10. The curriculum will change more rapidly in the future than it has in the past; changes will emphasize creativity, inquiry, learning concepts, and the use of a wide variety of new learning resources.

11. Teacher-education programs will place less emphasis on courses and regularly scheduled classes and more emphasis on individual study, small-group discussion, seminars, field experience, and working with children.

RECOMMENDED READINGS

Association for Supervision and Curriculum Development, *Freedom, Bureaucracy, & Schooling*. Washington, D.C.: A.S.C.D., 1971. Chapter 6 deals with impending changes in teacher education.

Chase, Stuart, *The Most Probable World*. New York: Harper & Row, Publishers, 1968. Identifies trends and predicts changes in many aspects of American life.

Drucker, Peter F., *The Age of Discontinuity: Guidelines to Our Changing Society*. New York: Harper & Row, Publishers, 1969. Chapter 15 deals with the new learning and the new teaching.

Foreign Policy Association, *Toward the Year 2018*. New York: Cowles Educational Corporation, 1968. A group of outstanding leaders in science and technology look fifty years into the future.

Hedges, William D., "Will We Recognize Tomorrow's Elementary School?" *N.E.A. Journal*, December 1967, pp. 9–12. Predicts that within three or four decades instructional terminals in the home will enable the student to master the skills at his own rate; the school will be primarily concerned with socialization.

Kahn, Herman, and Anthony J. Wiener, *The Year 2000: A Framework for Speculation on the Next Thirty-Three Years*. New York: Crowell-Collier and Macmillan, Inc., 1967. Speculates on what our world will be like in the twenty-first century.

National Society for the Study of Education, *The Curriculum: Retrospect and Prospect*. Chicago: University of Chicago Press, 1971. Chapter 7, by Harold D. Shane, deals with "Future-Planning as a Means of Shaping Educational Change."

Nesbitt, Marion, *A Public School for Tomorrow*, rev. ed. New York: Dell Publishing Company, 1967. Chapter 11 deals with educational expectations for the future.

Ragan, William B., and George Henderson, *Foundations of American Education*. New York: Harper & Row, Publishers, 1970. Chapter 17 deals with threats to our future: power, population, prejudice, and pollution.

Sand, Ole, "Schools for the 70's," *The National Elementary Principal*, September 1967, pp. 21–29. Defines the directions in which education is moving in areas such as deciding what to teach, organizing schools and classrooms, and evaluation and assessment.

Appendix

SELECTED FILMS

The following list of films is merely illustrative of the ones that can be used to supplement the various chapters in the book. The film library at the college or university nearest you can, no doubt, provide these and other films on a rental basis. Names and addresses of the producers are given below for the convenience of schools that may want to purchase the films.

List of Producers

Agrafilm (AF)
 P.O. Box 967
 Athens, Ga. 30601

American Federation of Labor and
 Congress of Industrial Organiza-
 tions (AFL-CIO)
 Department of Education
 815 16th Street N.W.
 Washington, D.C. 20006

Anti-Defamation League (ADL)
 315 Lexington Ave.
 New York, N.Y. 10016

Association Films (AF)
 347 Madison Ave.
 New York, N.Y. 10017

Bailey Films (Ba)
 6509 DeLongpre Ave.
 Los Angeles, Calif. 90028

Coronet Films (Cor)
Coronet Bldg.
Chicago, Ill. 60601

Davidson Films (Dav)
1757 Union St.
San Francisco, Calif. 94100

Educational Testing Services (ETS)
Rosedale Rd.
Princeton, N.J. 08540

Encyclopaedia Britannica Films (EBF)
1150 Wilmette Ave.
Wilmette, Illinois 60091

General Motors Corporation (GMC)
3044 W. Grand Blvd.
Detroit, Mich. 48202

Hayes Kruger (HK)
Louise Duffy School
95 Westminster Dr.
West Hartford, Conn. 06091

Holt, Rinehart and Winston (HRW)
383 Madison Ave.
New York, N.Y. 10017

Iowa State University (ISU)
Visual Instruction Services
Ames, Ia. 50010

McGraw-Hill (McGH)
Text-Film Department
330 W. 42nd St.
New York, N.Y. 10036

National Education Association (NEA)
1201 Sixteenth St., N.W.
Washington, D.C. 20036

National Educational Television
(NET)
12 Columbus Circle
New York, N.Y. 10023

Ohio State University (OSU)
1885 Neil Ave.
Columbus, Ohio

Pyramid Films (PYR)
Box 1048
Santa Monica, Calif. 90406

Roundtable Productions (RTP)
321 So. Beverly Dr.
Beverly Hills, Calif. 90212

Special Purpose Films (SPF)
26740 Latigo Shore Dr.
Malibu, Calif. 90265

Syracuse University (SU)
Syracuse, N.Y. 13210

Teachers College, Columbia University (TCCU)
525 W. 120th St.
New York, N.Y. 10027

United States Office of Education (USOE)
400 Marilyn Ave., S.W.
Washington, D.C. 20202

University of Michigan (UM)
Audio-Visual Education Center
Frieze Bldg.
720 E. Huron St.
Ann Arbor, Mich. 48104

University of Oklahoma (OU)
Audio-Visual Education
Norman, Okla. 73069

Wayne State University
Audio-Visual Department
Detroit, Mich. 48202

DESCRIPTIVE LIST OF 16MM FILMS

CHAPTER 1: *Learning To Live with Change*

America: The Edge of Abundance (NET, 59 min). Traces America's growth from a rural to an urban economy as viewed on British television.

America's Crisis: The Community (NET, 59 min). An evaluation of the cultural, educational, religious, and physical aspects of urban communities.

America's Crisis: The Individual (NET, 59 min). Presents the issues of man's search for identity in a complex, industrial society.

America's Crisis: The Parents (NET, 59 min). How today's parents are trying to find identity, purpose, and meaning in their lives.

Assignment Tomorrow (NEA, 32 min). Presents the role of teachers in school-community relations.

Education: The Public Schools (NET, 29 min). Discusses population mobility and explosion, new educational theories, increased government participation, and rising costs as forces shaping public schools.

Teachers (AFL-CIO, 20 min). Presents the responsibilities of teachers and how social and economic pressures affect these responsibilities.

CHAPTER 2: *Changing Estimates of the Human Potential*

Children Without (NEA, 27 min). Commentary on the disadvantaged child; based on Educational Policies Commission report.

Developing Self-Reliance (Cor, 20 min). A boy, accustomed to depending on others, develops self-reliance by assuming responsibility, recognizing goals, and making decisions.

Focus on Behavior: Learning about Learning (NET, 30 min). In developing new theoretical concepts about man's ability to learn, this film explores the work of Howard Kendler, Tracy Kendler, Kenneth Spence, Harry Harlow, and B. F. Skinner.

Heredity and Environment (Cor, 10 min). Overview of the interrelationships of cultural inheritances, genetics, and environmental influences.

Learning and Growth (EBF, 12 min). Arnold Gesell explains relationships between learning and growth.

Piaget's Developmental Theory (Dav, 28 min). Piaget's definitions of children's mental growth and development.

RAFE: Developing Giftedness in the Educationally Disadvantaged (NEA, 20 min, color). A gifted boy from a poor home environment receives special school help; open-ended film to be followed by audience discussion.

Social Development (McGH, 16 min). Analyzes social development at different age levels.

What Do I Know about Benny? (HRW, 10 min, color). Determining an elementary school child's academic aptitude and helping his mother accept it; includes the question of the reliability of standardized tests.

CHAPTER 3: *The Changing Elementary School Curriculum*

All in a Lifetime (NEA, 30 min). Schools of the past are compared with those of the present.

Education in America: The 17th and 18th Centuries (Cor, 16 min). Colonial schools are viewed as the early beginnings of education in America.

Education in America: The 19th Century (Cor, 16 min). Traces the development of free public school systems from the Northwest Ordinance to 1900.

Education in America: The 20th Century (Cor, 16 min). Traces the development of public education from the Industrial Revolution through World War II.

Horace Mann (EBF, 22 min). Presents important episodes in the life of the "father of our common schools."

CHAPTER 4: *Changing Teaching Strategies*

Broader Concept of Method, Part I: Developing Pupil Interest (McGH, 20 min). Presents a comparison of a teacher-dominated lesson with techniques for more student involvement.

Broader Concept of Method, Part II: Teacher and Pupils Planning and Working Together (McGH, 22 min). Illustrates how pupils learn to work together in functional groups.

Each Child Is Different (McGH, 22 min). An illustration of what teachers need to know of individual differences.

Experimental Studies in the Social Climates of Groups (ISU, 32 min). Shows the effects of autocratic, laissez-faire, and democratic climates on the attitudes and learning of junior high pupils.

Learning through Cooperative Planning (TCCU, 18 min). Presents the seven basic skills involved in cooperative planning.

Maintaining Classroom Discipline (McGH, 15 min). Shows how discipline depends upon the approach used by the teacher.

Teacher as Observer and Guide (TCCU, 20 min). How teachers can guide pupils through problems that promote growth and character.

CHAPTER 5: *Organizing To Maximize Learning*

Are Our Schools Up-to-Date? (NEA, 30 min). Presents the opinions of experienced educators on this question.

Personalized Education Series: Pt. III, Why Are Team-Teaching and Non-Grading Important? (SPF, 35 min). Team teaching and nongrading are explained.

Personalized Education Series: Pt. IV, How Can You Apply Team-Teaching and Non-Grading to Your School? (SPF, 35 min). Considers the decisions to be made in order to implement team teaching and nongrading.

Schools for Tomorrow (WSU, 27 min). Presents the use of citizens' groups, school personnel, and architects to build better schools.

CHAPTER 6: *Planning for Effective Teaching*

Effective Teaching in the Elementary School (McGH, 20 min). A fifth-grade teacher narrates some of her own experiences in making learning more effective.

Learning through Cooperative Planning (Cor, 18 min). Illustrates the value of preparation, participation, and keeping an open mind.

A Search for Learning (McGH, 13 min). Designed to show how to organize a classroom and present lessons using the discovery approach.

CHAPTER 7: *Utilizing Extra-Teacher Personnel*

Developing Leadership (Cor, 11 min). Illustrates the qualities required for effective leadership, how to become a leader, and how leadership in a democratic group changes with the will and interests of the group.

How To Get Cooperation (Cor, 11 min). A film presenting methods of securing cooperation in a school situation.

A New Supervisor Looks at His Job (USOE, 12 min). A young workman who has just been made a line supervisor is shown in an interview with the superintendent. He is told that in his new job he must learn to get results by working with people instead of with machines; the importance of the human element in supervision is made evident.

Overcoming Resistance to Change (RTP, 30 min). How administrators may overcome or prevent tendencies of employees to resent new ideas and procedures.

CHAPTER 8: *Research in the Elementary School Subjects*

Man and His Culture (EBF, 15 min). Shows how the earth might appear to visitors from another planet; considers the things that most cultures have in common, the ways in which cultures are transmitted from one generation to the next, and the ways in which they change.

Mathematics through Discovery (USOE, 25 min). Shows the use of the "discovery" method in teaching new concepts of mathematics at the elementary and secondary levels.

Movement Education in Physical Education (HK, 20 min). Through narration in question-answer form, two men teachers interpret movement education.

Science through Discovery (NET, 28 min). Presents the discovery method of teaching science in the elementary school.

Why Can't Jimmy Read? (SU, 15 min). The story of nine-year-old Jimmy and his reading problems as a typical case history from the Syracuse University Reading Clinic.

CHAPTER 9: *Instructional Technology*

Children Learn from Filmstrips (McGH, 16 min). Points out that the filmstrip doesn't take the place of anything in the curriculum, but, used with imagination, the medium can lead the child to a subject-into-learning.

Children Make Movies (McGH, 10 min). This segment of a film collection dealing with teacher education shows possibilities for children's film-making projects.

Choosing a Classroom Film (McGH, 18 min). Illustrations are given on how various film techniques such as photo-micrography and time-lapse photography supplement learning.

Creating Instructional Materials (McGH, 15 min). Shows that the creation of instructional materials can contribute significantly to the student's learning experience.

How To Use Classroom Films (McGH, 15 min). The basic principles for effective presentation and utilization of a classroom film are presented.

New Way to Greater Education (Cor, 16 min). How audiovisual teaching helps.

Teaching Machines and Programmed Learning (USOE, 13 min). The work of Pressey, Skinner, and others in devising machines.

Television in the Classroom (OSU, 10 min). A study of the utilization of television in the classroom.

CHAPTER 10: *Teaching Culturally Different Children*

The Coleman Report: Equality of Educational Opportunity (ADL, 55 min). Drs. Daniel P. Moynihan and Thomas Pettigrew lead discussions about the ramifications of the 1966 U.S. Office of Education report referred to as the "Coleman Report." The report indicates that quality education must of necessity be racially and socioeconomically integrated.

Portrait of a Disadvantaged Child: Tommy Knight (McGH, 16 min). A day in the life of a slum child; depicts some of the special problems, needs, and strengths of an inner-city child.

Portrait of the Inner City (McGH, 17 min). Shows home, school, and community aspects of an urban inner-city community; also shows how an inner-city boy found a middle-class role model.

Portrait of the Inner-City School: A Place To Learn (McGH, 19 min). Illustrates how teachers may unconsciously discriminate against culturally disadvantaged children; how textbooks discriminate through illustrations and materials which are unfamiliar to the inner-city child.

White Guilt: Black Shame (UM, 28 min). An analysis of how white guilt and black shame prevent community residents from overcoming barriers to integration.

Who Am I? (UM, 28 min). An examination of why the Negro child is constantly questioning and searching for his identity.

Worlds Apart (ADL, 16 min). Dr. Martin Deutsch, director of the Institute for Developmental Studies, designed the preschool curriculum shown in the film. It illustrates techniques for bridging the gap between the slum school and white, middle-class-oriented curriculum.

CHAPTER 11: *Creative Ways of Teaching and Learning*

Creative Attitude (GMC, 30 min). A member of General Motors' styling staff gives advice on creativity in individuals. He tells the difference between creative and analytical thought.

Why Man Creates (PYR, 30 min). An award-winning film that discusses and illustrates creativity as a basic and fundamental part of human existence. The film itself was produced in a highly creative fashion and is remarkably effective in making its points.

CHAPTER 12: *Effective Mastery of Skills*

The First and Fundamental R (HRW, 12 min). Deals with the problem of teaching reading to elementary school children in a low socioeconomic area.

Fundamental Skills in a Unit of Work (Ba, 20 min). How skills are learned in response to a felt need.

Making Learning More Meaningful (McGH, 11 min). How a teacher used the spontaneous interests of a class to develop arithmetic skills.

Science and Language Arts (McGH, 17 min). Emphasizes the importance of language arts skills in the teaching of science.

Science Study Skills (Cor, 11 min). Stresses the role of skills in measurement, observation, and record-keeping in teaching science.

Skippy and the Three R's (AF, 29 min). Presents an account of how children learn the three R's naturally and easily.

CHAPTER 13: *Individualizing and Personalizing Teaching*

Development of Individual Differences (McGH, 13 min). Reviews theories concerning the relative influence of heredity and environment.

Discovering Individual Differences (McGH, 25 min). Film shows methods used by a fifth-grade teacher in becoming acquainted with her class's individual needs and characteristics.

Each Child Is Different (McGH, 17 min). Dramatized incidents present a study of five fifth-grade children whose personalities and backgrounds present typical problems.

Individual Differences (McGH, 23 min). Wrong and right ways are shown in which a teacher can try to bring the shy, slow student into the mainstream of the class.

Personalized Education Series: Pt. I, Can Individualization Work in Your School System? (SPF, 41 min). Presents evidence that no other system can work so well. It goes into the kinds of changes in school organization, curriculum, and methods that may be required in your school system in order to provide individualization.

Personalized Education Series: Pt. V, How Can the Curriculum for Individualized Education Be Determined? (SPF, 35 min). Ties together the meaningful relationship of academic content, teaching skills, school organization, and individual differences of learners.

CHAPTER 14: *Classroom Management—Discipline*

The Aggressive Child (McGH, 30 min). An intelligent six-year-old is in constant trouble at home and in school because of fighting. Within this situation, the film examines the relationship between emotions and behavior.

A Child Who Cheats (HRW, 10 min). Handling a problem of cheating in the classroom.

Classroom Management (HRW, 18 min). A color film that illustrates Professor Kounin's method of research in his book *Discipline and Group Management in Classrooms* (1970).

Maintaining Classroom Discipline (McGH, 12 min). Contrasts poor and good discipline resulting from the teachers' varied approaches; importance of stimulating interest; handling of minor incidents.

CHAPTER 15: *Evaluating and Reporting Pupil Progress*

Administering a Testing Program (ETS, 13 min). A discussion of six points of a good testing program.

Interpreting Test Scores Realistically (ETS, 18 min). Discussion of the use of standard error and comparison of test forms in the interpretation of test scores.

The Public Relations of Testing (ETS, 11 min). Concerns ways of achieving good public relations with students, teachers, parents, and the community.

Report Card (HRW, 12 min). Explores the basis on which students in an elementary school should be graded.

Selecting an Achievement Test (ETS, 14 min). Deals with the selection of achievement tests by school personnel.

Using Test Results (ETS, 19 min). Shows ways to use test results to benefit instruction, guidance, and administration.

CHAPTER 16: *Schools for Tomorrow*

Assignment Tomorrow (NEA, 33 min). Place and importance of teachers in American life.

How Good Are Our Schools? Dr. Conant Reports (AF, 28 min). Dr. Conant reports on the deficiencies in American secondary schools and points out what he believes every secondary school should be prepared to do.

Report on Tomorrow (OSU, 26 min). Surveys the present educational situation and stresses the need for continuing growth and public support of the states' system of higher education.

Schools for Tomorrow (WSU, 22 min). Focuses on using citizens' advisory committees, school personnel, and architects to build better schools.

Author Index

Adams, James Truslow, 216
Adams, John, 53
Adams, Samuel, 53
Agar, Herbert, 53
Ahlbrand, William P., Jr., 77
Airasian, Peter W., 266
Alexander, William M., 94
Ames, Wilbur S., 162
Anzalone, Patricia Murphy, 263, 268
Austin, Mary C., 154

Barbe, R., 156
Barnard, Henry, 54, 58
Barnes, Fred P., 151
Beard, Charles A., 171
Beck, Joan, 336
Becker, James, 341
Begel, E. C., 64
Bell, Andrew, 56
Bellack, Arno, 47, 77
Berkeley, Governor, 49
Bloom, Benjamin S., 23, 36, 200
Blume, Robert, 344
Boocock, Sarane, 85, 197
Brameld, Theodore, 13
Brekke, Gerald, 155
Bronfenbrenner, Urie, 28
Brown, B. Frank, 97
Bruner, Jerome S., 25–26
Buckingham, Walter, 15
Burke, A. J., 168
Burns, Paul C., 27, 37, 160, 162

Cahill, Walter T., 159
Calvin, John, 48
Cardinell, Charles, 168
Carter, Alexander, 168
Carter, James G., 57
Caswell, H. L., 227
Chambers, J. Richard, 274
Chase, Stuart, 334–335
Clinton, De Witt, 56–57

Clymer, Theodore, 156
Coleman, James S., 85
Combs, Arthur W., 45, 220, 344
Cousins, Victor E., 58
Covington, Martin V., 156
Craig, Gerald S., 255
Crary, Ryland W., 242
Cunningham, Luverne L., 9
Cutts, Norma E., 265, 273–275

Dale, Edgar, 186
Dallmann, Martha, 253
Daugherty, Louise, 212
DeBoer, John J., 253
Dewey, John, 60ff., 95–96, 250
Dilorenzo, Louis T., 164
Drake, William E., 47, 49, 50
Drucker, Peter F., 4
Drummond, Harold D., 341–342
Dwight, Edmund, 57

Ebel, Robert L., 168
Edmund, Neal R., 159
Ehrlich, Paul, 6–7
Eikholz, G., 156
Engler, David, 339–340
English, Horace B., 29, 36

Faber, Nancy, 337
Fantini, Mario D., 208
Finn, James, 172
Foshay, A. W., 227
Frazier, Alexander, 342
Friedlander, Bernard K., 82

Gage, N. L., 168
Gagné, Robert, 200–201
Gardner, John W., 241
Gearson, John D., 84
Getzels, Jacob W., 233
Goldberg, Miriam L., 218
Goodlad, John I., 65, 241

Gould, Samuel B., 44–45
Gray, Roland F., 166
Gray, William S., 156–157

Hagaman, Neva, 78, 112
Hall, Samuel R., 57
Halliwell, Joseph W., 164
Hanna, Lavone A., 78, 112, 249
Hanna, Paul R., 13
Harris, Theodore L., 153–156, 158
Heathers, Glen, 3
Hedges, William D., 336–337
Henderson, George, 21, 63, 208, 210
Henry, Patrick, 53
Herman, Wayne L., Jr., 167
Herrick, Virgil, 158, 272
Hillson, Maurie, 91
Hoetker, James, 77
Holt, John, 245, 267
Horn, Ernest, 161–162
Howe, Harold, 11, 216
Hunt, Joseph McVicker, 21
Hunter, David R., 209
Hunter, Madeline, 269, 271, 273, 276

Jackson, Andrew, 52
Jackson, Philip W., 77, 233
Jarvis, Oscar T., 155
Jefferson, Thomas, 52–53
Johnson, A. M., 27, 37
Joyce, Bruce R., 168
Judd, C. H., 48

Kagan, J., 24
Kahn, Herman, 330ff.
Karplus, Robert, 64
Keislar, Evan R., 228
Kelley, Earl C., 62
Kennedy, D., 159
Kinzel, Augustus B., 333
Klein, M. Frances, 65
Klohr, Paul R., 39
Knight, Edgar W., 54
Kohl, Herbert, 268

Lancaster, Joseph, 56–57
Langemann, John K., 21
Lee, Dorris May, 225
Lee, J. Murray, 225
Leonard, George B., 19, 330
Lewin, Kurt, 153
Lewis, Frederick Allen, 60

Lipset, S. M., 14
Lumsdaine, A. A., 194
Lundsteen, Sara W., 161
Luther, Martin, 48

McAulay, John D., 257
McKendall, B., Jr., 207
McLendon, Jonathan C., 167
Madaus, George F., 266
Madison, James, 52
Mager, Robert F., 122, 200
Mann, Horace, 16, 52, 55, 57–58
Marcel, Gabriel, 261
Marconi, Guglielmo, 175
Martin, William, 159
Mattil, Edward L., 275
May, Frank B., 160
Melby, Ernest O., 318
Mills, Caleb, 58
Morgan, Joy Elmer, 60
Morrison, Coleman, 154
Moseley, Nicholas, 265, 273–275
Moss, H., 24
Mulry, June Grant, 159–160
Myers, R. E., 228, 230ff., 234

Nelson, Owen N., 344–345
Nye, Robert E., 275

Otto, Henry, 30–31
Owen, Robert, 55

Parker, Franklin, 215
Passow, A. Harry, 222
Penix, Findlay C., 167
Perrodin, Alex F., 163
Perry, William F., 58
Pestalozzi, Johann Heinrich, 55, 58
Piaget, Jean, 25
Pierce, John D., 58
Pines, M., 230
Pool, Ithiel Da Sola, 15
Porterfield, Denzil, 83
Postman, Neil, 246–247, 249
Potter, Gladys L., 78, 112
Preston, Ralph C., 256

Raab, Earl, 14
Ragan, William B., 21, 63–65, 81,
    163, 208, 210, 247, 255, 257,
    280, 304, 331
Raikes, Robert, 56

Redl, Fritz, 282, 285
Reisner, Edward H., 50, 81
Renner, John W., 64–65, 164, 247, 255
Riessman, Frank, 221
Rosenthal, Robert, 21
Rubin, Louis J., 243, 247
Russell, J. D., 48

Sanders, David C., 30–31
Sanders, Norris M., 68–69, 84
Scheckles, Mary E., 273
Schild, E. O., 197
Schiller, Sister Philomene, 167
Schmidt, Frederick B., 83
Schuller, Charles Francis, 193
Serra, Mary C., 156
Shane, Harold G., 159–160, 336, 344–345
Sheldon, Edward A., 55
Shepherd, Gene D., 331
Sherburne, E. G., 216
Sheviakov, George V., 282, 285
Shulman, Lee S., 227–228
Slawson, Wilber S., 274
Smith, Nila, 154
Smith, Robert O., 168
Spauldin, Robert L., 230
Spitzer, Herbert F., 166
Stafford, Donald G., 83, 164
Stahl, Dona Kofod, 263, 268
Stendler, Celia B., 242

Stevens, Romiett, 77
Stevens, Thaddeus, 58–59
Stoephasius, Renata Von, 65
Stowe, Calvin E., 55, 58
Stright, Virginia, 164–165
Swett, John, 58

Tabachnick, H. Robert, 160
Tanck, Marlin L., 26
Taylor, Stanford E., 160
Templin, E. M., 157
Thayer, V. T., 77–78
Tillman, Rodney, 329
Torrance, Paul E., 159, 226ff., 234
Travers, Robert, 202
Trow, William Clark, 173

Veatch, Jeanette, 155

Washington, George, 53
Weingartner, Charles, 246–247
Weinstein, Gerald, 208
White, John F., 177
Wiener, Anthony J., 330ff.
Wiley, Calvin H., 58
Wilson, John, 82–83, 164–165
Wilson, Woodrow, 11
Witherspin, Samuel, 56
Wittich, Walter Arno, 193
Witty, Paul A., 159
Worth, Witt, 24

Subject Index

Page numbers in italics indicate illustrations.

Activities, culminating, 117
  evaluation of, 118, *130*
  for groups, 71
  planning, 117–118, *118*–128
  teacher's participation in, 128–130
Administration, evaluation of, 307
  research in, 168–169
Age, as basis for grade placement, 92
  differences in multigraded schools
    and middle-school organization,
    94
American education, history of, 47–65
  reform movements, 3, 59–63
Anecdotal records, 312–314
Anti-intellectualism, in American so-
    ciety, 22
  in schools, 153
Appalachia, 215
Appropriate placement, 97
Art, classes, *33*
  individualizing, 275–276
  skills, 257–258
Assistant principal, 137–138
Audio-visual media, 116, 172–206
  filmstrips, 190–191
  motion pictures, 186–188
    list of, 350–356
    nontheatrical films, 187–188
    producers, list of, 349–350
    single-concept films, 187
  multimedia, 199–204, *266*
    evaluation, 203
    feedback, 203–204
    implementation, 202–203
    objectives, 200–201
    planning, 202
    preparation, 201–202
    role in future, 345
  overhead projectors, 189
    connection to tape recorder, 192

Audio-visual media (*Cont.*)
  phonograph records, 192–194
  scheduling of, 114
  tape recordings, 191–193
    connection to projectors, 192
    future use of, 338
  television, 175–186
  2 × 2 transparencies, 190
  See also Television
Automation, 5, 15, 22, 331–332

Basal-reading tests, 156
Behavioral statement in planning,
    121–122
Behavioral technology, 15–16, 20–21,
    331
Biological revolution, 6–7, 332–334

Canadian National Film Board, 187
Changes in American life, 2*ff*., 330*ff*.
"Changing American Child, The," 28
Checklists, in evaluation, 312, 314
Chicago ghetto schools, 212
Child-study instruments, 31*ff*.
Cities, growth of, 8*ff*.
  school district reorganization, 8
Classroom, management, 280–303
  physical arrangement of, 106–107
Communication skills, 250–251
Communism, 11
Community response games (*see* Sim-
    ulation games)
Comprehension (reading), research
    on, 156
Computer, 5
  future use in schools, 338, 340
  as simulator, 197
Concept learning, 24–25, 63
  in future, 341
  stages in development, 25

361

Conferences with parents, 33–34, 319–324
  check sheet, 322
  parents' role, 323
  preparation for, 321
Constitution of the United States, 51, 53
Consumer games (see Simulation games)
Content, 263, 269
  See also Curriculum
Continuous progress, 92, 96, 104
Copying in learning handwriting, 158
Creative writing, research in, 159–160
  skills, 253
Creativity, arts skills, 257–258
  in children, 227–229, 233–234
  defined, 226–227
  in future schools, 340–341
  and self-understanding, 245–246
  in teaching, 225–237
  See also Teaching creatively
Critical thinking, observed, 308
  in research skills, 248–249
  in science, 256
Culturally different children, 207–224
  American Indians, 213
  in Appalachia, 215
  discipline of, 211, 213
  extended family, 209
  identification of, 208
  lack of stimuli, 212
  language difficulties, 212–213, 220
  living conditions, 208–210
  self-concept, 213
  Southern Negroes, 211
  teaching, 210–224
  See also Slum schools
Cumulative records, 313–314
Curriculum, changing, 41ff.
  concept learning, 25
  content, relevance of, 6–7, 20, 42, 85, 125, 338
  defined, 39
  future, 340–342
  for gifted children, 10–11
  guides, 42–44, 113–114
  multiphased, 96–97
  nature of, 39ff.
  Ohio Association for Supervision and Curriculum Development bulletin, 22

Curriculum, changing (Cont.)
  organizational principles of, 41
  planning, 40ff.
    children's part in, 41–42
    groups, 41–42, 45–46, 107–108
    horizontal articulation (integration)
    of content, 41 (see also Unit teaching)
    implementing problems, 297
    teacher's role in, 41, 44–47
  reform
    federal funds for, 62–63
    1945–1947, 62
    1950s to present, 39ff., 62–63
    projects, 64–65
    research, 168–169
    single track, 10
    for slow learners, 10, 11
Custodian, school, 145

Daily lesson plans, 118–121
Daily work as evaluation of progress, 312–314
Decision making, 70–84
Democratic living, and discipline, 282–284, 287–289
  education toward, 51ff.
  evaluating progress in, 72–74
  and heterogeneous grouping, 101–102
  skills, 250–251, 256–257
  sociogram, 313–314
  stress, 297–302
  teaching for, 70ff.
  and unit planning, 117
Departmentalization, 99
Depression (1930s), effects of, 59–60
Desegregation, 94
Developmental reading, research in, 155
Dimensions of schooling, 262–267
Discipline, 280–303
  and competitiveness, 294
  defined, 281–292
  and democracy, 283–284, 287–289
  developmental system of, 286–287
  goals of, 282–283
  and individual differences, 284–285
  and morale, 294–295
  and rationale, 296
  versus repression, 293

Discipline (*Cont.*)
  and self-depreciation, 294
  and self-discipline, 291–292
Discovery, learning by, 65, 69–70, 80–84, 232
  in future schools, 341
  and mastery of skills, 247
Driver education, 196
Dynamic unit, 79–80

Early school years, importance of, 23–24
Education, goals of, 102
  for citizenship, 51*ff.*, 70*ff.*
  support for religion, 48–51
  as public responsibility, 48
Educational parks, 217
Elementary and Secondary Education Act of 1965, 337
Elementary education, history of, 47*ff.*
Emotional development of children, 28*ff.*
  in the middle school, 94
  and readiness in graded school, 92
Emotionally disturbed children, 30
Encyclopedia of Educational Research, 35, 153, 158
Environment, and effect on future schools, 330–331
  manipulation of, 6
Evaluation, 266, 304–328
  checklist for, 74–76, 312
  as a continuing process, 315
  cumulative records, 312
  by daily work, 312
  defined, 305
  feedback, 311
  goals of, 306
  in group living, 72*ff.*
  of individual, 73*ff.*
  by observation, 308–309
  and placement, 266–267
  principles of, 31
  and reporting performance, 304–328
    report cards, 316–318
  self-evaluation, 306, 315
  sociogram, 313–314
  student involvement in, 325–326
  teaching-learning triangle, 305
  techniques of, 308–314
  testing, 309–311
  See also Testing

Evaluation (*Cont.*)
  as a threat, 234
  written reports, 318–319
Experience unit, 79
Extra-teacher personnel, 133*ff.*

Family, extended, 209–210
  mother-centered, 210
Federal Communications Commission (FCC), 176
Films (*see* Audio-visual media)
Filmstrips (*see* Audio-visual media)
Ford Foundation, 187
Free School Society of New York, 54
Functional writing, 160, 253
Future of schools, 329–347
  new elementary schools, 336–342
  teacher training, 342–344

Gary Plan, 91
Geography, 256–257
  See also Social studies
Gifted children, 10–11, 19
  and creative writing, 159
  and testing, 311
Goals of education, 48*ff.*, 70*ff.*, 102
Grade placement of content, 63
Graded school, 91–93
  effect on reading achievement, 155
Group living (*see* Democratic living)
Grouping (inter- and intraclass), 101–103, 306
  heterogeneous, 101–103
  homogeneous, 102–103
  modified, 103
Guidance counseling, 30, 32, 70, 138–139

Handwriting, research in, 157–159
  skills, 253
  and videotape, 185
Harvard, 49
Health, classes, 32
  conditions in slums, 209
  records, 31
  scheduling, 121
  and school lunch program, 146
  services in future, 345
History of elementary education, 47*ff.*
Horizontal articulation, 42
Horizontal organization, 98*ff.*
  departmentalization, 99

Horizontal organization (*Cont.*)
  self-contained classroom, 98
  team teaching, 100

Independent learning, 63, 68–69, 97
  and reading techniques, 156
  and team teaching, 100
  and technological media, 339
  and testing, 311
Indians, American, 213
Individual differences, and creative
    teaching, 232
  and evaluation, 271, 307
  and grouping, 102–103, 263
  and unit planning, 124–125
Individualization, 3*ff.*, 22, 70, 93, 95,
    97, 103, 105–106, 261–279
  and discipline, 284–285, 289–290
  and evaluation, 271
  and instructional television, 179
  and multimedia, 266
  skills, 272–276
  in slum schools, 218*ff.*
  and tape recorders, 192
  and volunteer aides, 338
Infant school movement, 55–56, 108
Informational sources about school
    children, 31
Inquiry strategy (*see* Discovery)
Integrated curriculum (*see* Curricu-
    lum; Horizontal articulation;
    Unit teaching)
Intelligence, new concepts of, 21
  testing, 152, 309–311
IQ, 21, 152, 310
ITV (*see* Television, instructional)

John F. Kennedy School (Norman,
    Okla.), 339

Labor unions, 58
Language arts, 32
  skills, 252–253, 272–273
Laser, 5, 332
Learning potential, 19*ff.*
Learning styles, 263, 269
Learning theory, 20, 99
Left-handers, 159
Leisure, use of, 14–15, 233
Lesson plans, daily, 118–121
  weekly, 119–121

Librarian, school, 142
Listening, research on, 160–161
  skills, 252, 256
Lunch personnel, 145–146

Marking symbols, 316–318
Massachusetts Bay Colony, 3, 49–50
Mathematics, effects of teacher's atti-
    tude, 164–166
  emphasis on understanding struc-
    ture, 166
  individualizing, 273
  new math, 63–64, 166
  research on, 164–166
  skills, 253–254
Media, educational (*see* Audio-visual
    media)
Media specialists, 194
Medical personnel, 140, 142
Medicine, advances in, 333–334
Memorization, 50, 69–70
Monitorial system, 56–57
Milbourne High School, 97
Multigraded schools, 93
Multimedia (*see* Audio-visual media)
Music, 32, 121, 134
  individualizing, 275
  skills, 257–258
My Pedagogical Creed (John Dewey),
    60

National Education Act (1918), 15
National Education Association, 11,
    15, 60, 99
National Educational Television
    (NET), 177
National Science Foundation, 64
New England Primer, 50
New England town schools, 49–51
New math (*see* Mathematics)
New York City Board of Education,
    54
Nongraded schools, 91, 96–97
  effect on reading achievement, 155
  and mastery of skills, 244
Normal schools, 57*ff.*, 225
  See also Teacher training
Nova educational complex (Florida),
    336
Nuclear energy, 334–335

Objectives in planning, 120*ff.*
Observation (systematic), as information source, 32*ff.*
Ohio Association for Supervision and Curriculum Development bulletin, 22
"Old Deluder Satan Act," 3, 48–49
Open school, 105–108
Organization of elementary schools, 91–111
  as administrative device, 108
  combinations of forms, 104–105
  continuous progress, 92, 96
  effects on reading achievement, 155
  flexibility in, 108
  heterogeneous grouping, 101–105
  homogeneous grouping, 102–105
  horizontal, 92*ff.*
  implementation of change, 104–105
  versus middle school, 97
  open school, 104
  vertical, 92–96
Overhead projectors, 189

Paraprofessionals, 277
  See also Teacher aides
Parents, conferences with, 33–34, 319–324
  follow-up, 325
  groups, 320–21
  individual, 321–24
  manner, 324
  selection of environment, 324
  PTA, 144, 277, 320
  as volunteer teacher aides, 143–144, 277
  written reports to, 318–319
Performance standards, evaluation of, 123
  See also Testing
Pestalozzian influences, 55, 58
Phonics, research on, 155–157
Physical education, 32
  individualizing, 275–276
  skills, 258
Planning, 112–132
  arguments for, 112
  daily, 113, 118–121
  evaluation of, 130
  long-range, 113–115
  objectives of, 121–124
  problems of, 124–130

Planning (*Cont.*)
  rationale for, 113
  scheduling, 119–121
  statements of objectives, 122–123
  unit, 113, 115–118
  weekly, 119–121
Polarization, 13–14
Population trends, 7–8
Poverty, reflected in American schools, 10–11
Prejudice, 13–14, 207–208, 337
  See also Culturally different children
Power, uses of, 330
Principal, 136–137
  conferences on child's history, 32
  conferences with parents, 321–322
  creative leadership, 235
  and departmentalization, 99
  role of, in curriculum design, 41–42
Printing, invention and spread of, 48
Problem-solving, 245–247, 251
Programmed learning (*see* Technology [instructional])
Progressive Education Association, 60*ff.*, 243
Psychology, applied by teacher, 20, 30–31, 63
  self-understanding, 245–246
PTA, 144, 277, 320
Public School Revival, 52–55, 57–58
Public schools, failings of, 241–243
Puritan schools, 49–51
Purpose of school, 262

Questioning, as a skill, 248
Quincy School (Boston), 91

Readiness for school, 92
Reading, and creative teaching, 230
  to gather data, 249
  research in, 153*ff.*
    aims, 154
    basal-reading time study, 155–156
    comprehension, 155–156
    and creative writing, 159–160
    developmental practices, 155–156
    listening, 160–161
    spelling, 161–163
    teacher's role in, 154–155
    See also Phonics; Vocabulary
  and self-concept, 230

Reading and creative teaching (*Cont.*)
skills, 252
and videotape, 185
Recitation, 78*ff.*
Records, cumulative, 32, 271
samples of work, 35
Recreational resources, 270–271
Reform movements in elementary education, 3–4, 21, 55*ff.*
Remedial facilities, 154, 211, 214, 217
Report cards, 316–318
Research, educational, 35–36, 64–65,
151–170
bibliography (selected), 168–169
as common information source for
teachers, 152
defined, 151
futurists, 329, 244–245
limitations of, 152
in reading, 153*ff.*
related to discovery and self-directed
study, 82–84
theories
normative and empirical, 153
Research skills in elementary curriculum, 247–251
data gathering, 248–249
forming judgments, 249
questioning, 248
reading, 249
Resource unit, 79
Retention level, 160
Rules, 262–263, 268

School design, 339
School district reorganization, 9, 94
School Mathematics Study Group, 64
Science, 64, 82–83
research on, 163–164
skills, 255, 273
Science Curriculum Improvement
Study, 64–65, 82
impact on teacher education, 163–
164
Secretary (school), 144–145
Self-contained classroom, 98
Self-direction, 267–268
Self-discipline, 291–292
Self-understanding, 245–246
and self-evaluation, 306, 315
Seminars in teacher education, 344
Sensitivity training, 345

"Sesame Street," 177–178
Seven Cardinal Principles of Education, 15
Simulation games, 84, 197–199
implications of, 198–199
Simulations, 196
Simulators, 196–197
Singing, 275
Skills, basic, 243–258, 272
broader view of, 242–244
individualizing, 272–276
mastery of, 241–260
in old and new elementary
schools, 244
See also specific subject areas
Slow learners, 10–11, 19–20
and testing, 311
Slum schools, achievement in, 211–
212
cooperation with parents, 211–212
Chicago project, 212
language difficulties in, 212–213
materials and methods in, 219
problems of, 210–211
quality education in, 216–222
remedial facilities in, 208
teachers for, 219–222
preparation of, 222
Slums, living conditions in, 208–210
Social development of children, 27–28
teaching group living, 70*ff.*
Social studies, curriculum projects, 65
individualizing, 274
inquiry approach, 83
popularity of, 168–169
research on, 167–168
skills, 256–257
tests of study skills, 167
Social workers, 139, 212
Sociogram, 313–314
Space, as factor in teaching, 264–265
for learning, 339
utilizing, 270
Speaking, 252
and videotape, 185
Speech and hearing therapy, 32, 121,
140, 142
Spelling, mastery of, 244, 252
research on, 161–163
textbooks, 162
State Board of Education, Massachusetts (1837), 57

Stevens bill for free public education, 58–59
Student participation, in activities, 265–266
  with faculty on committees, 344
  as teacher aides, 276–277
Subject matter unit, 79
Substitute teachers, 141–142
Sunday School Movement, 56
Syracuse University teacher education program, 342–343

Tax support for schools, 54
Teacher, as coordinator of independent learning, 97
  as idea-giver, 68
  self-evaluation, 301–302
  as specialist, 134, 142
Teacher aides, 142–144, 277–278, 338
Teacher training, in curriculum planning, 47
  versus education, 226
  field experience, 344
  in future, 342–344
  seminars, 344
  sensitivity training, 345
  Syracuse University program, 342–343
  versus teacher education, 226
  and team teaching, 100
  University of Florida program, 343
Teaching creatively, 225–237
  conformity in United States, 226–227, 234–235
  creative experience, 232–233
  effects on children, 229
  encouraging originality, 226–227
  experience background, 233–234
  opportunities for creative expression, 235
  problem solving, 245–247
  pupil involvement, 234
  recognition for creativity, 234
  skills, 234
  relationship with pupils, 233–234
Teaching–learning triangle, 113, 305
Teaching machines (see Technology [instructional])
Teaching materials, 114
  for concept teaching, 26–27
  for culturally different children, 218–219

Teaching materials (Cont.)
  and departmentalization, 99
  evaluation of, 307
  in future, 337–338, 345
  grading of, 92
  inquiry-centered, 83
  to promote critical thinking, 22
  and self-evaluation, 306
  simulation games, 84–85
  teaching machines, 172–174
  textbooks
    basal readers, 156
    future of, 345
    mathematics, 254
    spelling, 162
    teacher's editions, 114
Teaching problems in slum schools, 211–212
Teaching strategies, 68–69, 135
  for slum schools, 218–220
Teaching unit, 79
Team teaching, 8, 68–69, 91, 100–101, 113
  and instructional television, 179
  and multimedia programs, 202–203
Technological advances, behavioral, 15–16
  communications, 5
  effects on future schools, 330ff.
  impact on leisure, 15
Technology (instructional), 171–206
  an area of study, 172–173
  contribution of, to quality education, 174
  defined, 171
  future of, 337–338, 345
  levels of, 173
  programmed instruction, 172–174, 194–196
    in mathematics, 254
  teaching machines
    impact of, 172–273
    tape recorders, 192
    teacher response, 174
  See also Audio-visual media; Simulations; Television
Television, 175–186
  commercial, 175–176
    advertising support, 175–176
    licensing, 176
    use in schools, 176

Television (*Cont.*)
  educational and public, 176–178
    children's programming, 177–178
    instructional, 178
      specific uses, 179
      effort-storing, 182–184
      equipment, 179–182
      feedback, 184–185
      front-row seat, 182
      videotape, 180–185
Testing, 309–311
  achievement, 309
  diagnostic, 310–311
  individual versus group, 310
  intelligence, 21, 152, 309–311
  with teacher-made tests, 310–311
Tests, record of child's, 32
Theoretical statements, 153
Time and scheduling, 264–265, 269–270
Time line, 257
Townsend Movement, 60
Transparencies, 190

Unit planning, 113, 115*ff*., 124–125
Unit teaching, 78–81
  versus departmentalization, 99

Unit teaching (*Cont.*)
  evaluation of, 130
  introduction of unit, 126
  involving students, 127
  organization of, 126
  plans for, 113, 115*ff*.
  preparation for, 125–126
Universal free schools, 51*ff*.
University of Florida teacher education program, 343–349

Vertical organization, 92–97
  appropriate placement, 97
  of graded school, 92–93
  of middle school, 97
  of multigraded school, 93
  team teaching, 100
Videotape (*see* Television [instructional])
Vocabulary, research on, 155–156

Weekly lesson plan, 119–121
Winnetka Plan, 91
Word-attack skills, research on, 155
Work specimen folder, 35
World War II, 11–12, 59–60
Writing (*see* Creative writing; Functional writing; Handwriting)

92399

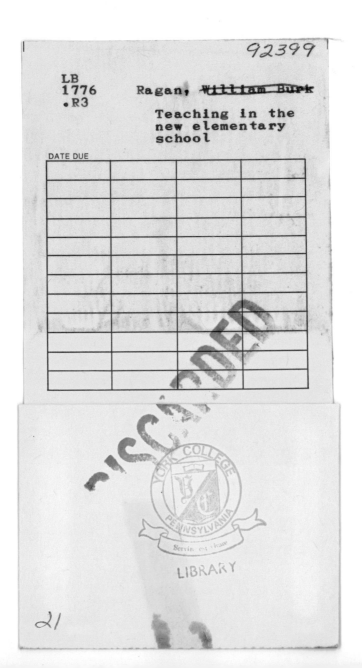

21